THE
SACRED
CHAIN

THE
SACRED
CHAIN

The History of the Jews

NORMAN F. CANTOR

HarperCollins*Publishers*

HarperCollins books may be purchased for educational, business, or sales promotional use. For information please write: Special Markets Department, HarperCollins Publishers, Inc., 10 East 53rd Street, New York, NY 10022.

FIRST EDITION

Designed by Alma Hochhauser Orenstein

Library of Congress Cataloging-in-Publication Data

Cantor, Norman F.
The sacred chain : the history of the Jews / Norman F. Cantor.
   p.   cm.
Includes index.
ISBN 0-06-016746-7
1. Jews—History.   I. Title.
DS117.C26   1994
909'.04924—dc20   94-25035

94 95 96 97 98 ❖/RRD   10 9 8 7 6 5 4 3 2 1

I dedicate this book to the memory of a fervent Canadian Zionist, my maternal uncle, Lieutenant Harry Niznick of the British Army. He died a hero's death on September 9, 1944, fighting the Nazi hordes in Belgium while crossing the Albert Canal, and is buried in a Belgian village. May his memory be enshrined forever among those over the centuries who died In Sanctification of the Holy Name.

CONTENTS

PREFACE

I have written this book for the lay reader, both Jew and Gentile, and the beginning college student. I have tried to make accessible the illumination of the Jewish past provided by both the classics of Jewish historical writing and the extensive new publications of the past two decades. I have sought to present a narrative that involves also intellectual criticism and historiographical assessments of leading themes.

My own inclination is toward historical sociology and cultural history, and I have tried to apply categories from these disciplines to Jewish history.

It was my son, Howard, who first suggested that I undertake this book. I have many times discussed with Howard and with my wife, Mindy Cantor, and my daughter, Judy Cantor, the issues found in this book. On some matters we all agree; on others there is a greater or lesser spectrum of disagreement. These family discussions over two decades prepared me to write this book and helped me to determine what to focus on.

I wish to thank my editor at HarperCollins, Hugh Van Dusen, and my literary agent, Alexander Hoyt, for encouragement and valuable suggestions.

I am grateful to my secretary, Nelly Fontanez, for her assistance and dedication to this project.

The Office of the Dean of the Faculty of Arts and Science at New York University provided secretarial and technical support.

Arthur H. Williamson of California State University, Sacramento, and Bennett Kravitz of Haifa University helped me with a critical reading of the manuscript. Norman A. Stillman of SUNY-Binghamton, Veronika Grim, Viscountess Samuel, of Wolfson College, Oxford, and Charles Dellheim of Arizona State University read a draft of some of the manuscript and provided helpful critiques. I am, of course, solely responsible for any errors in fact or judgment.

I want to thank the staff of the following libraries for their cooperation and unfailing courtesy: the Bobst and Law Libraries of New York University; the Princeton University Firestone Library; and Hebrew Union College (New York) Library.

Part of chapters six and ten originally appeared as articles in *Commonweal* magazine. I wish to thank the Commonweal Foundation for allowing use of this material here.

The translations from the Hebrew Bible are from *Tanakh: The Holy Scriptures* (Jewish Publication Society, 1988).

N.F.C.
SAG HARBOR, NEW YORK
APRIL 1994

Writing Jewish History

Jewish history for a lay audience began to be written in Germany in the mid-nineteenth century, drawing on the learning of the so-called Science of Judaism school headed by Leopold Zunz. Heinrich Graetz successfully combined this scholarly research with the romantic nationalist traditions of German historical writing. He added to the ingredients that shaped his multivolume history of the Jews his conviction that Jewish history witnessed the persistent record of Jewish superior morality and intellectuality as well as communal suffering, particularly at Christian hands. Translated into English and Yiddish, Graetz's work was read enthusiastically well into the twentieth century.

Meanwhile in the early years of this century the literary renaissance of Russian and Polish Jewry spread from novels and poetry to efforts at historical exposition by writers who were not academically trained but who made their living as journalists in Odessa, Warsaw, and other Eastern European centers. The most prominent of these Eastern European historians writing in Yiddish was Simon Dubnow, who was killed by the Nazis in 1941.

German Jewish historical learning flourished after World War I, abetted by activity in Vienna and commanding masterfully the methods of high-powered German academic scholarship in the humanities. In the 1920s and 1930s Zionist idealism and the Nazi threat drove the best of these German-speaking historians overseas to write there in a different language. Gershom Scholem was one of the founders of the Hebrew University and from that vantage wrote his seminal works on Jewish mysticism and messianism. Salo Baron was given a research chair at Columbia University, where he wrote an eighteen-volume social and religious history. Solomon D. Goitein worked first in Jerusalem and then in Philadelphia and Princeton. Using the genizah manuscripts from Old Cairo, Goitein published a massive five-volume study of Jewish society and economy between A.D. 1000 and 1300 in the Mediterranean world. Scholem was the most profound and provocative, Baron the most prolific and comprehensively learned of the Jewish historians in this century. Goitein was the pioneer in research into difficult documents that would reveal how a medieval Jewish society actually functioned.

From present perspective, these three giants of Jewish historical writing had their flaws. Baron had a fixation on technicalities of Jewish communal organization that makes for very difficult reading and a shortfall in relevance. Goitein was verbose, disorganized, and self-indulgent in his writing. Scholem was a brilliant writer and could, when called upon, be succinct and to the point. But his history of Jewish religion in the Middle Ages and the early modern era is deficient in examining the social causes for religious change; his work is too much a history of ideas.

Two other products of the German historical dispersion achieved prominence: Yitshak Baer at the Hebrew University, for his study of Jews in medieval Christian Spain; and Alexander Altmann at Brandeis University, for his work on the development of Jewish philosophy. Also important for the study of Jewish philosophy was an American, Harry Wolfson, at Harvard.

The Jewish Scientific Institute (YIVO) was founded in Vilnius and collected a magnificent research library for historical and sociological study. Fortunately most of the collection was transferred to New York before and after World War II. YIVO was also the base for many years of Rafael Mahler, a master historian, with Marxist leanings, of Eastern European Jewry; he ended his career at Tel Aviv University. Another pioneer—in Jewish historical sociology—was Jacob Katz at the Hebrew University, where this genre was perpetuated in the 1970s by Stephen Sharot.

The historical study of the biblical and interexilic eras had been inaugurated in the mid-nineteenth century by German Protestant scholars of the Higher Criticism school, and superior work in this area has continued to the present day in German-speaking and Scandinavian universities. Beginning especially in the 1930s additional contributions were made by American, British, and Israeli archaeologists, and new perspectives were opened in the 1950s by E. R. Goodenough at Yale and E. J. Bickerman at Columbia.

After 1950 the excitement, controversy, and data generated by the discovery of the Dead Sea Scrolls and the growing tendency of Catholic as well as Protestant scholars to look for the intellectual sources of Christianity in ancient Judaism generated an enormous body of literature on the early periods of Jewish history, much of it written by Gentile scholars.

A new era in Jewish historiography began in the 1970s and 1980s with the founding of Judaic studies programs at many American universities and colleges. This greatly increased the number of professorships in Jewish history and expanded rapidly the number of doctoral students in the field. Of major importance was the recognition both by commercial and university presses of the expanding market for works on Jewish history. The publication of monographs and their immediate acquisition by university libraries rapidly brought younger scholars to the attention of the academic world.

The quality of this broad new wave of Jewish historical scholarship was mixed, and by the early 1990s the field needed new paradigms to focus research and stimulate interpretation. But thanks to the proliferation of Judaic studies departments, a new academic visibility and respectability for Jewish history had been obtained. It moved within a period of two decades from the sectarian and esoteric margin to the mainstream of American academic life.

Despite the impoverishment of Israeli universities in the 1980s, the momentum in historical work begun there under the leadership of Scholem, Baer, and Goitein also sufficed to generate an active younger cohort of important scholars.

At the Hebrew University in Jerusalem, the school of Jewish history founded by Baer and Katz was developed further in the three decades after 1945 under the leadership of Samuel Ettinger and H. H. Ben-Sasson. Together with four colleagues, and with Ben-Sasson as general editor, the Jerusalem school published in 1969 an eleven-hundred-page *History of the Jewish People*. Translated into English and published in 1976 by Weidenfeld in England and a little later by the Harvard University Press, the Ben-Sasson and Ettinger volume effectively communicates to the academic world both the strengths and weaknesses of the Jerusalem school of Jewish historiography. Its main defects are a reluctance to examine religion closely, a dropping off of focus and attention in the modern period, and only marginal accessibility by the nonacademic educated public.

The Tel Aviv school of Jewish history, in cooperation with the French publisher Hachette and then in 1992 with Knopf in New York for the English version, responded with their own one-volume survey of Jewish history, *Historical Atlas of the Jewish People,* under the general editorship of Eli Barnavi. In two hundred twenty-nine oversize pages, this ingenious, at times brilliant work sets forth not only excellent original cartography but also a splendid set of color reproductions of Jewish monuments and a highly useful detailed time line. The main space is taken up with expository essays on important subjects in the Jewish past. The writing is more accessible than in the Hebrew University textbook, but still challenging for the lay reader.

Intellectually, the work's defects are a clouding of narrative line after A.D. 1100, making the book episodic and fragmentary in its discourse; a triumphalist Zionist tone in the latter part of the book; and a choice of emphasis that does not give European, especially Eastern European Ashkenazic, and American culture and society their appropriate due. We know we are reading an Israeli book when the Jews of Byzantium, the Ottoman empire, China, and India each get as much attention as or more attention than the Haskalah, the European Jewish Enlightenment of the eighteenth and nineteenth centuries (which ironically made Zionism and hence the state of Israel possible). The treatment given to American Jewish history is cursory and feeble. Nevertheless, the Tel Aviv volume should be praised for its maps and illustrations and for some of the essays, especially in the first half of the book.

Since 1980 the most important activity in Jewish historiography has been in the English-speaking world. Belatedly, postbiblical Jewish historical studies have begun to flourish in Britain, especially at Oxford and London universities.

Fostered by the American Jewish Historical Society and by academic recognition of Jewish history as an important subfield of U.S. history, knowledge of the American Jewish experience had progressed far enough for the publication in 1992 of the five-volume history entitled *Jewish People in America,* under the general editorship of Henry L. Feingold of the City University of New York. Extremely uneven in quality and uncertain in its voice, varying from the traditionally celebratory to the more intellectually valuable critical in tone, this series has the merit of consistent readability and close attention to the more recent era.

By the early 1990s Jewish historiography was greatly enriched by the availability of a whole new body of important literature, subsequent to the familiar names of the Scholem, Baron, and Goitein generation.

This body of historical writing is marked by the two-front advance that always characterizes a historical subfield experiencing major change. On the one side are detailed research monographs and on the other are insightful books of comprehensive interpretation. It is a good sign that significant contributions are being made to Jewish historiography by academics beyond those teaching in departments of Judaic studies. Among the half-dozen most original and interesting works on Jewish history published in 1993 were one by a professor of comparative literature and another by a professor of political science, both at American universities.

The numbers of new writers doing important work are evidence of the maturation of the field of Jewish history.

The ultimate test of the value of a historical field or school is integration with and influence on general cultural change and emerging ideology. This is the social challenge, as distinct from the more limited academic focus, that the Jewish historians face in the closing decade of the twentieth century. Out of their work should come not only the illumination of the past but implications for reconsidering the future of Israel and the Diaspora.

Making Jewish historiography an important ingredient of opinion-making within the American Jewish world will require historians to find distinctive voices and literary strategies by which the educated public can be addressed. Now that Jewish history has been fully habilitated in the American university, they will have the opportunity to do so.

Whether they will have the confidence and motivation is another question. The funding for chairs in Jewish history on American campuses has come almost entirely from the private sector, from wealthy

Jewish donors. As Jewish historiography reaches the edge of a highly sophisticated level of interpretation, it begins to penetrate subject areas and raise questions that are discomfiting to conventional views of the Jewish past with which affluent Jews are familiar and are fully comfortable.

The culture of American Jewish upper middle class, who pay for the professorships of Jewish history, is one that does not expect history to be a critical and a morally and politically challenging subject. In the medical schools they endow, sick Jews would not want nineteenth-century medicine to be taught, but nineteenth-century historiography is still fully acceptable to them!

They are used to a model of Jewish history that consists entirely of victimization and celebration—the Jewish past is sentimentally to be celebrated with appropriate mourning for Jewish suffering in the past two millennia at Christian and latterly Nazi hands. Jews are responsible for their own destinies only insofar as they occasionally accomplish great things intellectually and, in the twentieth century, in the case of Israel, politically and militarily. Otherwise there is really nothing problematic to think about in Jewish history, a litany of Jewish victimization.

This is the view of the Jewish past held by the American upper middle class who endow the chairs in Jewish history. It can be heard annually on the High Holidays sermons disseminated from the synagogue pulpits. It is a view that will come under strong scrutiny and significant challenge as the Jewish past is subject more closely to deep research and thoughtful reinterpretation.

American Jewish culture, open to new ideas in many areas, is not eager to attend to deconstructive ventures into the understanding of the Jewish past. The proliferation of recent publication on Jewish history from American campuses may already be running up against a glass wall of informal censorship, in which detailed uncontroversial explorations of particular subjects are be welcomed, but not visible challenges to the overall received victimization/celebratory model of Jewish history.

As long as historians, from the comfort of their endowed chairs, regurgitate the serviceable mythology of the past, the intellectual advancement of Jewish historiography and its instrumental value to reopen fundamental questions about Jewish life, present as well as past, will fall well short of its potential therapeutic, possibly reforming impact on Jewish culture and society.

Another limitation on the effectiveness of the current enhancement in the volume and quality of writing on Jewish history is organizational. The level of achievement of an academic field is determined by its institutional as well as its intellectual development. Jewish history is flourishing on the American campus but is spread too thinly among many universities. There are one, or two, or at most three productive scholars and teachers at each of a large number of universities. This thin spread is likely to increase as more universities receive endowments from Jewish benefactors for creating chairs in Judaic studies and compete for already well-established academic names to fill the chairs. The field of Jewish historical writing as a whole does not benefit when a prominent scholar is recruited from the Jewish Theological Seminary to Brown University, or from Brandeis University to New York University.

I am bemused at receiving three or four times a year letters requesting suggestions for candidates from deans at ambitious Southern or Midwestern universities, each engaged in a search to fill vacant chairs of Judaic studies. The letters always specify that the successful candidate be a well-known, well-published scholar. The professor of Jewish history is seen as an exotic bird on campus, to tweet away in a golden cage provided by a local millionaire Jewish family.

Socially this is a big advance on the situation of forty or even twenty years ago. Then the family would have put its charitable money into a hospital, and Jewish history, beyond a shadowy course offered on the side by the Hillel rabbi, would be absent from the curriculum. But getting stuck at the current level of supporting Jewish history on the campuses of America, even if the result is economically rewarding to established scholars, will not generate the great advancements in Jewish historical thought that are within reach.

What is needed is not more dispersion but more concentration. There ought to be three or four eminent departments of Jewish history in the United States, each staffed by at least a half-dozen active scholars of high distinction and supported by first-class libraries, funded journals, and an endowment committed to recruit and train graduate students. The emergence in the 1930s and 1940s of general history departments at Harvard and Columbia with this kind of intensive profile, modeled on the great European institutes, transformed American historiography. This kind of institutional takeoff is now needed in the field of Jewish history.

CREDO

All the laws and ordinances, all the blessings and curses of the Law of Moses, have but one unvarying object: the well-being of the nation as a whole in the law of its inheritance . . . One long chain unites all the generations, from Abraham, Isaac, and Jacob to the end of time.

AHAD HA'AM (ASHER GINSBERG), 1889
[TRANSL. STEVEN J. ZIPPERSTEIN]

To influence a people one has to be bone of their bone, flesh of their flesh; one has to have suffered their sorrows and felt their pain.

MENDELE MOCHER SFORIM (SHOLEM ABRAMOVICH), 1888
[TRANSL. CHARLES A. MADISON]

What, then, is religion? Just think what the Jews have suffered over the past two thousand years for the sake of this fantasy of theirs. Yes, it is this fantasy that holds people in its grip.

THEODOR HERZL, 1895
[TRANSL. ERNST PAWEL]

To be a Jew is . . . to remember that the world is unredeemed.

ABRAHAM J. HESCHEL, 1955

The greatness of this people was once that it believed in God, and believed in Him in such a way that its trust and love towards Him was greater than its fear.

HANNAH ARENDT, 1963

Unable to believe in the God of their fathers or to invest their emotional piety unreservedly in Israel, Jews born after 1945 discover themselves to be atheists in search of a synagogue, at least in the sense of a place of common recognition.

FREDERIC RAPAHEL, 1994

THE
SACRED
CHAIN

CHAPTER ONE

The Origin of the Jews

The Romans incorporated the eastern end of the Mediterranean into their expanding empire in 63 B.C. They called the land on the southern part of this Mediterranean extremity, lying between Syria and the Egyptian desert, Judea, and hence its people became known in the Roman world as Judeans, hence Jews. This Roman appellation accorded with Hebrew people's reference to themselves as members of the tribe, and later kingdom, of Yehudah.

The Romans found the Jews querulous, recalcitrant, divided among themselves, and difficult to govern. But the Jews had a book of historical and religious writings that aroused the interest and stirred the admiration of the more literate Romans. Among the many peoples the Romans conquered, only the Greeks had an ancient literature of, in their eyes, comparable quality. The Jewish book told a long story about, among other subjects, the origin of the Jews.

The Hebrew Bible we read today is the Masoretic ("traditional") text that was written down around the year A.D. 1000. But we have a Greek translation (the Septuagint) prepared for the large Jewish community of Alexandria, Egypt, around 250 B.C. that coincides ninety-five percent with the Masoretic text. And the texts of the Bible possessed by the Qumran community along the Dead Sea—the famous

Dead Sea Scrolls, discovered in the late 1940s—give us at least fragments of nearly every book in the Bible in the original language
(normally Hebrew) and date probably from the period 300–100 B.C.

The biblical texts from Qumran remarkably confirm the ancient
authenticity of the Masoretic text that Jews have regarded as authoritative since the eleventh century A.D., which is used in Jewish synagogues and schools today. This discovery has been a great relief to
the rabbis. The ancient Qumran texts of the Bible and the medieval
Masoretic text coincide by a factor of ninety-eight percent.

The Hebrew Bible (Tanach) presents a historical narrative of the
Jewish people through fifteen centuries before the Common or Christian era, with a rhythmic thrust, a graphic detail, and a clarity of
overriding conception that is found nowhere else in the literature of
the ancient world. Nothing like such a thick, confident, and obsessive historical myth would again be invented until the rise of European nationalist histories in the nineteenth century. Biblical history
has therefore continued to be preached with confidence in Jewish
synagogues and taught in Jewish schools down to the present.

Furthermore, in the period from 1935 to 1965 a prominent American archaeologist, William Foxwell Albright, as well as Israeli
archaeologists like Y. Yadin, and some German scholars, asserted
that modern archaeological excavations had confirmed some key
events in the Bible, such as the fall of Jericho to the Israelites when
they allegedly swept into Canaan under Joshua's leadership from
their forty years of tarrying in the Sinai desert after the Exodus from
Egypt.

The mute stones dug up out of the ground, it was joyously
claimed, now spoke and confirmed the fundamental historicity of the
Bible in the second millennium B.C., the age of the Patriarchs and
Judges. In the 1960s a German writer knowledgeable in archaeological literature, Werner Keller, put all this information together in one of
the all-time best-selling history books, *The Bible as History*, and was
still stubbornly bringing it up to date in a revised edition in 1981,
which is today still passionately espoused in the Old Confederacy.

Unfortunately, a brilliant, dour British archaeologist, Kathleen
Kenyon—a fervent anti-Zionist who worked under Jordanian patronage—around 1960 made a hash out of Albright's Jericho argument.
The burned city that Albright discovered was from a much earlier era
than the time of Joshua's invasion of Canaan, Kenyon demonstrated.

Similarly, all the claims for archaeological verification of the first millennium of Jewish history as told in the Bible have eroded. Abraham, Isaac, Jacob, Moses—if they ever lived, if they were real historical figures, there is no basis for believing so outside the Hebrew Bible itself.

Even the famous Exodus from Egypt when Jews were slaves unto Pharaoh, the liberation celebrated each Passover—more than one hundred years of determined and immensely expensive historical research and archaeological quest in the Nile Delta have not yielded one single shred of verification to this story that has fired Jewish (and sometimes Christian) imagination through the centuries.

All we are left with are two weak and nonverifiable arguments to support the Bible's history. First, the thickness of detail and dramatic persuasiveness of the biblical history "could not be" mere fictive myth. "It must have" a kernel of fact, a basis in actual events, no matter how embellished in the telling. The learned scholars of Tel Aviv University in their 1992 *Historical Atlas of the Jewish People* claim that "even the least historically authentic biblical traditions clearly represent real events, social processes, and flesh-and-blood figures." By this they mean that the biblical stories of early Jewish history in the second millennium ·B.C. are not at face fantastic and impossible. They could have happened.

That does not mean, however, that they did happen. Empirical research has not been able to establish this historicity. What is given in the Bible about Jewish origins are made-up stories created from a much later time, as long as a thousand years after the events allegedly occurred.

The second argument for the historicity of the Bible consists of parallels and references in other peoples' ancient history. Certain events in the Bible "fit in" with well-known general or particular non-Jewish trends or happenings in the history of the ancient Near East. Thus the Egyptians for a few years had a pharaoh who appears to have been a monotheist (the Egyptian priests wouldn't buy into this, and after Pharaoh Ikhnaton's death, Egypt reverted to its traditional polytheism). That Abraham came from the "Ur of the Chaldees" in the Tigris-Euphrates valley is made plausible, some argue, by the thick settlement there in the early or mid-first millennium B.C., when Abraham is thought to have lived there before migrating with his clan westward. Mesopotamian religion contains certain historical myths, particularly the story of the flood (Noah), that are also told in similar fashion in the Hebrew Bible. Maybe the Jews brought Mesopotamian stories with them to Canaan.

Again, if the Jews made their way to Egypt and were welcomed by good pharaohs and were later enslaved by bad pharaohs, this coincides with the Hyskos interlude in Egyptian history in the twelfth century B.C. The Hyskos were a sea people from the eastern Mediterranean, thought to be "Semites" like the Jews (whatever these rigid nineteenth-century racist categories might mean). And so the Jews lived comfortably under Hyskos rule for a century or so, after which a native Egyptian dynasty resumed power and naturally oppressed and conceivably enslaved the Jewish allies of the now overthrown Hyskos rulers, until under a great leader, who may not have been Jewish, the Israelites escaped into the Sinai desert and slowly made their way back to Canaan, the land God had promised to their forefather, the patriarch Abraham, according to the Bible.

The historicity of the Bible before 1000 B.C. is very thin indeed. It depends on anxious speculations like these. The only useful archaeological find that has turned up is that of a stone inscription stating that around 1200 B.C. an Egyptian pharaoh destroyed an army of Israelites in Canaan—not a particularly glorious verification of the Bible! But apparently the Jews were there, in Canaan. What they were doing there is another matter.

After 1000 B.C. the darkness begins to lift, but only just a little before 800 B.C. An Egyptian source refers to fighting against the people of Asher around 950 B.C.; Asher was the name of one of the twelve tribes of early Israel. In 1993 exultant Israeli archaeologists reported the discovery of a stone inscription from the time of what would have been King David's great-grandson, referring to the "House of David." There is cause for celebration because, despite the lengthy novellike account of David's life (probably two separate stories mingled together) in the Bible, this discovery is the first actual authentication of his existence, or at least memory of his existence.

Today the Israelis agonize that under their soil, despite decades of dry-hole drilling all over the country, seems to be one of the very few places in the Near East without a substantial pool of oil. Perhaps one day now the gusher will come in. And perhaps any year now great archaeological finds will be made verifying the Bible's account of Jewish historicity between the patriarch Abraham and King David.

Most likely David did live, and rule, and his overambitious son Solomon did build the First Temple in Jerusalem.

But until the glorious day dawns of archaeological verification for the line of Abraham, we have to stipulate that all of Jewish history of the first millennium B.C.E. and some of it for a century or two after that, as told in the Bible, is one of the great masterpieces of imaginative fiction or artfully contrived historical myths of all time. From empirical evidence, it did not happen.

Somewhere around 800 B.C.E., in the court of King David's great-grandson, a writer of genius—quite possibly a woman of the high aristocracy—contrived this astonishing novel about the rise of the Jews. Perhaps she adapted some fragments of stories that were already circulating. Perhaps she made it all up. When the Jews went into Babylonian exile in the sixth century B.C. (where the patriarch Abraham supposedly originated, so the Jews in a sense went conveniently back to their geographical roots, according to the Bible), the rabbis and scribes worked overtime to expand on this novelistic history and give it the theological twist they wanted. After some Jews came back to Jerusalem under benign Persian rulers in the fifth century B.C., the biblical history of the Jews was given the final form we read today by rabbis and scribes on-site in Jerusalem, particularly by the scholar and communal leader Ezra.

In addition to the so-called Book of J (for Jehovah), the grand text by the aristocrat from the time of King David's great-grandson, Ezra and his scribal associates stitched into the final biblical version, not always neatly, selections from three other earlier sources.

This is what the best biblical scholarship teaches today, as summed up recently in brilliant books by Richard Elliott Friedman, Harold Bloom and David Rosenberg, and Robin Lane Fox. The "Bible as history" doctrine, based on the work of W. F. Albright and Israelis like Y. Yadin, which flourished in the 1960s and was feverishly popularized in Werner Keller's naive book, has bitten the dust. Even the gung-ho Israeli archaeologists are cautious about biblical historicity these days.

The "Bible as history" has in the early 1990s been replaced by the "Bible as literature" theme, propounded by Robert Alter, a prominent literature professor at Berkeley and a frequent contributor to *Commentary* magazine, the leading Jewish American journal of cultural criticism. Alter's argument runs: Don't worry about verifying pesky little details in the Bible by digging up stones in Israel. Don't even worry about the way in which the Masoretic text of the Bible was composed and edited over several centuries and has identifiable pastiche qualities. Let us read the wonderful standard text that we have as a integral work of literature and define its composite literary structure and synthetic intellectual meaning.

Why not? This won't harm anyone and will give pleasure and inspiration. It is a kind of ahistorical literary neofundamentalism and it had become fashionable among the more progressive rabbis who now know, deep down, that Keller is mistaken.

The lack of historicity of the biblical account of Jewish origins, from the time of Abraham and until just before King David (i.e., before 1000 or so B.C.) is cryptically forecast in the Pentateuch itself: "The people [Hebrews] shall be alone and shall not be reckoned among the goyim [other nations]" (Numbers 23:9).

Who then were the Jews? Where did they come from? Modern scholarship offers three choices. The first is the familiar claim that the Jews came out of the desert: The Jews (Israelites, Hebrews) were originally a seminomadic desert people living off their flocks of sheep (and possibly camels) who invaded Canaan and pillaged the rich old neolithic cities in the Jordan valley and on the coastal plain.

There is a bit of an archaeological obstacle to this Bible-based view—a nomadic culture in the ancient Near East is a camel-based culture, and archaeology seems to indicate that biblical chronology places Abraham and the other patriarchs several centuries before the appearance of the known domesticated camel. Yet seeing the first Jews as nomads from the desert, alien attackers upon the soft heathen Canaanites with all their obnoxious idols, was and is psychologically satisfying. It does tend to confirm the close ancient kinship of the Jews and the Arabs of the desert, the latter also being progeny of the patriarchs, according to the Bible.

Another explanation of the origin of the Israelites is that they were just a Canaanite subgroup who—according to Martin Noth—gathered around innovative altars on certain hilltops. They came to adhere to a distinctive, more spiritual, and less idol-ridden religion and then invented a historical past by which, collectively, through Yahweh's will, they separated their group from the common run of abominable Canaanites. But they were Canaanites, just sectarian ones.

Or if, like N. K. Gottwald, you prefer a Marxist explanation, the origin of the Jews lies in proletarian revolt. They were *hapiru* (a Mesopotamian word from which possibly Ivri, Hebrew, stems), an assemblage of rebellious peasants, mercenaries, and other socially underprivileged people contending against the ruling classes in the Canaanite city-states.

A prominent Israeli archaeologist, I. Finkelstein, in 1988 tried to sum up a century of archaeological work on the earliest Hebrews and to conflate all these theories of Jewish origins into one synthetic proposition. The Israelites were at first "sedentary," he said, then "pastoralist," and finally they underwent "resedentarization." And so the apparently simple image of Father Abraham leaving the Ur of the Chaldees and eventually entering the Promised Land of Canaan with his family and flocks—this image of the people of the desert penetrating the cities of the plain—turned into a complex story indeed.

Some of the Jews at one point, perhaps recruited by their Hsykos kinsmen, we may acknowledge, found their way to Egypt for a while and then came back after the Hyskos lost power. This subchapter was exaggeratedly memorialized in a great liberation myth of (wrongly) the whole or even a majority of the Jews being slaves unto Pharaoh, possibly Ramses II (d. 1204 B.C.), the obsessive pyramid builder. Or the whole Egyptian sojourn was made up in later centuries for some ideologically conditioned or socially advantageous purpose.

If you believe in science, if you want your history to be based in empirical evidence, there was nothing ethnically or sociologically special about the earliest Jews. They were just another group living in the eastern Mediterranean, until at some point between 900 and 300 B.C. they developed a distinctive religion with its monist providential doctrine, its puritan ethic, its insistence on male circumcision, and its strenuous dietary taboos. Then a history going back a further thousand years was created to give substance and conviction to the Law that went forth from Jerusalem.

At a certain point in the mid-first millennium B.C. Jewish intellectuals, writers, and religious leaders had created a unique culture, a singular religion, a distinctive view of human behavior. And they invented a history and a theory of history to justify and give narrative depth to all the other facets of their culture. This invented history, incorporated in the Hebrew Bible, was later appropriated into Christian thought and became for many centuries an unquestionable ingredient of the sensibility of European culture.

This long-term impact and high degree of practical credibility does not, however, verify the historicity of the Bible's account of the era before King David. And even for the period during and after David's reign, much in biblical historiography is problematic and requires close scrutiny.

Scrutiny comes from anthropologists as well as others. It is claimed that all the care and idealism of Ezra and his redactor colleagues could not entirely eliminate from the Tanach glimpses of cultural primitivism embedded in popular discourse. A young Stanford University anthropologist, Howard Eilberg-Schwartz, in 1990 found it relatively easy to ferret out traces of common primitive or savage religion in the Masoretic text of the Hebrew Bible that was finished around 300 B.C.:

> Israelite religion had its own form of totemism. [That is], as in "primitive" societies, animals provided the foundational metaphors through which the Israelites articulated the understanding of who they were and what they wanted to be. These metaphors, which provided an idiom for theological, national and social reflections, fundamentally shaped the practices of Israelite religion. Fertility, procreation and reproduction . . . were critical to the conception of the covenant between Israel and God . . . Jews have frequently been presented as a "People of the Book." But it would be equally appropriate to describe them as a "People of the Body."

In biblical religion then, according to anthropologists, can be found traces of totemism and fertility cults and bodily extrapolations common to all religions of the ancient Near East and indeed to the savage mind universally.

Yet these savages never wrote the Bible. The other ancient Near Eastern peoples, who in some instances in the Mesopotamian and Egyptian Deltas fastened on religious concepts close to essential Hebrew ones, still fell far short of ancient Judaism. The Jews may have begun with consciousness of their body as a way of articulating their religious concepts, but they finished by 300 B.C. with an infinitely complex consciousness foregrounding ethics and spirituality.

The Jews began like everyone else. They ended up, around the time when what became the Masoretic version of the Bible was completed in Jerusalem in the fourth century B.C., different from everyone else.

Both points are important. Anthropologically the Jews in the late second millennium B.C. appeared to be just another named group in ancient Near Eastern society, like the Canaanites and the Philistines. Somewhere along the way in the first eight centuries before the Common Era they changed in accordance with their unique religion set down in the Tanach, their holy scriptures.

This is how history transcends and diminishes anthropology and separates from it. For history it is not the universal sameness of base that counts—the bodily and animal metaphors that savage societies employ to represent their perception—but the particular differences in developed cultural superstructures, discontinuous with the anthropological base, that are meaningful.

People articulate their ideas in a frame of reference of what they know. The savage mind knows the body relative to its physical environment. So all its religious discourse is laced with bodily metaphors, with reference to animals, copulation, menstruation, food, and so forth. Later other, less bodily and eventually spiritual frames of reference are determined and become the focus of articulation. Some bodily references endure. They have become conventional focuses of symbolic speech and still have superior resonance.

But this marginal symbolic durability does not make the Jews the People of the Body. From some point between 600 and 300 B.C. (if not earlier) they were the People of the Book. And these holy scriptures represented a culture that featured providential monotheism, puritanical ethics, and a rigorous behavioral code.

The Jews of the mid-first millennium B.C., when the Bible as we have it was written, sensed something special about themselves, something that organically separated the Jews from other peoples. They needed a story of their origins, a narrative myth to account for this specialness, for their moral fiber, their intelligence, their intense communal sensibility, their durability in the face of onslaught and exile.

Today they might imagine that sometime in the distant past a spaceship from another planet landed on this earth carrying an extraterrestrial people initially called Hebrews and later Jews. Today they might hypothesize and fantasize that this extraterrestrial immigration accounts for the obscurity of Hebrew origins, the inability of archaeologists with all their data and excavations to explain the strangeness of the Jews, their astonishing vitality, creativity, and capacity for survival against severely overwhelming odds.

But the idea of extraterrestrial origins for earthly beings was not in the arsenal of ancient Jewish mythology. The Hebrews had to project their singular strength onto the intervention of an omnipotent, universal deity, as in the words of the 44th Psalm:

> We have heard, O God, our fathers have told us the deeds You performed in their time, in days of old.
>
> With your hand You planted them, displacing nations . . .
>
> It was not by their sword that they took the land, their arm did not give them victory, but Your right hand, Your arm, and your goodwill, for you favored them . . .
>
> Through You we gore our foes; by Your name we trample our adversaries . . . it is not my sword that gives me victory; You give us victory over our foes.

They had to use what ancient Mediterranean culture gave them in the way of explanatory myth: the power and will of a transcendent deity.

Today what is called science fiction would provide another story, and perhaps a more persuasive one, certainly a more humanly circumstantial and less abstract and bleak one. But they were stuck with the provenance myth they developed and it became the root and branch of their religion, morality, and culture for the ages to come.

Jewish history in its intellectual and cultural manifestation consists of efforts to habilitate, to live with this myth of divinely ordained beginnings, of the impact of a transcendent deity upon a small, obscure people of shepherds and farmers.

The Bible celebrated the organic superiority of the Jews' persistence in comparison with other ethnic groups, their stern morality and astounding literary intelligence, by transferring the source of this power from their human nature to a divine being who idiosyncratically by his own will chose a weak and obscure people for a long march through the fertile crescent of the ancient Near East and its early inheritance of a now designated Holy Land. This is the myth that the ancient Jewish scribes, prophets, and rabbis employed to explain and hide the ultimate secrets of their people's origins.

Sometime in the early centuries of the second millennium B.C. Abraham and his family lived in Ur in the southern point of the Tigris-Euphrates valley, not far from the Persian Gulf. He journeyed north through Babylon and came to Haran, at the northern end of the Tigris-Euphrates valley. God told him to go to Canaan, which he did. His son Isaac lived in Beersheba, an oasis in the Negev Desert in what is today the southern part of Israel, but Isaac's son Jacob and his family resumed the Jewish wanderings, returning temporarily to Haran, where he resided for a while with an uncle, and ultimately coming to Egypt, where one of Jacob's sons, Joseph, held a high position in the government. But then came a pharaoh "who knew not Joseph" and enslaved the Jews. Ultimately under the leadership of Moses around 1300 B.C., the Jews left Egypt to return, after crossing "the Sea of Reeds" to the Promised Land of Canaan, which they finally entered and conquered forty years later, just after Moses died.

Such is the biblical story, whose verification defies the course of historical and archaeological science. It is a romantic fantasy.

The modern anti-Semites claimed the Jews were outside humanity. Hitler said they were a bacillus in the bloodstream of civilized peoples and had to be excised from the face of the earth. In their perverted hate-filled way, the anti-Semites sensed the truth of Jewish history, the specialness of the Jews, their strangeness on the face of the earth. The anti-Semites could not stand to witness all the good things the Jews had brought mankind because that would remind these inferior people of their own underdevelopment and depravity compared to the Jews. They sought to kill them all, but as in the case of previous massacres and catastrophes in Jewish history, their effort at extirpation of the Jews, with active or silent complicity of many nations, did not succeed.

Jewish survival in the face of the advanced technology of genocide was the recent historical demonstration that universal hatred for the Jews could not surmount their superhuman strength, intelligence, and durability.

The ancient Hebrews knew that the special quality of their origins was somehow grounded in the uniqueness of their provenance. This had to be kept secret, and could only be handed down by the scholars and rabbis to later generations in impenetrable code. For now, in the mid-first millennium B.C., the Jewish teachers and writers had to prevaricate. Curiosity-seekers inquired where and how the Jews came to Cannan long ago, and so the Jews invented the powerful narrative line of Mesopotamian origins, travail in Egypt, national liberation, and the penetration and finally conquest of Canaan under the leadership of Judges, among whom is a certain Deborah, "mother in Israel."

Some biblical scholars see Deborah's heroic poem in the Book of Judges as an authentic archaic survival from early times. It may just as well be consciously contrived as a pseudo-archaic literary device from the middle of the first millennium B.C., a thousand years later, with just a note of sardonic hyperbole:

My heart is with Israel's leaders, with the dedicated of the people—Bless the Lord!

You riders on tawny she-asses, you who sit on saddle rugs, and you wayfarers, declare it! . . .

Awake, awake, O Deborah! Awake, awake, strike up the chant!

A similar contrived archaism to give plausibility to the biblical story may be perceived in the murky, incomprehensible dietary legislation (kashruth) in the Book of Deuteronomy that seems at times to be grounded in health reasons, at others in anthropological taboos based on blood revulsion and structural duality.

The biblical version of Jewish origins was sufficiently historical-sounding in the context of ancient Near Eastern narratives to forestall further inquiry as to how this people of distinctive quality, superhuman in their fortitude and literate intelligence, came to be where and what they were. All the Jews' unique mental and physical capacity in comparison with the other peoples of the earth, the Gentiles, were attributed to the will of a single and singular God. The Jews' innate superiority, their organic power, was projected onto Yahweh, a strange omnipotent, fastidious deity.

Once this myth was in place, elaborately narrated in holy scriptures that became the text of advanced education, as well as spiritual reading, the Jews had to live with it. They had to build a culture and society on God's covenanted connection to a people thereby perpetuated through time in a sacred chain.

After about 200 B.C., satisfied with the elaborate historical myth of Jewish origins, the intellectual and religious leaders of Israel cut off further historical exposition and explanation. Significantly, the Tanach, the Hebrew Bible, is suffused with historical thinking and narrative, but the elaborate commentaries on it, concluded in Mesopotamia in the sixth century A.D. in the form of the Babylonian Talmud, rigidly excised history from the seemingly endless dialogues of the learned rabbis that comprise the Talmudic multivolume text. This could not be fortuitous. The discoursing rabbinical legalists and ethicists may have had little taste for historical disquisition. But the unhistoricity of the Talmud, with its infinite rabbinical chatter on just about anything as compared to the ultrahistoricity of the Bible, could not have been accidental. It seems that redactors and editors consciously excised almost every historical reference that slipped out of rabbinical mouths.

This rabbinical censorship of history results in some curious anomalies. The Second Book of Maccabees, discussing the later history of the heroic Hasmanean family, did not make it into the canon of the Hebrew Bible. It comes down to us in the Christian Bible in a Greek translation. The later Maccabees were not moral paragons, and the redacting rabbis apparently thought the history of this late Jewish royal dynasty should fade out with an account only of its earlier, more positive era—the one celebrated in the festival of Hanukkah.

The excision of history resulted in further anomalies. The Jewish war of national liberation against Rome in 66–70 B.C. resulted in the destruction of the Second Temple. The latter catastrophe was—and is still—memorialized in the fast day of Tisha B' Ab (falling in August), but amazingly there is no account from Talmudic sources of the revolt against Rome and the Roman destruction of the Temple. After the redactors and editors of the Talmud finished censoring postbiblical history, the only circumstantial source for the greatest catastrophe in ancient Hebraic times was a partisan, self-serving, although brilliantly written account of the Jewish Wars by Josephus Flavius, a treasonous aristocratic Jewish general. Because Josephus's field of action was in the north, in Galilee, and he never joined the freedom fighters in Jerusalem, the disastrous splits among the liberation front in Jerusalem are not clear to us.

The Talmudic rabbis also tell us next to nothing about the last Jewish rebellion against Rome in A.D. 135 led by Bar Cocheba, even though he was supported by a prominent rabbi of the time, Akiba. We only learn in cryptic, heavily edited Talmudic discussion that the Roman vengeance for this last rebellion was extremely bloody, and one rabbi also expresses personal contempt for Bar Cocheba, an editorial slip-up.

The even more important rebellion against Rome that occurred in the Diaspora, and especially in the great Jewish community of Alexandria, in A.D. 115–17, which in the end devastated the Alexandrian Jewish community and probably others in the eastern Mediterranean and constituted a critical turning point in Diaspora history, is passed over in silence by the Talmudic rabbis.

Therefore a stark polarity exists in rabbinically redacted Jewish historiography between the elaborate accounts of events stretching from Abraham in the early second millennium B.C. to the early history of the Maccabees in the third century B.C. and what followed. After the earlier historicizing era, rabbinical Judaism prefers silence on history and turns to legalistic and ethical analysis as its form of discourse, a legalism and a moralizing without developmental consciousness, a static kind of thinking in which the laws of Moses and legal decisions of rabbis in the early centuries A.D. and beyond are treated as if they were contemporary with each other.

From being overly historicized with fanciful narrative in the Bible, Judaism swings radically to become a religion without history by not later than the second century A.D. This prejudice against history continues unabated until the pogromist catastrophe inflicted by the French crusaders on the flourishing Jewish communities in the Rhineland in A.D. 1096, which stimulated a modicum of Jewish historical writing, as did subsequent catastrophes—the expulsion from Spain in 1492, the Cossack massacres of Polish Jews in 1648, and the upheavals produced in Jewish communities in several countries as the result of the controversy over the messianic movement led by Sabbatai Zebi in the 1660s.

But by and large the Jewish blackout on historical writing continued into the nineteenth century when narrative of the Jewish past by secular-educated Jewish scholars was inaugurated in Germany under the influence of aggressively historicizing Protestant culture.

Even today Jewish prejudice against history, inaugurated by the postbiblical sages who created the Talmud, continues. Listen to the synagogue sermons of even a learned, academically trained Reform rabbi and you are very likely to hear the familiar narrative of Abraham to the Maccabees as the pool of instructive historical anecdotes, supplemented only by later catastrophe references, with 1492 and the Holocaust of the 1940s the prominent ones.

None of the great names in modern Jewish historical writing, from Graetz and Dubnow to Baron and Goitein were practicing rabbis. In the nineteenth and early twentieth centuries the writers of history were publicists and journalists; since then they have been academics. The rabbinical mind, even in its contemporary American Reform variant, cannot bring itself to supersede the essentially antihistorical way of thinking that the authors of the Babylonian Talmud implanted in high Jewish culture.

Postbiblical Judaism remains a culture with a rigid, obsolete historical dimension, satisfied with the brilliant, elaborate romantic fantasies developed by the scribes and rabbis between 600 and 300 B.C. to explain the origin of the Jews. This historiography, matched for quality of invention and persuasion in ancient literature only by Greek and Roman epics and historical narrative, became a congealed structure of hypostatized narrative culture that sufficed for nearly all Jewish historical speculation and time-sequential theorizing until the present day.

Realistic, truth-telling history of the Jews is even now not welcome in the ruling circles of the American and Israeli Jewish communities, among the rabbis, the billionaire patriarchs who heavily patronize and enthrall them, and the prominent politicians. When Ellis Rivkin in the 1950s was invited to teach Jewish history at Hebrew Union College in Cincinnati, then the academic center of American Reform Judaism, he had to gain beforehand a promise from the head of the college that his boldly deconstructive class-struggle version of Jewish history would not be censored or censured.

In the two Israeli universities of distinction, in Jerusalem and Tel Aviv, both of which boast large complements of historians, Jewish history is segregated, in the form of a separate department, from all other history; thus, the faculty in the latter departments, trained at Oxbridge, the Sorbonne, the University of Munich, and prestigious U.S. universities, do not have to be responsible or feel professionally contaminated as the Israeli historians of the Jews wrestle, not very cleanly, with the biblical mythology. This they cannot verify by the standards and procedures of empirical scientific history, but they fear to discredit it decisively in the face of expected angry reaction from Jewish opinion-makers in Israel and America.

History provides entertainment (a good story) and inspiration (modes of heroic deportment). But it also can be corrosive, which is why it was so favored by the nineteenth-century liberal bourgeoisie in attacking the old aristocratic European order. History can raise troubling questions that press for an answer and can stimulate a public discourse that embraces and gives therapeutic solutions to angularity, marginality, and discordance.

Postbiblical Jewish history can be construed as a long litany of victimization, from the Romans to the Germans and Arabs, and it is conventional to do so. Yet the Jews were not entirely the blameless victims of history. To a disputable but minimally real extent, they contributed to the fashioning of their own destiny.

When the pages of postbiblical Jewish history were all but emptied of significant content by the intellectual leaders of Jewish culture until the mid-nineteenth century, and what was not blotted out was diminished and narcotized into a recital of unprovoked victimization, the rabbis had an easy time of dealing with the challenge of historical thought—they had enough to do otherwise. So they quit while they were ahead, stressing the perpetually relevant significance of biblical history in an ever-present litany of creation and early development. They did not feel pressed to assess the awkward and indeed troublesome questions of postbiblical development. As it were, they bowed out of historicity while they were ahead.

Only when modern historical science, using intense archaeological pursuit, came up empty in trying to verify the Bible's account of Jewish history in the second millennium B.C.—which became decisively evident by the 1970s—was the romantic fantasizing of the ancient sages between 600 and 200 B.C., and especially between 400 and 250 B.C., fully revealed. This aversion to recognizing a negative discovery, even in the textbooks prepared by the impressive Jewish history departments in Israeli universities, is understandable in view of what such a realization would induce: a troublesome and not easily controlled reappraisal of the whole course of Jewish history and the meaning of Judaism, based on what now appears to be a historically grounded religion paradoxically founded on fictional history.

Would it be now possible boldly to replace the migrations of the patriarchs with some other hypothesis, such as the arrival of the Jews from another planet? Aside from the conventional predilection to favor Jewish origins in innocuous Mesopotamian shepherds rather than in awesome extraterrestrial beings, there would be the fear that this innovative fiction model would erode the whole ethos of Jewish combating of modern anti-Semitism through a claim of Jewish similarity to other peoples, even though Orthodox Jews in their early morning prayers daily thank God for making the Jews "different than the peoples of the earth."

So silence on postbiblical history and the perpetual ringing of the bells on the mythical migrations of the patriarchs and the romanticized heroism of David and the Maccabees appears the wisest course.

It remains to be seen what the general impact of the proliferation of Jewish historical writing from the new Judaic studies departments will be. Since half of these scholars have had rabbinical training and nearly all the chairs they occupy were funded by the billionaire patriarchs, an early upheaval in Jewish historical consciousness leading to a cultural revolution should not be anticipated.

CHAPTER TWO

The People of the Covenant

Whether the Israelites of the early first millennium B.C. were a nomadic people who came out of the southern desert to overrun the urbanized Canaanites along the eastern littoral of the Mediterranean, or whether they were originally a religious or social subgroup among the Canaanites themselves, they became bound together in a loose political confederation. More important they had a religious identity—their devotion to their god Yahweh (YHWH, Jehovah) and the belief they were bound to him by a covenant (B'rit).

Whatever had been the origin of these people called Israel, they were now a people collectively and identifiably called by God. Yahweh would protect the tribes of Israel, and in return they must obey certain religious commands set down by him. The Jews also cultivated a memory (however invented) of the captivity of some of their tribes in Egypt and their rescue from Egypt by Yahweh through the leadership of Moses. Despite a tendency to confuse Yahweh with local gods and to worship according to the forms practiced by the Canaanites, these traditions were assiduously cultivated.

The covenant was not a negotiated contract—the Jews had not entered voluntarily into a compact with Yahweh, nor could they withdraw from their obligations to God. Of his own inscrutable will, Yahweh had chosen this obscure people as his own.

Parallels drawn by W. F. Albright and others between the Jewish covenant with God and ancient Near Eastern business contracts and diplomatic pacts are not convincing. The B'rit is not the outcome of a deal between two free parties. It is an act of providence unilaterally imposed by divine majesty upon the Jews.

The covenant idea was that God had given to the fathers of the tribe—Abraham, Isaac, and Jacob—the land of Canaan as their own land, and when the Jews were slaves of Pharaoh in Egypt, he had sent Moses to lead them out of captivity and back to the Promised Land. Yahweh had also imposed on his people his ethical norms and religious commandments, beginning with the tablets accorded Moses on Mount Sinai. The Jews had no choice but to maintain God's covenant—this was their burden and their glory.

The power and meaning of the covenant is adumbrated early in the Bible in the story of Abraham's willingness to sacrifice his son Isaac at God's command. Of course, divine intervention precludes this killing of the child, but that Abraham was willing to perform this heinous ritual at God's command is held to be meritorious and worthy of immense reward. The covenant has been upheld, even to the point of death, and Yahweh is immensely pleased:

> By Myself I swear, the Lord declares: Because you have done this and have not withheld your son, your favored one, I will bestow My blessings upon you and make your descendants as numerous as the stars of heaven and the sand on the seashore: And your descendants shall seize the gates of their foes. All the nations shall bless themselves by your descendants, because you have obeyed My command.

The story of the sacrifice of Isaac had a profound message for the Hebrew mind down through the centuries.

In biblical history, the people complained often enough and aroused God's wrath frequently enough by violating the covenant, even to the point of worshipping idols and false gods. But the people had been called, and they could not repudiate the covenant. The prescribed circumcision of all Jewish males memorialized the eternity of the covenant. The benign Sabbath symbolized the covenant's continuing humane value in Jewish life.

In this land of Canaan that God gave to Abraham, his seed

would prosper and multiply. Abraham would be "the father of a multitude of nations." Canaan would be "an everlasting holding" of the people of the covenant:

> I am God Almighty. Live always in my presence and be perfect, so that I may put my covenant between me and you . . . I am setting up my covenant between me and you and your descendants after you as an eternal covenant, to be your God and the God of your descendants. And I am giving you and your descendants after you the land where you are now aliens, the whole of the land of Canaan as an eternal possession, and I will be God to them . . . You shall circumcise the flesh of your foreskin, and this shall be the sign of the covenant between me and you.

These words of Yahweh to Abraham in the Book of Genesis are the foundation myth of Jewish history, the idea out of which the sacred chain of self-imposed collective Jewish destiny was forged.

This theme is reinforced in the Book of Exodus by God's message to the people of Israel assembled at the foot of Mount Sinai:

> And now, if you hear my voice and observe my covenant, you shall be my possession before all the peoples; for the whole earth is mine. You shall become to me a kingdom of priests and a holy people.

The covenant idea is the polar opposite of democracy, multiculturalism, and ethnic equality. It is intensely elitist. It singles out the people of Israel and raises them uniquely above all other people as a holy community of priests designated to witness God's word in the world, as summarized in the Decalogue, the Ten Commandments that Moses received from Yahweh on Mount Sinai:

> I am the Lord your God.
> You shall have no other gods besides me.
> You shall not make for yourselves an image of God.
> You shall not take the name of the Lord your God in vain.
> Remember the sabbath day to keep it holy.
> Honor your father and mother.

You shall not kill.

You shall not commit adultery.

You shall not steal.

You shall not bear false witness against your neighbor.

You shall not covet your neighbor's house.

You shall not covet your neighbor's wife . . . or anything that is
   your neighbor's.

Bound together by these beliefs and moral law, the Jewish tribes overcame the power of hostile Canaanites, we are told. In the tenth century B.C. the tribes of Israel, faced with a great threat from the Philistines, united into one kingdom. David, later remembered as their greatest king, was able to defeat the enemies of Israel and to establish a hegemony in the land. He captured the hill city of Jerusalem and made it the capital of his empire. In the reign following David's, his son, rich and mighty Solomon, built the Temple, which was to become the center of religious observance in Israel. The rise of David's monarchy (tenth century B.C.) can be perceived from circumstantial biblical accounts reinforced by meager archaeological data.

The emergence of kingship among the Israelites in the ninth century B.C. was the consequence of the invasion of Canaan from the Mediterranean side by a sea people, the Philistines, who possessed superior iron weapons. The Philistine center was along the southern coast in places like Ashdod and Ashqelon. In response to this threat, the Hebrews could no longer rely on the leadership of "judges," ad hoc military leaders (some of them peculiarly women, perhaps reflecting, as feminists claim, an earlier matriarchal society). The Hebrews needed the continuity and strength of a united monarchy.

The first such king, Saul, was given divine sanction for his rule over the people by the ceremony of anointment, wherein the high priest Samuel poured holy oil on Saul's head. Even though Saul came from the smallest of the Hebrew tribes, his anointment to the kingship and some early success against the Philistines won him popularity and loyalty. The ambitious leader of a powerful mercenary band, David, from the largest of the tribes, Judah, would not raise his hand against anointed Saul and try to overthrow him, despite increasing tension between the two power brokers.

When Saul and his sons fell fighting against the Philistines, David took the kingship, defeated the Philistines (from whom the Jews learned iron-making and to whom they gave their alphabet), and set up his capital in the newly conquered citadel of Jerusalem, on the high arid inland plateau. A convenient court seer proclaimed the durability of David's line despite the king's boisterous sexual behavior. An elaborate system of cisterns and wells, now again visible after recent archaeological discovery, provided water to the new Jewish citadel.

Solomon, the son produced by the most scandalous of David's numerous unions, ruled temporarily an imperial territory larger than Israel itself. Solomon generated high-glitz court glamour, and he too enjoyed a multitude of wives and concubines. He imposed heavy taxation on the people to build the Temple in Jerusalem. Here was centralized the sacrifice of animals to Yahweh. And the Temple priesthood came to play a dominant role in religious life.

Nothing in the story of David and Solomon, told with elaborate detail in the Bible, distinguishes them from any other minor dynasty of the ancient Near East—except the commitment to Yahweh and the covenant, even though Solomon had a relish for Gentile women.

The period of a united empire was brief. After Solomon's death in 931 B.C. the empire disintegrated into two kingdoms—Israel in the north and Judah in the south, reflecting long-standing separatist tendencies. Neither kingdom was able to retain its independence for long. The two kingdoms were so placed between Egypt and the Mesopotamian empires that they were frequently the scene of recurrent battles between the contending great powers. Finally, Assyria extended its predominance from Mesopotamia and reduced the two Jewish kingdoms to a state of vassalage.

During the period that Israel and Judah were menaced by the great powers, Jewish religious practices and beliefs changed—partly in response to the foreign threat and partly in reaction to conditions within Israel itself. Along with the worship of Yahweh, there had also been, from the tenth until the eighth century B.C., worship at other shrines. Intermarriage with foreigners was frequent, and because Yahweh was worshipped at local shrines, there was a tendency to fuse him with the gods of the locality. There was another significant social change: In contrast to the conditions of relative social and economic equality that had prevailed in primitive tribal times, the community was becoming increasingly separated into rich and poor. The characteristic Near Eastern social conflict of landlord against peasant, town against country, royalty and priesthood against commoner prevailed.

The prophetic movement of the eighth to the sixth century B.C. attributed the impending misfortunes of Israel to its forsaking of the covenant with Yahweh. The prophets were visionaries and rigorous moralists who made public pronouncements communicating Yahweh's current message to the people of the covenant. The prophets did not advocate simply a return to the practices and way of life of earlier times. They were progressives who demanded fulfillment of morality and social justice and the pure worship of Yahweh. To save the nation, it would be necessary to purify national life and reform society.

Some of the prophets were associated with the Temple. Some represented political factions within the nation. Yet they were always individuals whose personal experiences led them to believe that they were chosen by Yahweh to speak to the nation on his behalf. Often they experienced communication with Yahweh through ecstatic visions, and they felt compelled to convey his message to the nation regardless of its reception or the consequences. Unfortunately, the writings of the major prophets in the Hebrew Bible were much edited in later centuries, and texts do not well disclose the individual personalities of most of the prophets.

The prophets spoke out to the Jews in the mid-eighth century B.C. with a common message. In the northern kingdom of Israel, two prophets, Amos and Hosea, foretold the destruction of Israel. Amos asserted that the demands of Yahweh were moral and spiritual, spoke against the oppression of the poor by the rich, and attacked the ritualistic practices of Israel. His contemporary, Hosea, explicitly named the Assyrians as the instrument by which Yahweh would destroy Israel if it did not repent. In the kingdom of Judah to the south, the warnings and demands of Amos and Hosea were echoed by the prophet Isaiah, who identified the sin of Israel as its rebellion against Yahweh, and by Micah, who, like Amos, called for an end to chronic social grievances.

The prophets did more than attack the syncretic blending of the Hebrew faith with other cults and excessive attention to ritualistic externals. They insisted that Yahweh was the one and only God and that obedience to Him and fulfillment of His ethical demands was the only possible course for the salvation of the Jewish nation. Eventually their calls for reform profoundly influenced the official—priestly and royal—position that they sometimes criticized. The oppositional character of prophecy was steadily moderated into one of cooperation with the ruling group.

The destruction of the northern kingdom of Israel at the hands of the Assyrians under Sargon II in 721 B.C. made more insistent the prophets' religious demands in the surviving Judean kingdom in the south.

The Hebrew word for prophet is *nabi*, one who calls or is called. A prophet in ancient Judaism is not someone who predicts the future, although the Hebrew prophets did plenty of that. It is rather someone called by God to proclaim or communicate his word. Therefore the prophets are God's chosen successors to Abraham and Moses as truth-speakers of divine intelligence. It was, and still is, the tendency of Christian interpreters of the Hebrew Bible, in the Middle Ages and in modern times as well, to view the prophets as oppositional to priestly Judaism. Thereby the Christian interpreters can claim that the prophets were envisioning a more liberalized and ethically based Judaism and downplaying the importance of the legal code derived from the covenant, and so were allegedly preparing the way for Jesus and the New Testament, the new dispensation that abandoned much of the old code of religious law. In the nineteenth and earlier twentieth centuries there was a tendency in Reform Judaism to go somewhat along this interpretive road, viewing the prophets as advocating a more ethically centered Judaism, less focused on the legal demands of the covenant.

Some Reform rabbis and secular commentators still take this position, but in recent years there has been an overwhelming tendency among Jewish interpreters of the Bible to view the prophets as within the mainstream of priestly and legalistic Judaism and to downplay the oppositional character of the prophetic movement.

The most interesting text in this regard is in the Book of Isaiah, where God seems to look askance upon fasting in comparison with activist social justice:

Is such a fast I desire a day for men to starve their bodies? Is it bowing the head like a bulrush and lying in sackcloth and ashes? . . .

No, unlock fetters of wickedness, and untie the cords of the
yoke, to let the oppressed go free . . .

Today the almost universal view among Jewish scholars is that
Isaiah is not placing justice over a code of prescribed religious
praxis, but instead is saying that the latter must be fulfilled by the
spirit and sensibility of the former. A behavioral code without intense
moral consciousness is not the Jewish way. Law fulfilled by justice is
the Jewish way.

Already in ancient times, this section of Isaiah was read aloud to
the congregation on the Day of Atonement to remind the community
that the Law must be fulfilled inwardly as well as outwardly. This is
the prophetic message, so that even if the prophets may have started
out as critics of the priesthood, the two religious ways rapidly coalesced. Today this is the consensus view of the prophets among Jewish biblical scholars.

The essence of biblical Judaism is the blending of a legalistic
with a prophetic tradition—a religion of command with a religion of
moral commitment. In the Book of Deuteronomy, drawn up in its
present version in the seventh century B.C., after the era of the great
prophets, this blending of law and prophecy, command and commitment, takes the definitive form of God saying: "I have put before you
life and death, blessing and curse. Choose life . . . by loving the Lord
your God, heeding His commands and holding fast to Him."

The prophet Isaiah blends the covenant ideas with Israel's designated role in spreading God's message of justice and love to the
whole world:

This is My servant, whom I uphold, my chosen one, in whom I
delight. He shall teach the true way to the nations . . .

He shall not grow dim or be bruised till he has established
the true way on earth . . .

I the Lord, in My grace, have summoned you, and I have
grasped you by the hand. I created you and appointed you a
covenant people, a light of nations.

This synthesis of legal tradition and prophetic enthusiasm provided emotional sustenance during the difficult days of the later
eighth century B.C., when the political life of Judea was marked by

conquest, revolt, and internal conflict. The Assyrian siege of the city of Jerusalem was broken in 701 B.C. when the forces surrounding the city were struck by plague and forced to withdraw, leaving Jerusalem the only unconquered city in the Jewish realms. The status of Jerusalem and the Temple were thereby greatly increased, and the national god Yahweh was regarded as the defender of his city against the invader. But the brief respite that followed the siege was only the prelude to a period of demoralizing vassalage to Assyria, whose military strength was much too great for the Jews to resist.

Some members of Hebrew society went beyond cooperation with the conquerors. Some even worshipped Assyrian divinities, assigning to Yahweh the highest place in the Assyrian pantheon. New prophets arose to condemn such abuses. In the late seventh century B.C., Jeremiah prophesied that Solomon's Temple would be destroyed because the singular worship of Yahweh as set down in the covenant had been forsaken.

In response, under the leadership of the ruler Josiah (639–609 B.C.), a reforming movement in Israel achieved concrete and immediate results. Josiah was bent on reforming worship, and his major undertaking was the plan to centralize all worship in the Temple at Jerusalem. The shrines that dotted the mountains of Judah were destroyed, and the priests who had attended them were brought to Jerusalem and made subordinate to the priests of the Temple. The Temple itself was purified, and an austere ritual was mandated. Once all worship was restricted to the Temple in Jerusalem, the practice of accompanying almost every significant action with ritual magic had to stop. Josiah's reforms served to infuse some of the prophetic ideals into official religious observances.

King Josiah gave royal legitimacy to the newly completed Jewish behavioral code, the book of religious law that we now know as the Book of Deuteronomy in the Bible. During Josiah's reign priests and scribes, drawing on some ancient sources, but adding much of their own, presented the Deuteronomic book as having been newly discovered in the Temple and received legitimation and authority for this priestly ordained code from the king.

The official story was the discovery, in the course of purifying and repairing the Temple, of a law book that outlined how the blending of prophetic and traditional practices could be accomplished. This was the book that Josiah attempted to follow in his reforms. It represented the first written segment of Torah (Law, literally instruction), the final and sufficient word of God. From this time forward (although it would undergo important changes after the death of Josiah), the religion of Israel depended more and more on the strict observance of God's law as described in the Torah.

The reforms of Josiah had only begun to be implemented when he died. The time was too short for extensive implementation. Jeremiah's incessant prophecy that the Temple would be overthrown soon came to pass. This time the Babylonians, who had replaced the Assyrians as rulers of the Near East, besieged Jerusalem. The city fell to Nebuchadnezzar in 586 B.C., and Solomon's Temple was destroyed. Most elite members of the Judaic population were sent into exile in Babylonia, where they established a colony. Jeremiah took refuge in Egypt. Passive elements were left in Judea, and new colonies were brought in by the Babylonians, who thus removed the possibility of effective opposition.

"Lonely sits the city, once great with people. Judah has gone into exile . . . ," lamented old Jeremiah in his Egyptian exile. Yet those who had gone to Mesopotamia, we are told in the Bible, swore that they would never forget Zion. By the waters of Babylon they sat down and wept and swore a mighty oath that the covenant between Yahweh and the Jews would not be abrogated.

Despair is mitigated by hope of redemption and restoration in the future. Destruction and exile would in time be succeeded by return to Jerusalem, and restoration of David's royal line. In Jeremiah's lyrical pronouncement:

> He who scattered Israel will gather them, and will guard them
> as a shepherd his flock. For the Lord will ransom Jacob, redeem
> him from one too strong for him.

The recurring cycle of defeat and triumph, of exile and restoration, of destruction and redemption, here articulated by Jeremiah, became a central motif of resurgent theology in biblical and all subsequent Jewish thought.

The destruction of Judah and the Babylonian willingness to allow Judeans to settle throughout their empire provided impetus to dispersion of the Jewish population. The most vital group was the Jewish colony established in Babylonia. Living in a foreign land, they were

deprived of worship in the Temple, but instead of losing their identity and becoming assimilated into the native population, they developed a highly self-conscious religious community. Many Jews, of
course, were assimilated into Mesopotamian culture, but for the rest,
obedience to the Law was held as the source of the distinctiveness of
the Jews. Circumcision and observance of the Sabbath became more
central than ever, as did observance of dietary restrictions, to
strengthen Jewish identity while Jews lived in multicultural exile (circumcision was common in the ancient Near East, but the Babylonians did not practice it, so for the Jews it became even more important than before).

The foundations of the synagogue, which would become critically important in later Judaism, can be traced to the meetings of this
Jewish community in exile from Jerusalem. In the absence of the
Temple, religious meetings had to forsake ritual and rely on prayer
and reading of religious texts.

In Babylonia, the Jews spoke Aramaic, the common language of
the country. Aramaic is a Semitic language that closely resembles but
is still distinct from Hebrew. After some of the Babylonian community returned to Judea, they took Aramaic with them, and it became
the language of the Jewish populace for several centuries. The Jewish prayer for the dead is still recited in Aramaic, reflecting its sometime popular use.

Some modern scholars, like Manchester's John Allegro and
Columbia's Morton Smith, have speculated that what the Jews
learned in Babylonia was more than Aramaic and synagogue worship. Rather it was there, in the valleys of what is today Iraq, that the
Jews in the middle of the first millennium B.C. are said to have
learned much of their monotheism and to have written drafts of most
of the Pentateuch's narrative text, which they later brought back to
Jerusalem. The Bible symbolically hints at this derivation by placing
the homeland of the patriarch Abraham in Iraq.

By this view, well-speculated but unproven, Judaism was a
derivation from Mesopotamian religious culture. Allegro and Smith
also contend that Jews brought back with them from Mesopotamia a
volatile brand of esoteric religion to go with the more sedate biblical
religion we recognize.

Even in Babylonia the prophets continued to speak out, but after
the destruction of Jerusalem their preaching took a new tone. Instead

of prophesying the destruction of Jerusalem, they explained that the misfortunes of the Jews were punishments for their sins and anticipated the eventual restoration of Halakah (religious law) in Jerusalem. Ezekiel had foretold the destruction of Jerusalem, but writing as an exile, he also denied the idea of collective guilt and claimed that each individual received retribution for his own sins. At the same time, for Ezekiel the Israelites were the chosen people of a universal God, and he looked forward to the redemption of the nation.

The later prophets who wrote in exile not surprisingly tended to give universal significance to the Jewish faith, a trend illustrated by the writings of Second Isaiah. Deutero-Isaiah enunciated the idea that Yahweh, the universal creator of the universe, had chosen Israel to be his witness among the Gentiles. Just as the Hebrew people's suffering had been a lesson to mankind, so would its restoration be brought about as a sign of a new age of universal peace and justice. In order that war might end and nations beat their swords into agricultural implements, the word of God must again go forth from Zion and the Law be proclaimed from Jerusalem.

The prophets who wrote in exile recognized a common brotherhood of all peoples and Yahweh as the father of all mankind. Yet this kind of universalism did not detract from or erode faith in the Jews' covenanted destiny as God's chosen witnesses to mankind. On the contrary, it enhanced the strength of this belief. The Jews must return to Jerusalem and restore the Temple so that mankind might enjoy peace and justice.

The hopes of the exiles were answered in 539 B.C. when the Persians took the city of Babylon and established their control over the Babylonian empire. Since the Persians' policy encouraged local religious organizations within their empire, the Jews were allowed to return to Jerusalem and were even permitted to rebuild their Temple. But after two generations of exile, the return to Jerusalem was slow, and the population dwelling on the land was not especially eager to restore the Temple. Neither the returned exiles nor the indigenous Jews had the kind of funds required for the restoration of Jerusalem. Reconstruction was begun by Zerubbabel, under the Persian king Darius I, and the new Temple was consecrated in 515 B.C. But not until the administration of the Persian governor Nehemiah, in the mid-fifth century, was real reconstruction carried out and the enforcement of religious law achieved. Nehemiah was empowered by the Persian king to institute important reforms. He prohibited marriages with non-Jews, provided for the payment of tithes and the observance of the Sabbath, and allowed for the remission of debts to lift the heavy burdens that oppressed the poor. Finally, Nehemiah saw to the rebuilding of the walls of Jerusalem.

Those who had remained in Judah as well as those who had, under Babylonian rule, been assimilated into the population from abroad were not eager to see the power of the Temple restored, for this would mean the predominance of the returned exiles. Therefore they opposed Nehemiah's reforms and continued to live much as they had during the exile.

To counteract their obstructionism, Ezra, a member of the group of exiles in Babylonia, early in the fourth century undertook a commission from the Persian king to restore the systematic observance of Jewish law in Judea. As a result of his work, the books of the Law, the Pentateuch (the so-called Five Books of Moses), incorporated the results of the exile experience with the reforms of Josiah and the prophetic tradition. The Law now began to take on its final form. In the future, mainstream Judaism would be a religion of the Law that religious leaders insisted was binding on all of the Jewish nation.

As far as practice was concerned, the most important change in this amended version of the Law was the observance of the Day of Atonement. In doctrine, the most important addition was the development of an eschatological view of history—the view that a Messiah would come forth to lead the Jewish nation in the Day of the Lord. Yahweh was no longer the national champion of Israel but rather the judge of the entire world, a universal God whose will was absolute justice. The judgment of God was worked out in history, and His commands were expressed in the Law of the Jewish nation, whose misfortunes were a lesson to all mankind and whose eventual triumph was assured because they were the chosen people of the Lord.

In the meantime, the Jews remained a conquered nation—the vassal state of the Persians, and then of Alexander the Great and his successors, the rulers of the Hellenistic kingdoms of the Near East that emerged in the fourth century B.C.

In a couple of decades before his death in 323 B.C. Alexander of Macedon created the largest empire the ancient world had known, stretching from Greece to northern India. Judea was early on incorporated into the realm of the world conqueror, who treated the Jews generously. After his death, his empire broke up into three political entities. Judea was initially under Egyptian rule, but this was soon superseded by incorporation into the Syrian empire of the Seleucid dynasty.

The differences were political but the culture of the post-Alexander Hellenistic world was largely the same everywhere in the Near East. Hellenistic civilization was a urban-centered blending of the religions and lifestyles of the eastern Mediterranean, bound together by Greek language (in postclassical, vulgarized form) and, among the educated class, by Platonic philosophy.

Within Judaism itself in the Hellenistic era, numerous divisions and conflicts centered around the priesthood. With the reorganization of the Temple, the high priest became the most important official in the state, but the power struggle within the priesthood meant that there was no peace within the Jewish nation. Most conflicts were fought around one crucial issue: Would the integrity of Jewish religious culture be preserved despite a growing tendency toward absorption into the Hellenistic world?

Jews were given a privileged position in the Hellenistic kingdoms. They were allowed to settle freely in the cities of the Near East and were granted social and economic privileges second only to those of the Macedonian and Greek conquerors. The attraction of the Hellenistic cities was very powerful, and large colonies of Jews dotted the Near Eastern world. But even this dispersion did not cause the Jewish colonies to lose their identity. Instead, synagogues were established, the Law was respected, and proselytes were added to the ranks of the faithful. Converts who attended the synagogue and observed some of the Law—omitting the more stringent requirements such as circumcision—also swelled the ranks of the Jewish community.

Within Jerusalem itself, Hellenizing influence took a political form expressed in cooperation with the foreign monarchies and a cultural form expressed in the adoption of Greek language and lifestyle. The Pentateuch was translated into Greek by Alexandrian Jewish scholars in the Septuagint version. There was even a Greek gymnasium in Jerusalem, where the young men of Israel took part in athletic contests in the Greek manner. Some Greek preference for nudity was particularly appalling to the faithful, though all the Hellenistic innovations were widely opposed by the more conservative elements of the Jewish population.

Political and cultural discontent flared into open rebellion in 168 B.C. when Antiochus IV Epiphanis, the Seleucid ruler of Syria, came to Jerusalem and flagrantly polluted the Temple. The old shrines began to be converted to the worship of new Hellenistic gods, and the population was threatened with adoption of new Greek observances. Possibly Antiochus's motives were political rather than ideological—he was trying to extort money from the Jews to pay for his military campaigns—but a bitter conflict erupted.

At first, widespread compliance was broken only by martyrs who refused to take part in the new rites, but in 166 B.C. open and organized revolt began. At the outset of the struggle, the rebels merely retreated to the hills and engaged in occasional guerrilla warfare against the foreign officials, but under the leadership of Judas Maccabeus the rebels won several battles. The military skill of the Maccabean family gained for them the open support of Jews who were deeply opposed to the religious oppression by their Syrian overlords but who had initially been cautious about the possibility of rebellion.

The Book of Daniel, which was written at the time of the Maccabean revolt, indicates the highly emotional, apocalyptic speculation that accompanied the conflict against the Syrian empire. The latter was seen as the fourth and final empire in history; it would be replaced by the kingdom of God.

The revolt spread rapidly, and because of troubles within the Syrian empire, the Maccabeans were able to gain recognition of Judea's virtual independence, and the state that they established lasted for almost a century, until the Roman conquest in 63 B.C.

The symbol of Maccabean rule was the menorah, the seven-branched candelabra on a three-legged base. Later, under Roman rule in Judea, a solid base for the menorah became fashionable, and in this modified, post-Maccabean form the menorah became the symbol of the modern state of Israel.

A special expanded menorah, allowing a light for each day of Hanukkah, the eight-day festival of lights, is used to commemorate the Maccabean reconquest of the Temple from the Syrians and the Temple's cleansing and renewal. Traditional legend told of the discovery of a flask of holy oil in the Temple, enough to burn for eight days.

Joyous celebration of the Maccabean military triumph and spiritual rededication ignores the sad later history of the Maccabean (also called Hasmonean) dynasty, whose kings turned out to be just another family of greedy, manipulative, and often inept rulers.

Much of the support for the rebels and the new ruling dynasty had come from those elements in the population that were particularly concerned with establishing pure religious beliefs and practices, but once independence was won, the Maccabean kings were mainly interested in preserving their own independence and political power. The new monarchy was torn by factional struggles and was forced to play politics with the Syrian empire to maintain its independence.

This situation did not change when the Romans under Pompey established their hegemony in Judea in 63 B.C. Although the Jews were allowed to continue their religious life, the policies of the Roman governors and the puppet kings they set up frequently came into conflict with the beliefs and practices that made the Jews unique within the Roman Empire. Revolt was always just below the surface of Jewish political life in the late first century B.C. Even among the aristocrats and wealthy groups, many never completely accommodated themselves to Roman rule. Roman pacification of Judea was incomplete.

Such a political situation offered no solution to the controversies that tended more and more to split Judaism into religious factions and sects. The reliance on written law gave rise to the predominance of scribes, men of learning who studied and interpreted the Law. It also fostered religious controversy, which focused on two groups of interpreters, the Sadducees and the Pharisees. The Sadducees were the more aristocratic of the two groups. They dominated the Sanhedrin, the Jewish high court in Jerusalem. The Sadducces refused to recognize anything not explicitly stated in the written Law. They appear to be descended from the Zaddokites, family members and their allies who had controlled the priesthood from the time of a certain Zaddok, high priest in the time of King Solomon. Possibly the term "Sadducees" is a derivation from "Zaddokites."

When the Maccabees defeated the Syrians and gained Jerusalem, they evicted the Zaddokites from the priesthood and put their own men in charge. This Maccabean move greatly disturbed the Zaddokites, and a militant wing of the Sadducees, the Essenes, plotted a revolution in response.

The Pharisees were eager to supplement the text of the Law with oral tradition and rabbinical interpretation. In that sense they were liberal and progressive. The Pharisees insisted that in addition to the written Law (Torah), which Moses and the Israelites had received from Yahweh on Mount Sinai, the Jews had received an oral law of equivalent importance, and it was the obligation and privilege of the learned scribes, the rabbis, to interpret the oral law and make it fully compatible with the written Law. Through interpretation, the Pharisaic rabbis would bring this double-faceted legal heritage up-to-date and apply it to current needs and issues.

Therefore while the Sadducees held to a rigid and literal reading of the written Law, the Pharisees were malleable and progressive updaters of the Law, a large part of which, they claimed, was orally received. This Pharisaic view has remained the basic assumption of rabbinical, or Orthodox, Judaism. While in general the Pharisees were also more strongly opposed to Hellenistic influences than the Sadducees, the Pharisees borrowed from Mesopotamian religion the popular doctrine of personal immortality and resurrection of the dead, which is absent from the Torah.

The Pharisees were a middle-class phenomenon. They were laymen, not priests or members of aristocratic priestly families, as were the Sadducees. The Pharisees were scribes and teachers, the lay, nonpriestly community leaders whom the Jews called by various names but most commonly and persistently referred to as *rabbis*.

The Pharisees banded together in fraternities and clubs to discuss the implementation of the Law. They divided into two schools, led by the teachers of the Law Shammai and Hillel. The school of Shammai was more rigorous and legalistic, that of Hillel more pragmatic and humanistic. It was Hillel who responded to the scoffing request of a heathen to teach him the whole Torah while the heathen was standing on one foot: "What is hateful to you, do not do to your neighbor: that is the whole Torah; the rest is commentary."

Both the Sadducees and the Pharisees accepted the rule of a foreign power as a necessary evil, though the more socially upscale Sadducees were more willing than the Pharisees to collaborate with the Roman conquerors. But other Jewish groups were unwilling to compromise. The Zealots continued the tradition of revolution against foreign domination that had characterized the early phase of the Maccabean resistance. They demanded political independence for Israel and refused to pay taxes to the Roman emperor, claiming that they owed allegiance only to the one true God. Members of this minority movement used terror and guerrilla activity to stir up resistance to the oppressors. They became Sicarii (assassins). They sought a war of national liberation from Roman rule.

While the Zealots represented a breakaway from the majority of the Pharisees toward a more radical political position, other groups inclined toward a more radical spiritualism. The desire to lead a pure life of obedience to God's will led the Essenes to withdraw from the Jewish community altogether. As an elect community of the pure, they established themselves at Qumran in the desert along the Dead Sea, where they tried to fulfill the Law in spirit as well as form. The Qumran community's library, the so-called Dead Sea Scrolls, was discovered in caves along the Dead Sea in the late 1940s.

A New York University expert on the Dead Sea Scrolls, Lawrence Schiffman, believes that the Qumran community was founded around 150 B.C. by a group of pious Sadducean priests who rejected Pharisaic canonization of the oral law. Believing themselves to be living in the last age, the Essenes under the charismatic leadership of a "Teacher of Righteousness" practiced a highly disciplined form of asceticism. They held property in common. Some of the Essenes did not marry and refrained from sex—a monastic disavowal unique in ancient Judaism.

The Qumram community represented a strenuous attempt to fulfill the prophetic demands for righteousness through obedience to the will of God. Yet even in their own day, some saw in Essenic activism the influence of ideas from Hellenistic philosophy and religion, from non-Jewish culture.

The proliferation of factions and sects among the Jews in the era of Roman domination reflects the extreme threat to the integrity of the Hebrew faith presented by the power and attraction of Roman and Hellenistic civilization. How far the Jews could collaborate with Roman power, how much they could compromise with Hellenistic culture and still remain true to Yahweh and his Law, was the agonizing question they encountered daily. Giving additional force to this dilemma was the widespread belief in Judea at the end of the first century B.C. that the final, crucial stage of history had been reached, that God was about to judge among all the nations and particularly to call the Jews, his chosen witnesses, to account. Some kind of Messiah (Redeemer) would be God's chosen instrument to achieve these things.

Among the Jewish aristocracy, particularly those descended from the Maccabeans, there were collaborators with Roman power, and some Jews were powerfully attracted by the wonders of Hellenistic art, literature, and philosophy. The majority, however, under Pharisaic leadership, held out against both acquiescence to Roman rule and absorption into Hellenism. They marched to a different drummer and did not go the way of all the other peoples of the Mediterranean world. They continued to believe that as God's chosen people they had the duty to fulfill his will at all costs; their reward would come when the Day of the Lord was established. This Jewish intransigence and separation, so irritating to the Romans, so repulsive to the Greeks, made the people of the covenant unique in the Mediterranean world.

Gentile commentators admired the Jews for their holy scriptures and their steadfast devotion to the Law of the covenant. Yet the Jews were also regarded in the Mediterranean world as arrogant, subversive, and untrustworthy. The leaders of the Jewish community did not calculate the consequences of their removal from paganism. In their view, there was no other way to live than by the Halakah, God's law, by which the covenant was fulfilled. This meant in practice that many hundreds of thousands of Jews, especially those living in the Diaspora outside Judea, who found Mediterranean culture more meaningful and accessible than strict biblical teaching and Pharisaic law, drifted away and were completely assimilated into the surrounding population. The adherents of the covenant became the Orthodox voice of Judaism.

For the past one hundred twenty-five years a legion of scholars, both Jewish and Christian, have tried to establish clearly the development of the Hebrew faith between King David and Jesus Christ, spanning the last millennium before the Common Era. The details remain uncertain in many aspects, and in general it is not a happy story.

But the prime ingredients of ancient Jewish history in the first millennium B.C. are evident enough: the priestly code of behavior promulgated by the kings and clerics who commanded the Temple in Jerusalem; prophetic pronouncements on ethics, universal history, and expectations of the future, which over time coalesced with the priestly code; the demotic experience of the Diaspora, beginning with the Babylonian exile, when divinity had to become less physically rooted and a communal synagogue became the prime place of worship of an immaterial God; and a belief in personal immortality and resurrection of the dead, which only filtered into Judaism in the two or three centuries before the Common Era.

Alongside these fundamental attitudes were messianic expectations. The Redeemer was either the Jewish people as a whole, "the man of sorrows" who vicariously suffered for and cleansed transgressions of the rest of mankind; or a charismatic individual, descended from the "Tree of Jesse" (House of David) who would restore the glorious old ramshackle monarchy; or some conflation of these two ideas.

By the later years of the first century B.C. these had become the key doctrines propounded by the Pharisees, whose successors were the teaching and judicial rabbis left standing after the destruction of the Second Temple in A.D. 70 and another massive forced exile of the Jews. Today we call this Pharisaic and rabbinical Judaism the Orthodox or canonical (Halakic) faith. Even though in A.D. 100 (as today) the majority of Jews, probably a great majority, in the world were not full adherents or strict practitioners of Pharisaic-rabbinical-Orthodox Judaism, it is right to call this mainstream Judaism.

At least two alternative forms of Hebrew faith existed alongside rabbinic orthodoxy: Essenic, apocalyptic, and mystical Judaism (as in the religion of Qumran, of the Dead Sea Scrolls), advocated vehemently by very small but intense minorities and a culture that in the Middle Ages and early modern times occasionally sought to unite with and embrace the Orthodox tradition; and the philosophic, Hellenistic, assimilating Judaism of the Alexandrian and other great eastern Mediterranean communities. Hellenistic Judaism resembles the liberal and Reform Judaism of today.

The threefold split in Jewish religious culture, which was to prevail into modern times, was already evident in the first century B.C. We call rabbinical Judaism mainstream because it is a direct outgrowth of the previous millennium of Jewish history. It has a closely held, deeply textured, continuous history down through the centuries, and it flourishes today again in Jerusalem as well as in New York. In the first six centuries of the Common Era it generated the Talmud, and it became the dominant religious faith and practice of the great Eastern European communities from the seventeenth century into the twentieth century.

Pharisaic-rabbinical Judaism was the faith and culture against which the other communities of believers measured and defined themselves. This was the core culture. Efforts are constantly made, both in learned treatises and in the sermons of Orthodox rabbis, as well as in guidebooks for the suburbs on "Jewish literacy," to define the nature of mainstream Judaism. Yet the most insightful effort was made by the German Protestant sociologist Max Weber in 1906 in his book *Ancient Judaism*. It has never been superseded.

The most important characteristic of mainstream Judaism is that unlike all the other religions of the ancient Mediterranean world, including Christianity, it does not involve magic. The word "magic" in anthropology means that some physical act like a sacrament or faith healing or astrological calculation or touching of some object is being used to bring divine assistance to mankind. Mainstream Judaism recognized only prayer and righteous conduct as a form of communication with the divine. It is true that for centuries animal sacrifices had been offered at the Jerusalem Temple altar, which is a low-grade form of magic. But the developing Pharisaic-rabbinical Judaism jettisoned the intercession of all magic to summon divine favor and help. Probably this nonmagical mode had begun in the two centuries between the First and Second Temples, when burnt offerings could not be made in Jerusalem. And after A.D. 70 there was again no Temple. So rabbinical mainstream Judaism had to rely on a purely spiritual relationship between God and the people of the covenant.

Yet the development of Judaism as a nonmagical religion was not only a reaction to the absence of the Temple and its altars. Ingrained in the prophetic tradition was God's disavowal of his pleasure in sacrifices and other magical rituals and insistence on the human supplication of God in purely spiritual and moral terms.

In 1960 Yehezkel Kaufman of the Hebrew University confirmed Max Weber's interpretation of ancient Judaism:

> The religious idea of the Bible . . . is that of a supreme God who stands over every cosmic law, every destiny and every compulsion: unborn, uncreated . . . a God who does not fight against other deities or power of impurity, who does not sacrifice, predict, prophesy and practice witchcraft; who does not sin and needs no atonement; a God who does not celebrate the festivals of his life. A free divine will that transcends all that is—that is

characteristic of biblical religion, and that makes it different from all other religions on this earth.

God is Who He Is—absolutely transcendent, and beyond effects of human magic to summon or influence, the eternally self-subsisting One. "Hear O Israel, the Lord our God, the Lord is One." This became the essential declaration of Jewish faith. This is probably not where Judaism started in the late second millennium B.C., but it was where it arrived in the Pharisaic, mainstream form by 200 B.C.

This antimagicality is the distinctive quality of the Hebrew covenant religion as it took its definitive form toward the beginning of the Common Era. This too is the ultimate reason for the rise of ideological anti-Semitism at the same time. The Jews in their mainstream faith had chosen a radical course different from the religion of all other Mediterranean communities, including the Christian one, and thereby the Jews challenged the legitimacy of these other cultures.

At some point in the Christian era, all Orthodox Jews became accustomed to begin the day with a prayer of thanks that God had made them different from the Gentiles, even when—or especially when—the Gentiles had the wealth and power and were persecuting or even exterminating the people of the covenant. Living under the covenant, in accordance with the Pharisaic-rabbinical-Orthodox faith, indeed made the Jews different from the Gentiles, "the peoples of the earth." The difference is obvious in circumcision, the dietary laws, and the observance of the Sabbath and the Day of Atonement.

The crucial difference lies also in a mentality, a consciousness that mainstream Judaism engendered. First, the Orthodox Jew had no physical or ritualistic crutch. He could not rely on a dying and reborn divine savior incarnated in human form, in a material sacrament to unite him with this savior God, in astrological calculation, in touching of sacred objects and other familiar facets of magic. He could rely only on the goodness and majesty of God. If bad things happened to good people, the Jew had to accept these disasters and go on with living as best he could.

He had to rationalize a disaster in one of several ways. He, the Jew, was really at fault after all. On second thought he had acted badly, if only by being too self-confident and self-righteous in his goodness, and Yahweh was rightly chastising him. Or suffering was a learning process and an act of purification and he, the Jew, would come out of it a better person and better able to fulfill God's commandments. Or the suffering of the Jew was somehow for the benefit of mankind, a vehicle for communicating God's word to the Gentiles and a strategy for implementing God's mercy.

In the last two centuries B.C. these rationalizations for why the Jews suffer collectively and why bad things happen to ostensibly good individuals prevailed in the Jewish dialogue and were embedded in their consciousness. This "theodicy" (justification of the ways of God to man) was to have a very long and intense workout in Jewish history. There is no more continuous intellectual theme in the exercise of the Jewish imagination. All of Jewish history is a theodicy.

The second most critical ingredient of the mentality that mainstream Judaism engendered was historicity. For the pagan cultures of the ancient Mediterranean the time was always now, always the eternal present. The Jew saw himself as part of a very long and tempestuous continuity reaching from the patriarchs to the present. Everything the Jew did he did in the context of this extended temporal dimension, replicating and perpetuating it and interacting with it.

We have seen that Jewish historicity is a peculiar one, a backward-bending historical curve, in the sense that the details of historical information terminate with the early Maccabees. After that the Jews still function very much within a temporal dimension, but the details of the post-Maccabean era in Jewish history are left mostly blank, because these details would arouse too many questions and too much controversy, some of it uncomfortable for the rabbis.

Jewish historicity has a plenitude, indeed a plethora of historical information about the earlier history of the Jews (much of it fictional or heavily romanticized) and a sparse deficiency for the post–early Maccabean era. This was the model of Jewish historicity that existed until the beginning of modern historiography in the early nineteenth century, and this backward-leaning historical curve still conditions the sermons of rabbis of all persuasions.

The Jewish mind-set also stressed community. No man was an island. The individual's acts were made significant in a group context. This attitude per se was far from unique; the Greeks insisted that we are all social or communal beings. The difference in Jewish thinking was that their community was temporal as well as spatial in dimension. Their community was on a move through time, was on an unbroken pilgrimage route somewhere, sometime to the end of days. Thereby the community in which the Jew was immersed was not only the current large group but the whole retinue of the Jewish people through two millennia from Abraham through Moses, David and Jeremiah to the present. Every act of every individual had to be imagined and judged in the perspective of whether it advanced or impeded the pilgrimage of the community through time.

The psychic burdens of theodicy and historicity were severe and unyielding. Anyone who had to rethink continuously and fundamentally the divine and historical significations and their relationship to personal feelings and present personal conduct would become stressed to the point of madness. The practical solution for everyday living that mainstream Pharisaic-rabbinical-Orthodox Judaism offered was minutely listed mitzvoth, or good points of conduct (ultimately six hundred thirteen of them), that codified the behavior of the devout Jew from the moment of waking in the early morning to falling asleep (and beyond) at night.

The tremendous psychic pressures of Jewish theodicy and historicity meant that this was a religion that rejected all the magical props of other cultures and faiths and yet offered an extremely detailed, obsessive code of human behavior to make daily life endurable. Thus the great paradox of the covenant religion as both an extraordinarily liberating and a compulsively confining culture.

There was a time, in the late nineteenth and early twentieth centuries, when the covenant theology aroused deep reservations in some Jewish intellectual circles with reference to the problematics and anxieties it created for daily living in a difficult and imperfect world. That is not the case anymore. All those from Jewish quarters who comment on covenant theology do so in the temperament of uncritical praise. The droves of Judaic studies programs on American campuses that have been established with generous endowments in the past twenty years are insistent in their unwavering praise of the idea of the Jews as people of the covenant.

To these Jewish voices of very strong covenant affirmation are added those of Protestant commentators on the Bible. Since the 1920s there has been a great revival of seventeenth-century Protestant covenanting theology, and if this presents some awkwardness for Protestant thinkers because it has to be integrated somehow with the doctrine of the incarnation of God in human form, a very contrary and quite hard-core magical belief, they try hard to overcome these tensions, or simply ignore them. A thriving, well-subsidized American Protestant press exists in Philadelphia to publish lengthy treatises with titles like "The People Called."

One of the favorite paperback books in current American Judaic studies programs is *Exploring Exodus* (1986) by Brandeis University's Nahum Sarna. In this book we read, along with the conventional but doubtful claim that the Jewish covenant is "expressed" in contemporary legal instruments of diplomacy and business, this enthusiastic generalization: "Covenant . . . describes nothing less than the assertion of the conclusion of an eternally binding pact between God and His people." Sarna is so pleased with this idea that he does not explore its psychological and sociological significance for Jewish history.

The authors of the Bible were more realistic. The tensions and distresses of living with God's covenant are recognized in the Bible. The Book of Exodus described how while Moses was up on the mountain receiving tablets of the Law from God, "the people were out of control" and made an idol, a golden calf to worship, and Aaron, Moses' brother and the high priest, "had to let them get out of control." When Moses returned, in his fury, he not only destroyed the idol but also turned loose the Levites, the priestly tribe, on the people, and the Levites proceeded to slaughter three thousand of them. There is obviously a downside to the eternally binding pact between God and His people. Break it and be slaughtered by Yahweh's priestly shock troops.

That Ezra and the final editors of the Bible let this violent story stand indicates their attitude to those in the Jewish community who visibly violated the covenant. There will be covenant breakers, the redactors are saying—the people will get out of control. Punishment must be used to restore discipline when necessary and where possible. This is a realistic assessment of the difficulty of maintaining the covenant.

Ezra and the redactors of the Bible also let stand in Genesis the chilling story of the sacrifice of Isaac to communicate the demand enforced on every Jew to accept Yahweh's dictates, even if they are inhuman.

The scribes and rabbis also included in the biblical canon the late work Ecclesiastes (Ko Hi-Lot) with its deep pessimism:

> A season is set for everything, a time for every experience under heaven . . . A time for being born and a time for dying . . . A time for crying and a time for laughing . . . A time for loving and a time for hating . . . I realized that the only worthwhile thing there is for men is for them to enjoy themselves and do what is good in their lifetime.

Some modern commentators have seen Ecclesiastes as an anomalous work in the Hebrew Bible. It is held to reflect the fatalistic sentiments of Stoic philosophy and so was a product of Hellenistic influence on Jewish thought. But it conforms to the fatalistic sensibility behind the story of Isaac's sacrifice. It does not seem to be outside the parameters of Pharisaic mentality.

Similarly, the whole of the Book of Job, written probably around 300 B.C., is devoted to the problem that covenant theology raises: Why do bad things happen to a good person? It never really answers this question. In the end a voice comes out of the whirlwind and tells the distraught Job to shut up, have faith in God, and stop whining. At the end of the book an epilogue (probably by a later author) restores Job to his wealth and health. The immensely learned historian of later ancient Judaism, Elias J. Bickerman, calls Job, along with Ecclesiastes, one of "the four strange books of the Bible": What is it doing there in the canon, raising contrary anxieties? The rabbis must have had enough of such concerns themselves to put Job in the Masoretic canon.

The fifty-third chapter of the Book of Isaiah (written by Deutero-Isaiah in Babylonian exile around 525 B.C.), which later so excited the disciples of Jesus of Nazareth, tries to explain the suffering of the Jews as the means of mankind's redemption:

> He was wounded because of our sins, crushed because of our iniquities, he bore the chastisement that made us whole, and by his bruises we were healed.
>
> And the Lord visited upon him the guilt of all of us . . . He bore the guilt of the many and made intercession for the sinners.

So in imposing the covenant unilaterally on the Jews, God was going to use this people as "a sheep led to the slaughter," says

Deutero-Isaiah, a sacrifice for mankind "that through him the Lord's purpose might prosper." By the covenant the Jews not only are given a hardship post in that they are meant to bear the agonies of life without the therapeutic provided by magic but also are sent on a sacrifice mission for the benefit of the human race.

This is a hard message but again a realistic assessment of reality. The Jews are not powerful. They will be beaten down by the great forces, by the megaton empires. The covenant means sacrificial suffering. Be prepared to endure it in God's Holy Name.

The covenant idea is as far as you can get from romanticism although it is normally interpreted today in an upbeat, sentimental manner in the American suburban synagogues. The old rabbis knew better. They knew what the Jews were in for in the long pilgrimage through Gentile territory. Their realism prepared the Jews to face their difficult and at times cruel destiny. Only this kind of tough-minded, realistic temperament could have preserved the people of the covenant down through the centuries of defeat and Diaspora.

The 74th Psalm frankly recognizes the hatred that the Jews incur on all sides from the Gentiles:

Your foes roar inside Your meeting-place . . .
They made your sanctuary go up in flames; They brought low in dishonor the dwelling place of Your presence . . .
They burned all God's tabernacles in the land.

Shoah, destruction, holocaust, is an ever-present prospect for the Jews. Nor can God's people find solace anymore in the preaching of the new prophets. The age of the prophecy is over:

No signs appear for us; there is no longer any prophet; no one among us knows for how long.

A deep social pessimism, an awareness of ever-impending disaster is central to the ethos of Pharisaic Judaism. In response, mainstream Judaism fashioned a defensive code of behavior, a wall of religious law, against the consequence of the Jew's sacrificial and redeeming role in history. The Torah separated the Jews from the goyim, the other peoples of the earth, by insisting on circumcision of all males, by mandating complete rest from labor every seventh day, by implementing an elaborate system of dietary taboos, by calling for fasting on the Day of Atonement.

In addition, after the return from Babylonian exile and the building of the Second Temple were imposed the requirements that all males engage in communal prayer each morning and evening, that all male children be sufficiently educated to read the Word of God in the holy scriptures, that the primal creed ("Hear, O Israel, the Lord our God, the Lord is One") be posted in a mezuzah (ornamental box) on all doorposts and that God's word similarly be placed in a phylactery (leather-covered box) that hung between the eyes in morning prayer.

Writing in 1979 Jacob Neusner, one of the most learned and prolific of the new wave of Jewish studies scholars on American campuses, stressed the centrality of prayer as the way of the Torah:

> Life under the law means praying—morning, evening, at night, and at mealtimes, both routinely and when something extraordinary happens . . . The way of the Torah is the way of constant devotion to God.

A good Jew in the mainstream, Orthodox tradition is a penitent Ba'al T'Shuva, a master of penitential prayer.

A religion based on a diurnal discipline of frequent prayer, unmodified by magic ritual, forms a temperament characterized by determination and reticence. What is to be done is known by the prescriptions of the written and oral law. God is beseeched to fulfill the covenant by rewarding good behavior and refined sentiments.

But God is too transcendent to be predictable. There is faith but not assurance that individual fulfillment of the Law will produce personal blessing. There is no known practical alternative to beseeching Yahweh the Good, One, and Omnipotent to succor and reward.

Constant prayer has embraced the individual in a behavior pattern and a sensibility that is the core of personal being, and such a program of prayer persists and sustains even in the face of personal defeat and disappointment and seeming injustice. Prayer for the observant Jew also has the effect of encouraging communal action. The more elaborate and full schedule of prayer only occurs in a minyan, a group of ten adult Jewish males, fostering group dialogue and comity.

Looking outward from the individual toward group solidarity was also stressed by the Pharisees' confirmation of the prevailing prophetic injunctions toward social justice. Mainstream Judaism did not condemn competitive business enterprise, the holding of slaves, the accumulation of wealth, or a hierarchic class structure. Since the absence of magic left the individual to make rational, purely human choices for himself, Judaism produced a mind-set that was highly conducive to market enterprise based on calculation of rational choices. Judaism and capitalism were fully compatible.

But there were heavy communal demands that the strong, affluent, and fortunate exercise charity (tzedakah) toward the weak, poor, and downtrodden. The widow, the child, the physically afflicted were not only to receive substantial aid but also to be treated with dignity. Poverty and affliction were never to be shamed.

Mainstream Judaism allowed for capital accumulation but imposed strictures on the rich not only in terms of charitable giving but also by demanding postponed gratification and condemning conspicuous consumption and personal indulgence.

The prophets and later the rabbis were deeply concerned with the social and moral consequences of the flaunting of wealth and of the humiliation that accompanies poverty. Their psychological insight into the culture of poverty was a keen one, and they sought to excise such a downside culture from the Jewish community, whatever its modest economic circumstances.

The leaders of the Jewish community, the masters of prayer, the redactors of the Bible, the rabbinical interpreters of the Law, were all males, whereas in many pagan religions, including the Roman, priestesses played an important role. Circumcision, the mark of the covenant, was a Jewish male rite. Pharisaic Judaism honored women as mothers and daughters, but essentially it placed women in a secondary and marginalized position within the family and community. To the present day, Orthodox Jews in their daily morning prayer thank God not only for not making them Gentiles, but also for not making them women. The Halakah is very concerned to prevent sexual intercourse with a menstruating woman. A woman in the full exercise of her sexuality is taboo.

At the beginning of the first millennium B.C., as was common in the ancient Near East, there likely were priestesses in Israel, presiding over local altars. In the age of the judges, there were women military and political leaders. The Book of J, the core narrative of the Pentateuch, may have been written by a royal princess, and it accords with a feminine mentality. By 150 B.C., when Pharisaic Judaism had fully crystallized, there was no social or intellectual leadership of women within the religious community, and assertive and prominent women in royal families in the later decades of the era of the Second Temple were not fondly viewed by scribes and rabbis.

To the present day, the architecture of Orthodox synagogues preserves the ancient rabbinical propensity toward the marginalization of women in the Jewish community. Women sit in a segregated balcony, separate from their husbands and sons. In mainstream, Orthodox Judaism, women may not be at the back of the bus, but they are segregated in the synagogue. Orthodox Judaism is tolerant of divorce, but it is granted only to males. Wives on their own cannot obtain divorces.

Pharisaic Judaism insists that descent in the Jewish community comes through the mother—to be a Jew, the Orthodox still insist, you must have a Jewish mother. This is sometimes cited as evidence of the high esteem in which women are held in the Jewish community. But it actually reflects toleration of the double standard of sexual behavior, so alien to women's equality. Because men in ancient Israel produced children by relations with Gentile slaves and concubines, the only way in which purity of Jewish blood could be scrutinized was by the rabbinical ruling that Jewish descent had to go through the legitimate Jewish wife. Unless a Gentile wife of a Jewish male converted, her children were not regarded as Jews.

The husband was relatively free to have sexual contact with partners other than his wife, and this frequently involved Gentile women. These mamzerim (bastards) whose mothers were Gentiles were excluded from the Jewish community. It was a nice question for later rabbinical courts whether bastards engendered by Jewish male adulterous relations with Jewish women were full and equal members of the Jewish community. Most courts said no.

In return for the burdens and strictures of living according to the covenant and Halakah, in return for being God's witness in the world, a light to the nations, and a sacrificial lamb to cleanse mankind, what did mainstream Judaism have to offer in the way of reward to the prayerful, observant Jewish male? The following: that God would give the Jews the land of Israel; that the seed of Abraham would be fruitful and multiply; that the observant Jew would feel satisfied he was a righteous person walking in the way of the Lord; that he belonged to a community, a people who were something special, who were separate from the Gentiles, and divinely designated.

That this reward system in ancient Judaism was not entirely adequate to compensate for the burdens of the covenant is indicated by the quiet acceptance after 200 B.C. into the rabbinical mainstream of the widespread Near Eastern belief in personal immortality and resurrection of the dead. This was not a doctrine vehemently preached among the Jews. It was more like a concession marginally allowed to the anxious masses by their religious leaders. Personal immortality has rarely been vigorously propounded in the Orthodox tradition; it is more of an add-on reward, a bonus, than a prime inducement to observance of the covenant.

The only clear statement about the resurrection of the dead in the Bible occurs in the Book of Daniel, the last work in the Masoretic text to be written, about 160 B.C., during the Maccabean revolt: "Many of those who sleep in the dust of the earth will awake, some to everlasting life and some to the reproach of eternal abhorrence." This tepid statement indicates how awkward, tardy, and undeveloped was the intrusion of personal immortality into ancient Judaism

The burdens and sacrifices of being a fully observant male Jew cannot receive adequate reward within mainstream Judaism. You are a Jew because God chose you for this role in history and society, not because of the compensation system.

The belated introduction into Pharisaic Judaism of the doctrine of personal immortality as compensation for the suffering of the just person in this life did not fit easily into mainstream Jewish belief. Contrary to Hellenistic and Persian beliefs, the Bible does not separate the soul and the body but rather conceives of *nefesh*, the integrated human being. Personal immortality raised the issue of dividing soul from body that generations of rabbis and philosophers now had to contemplate, without clear consensus.

The essential idea of Pharisaic Judaism is not expectation of reward through immortality but complete faith in the majesty and goodness of God as affirmed in the tragic heroism of the 23rd Psalm:

The Lord is my shepherd; I shall not want . . .

Yea, though I walk through the valley of the shadow of death, I will fear no evil . . .

Surely goodness and mercy shall follow me all the days of my life; and I will dwell in the house of the Lord forever.

Mainstream Judaism that developed after 600 B.C. had such strong and positive qualities that, short of physical elimination of the Jews, it was almost bound to continue and to evolve after the destruction of the Second Temple by the Romans in A.D. 70. Indeed, in the midst of the ill-fated Jewish wars against the Romans in the first and early second centuries A.D., the austere Orthodox rabbis, led by Yochanan Ben Zakkai, secured from the accommodating Romans permission to set up religious schools elsewhere in Judea even as the Romans assaulted Jerusalem, destroyed the Temple, and dispersed the population.

This withdrawal of the rabbis from the political fate of the homeland was the end result of what was already clear in the first century B.C. Pharisaic Judaism was a self-subsisting culture and a kind of mobile religious and moral tabernacle that could function autonomously and perpetually almost anywhere that Jews had a modicum of physical security and economic opportunity. This was to be the single most continuous and important theme in Jewish history until modern times, the sacred chain that binds the generations together.

But the downside of mainstream Judaism was also evident in the last two centuries B.C.—the very severe demands it made on its adherents and the psychological stress and social difficulties under which it put them. This meant that alternative forms of Judaism would be sought within the homeland, and in the already large Jewish Diaspora in the eastern Mediterranean there would almost inevitably arise a more liberal and softer kind of Jewish faith that would make life easier for its adherents and allow them a greater measure of participation in Gentile culture and society.

The outcome of the first era of Jewish history, down to the beginnings of the Common Era, is therefore a deeply ambivalent one. That is not the way it is taught today in synagogue schools or articulated from Jewish pulpits. In these forums, the Bible's second millennium B.C., from Abraham to King Saul, is treated as straight history; King David and King Solomon are extolled as splendid rulers and fascinating people, and even the succeeding long period of disunity, defeat, exile, and return only to experience further alien conquest is presented in a highly upbeat fashion, culminating in the Maccabean triumph, which since 1967 has been viewed through the triumphalist prism of the Six-Day War and other Israeli gains.

The best and most dispassionate historical scholarship, however, greatly deflates the authenticity of this traditional perception of early Jewish history. The first millennium of Jewish history as presented in the Bible has no empirical foundation whatsoever. It was made up later as a work of the imagination and shaped by doctrinal and political needs. King David lived, but the colorful figure in the Bible can only be validated to the extent that he was just another small-time, modestly successful Near Eastern ruler. The glorious imperialist Solomon, builder of the Temple, also existed, but at the very least the Bible inflates a second-level Near Eastern monarch to one who operates at a very high level of grandeur, power, and wealth. This cannot be confirmed, and it is highly unlikely.

Circumstantial Jewish history, which has many gaps but also strong, empirically sustainable segments, begins with Solomon's death in 931 B.C. and the split into the two kingdoms north and south. Thus authentic ancient Jewish history begins with an event of negative value, the start of political decline, and with two exceptions—first, the return from exile under Persian auspices, the building of the Second Temple, and the completion of the text of the Bible under Ezra; and second, the early triumphal years of the Maccabean dynasty before it crumbled into corruption and decay—this long history is neither happy nor glorious.

Yet out of this millennium of frequent political defeat and only occasional social progress emerged a thick culture of mainstream Judaism around which subsequent Jewish history turns and develops.

Pharisaic-rabbinical Judaism also slowly fomented an ethnically identifiable people—a nation grounded in blood, Martin Buber called it in the early 1920s before the rise of Nazism made such racial discourse politically incorrect—out of the motley array of Canaanites and other Near Eastern peoples who lived in ancient times between the Golan Heights and the Negev Desert.

Within Judea, the consistency of Jewish ethnic stock after 100 B.C. was not mitigated by a significant number of conversions from the Gentile population. Pharisaic Judaism welcomed converts, but within Judea, among the urban population of Greek-speaking Gentiles that the Romans established along the Mediterranean coast, its efforts at proselytizing were only mild and haphazard.

Full conversion of Gentile males to Judaism was rare because of the painful and hazardous requirement of adult circumcision. Occasionally an observant Jewish male married a Gentile woman convert, and, as the rabbis today never stop telling us when they find themselves on multicultural panels, one of the lesser books of the Masoretic Bible is devoted to the story of such a convert, Ruth the Moabite, whom biblical legend embroidered into an ancestor of King David. But the strictures of life according to the Law and total rejection of part-Gentile children of Jewish males from the community of the faithful (unless they converted), meant that over time observant Jews became an extremely endogamous group, marrying within a very limited circle of choice.

Consequently, by the beginning of the Common Era Jews who observed the written and oral law were not only a compactly organized social and religious group, but also had become an ethnically homogeneous people, separated by blood as well as culture from other peoples.

In origin the Jews may very well have been merely a sectarian or subversive subgroup among the Canaanites. But in time they had become a distinct race, an ethnic group.

Around the year 1000 B.C. there was nothing distinctive about the Jews ethnically, linguistically, politically, or economically. They were one among several small groups in the eastern Mediterranean, and their behavior and structure in these social categories was typical of that part of the ancient world. What distinguished the Jews by 800 B.C. were the essentials of their religious experience and expressions that were beginning to emerge.

By 500 B.C. this religion had become elaborately articulated into biblical Judaism and continued to develop in Babylonian exile. Half a millennium later, at the beginning of the Common or Christian Era, the now established text of the Bible, combined with the traditions of oral law as interpreted by the scribes and teachers who comprised the Pharisaic rabbis, spoke for a nation distinctive ethnically and genetically as well as spiritually—a people bound together in both blood relationship and cultural forms.

To view the outcome of ancient Jewish history as the formation of a race, a distinct ethnic group genetically bonded, will arouse discomfort in some circles. It will be claimed that the concept of race and an attitude of genetic gouping is thoroughly obsolete, morally discredited by the vicious use to which it was put by the Nazis in the 1930s and 1940s, and thoroughly repudiated by the best anthropological science.

This absolute exclusion of race from historical discourse peaked in the 1960s but is now itself vulnerable. The emergence of a younger generation of anthropologists and the discovery of DNA genetic typing has renewed a scientific drift toward viewing positively a genetic influence on human behavior and—even more controversial, but also propounded—specifically on human intelligence.

In a well-balanced recent book that surveys the history of the idea of race and genetic impact, physical anthropologist Pan Shipman asks the bottom-line question: "Can genetics and anthropology untangle this troubling snarl of conflicting beliefs, incomplete information and moral quandary" involved in the concept of race? Shipman replies, "Not yet." She cites, however, recent studies pointing to the conclusion that "the emerging pattern is one of genetic influence over complex behavior rather than genetic control." This careful statement attributes to genetic makeup important influence, along with environmental and social circumstances, in the development of a population.

The Harvard biologist Ernst Mayr claimed that "a species was a circumscribed collection of individuals who exchanged and recombined their genetic material in a single gene pool." This is what the Jews did after 200 B.C., if not earlier. Another prominent biologist, Theodosious Dobzansky, remarked that "race *differences* are a fact of nature." And the Jews, stretching from antiquity into this century, appear to have been different, a distinct ethnic or racial group.

These comments from biologists and anthropologists are not cited to show that the great scientific debate on the genetic composition of human populations has been settled. But the further we travel from the monstrosity of Nazi misuses of the racial concept and the more genetic applications are investigated, the more does a scientific sanction for viewing the Jews as a distinct genetic group, and furthermore one exhibiting an extraordinarily creative behavior pattern, come within the parameters of legitimate discourse.

Until the scientific issues are settled, tradition and sensibility will sustain racial and genetic assumptions about the Jews. Ideological sensibilities rooted in the Bible and the course of Jewish history itself endorse this view of the Jews as a people joined together by blood and genes, by hearts and minds, and not only by environmental, cultural, and social circumstances. This is a thematic outcome of ancient Jewish history, and it is confirmed by later developments.

CHAPTER THREE

Jewish Diversity

Two prominent historians began to publish in the 1930s and presented a then novel and radical view of ancient Jewish history from the second century B.C. into the early centuries of the Common Era. They were Elias J. Bickerman, by origin a Russian Jew, educated in Germany, who taught in France until he fled from the Nazi invasion in 1940 and then at Columbia University for a quarter of a century; and Erwin R. Goodenough, an American Gentile and committed Christian, trained at Harvard, who held a research chair at Yale for thirty years.

Bickerman's main interest was the history of the Maccabean revolt of the mid-second century B.C. and the dynasty (also called Hasmonean) that ruled for another century, until the Roman conquest of Judea in 63 B.C. Goodenough devoted himself principally to studying minutely the material contents and implications of a massive archaeological discovery, the well-preserved ruins of a great Jewish synagogue in the provincial Syrian town of Dura-Europos, dating from the third century A.D. Goodenough published many volumes on Dura-Europos, particularly trying to understand the religious and intellectual implications of the imagery in the elaborate mosaics that decorated the floor and walls of the synagogue.

Bickerman and Goodenough held chairs in ancient history at respectively Columbia and Yale; they predated the founding of Judaic studies departments on American campuses. What they had to say was immensely important to and extremely controversial for Jewish history and remains so today.

Essentially they were presenting, in regard to different eras, the same thesis: that retrospectively we may identify Pharisaic-rabbinical-Orthodox Judaism as mainstream, but to regard it as exclusively the important form of Judaism is a one-sided and vulnerable view of Judaism in antiquity. Within the context of ancient times after 200 B.C. an alternative Hellenistic Judaism, the elaborate and profound integration of biblical tradition with the philosophy, theology, and magic of the Hellenistic world, was highly active. In the case of Jews living outside Judea in the Diaspora, Hellenistic Judaism was the faith practiced by the majority of Jews. The Bickerman-Goodenough theme is therefore one of cultural and religious diversity.

Bickerman began publishing on the causes and significance of the Maccabean revolt in 1937 and was still publishing books and articles on facets of the Hasmonean dynasty and the culture and religion of that era in the 1970s. He saw the traditional view of the origins of the Maccabean revolt in the putative oppressive and sacrilegious policies of Antiochus Epiphanes as simpleminded. In his view, the source of the conflict that led to the Maccabean movement for independence from Syria was a religious and cultural split within the Jewish elite, and indeed among the high priests, between those who insisted on what became Pharisaic-rabbinical purity and those who, not only to ingratiate themselves as collaborators with the occupying Hellenistic power, but also for intrinsic cultural and religious purposes, sought a reconstruction of the biblical faith through wide-ranging Hellenization in belief and ritual.

Benedikt Otzen, a Danish scholar who vehemently supports Bickerman's view of Maccabean times, in 1990 summarized this still controversial thesis:

> The Hellenists in Jerusalem regarded the Jews' tendency to isolate themselves, culturally and religiously, as a hindrance to progress and development. The wish to break out of this isolation and be accepted into the society of nations, that is, to distance themselves from a form of life which the Greeks would

only regard as barbarous, was the ultimate impetus behind the efforts of the Jewish Hellenists . . . In principle what took place was a civil war between two factions within Judaism itself.

The attitude of the Jerusalem Hellenists speaks for the principles of liberal Judaism in all times and places.

The Maccabean victory over the Syrians and the gaining of Jewish independence for several decades represented a check to aggressive Hellenization in Judea and provided the political and polemical context for the rise of Pharisaic Judaism as the mainstream faith. But the magnetic attraction of Greek language, literature, philosophy, science, and astrology, as well as a seductive pastiche of Oriental sacramental religions integrated into Hellenistic culture, continued in the late first century B.C. to exercise a powerful attraction for the educated elite in Judea. During the reign of the Roman client-king Herod the Great in Jerusalem from 37 B.C. to 4 B.C., there was a renewed boost to cultural Hellenization with theosophic implications.

Herod was the wealthiest and most extravagant Jewish ruler, with the most elaborate court, since Solomon. His family, ethnically from beyond the Dead Sea (what is today Jordan) and not Jewish but converted to Judaism, rose in the service of the later Hasmoneans and ultimately replaced them by skillful political maneuvers in Jerusalem and Rome.

Herod rebuilt Nehemiah's modest fourth-century B.C. Second Temple to exceed Solomonic proportions and to make it renowned for splendor. The famous Wailing Wall in Jerusalem today is a remnant of the mere outer wall around Herod's huge and lavish structure. But Herod was a dedicated multiculturalist who also donated resources (derived from his oppressive taxation of the Jewish people) to pagan temples within his kingdom and abroad. His reign and patronage provided opportunity and impetus for a renewed Hellenizing thrust in the Jewish kingdom. This revived the cultural civil war of the mid-first century B.C. and helped to set the stage for the ill-fated Jewish rebellion against Rome that broke out in A.D. 66 and ended in the destruction of Herod's Temple four years later.

Within Judea the two centuries of intermittent struggle between the Hellenists, who sought to integrate Judaism within the structure of Hellenistic culture, and the Pharisaic rabbis, who shielded the written and oral law as defined by Ezra and his rabbinical successors, ended in a kind of victory for the latter, but within a context of disaster. The mostly apolitical Pharisaic tradition was intensely cultivated, with Roman approval, first at a rabbinical school at Jabneh near Jaffa on the Mediterranean coast and later in the Galilee. But Jewish political autonomy was eliminated, Jerusalem as a Jewish city superseded, the Temple burned to the ground and—after the massacre of many thousands of freedom fighters and civilians—most of the Jews driven into the second exile that endured for two millennia.

Goodenough's thesis was that when the refugees from this Roman holocaust got to Alexandria or the other prominent centers of Jewish settlement in the eastern, Greek-speaking Mediterranean (plus an emerging Jewish community in Rome itself), they discovered the dominant form of Jewish faith and culture in the Diaspora was close to the Hellenistic variety of Judaism that had contended so bitterly for two centuries against the Pharisaic puritan tradition in the Jewish homeland and that in the end had lost out to the rabbinical mode.

Goodenough called attention to the Dura-Europos mosaics in relation to other archaeological and literary evidence and argued for recognition of the authenticity of an alternative variety (or varieties) of Judaism that existed among the vast Jewish population of the Diaspora.

The Dura-Europos decorative artworks not only transgressed against the Orthodox proscription of images in synagogues, but they also portrayed alongside biblical religious imagery motifs derived from the theology and astrology of the pagan Greco-Roman world. Goodenough was saying that in antiquity, in addition to what we call mainstream rabbinical Judaism, there was a liberal Judaism extensively integrated with leading facets of Hellenistic culture, just as nineteenth- and twentieth-century liberal or Reform Judaism recast Jewish doctrine within the progressive, secular culture of modern times. It is significant that the Dura-Europos synagogue did not have a separate balcony for women.

The Dura-Europos mosaics rank for Goodenough among the great monuments of Jewish culture. In his view, they were not just fashionable decoration but meaningful symbolism that exhibited the integrative kind of Hellenistic Judaism he admired, synthesizing Jewish and pagan traditions:

[The rabbis] aspired to much power in regulating the lives of Jews, and eventually got it, but . . . for centuries even in Palestine [they] fought a hard battle for popular prestige and support . . . The picture we have got of this [Hellenistic] Judaism is that of a group . . . which . . . built its synagogues with a marked sense that it was a peculiar people in the eyes of God, but which accepted the best of paganism . . . When the religious symbols borrowed by Jews in those years [early centuries A.D.] are put together, it becomes clear that the ensemble is not merely "a picture book . . . ," but reflect a lingua franca that had been taken into most of the religions of the day . . . as well as by Christianity later.

In Goodenough's view, this glorious efflorescence of "inclusive" Jewish culture with its symbolic unification with pagan thought and art, although largely suppressed by the rabbis in the early Middle Ages, attains a partial recovery in the late medieval mysticism of the Cabala.

Goodenough's early work was a study of the voluminous writings of Philo the Jew, a leader of the Alexandria Jewish community in the first half of the first century A.D. Philo, who wrote in Greek, developed an elaborate synthesis of biblical doctrine and Platonic philosophy. Goodenough noted—and Harry Wolfson, who held the chair of Jewish studies at Harvard for three decades after 1930, fully adumbrated—that Philo's synthesis of Judaism and Hellenism provided the model of the development of Christian theology in the two centuries after A.D. 150, beginning with Clement of Alexandria, a Christian intellectual disciple of Philo the Jew. Goodenough, however, was more interested in Philo's significance for Jewish culture and religion than for Christian doctrine. In his view, Philo stands for the integrative, culturally diversified, Hellenistic Judaism of the Diaspora that is eventually represented in the elaborate mosaics of Dura-Europos.

The fortunate archaeological find in that provincial Syrian town stands for the thousands of similar liberal, culturally diversified synagogues that stretched over the eastern Mediterranean in the first half-millennium of the Common Era. Fragments of others remain, but only in relatively remote Dura-Europos was the later predilection of triumphal Christian churches to pillage the artworks of Jewish synagogues and the ravages of centuries of historical conflict fortunately avoided. The synagogue at Dura-Europos was abandoned by its congregation so that later generations of Greek Jews, persuaded by rabbinical principles, did not have the opportunity to remove the artwork with its elaborate Hellenistic pagan symbolism.

Goodenough's view of ancient Jewish history was ill-received in the 1930s, 1940s, and 1950s in the Jewish seminaries that were then the vortex of Jewish historical study in America, and it has been at best marginalized in the succeeding Judaic studies programs of more recent vintage. The Goodenough thesis of a Hellenistic Judaism as important in ancient Jewish history as the rabbinical kind has paradoxically received greater toleration among Israeli scholars, but they have downplayed its impact by concentrating almost exclusively on the Jewish community in the ancient homeland and dealing little with the immense Diaspora community.

This has also been the approach of the authoritative, highly readable survey of Jewish history *From the Maccabees to the Mishnah* by Shaye J. D. Cohen, for a quarter of a century the professor of ancient Jewish history at the Jewish Theological Seminary in New York, and now the holder of the prestigious chair of Jewish studies at Brown University.

Cohen explicitly rejects the antinomy of Palestinian and Hellenistic Judaism and refuses to use the latter term, which he finds too vague to be sustainable as a historical concept. He believes that all Judaism of the time near the start of the Common Era was more or less touched by Hellenistic culture. Hellenistic Judaism is therefore in Cohen's view a general context, not an identifiable intellectual and religious movement opposed to traditional Pharisaic Judaism. Yet Cohen does acknowledge that "The synagogues revealed by the archaeologist, with their carvings, mosaics, and paintings, are not the sort of buildings that rabbinic evidence had led us to expect." This undercuts Cohen's refusal to regard Hellenistic Judaism as a cultural entity ranged against rabbinical Judaism.

Writing in 1990, Jacob Neusner, the previous holder of the Brown chair, explicitly endorsed Goodenough's pluralistic view of Judaism in the first six centuries A.D. He agreed that "the manifestations of the Jewish religion were varied and complex." Neusner supported Goodenough in balancing Talmudic Judaism against "Hellenistic-Jewish mystic mythology." Neusner then audaciously claimed that the rabbinical legists and commentators who continued and enriched the Pharisaic tradition in the first six centuries A.D., while they used no terms from Greek philosophy in their economic and political doctrines, were themselves influenced by Aristotle, who was along with Plato the master of the Greek philosophic tradition. This claim is more supportive of Cohen than Goodenough.

Goodenough's paradigm of an antinomy of Hellenistic Judaism of the Diaspora as against rabbinical Judaism in Judea remains highly controversial and particularly problematic for Jewish scholars of rabbinical background. As is characteristic of all high concepts in cultural history (e.g., Was the Italian Renaissance of the fifteenth century late medieval or ideologically postmedieval?), a major issue is embedded in what may seem to be mostly a semantic dispute. Consciously or subconsciously what bothers Jewish scholars is that the polarity of Hellenistic versus Palestinian Judaism looks like the Christian Old versus New Testament idea raising itself again in amended form, and that carries too much partisanship tending to disparage traditional Judaism to be admitted into the academic arena.

As in the case of all paradigmatic controversies in cultural history, close scrutiny of the social context is helpful. An examination of the social context immediately reveals that concentration on the history of the Jews in their homeland and historical marginalization of the Jews in the Diaspora contravenes demographic reality.

The history of Jewish life in the Galuth (Diaspora) at the beginning of the Common Era is shaped by an astounding demographic fact. Of a population of some sixty million people in the Roman Empire, as much as ten percent and not less than eight percent were Jews. At the time Jesus of Nazareth lived and died and Herod's Temple was destroyed, some six million Jews lived in the Roman Empire, according to social historian Salo W. Baron. Of these, two-thirds were living in the Diaspora. And of the Jews living outside their ancestral homeland, close to ninety percent were living in the eastern Mediterranean in the Greek-speaking culturally Hellenistic part of the Roman Empire.

The Egyptian metropolis of Alexandria, with a million people, was one-third Jewish. In the teeming cities of Asia Minor—today the non-European part of Turkey—which was still a very prosperous and heavily populated region (before it was ruined by centuries of bad government and possibly climatic deterioration), there were many large and prosperous Jewish communities in the first half-millennium of the Common Era. Large Jewish communities, going back to the first exile of the sixth century B.C., still existed in Mesopotamia ("Babylon," as the Jews called it), which lay outside the Roman Empire; here the Jewish population was a million.

How did these five million Jews of the Diaspora at the beginning of the Common Era make their living? Much like the rest of the population, with the exception of the Gentile holders of the high office and the aristocratic landlords. Jews were prominent in all middle-class occupations—they were farmers, craftsmen, and mercenaries in the army. They had already come to play an important role in what European Jews many centuries later would call *handel,* a word that embraces all kinds of trade, from ambitious, risky, and highly capitalized long-distance commerce, such as the silk import trade from East Asia, to local trade and selling in the open-air markets that still move most small merchandise in the Near East.

Lest we think of the ancient Jews as mainly soft-handed merchants and shopkeepers, it is worth noting that in the Hellenistic world the Jews, like Israelis today, were regarded as tough guys— they were valued as mercenary soldiers. Two hundred miles up the Nile, near the location of the present Aswan dam, there existed for two or three centuries a Jewish mercenary army encampment that built for itself, sacrilegiously, a miniature temple where animal sacrifices were conducted.

How were the Jewish communities of the Diaspora organized and governed? Tightly or loosely, hierarchically or democratically? Salo Baron, originally a Viennese Jew, who for thirty-five years from the late 1930s held the chair of Jewish history at Columbia (specially endowed, like Harry Wolfson's at Harvard, from Jewish philanthropic sources, not paid for from the regular university funds controlled by the then anti-Semitic trustees of those prestigious universities), devoted many years to trying to find out. The picture is not clear. Baron, influenced by the liberal statism of the New Deal ideology adhered to by his colleagues in the Columbia history department, probably exaggerated the degree of close organization and territorial cohesiveness as well as the consensual quality of Jewish community structure.

A great part of Jewish community organization depended on the synagogues. In addition, at various times and places, certain communal councils and office-holders were given governing mandates over the Jewish population by state authority. It is hard to know, however, what these high-sounding titles such as "prince" or "exilarch" meant in practice. Reading the Anglo-Jewish press in the United States or Canada today would give a somewhat unreal impression of a contemporary community highly organized along the lines of consensual democracy.

Then and now, the important institution for Jewish life outside the family was the synagogue, which provided social (education, charity for the poor and the aged) as well as religious services. A small group of wealthy families dominated synagogue governance, and the rabbi was drawn from one of the dominant families or otherwise selected by them. Occasionally a wealthy, well-educated, prominent Jew could receive a high-sounding title from the government as spokesmen for all the Jews in the town, region, or even country, and these elaborate titles became desirable family possessions that were handed down from father to son along with other prized belongings. Periodically the titular leaders of the Jewish community summoned representatives to council meetings, where the representatives would speak for the wealthy families whom they consulted.

However, these extra-family or extra-synagogue governing mechanisms within the Jewish community, while probably meaningful to the prominent Jews involved, or their families, were likely of small moment in the lives of the great majority of the Diaspora Jewish millions. They pursued their craft or business, attended synagogue frequently or occasionally, educated their children in a Jewish tradition carefully or haphazardly, more or less respected the Sabbath, and lived out contented or desperate lives.

The great majority of Alexandrian Jews in A.D. 200 spoke Greek, could read Hebrew not at all or just enough for a few prayers, loyally attended religious services that were almost entirely conducted in Greek, circumcised their male children, observed Passover, Hanukkah, and the Day of Atonement (but not commonly by fasting), and still thought of themselves as Jews. They were therefore similar to Jews in America today. And as in America, hundreds of thousands, particularly in smaller towns in the hinterlands, slipped away from Judaism and became completely assimilated into the Gentile world into which they readily intermarried.

In the larger cities observance of the Jewish dietary law (kashruth) was widely but far from exclusively practiced. It was not hard for the people in the larger Jewish communities of the Diaspora to maintain the dietary laws, the essentials of which were prohibition against pork and shellfish and required ritual slaughter of cattle, sheep, and fowl. But pork was a common Near Eastern taboo (also maintained later by the Muslims). The Mediterranean is not overly supplied with shellfish, and plenty of the other kinds of fish were available before the infusion of warm water from the Red Sea after the opening of the Suez Canal in the mid-nineteenth century killed off many varieties. Near Eastern diet, then as now, did not critically involve beef, so the cumbersome problem of kosher slaughtering of cattle was a modest one, as it is also not a big issue in Israel today.

Lamb was a precious commodity privileged for the rich or for ritual occasions at the Temple in Jerusalem. The staple diet of the Near East then and now is rice and other grain topped off with a little bit of fowl (easily slaughtered by kashruth method) or fish, and supplemented by a lot of vegetables and fruit. This is still the basic diet of the great majority of Israelis today, as anyone can verify by standing at the busy checkout line of a Tel Aviv supermarket on a Thursday afternoon or a Friday morning.

Only when Jews later came to live in the northern world of Europe did observance of kashruth became a difficult thing in that much more carnivorous, beef-eating environment. Observant Jews serving in the Roman army in the second century A.D. were less bothered by dietary restriction than Jews serving in the American army today.

Reform and Conservative rabbis in modern times rationalize the Jewish dietary laws by claiming that eating pork in the hot climate of the Near East is unhealthy, and shellfish might come from polluted waters. But scholars today believe the injunction against pig meat (the requirement was that a slaughtered animal for Jewish consumption had to have a cloven hoof) is simply the random survival of a primitive taboo. Nobody has explained the odd shellfish prohibition. Robin Lane Fox has mischievously suggested it was due to an ancient scribal error.

Concern about diet is one explanation for the remarkable fecundity of the Jewish population in the early Roman Empire. People aware of divinely ordained dietary law will always be careful what they put in their mouths; they will be fussy and therefore healthy eaters.

The large Jewish minority in the Roman world is further explained by strong family bonds, resulting in the care of infants and children and elderly people, and by injunctions on behalf of charity and the communal concern for the poor, weak, abandoned, and old. The impact on population growth of the traditional Jewish code of personal and social behavior is similar to that engendered in urban America today by welfare and public assistance programs—it augments life expectancy and by care for infants produces a low infant-mortality rate.

Rabbinic Judaism gives no privilege to sexual abstinence. It encourages sexual relationships, always within marriage, which means a high birth rate. It fosters a strong, caring family environment, which means nourishment of infants and young children.

The Roman governing class was impressed by Jewish scriptures, prayer, and spirituality at the same time they were disturbed by Jewish exclusiveness and self-imposed separation from much of the activity of the rest of society. There was always something troublingly arrogant and superficially subversive about the Jews. But the Roman Empire, before it went Christian in the early fourth century, treated Jews generously. Judaism was a legally sanctioned religion, and Jews were normally not required to sacrifice at the altars of the imperial cult. The latter had more political than religious significance; it expressed the unity of the Roman world. Freeing the Jews from the obligations to participate in the imperial cult was equivalent to the American federal government passing a law freeing Jews from taking loyalty oaths, singing the national anthem, and reciting the Pledge of Allegiance to the flag.

The Romans respected the Jews and normally (if the Jews did not rebel or create civil disorders) treated them well, in part because the Jewish religion was very old and centered on holy books. These qualities appealed to the Roman aristocracy.

But the main reason that the Jews received favorable treatment in the Roman Empire was the huge size of the Jewish population and their location in the major cities of the eastern half of the empire as well as in Rome itself, followed by slow migration into the urban areas of the western Mediterranean and in Spain into the interior of that country.

By their number and location the Jews could make a lot of trouble for imperial and local Roman government if they became unruly and oppositional. This indeed occurred in Judea itself in A.D. 66 and 132 in the form of attempted revolutions of national liberation. They failed, but the first one especially was costly and troubling for Roman power. In the eastern metropolis of Alexandria in A.D. 115 another Jewish uprising produced civil war in the streets. It appears to have been the consequence of long-standing tension between the large Jewish minority and the rest of the population jealous of Jewish privilege and wealth.

The Romans appreciated the Jews' demographic clout and recognized that when not aroused the Jews were hard workers and responsible citizens. It was wise to treat them reasonably well, although never totally freeing them from criticism for their peculiar behavior.

The educated Jewish elite in the Diaspora cities of the eastern Mediterranean wanted to mollify their pagan critics by a synthesis of Judaism and Hellenism. Among the wealthy and well-educated Jews of Alexandria, the world of Greek literature, philosophy, and science in which they were immersed offered compelling ways of reinterpreting Jewish doctrine that did not place them outside the Hellenistic culture's essential discourse and at the same time achieved an intellectual and religious expression that offered a radical alternative to the Pharisaic formulation.

The philosophic spokesman for Hellenistic Judaism of the more elevated, philosophical kind was Philo, who died around A.D. 50. He was therefore an exact contemporary of the Pharisaic rabbi Hillel in Judea, as well as of Jesus and Paul. He came from one of the wealthiest Jewish families in Alexandria and was a prominent community leader, chosen at one point as a member of a delegation to go to Rome and petition the emperor.

How observant a Jew Philo was is uncertain. He had a thorough knowledge of the Bible in the Greek (Septuagint) translation, attended synagogue regularly, and spoke respectfully of Sabbath observance and circumcision. But while formally condemning intermarriage with Gentiles, he spoke against hampering "the fellow feeling and intercommunion of men with men . . . Intermarriages with outsiders create new kinships not a bit inferior to [endogamous] blood-relationships." This is not a Pharisaic rabbi talking, but the more radical kind of American Reform rabbi. It is not hard to imagine Philo speaking thus from the pulpit in Beverly Hills or Great Neck to enthusiastic upscale audiences. While sympathetic to rabbinical doctrine, Philo regarded it as the expression of the simple faith of the common man. For intellectuals like himself there was another kind of Judaism, expressed through the ideas of Greek, especially Platonic and Stoic, philosophy.

The two sides of Jewish faith were made compatible in Philo's view by an allegorical reading of the Bible in which Greek theory was discovered within the literal superficial biblical text. This allegorical method for interpreting the Bible was to have wide currency in both Jewish and Christian culture until the twentieth century.

The essentials of Philo's view of God is that He is light: "God is the fountain of the purest radiance, and so when He reveals Himself to a soul the rays He puts forth are free from all shadow and are of intense brightness." [transl. R. Williamson]

To bridge God and man in Philo's system there is an intermediary Logos (word, idea), "a second God." This is pure Platonism:

> To his Logos, his chief messenger, highest in grand honor, the Father of all has given the special prerequisite to stand on the border and separate the creature from the creator. This same Logos both pleads with the immortal [God] and acts as suppliant for afflicted mortality [mankind] and acts as ambassador of the ruler to the subject [people]. [transl. P. Fredrikson]

God is absolutely unique and transcendent, "the Alone." The Logos, as God's self-expression and purest emanation, provides the bridge between mankind and the transcendent and unique God. Philo is applying Platonic theory to Jewish faith, but he is also responding to an emotional and psychological need that traditional Judaism aroused in many: how to approach the unique, self-subsisting deity, how to find a way to communicate with God and personally experience His love and care.

The intellectual route to Philo's Logos was prepared by the Jewish "wisdom" literature of the second century B.C. A cosmic force called wisdom emanating from God imposes itself on the earth. Thus *Sirach,* written c. 180 B.C. in Jerusalem: "I am the word which was spoken by the most high; It was I who covered the earth like a mist. My dwelling-place was in high heaven."

The Pharisees regarded nearly all the wisdom literature as a Hellenistic intrusion and excluded *Sirach* and other such works from the biblical canon. Philo, by using the Platonic theory of forms, articulated the sentiments of the wisdom literature into a theology of Hellenistic Judaism.

Later the rabbis will speak of the Shekinah, God's emanation upon the world through which His presence is felt. This is not far from what Philo was saying, but the Greek term "Logos" carries a heritage of Platonic theory of forms, and this discourse distinguished it from rabbinical Shekinah. Language makes a difference; terms determine.

Philo's legitimation of what Roland Williamson has called "a two-tier Judaism," the simple faith of the ordinary believer and the philosophic faith of the intellectual, and his effort to find a way to attain a mystical union with the godhead—both characteristics place him within the mainstream of Jewish history. Two-tier Judaism, in which one tier was a refined, esoteric, and learned mysticism, was to become a broad avenue in Jewish cultural history.

Philo's dualist view of human nature is also Platonic and, despite the Pharisees' previous recognition of personal immortality, it constituted a radical departure from Hebraic anthropology, with its core concept of *nefesh,* the integrated human being and the unity of soul and body. In Philo's view the human being is split—a spiritual soul exists within the prison of the material body and yearns for liberation. This too is characteristically Hellenistic, and it marks a radical departure from the biblical image of *nefesh,* the unified human being.

In consequence of Philo's dualist perception of human nature, he speaks of sexuality in terms of extreme emotional revulsion that flowed from Hellenistic Platonism and Stoicism into Christianity. Not even Philo's references to sexuality within marriage are enthusiastic.

Philo is the prototype of the liberal or Reform Jewish intellectual: While remaining respectful of the essentials of the old religion, he has reinterpreted it in a way that perceives it in an entirely distinct manner and has overlaid it with philosophical assumptions from a thoroughly different contemporary culture. Intellectual truth rather than everyday experiences within the traditional Law is his goal. These are characteristics of liberal as distinguished from Orthodox Judaism at all times and places, including twentieth-century America.

The subsidiary purpose of Philo's teaching was to attract more

Gentiles to the Jewish faith, either to be fully proselytized or as "God-fearers" who participated in Jewish thought and learning in varying degrees while avoiding circumcision and full-scale conversion. Alexandria boasted a significant number of both kinds of converts.

Hellenistic Judaism was a self-consciously proselytizing religion, aggressively more so than Pharisaic Judaism. Did it gain more converts than the numbers lost to the Jewish community of the Diaspora by assimilation and intermarriage? Probably not. But Philo was enthusiastic about the prospects of making Judaism in his Hellenistic form into a missionary faith. This was the way he explained God's purpose in allowing the great dispersion of the Jews in the Roman Empire—the Diaspora was intended by Logos to facilitate the conversion of the Gentiles to revealed truth.

Facilitating the adherence of proselytites was, however, only the secondary purpose of Philo's teachings. He was mainly responding to felt needs within the Jewish world of his time—to bridge God and mankind, to formulate an anthropology that liberated the spiritual soul from the corrupting and ephemeral physical side of human nature, to articulate Judaism in the language and concepts of the then predominant Platonic philosophy and thereby elevate its legitimacy among the intellectual class.

Philo has had many successors in Jewish history. You can hear them any Friday evening preaching from the pulpit of any Reform synagogue and most Conservative synagogues in the United States or Canada. If they don't sound exactly like Philo, that is because the philosophy with which they are integrating Judaism has long since moved on from Hellenistic Platonism to some twentieth-century cultural theory that is a derivation from the eighteenth-century liberal and secular enlightenment.

It accords with Philo's historical role as the prototype of liberal Judaism that his teachings were less controversial among the Gentiles than among the Jews. This has also been the experience of modern Reform rabbis who still have no officially recognized status in the Israel of today.

Philo's doctrine of Logos as an intermediary second God resembles the Christian view of the relation between father and son in the Trinitarian godhead. The Gospel of John, one of the four Gospels that aimed to portray the life of Jesus, written around A.D. 100 by a

Gentile in either Asia Minor or Philo's own city of Alexandria, proclaims at the outset a discourse that sounds Philonic: "In the beginning was the logos [word], and the logos was with God, and the logos was God."

Philo's separation of soul and body and discomfort with sexuality are also characteristically early Christian sentiments. Philo's advocacy of a highly allegorical interpretation of the Bible became the dominant Christian way of understanding the Bible until recent times.

It would be naive to say that Philo was the intellectual molder of early Christianity. Philo and the Christian thinkers were drawing from the common source of Hellenistic culture and its core of Platonic mysticism. Nevertheless, Philo's direct impact on Christian thought was unquestionably great. That is the prime reason that his voluminous writings have survived intact, not just because they were written in Greek. What he said was compelling and authoritative for the ancient and medieval Christian Church, which preserved, copied, and published his work.

Philo's Platonic separation of soul and body is a kind of dualist philosophy. Dualism is a theme that looms large among the alternative voices and places of Judaism around the beginning of the Common Era. Essenic (or whatever) Judaism of the Qumran Dead Sea community that evolved from the mid-second century B.C. until the Dead Sea group was dispersed in A.D. 68 by the Roman kittim (evil hosts), as the conquerors are called in the Dead Sea Scrolls, presented another kind of dualism, different from Philo's, but also in contrast to Pharisaic monism.

The traditional Jewish view was one God and one chosen people. The others are just the peoples of the earth, God's instruments and recipients of the Jewish witness of God's words. The cosmic apocalyptic vision of the Qumran sectarians, on the other hand, sharply divided the whole world into the children of light and the children of darkness. The struggles of these two camps within accelerating time represents for Qumran the main theme of history that is nearing its end.

There were indeed motifs in the biblical prophetic writings of the struggle between the good and the bad in society. But the Qumran texts echoed the apocalyptic literature of the interexilic period that the rabbis excluded from the Hebrew canon (with the exception of the Book of Daniel, the earliest such apocalyptic writing).

Qumran went far in the direction of a dualistic-apocalyptic-eschatalogical doctrine. The world is approaching its end, the children of light alone will prevail. The children of darkness—rejected Jews along with goyim—will be dammed. The "congregation of uncleanness," the "community of wickedness" shall be annihilated along with cursed Satan. But: "He caused some of the sons of the world to draw near him . . . as a congregation of holiness in service for the eternal life." This is not an absolute departure from traditional Judaism. Yet it is a major evolution within it, subtly replacing historical monism with cosmic dualism.

Historical monism was the biblical idea. It posited a providential God directing the course of Jewish destiny among the nations. Cosmic dualism exhibited in the Dead Sea Scrolls is apocalyptic—it uncovers an inner, more important story that is eschatalogical—it perceives the coming end of the world. It is cosmic—it transcends Jewish history and encompasses the universe. And it is dualistic. It makes world society the theater of struggles between two communities, the children of light and the children of darkness.

This bends drastically the traditional form of Jewish history and focuses on a universal frame. History does not in the Qumran view concentrate on Jewish destiny. It takes a universal, cosmic perspective. Qumran supersedes the long linearity of Jewish history with stress on what is happening now universally and is about to happen in the future.

The Qumran ethos is extremely angry and pessimistic. Man lives as a stranger in an evil world ruled by the devil. Only a cosmic upheaval can give comfort and peace to man. The angry dualism is a significant modification of the Pharisaic temperament. The calm reticence and secure feeling within the bonds of the Law have been superseded, replaced by paranoid visions of furious war to end all things:

> Thou wilt deliver in the hands of the poor the enemies from all lands, to humble the mighty by the hand of those bent to the dust . . . We will despise kings, and we will mock and scorn the mighty . . . The prince of light thou hast appointed from ancient times to come to our support . . . But Satan, the angel of malevolence, thou hast created for the pit . . . Thy mighty hand is with the poor . . . And [the children of light] shall cleanse themselves of the blood of the bodies of the ungodly. [transl. G. Vermes]

Qumran culture is Pharisaism in hysterical overdrive, or an extremely paranoid version of Jeremiah. The Qumran mentality can be seen as a resurgence of the most radical strand in the prophetic tradition, become more polarized and confrontational under the pressure of class conflict and oppression by the Roman kittim in troubled Judea.

Less certainly, it may also be seen as mainstream Judaism coming under the influence of Hellenistic ideas (Qumran's prince of light is not all that remote from Philo's Logos) and the characteristic, long-standing Iranian dualistic religion. The Iranian ideal posited a perpetual struggle between the god of light and the god of darkness until the end of time. This is called Zoroasterism and Manichaeism.

Whether the Qumran community actually came under the influence of Iranian dualism is an unresolved possibility. It may even be speculated that this theological dualism had been brought back from Mesopotamia to Jerusalem when the first exile was ended under Persian auspices and had remained as an underground sectarian persuasion until it surfaced in the Dead Sea Scrolls.

Qumran's dualistic apocalypticism is a prime foundation of Gnosticism (from Gnosis, knowledge), the alternative, subversive dualistic theosophy that had a long history not only in Christianity but also in Judaism down into the writings of Israeli Gershom Scholem and Scholem's self-designated disciple, the American Jewish critic Harold Bloom, in our time.

Gnosticism is dualistic; it posits the world as a struggle between good and evil cosmic forces. Kurt Rudolph in 1987 in his definitive study of Gnosticism concluded that "Qumran offers a certain link on the fringe of Judaism for the illumination of the origin of gnostic ideas." The great historian of Jewish mysticism, Gershom Scholem, believed that Gnosticism was non-Jewish and Hellenistic in origin. It vitalized Jewish religion in the late Middle Ages. But a recent highly innovative study of Jewish mysticism by another Hebrew University scholar, Moshe Idel, argues that Gnostic mysticism itself has indigenous roots in Jewish religious culture, a strain of mysticism, largely suppressed by the rabbis, that contributed powerfully to the shaping of early Christianity and broadened out within Christianity's powerful opponent, the heretical Gnostic church of the second century A.D.

Idel's major amendment of Scholem's history of Jewish mysticism has been endorsed by I. G. Marcus of the Jewish Theological Seminary. It appears that Gnosticism partly represents a supra-Orthodox ancient Jewish mysticism.

Both Scholem and Idel believe that Cabalistic Jewish mysticism of the later Middle Ages is rooted in an esoteric movement within Judaism that goes back to antiquity and came out of the closet and flourished in the open, and fully developed its doctrines between the thirteenth and fifteenth centuries. What separates them is Scholem's view that the Jewish ancient mystics learned from Gentile Gnostics, while Idel proposes the opposite: that the mystical doctrines "were originally Jewish ones that afterward infiltrated Gnostic circles and were simultaneously passed down among the Jews until the emergence of the historical Kabbalah" after A.D. 1200.

What was in what became known as Gnosticism that would have appealed to Jewish religious thinkers in the first two centuries A.D.? Principally three things. First, it expounds the idea that the world is a scene of struggle between divinely empowered forces, good and evil, light and darkness. This is a dualistic theme that also prevailed in Qumran literature. It was a way of explaining why so much evil exists in the world. The Pharisaic-rabbinical tradition always had trouble explaining the origins of evil and why bad things happened to good people. Jewish Gnosticism would not have trouble today explaining the divine significance of the Holocaust, which so bothers rabbinical theodicy: The Holocaust was an emanation from the god of darkness, an ultimate realization of evil in the world, the Gnostics would say.

The second appealing aspect of Jewish Gnosticism in about A.D. 100 was the belief that some human beings have a spark of the divine light waiting to be liberated, the result of a primordial cosmic accident. This supports a social elitism—some humans have the divine spark, others do not.

A third appeal of Jewish Gnosticism was the embedding of this mystical doctrine in astrological cosmology. Astrology was immensely popular at the time (and for many centuries thereafter) among Jews as well as Christians. Pharisaic-rabbinical Judaism recognized astrology but rejected it as magic. In the later Middle Ages a more fully developed Gnosticism doubled back and influenced the development of the Cabala, Jewish mysticism, and carried astrological systems into Jewish mystical theosophy.

Moshe Idel's recent modification of Gershom Scholem's paradigm of the development of Jewish mysticism does not detract from the magnitude of Scholem's accomplishment. Scholem's *Major Trends in Jewish Mysticism,* published in 1941, followed by his studies of mystical and messianic movements in the later Middle Ages, published in the 1950s and 1960s, comprise the single greatest achievement in twentieth-century Jewish historiography because they opened up a new perspective on the religious and cultural history of Judaism from the early centuries of the Common Era until 1800.

What Scholem did was to focus on the internal history of the Jewish people and examine the phenomenon of their religious experience and articulations of their spiritual consciousness. He demonstrated unimpeachably that the Pharisaic-Talmudic-rabbinical tradition may have been the mainstream but that in addition to this learned and authoritarian hegemony, a set of alternative Judaisms developed in complex and intertwined fashion around the phenomenon of mystical experience and at certain points, especially in the later Middle Ages, interacted and combined with the clerical Talmudic tradition.

The internal history of the Jews thereby became a much more exciting, provocative, and, for the twentieth century, meaningful study. In sum, what Scholem—a secularized German Jew trained in the great humanities faculties of the German universities, who migrated to British Palestine in 1924 and was one of the founders of the Hebrew University—defined for the history of Jewish culture was that the word "diversity" is as important as the word "tradition." His paradigm of Jewish religion and cultural history places him in collaboration with Bickerman and Goodenough as the classical proponents of diversity in Jewish history.

Covenant theology as articulated by the Pharisaic scribes and rabbis was the mainstream of Judaism in the ancient world, the sacred chain that binds the generations of Jewish history. It is a nice question, unresolved and probably never to be answered, how much of this traditional Judaism itself owed to surrounding Near Eastern culture, particularly to Mesopotamian religion. Yet we can confidently affirm that covenant religion was largely or even overwhelmingly an indigenous Jewish phenomenon, with the exception of the late importation of the idea of personal immortality and the resurrection of the dead. This assessment, flattering to the modern Orthodox community, should not, however, blind us to the immense diversity of ancient Judaism and the articulation of distinct strands of Hellenistic Judaism that not only represent a cultural and intellectual Jewish interaction with the Greek-speaking world and its consciousness, but also constitute highly creative alternative worldviews with Judaism itself.

Philo's philosophy and the Qumran scrolls, located respectively in Alexandria and the Judean desert, were the most prominent of these other varieties of religious experience in the Jewish world of that era. They shade off along a spectrum that includes wisdom literature, apocalyptics, and Gnostic speculations. We are involved here in an immensely complex, vibrant world of mystical and theosophical imaginings and discourse that preoccupied the intellectual and religious elite in the great Diaspora population as well as in Roman Judea, affecting and affected by the Jewish masses, and to a degree acted back upon the rabbinical mainstream itself at the beginning of the Common Era and for many centuries thereafter.

Historical Judaism was therefore a combined product of inward-looking Pharisaic-rabbinical culture and a variety of other Jewish cultures that at the margin dynamically integrated the covenant tradition with alternative religious and intellectual systems arising from the Hellenistic world.

Another way to state this central historical phenomenon is to say that the impelling cultural force that came out of ancient Judaism was a fervent effort by the rabbis to make Judaism as thick, homogeneous, inward-looking, and self-subsisting a culture as possible, a dense, heavy, and controlled mass we call mainstream, Orthodox, traditional Judaism. But other voices in Judaism in many places were doing the opposite, opening up the covenant religion to interact and synthesize with philosophic, apocalyptic, dualistic, and sectarian cultures. They were making forms of Judaism that were plastic, malleable, uncontrollable, unfinished, open-ended.

In this split between diversity and polarity lies a cultural dynamic of Jewish history to the present day. Jewish intellectuality was impelled by a simultaneous and contradictory combustion, the implosion of rabbinical faith and the explosion of alternative systems, of which Hellenistic Judaism and Qumran apocalyptic dualism are the most memorable in ancient times.

Both the implosive and explosive kinds of Jewish cultures have in bygone and contemporary times made claims to authenticity, legitimacy, and superiority. Such a claim cannot be exclusively adjudicated to one or to the other. Implosive and explosive Jewish cultures indiscriminately and without prejudice must be recognized for their sincerity, dignity, and creativity.

Both in the past and today some Jews want to define Judaism as an exclusive religion that shuts out other cultures, and some Jews want to make of Judaism an inclusive religion that incorporates all sorts of progressive ideas and attitudes from the surrounding world in which Jews live. Exclusiveness has never been nor can be absolute—bits and pieces of other cultures slip into the Orthodox structure, and the complete success of exclusiveness would lead to rigidity and boredom. Inclusiveness never is as satisfying as the liberal synthesizers hope; anomalies and inconsistencies and indigestible paradoxes and contradictions persist.

The privilege of superior authenticity cannot be accorded to either exclusive or inclusive Judaism. Rabbinical Judaism deserves to be called mainstream; the other kinds deserve to be recognized as dynamic and intellectually creative. Jewish history recognizes the multifaceted gains of both cultural exclusion and intellectual inclusion. In the words of the 119th Psalm:

> Open thus mine eyes that I may behold wondrous things out of
> Thy law . . .
> And I will walk at liberty: for I seek Thy perception.
> I will speak of Thy testimonies also before kings, and will
> not be ashamed.

Hellenistic Judaism attempted to bridge the covenant religion and prophetic ethics with Hellenistic lifestyle and Platonic philosophy. It was a liberal and progressive culture and the prototype for all such forms of liberal Judaism in later eras and today, which have always stood for the party of humanity.

Qumran, apocalyptic, and Gnostic Judaism was not benign and bourgeois. It was intense, brooding, angry, problematic. It anticipated subsequent radical movements in Judaism, which have stood for the party of the Messiah and mystical discovery.

And what of Pharisaic-rabbinical Judaism? Its observant adherents were what they were, a unique and incomparable and inwardly sustaining group. They resisted incorporation into Hellenistic culture.

They downplayed messianic speculation and mystical effusions. They lived their faith with its stern behavioral code and were reticent about many of its theological implications. They were the covenanted party of God.

The exclusiveness, discipline, abstinence, stability, prayerfulness, reticence, and inwardness that characterized the thick culture and repressive behavior patterns of rabbinical Judaism absolutely marked it off (and still does so today) from the world of the goy, from the world of the Gentiles. This was not the case with Hellenistic Judaism, which all along its activated margin blended into and interacted with what it regarded rightly as the more attractive, permissible, and creative facets of Gentile culture and society.

The fatal attraction of Greek thought and language eroded the Pharisees' sharp demarcation from the Hellenistic way of doing and thinking, and this risked encouragement of Jewish apostasy, intermarriage, and assimilation into the magnetic field of Hellenism just as the hypnotic attractions of twentieth-century American secular civilization have in our time drained away millions of Jews from the faith of their fathers.

Yet the motion of transference and abandonment worked both ways in the early Roman Empire much more proportionally than in modern America. Hellenistic Judaism was a success as a proselytizing religion in the eastern Mediterranean world and as a cultural beacon and attraction, to such an extent that it aroused the paranoid fears of leaders among committed pagans and envious Christians in the first century A.D. They imagined the threat of the Judaizing of the Roman Empire. These fearful imaginings inspired countervailing efforts and incited anti-Jewish polemics and libel and pogromist riotings in the streets of Near Eastern cities. If liberal Judaism were now aggressively and successfully involved in conversion efforts in contemporary America, there would be a similar reaction from pulpit, university, and media.

Qumran apocalypticism did not envisage the conversion of the Gentile world but rather militant confrontation with it and physical destruction of it, as the children of light, in some kind of eschatological and messianic upheaval, overcame the followers of darkness and the devil. Qumran also wanted to cut off the traitors within the Jewish fold. Qumran culture, like Philonic Hellenism, was distinct from Pharisaic-rabbinical Judaism, but for other reasons.

Against rabbinical stability Qumran sought social and political destabilization. Against benign acceptance of suffering it wanted an immediate therapeutic resolution that would terminate Jewish deprivation and agony. Against a religion grounded in patience and behavioral repetition, Qumran sought release, liberation, and primal gratification.

Qumran's ultimate heir is political Zionism. The effects of the Qumran disposition, its grandiosity, impatience, fanaticism, and boldness, endure today in the Israeli empowered elite.

CHAPTER FOUR

Destruction and Redemption

On the ninth day of Ab in A.D. 70, under the hot August sun, Jerusalem was burning. It was in the course of being devastated by the armies of the Roman general Titus, the son of Emperor Vespasian. Herod's magnificent Temple was burned to the ground, just as on the ninth of Ab in 586 B.C. the First Temple was destroyed by armies of the Babylonian ruler.

The next five centuries after the destruction of the Second Temple were a time of disaster and deterioration for the large Jewish population of the Mediterranean world, both in Judea and in the Diaspora, countervailed only by the elaboration of Talmudic culture as a redemptive force in Jewish life. The Jewish decline in the first half of the first millennium A.D. exhibited five identifiable stages.

First, the failure of the great Jewish rebellion of 66–70 B.C. against Roman rule in Judea resulted in the leveling of the Second Temple, leaving only the ruins of its outer wall (today's Wailing Wall), the desolation of Jerusalem and its repopulation by Gentiles under Roman imperial aegis, the death or selling into slavery of hundreds of thousands of Jewish inhabitants of Judea, the exile of even greater numbers of Jews, and the long-term impoverishment of the remaining Jewish population in their homeland. Judea, David's proud realm, now became Roman Palestine, and it retained this insulting name, so abominably reminiscent of the ancient Jewish enemy that David had vanquished, until 1948.

Second, the defeat of the second Jewish rebellion against Rome in A.D. 135, and the death at Roman hands of its military leader Bar Cocheba and its spiritual guide Rabbi Akiba, was followed by Roman prohibition of entry of the circumcised to Jerusalem, now given a heinous Latin name, and the shrinking of the Jewish population in its homeland to a minority of the population.

Third, under the leadership of Rabbi Saul of Tarsus (Saint Paul), the small Jewish sect who venerated Jesus of Nazareth in the 50s and 60s began the rapid conversion of uncircumcised Gentiles and by mid-second century A.D. had become a powerful rival to Judaism in the Roman world. Therefore the determination of this Pharisaic rabbi Paul to make Christianity a religion for the Gentiles as well as Jews was a cataclysmic event for the Jews. As Gentile leadership took over the Christian Church, and as it mixed its Jewish heritage with Greek and other pagan traditions, the Church became more and more estranged from the Jewish communities and, by A.D. 200, their bitter antagonist. The conversion of Saint Paul the Jew to the Nazarene sect and the success of his universalist missionary teachings therefore represent an important and disastrous chapter in Jewish history.

Fourth, the great Jewish community of Alexandria suffered major losses in the street conflict of A.D. 115, partly a civil war with the Greek pagans, partly a reverberation of the anti-imperial rebellions in Judea. This conflict was followed by persecutions and pogroms against the Alexandrian Jews, the drastic diminution of their number, and their economic and cultural decline. Other great centers of Hellenistic Judaism also deteriorated.

The fifth and final stage of this destructive process was the accession to the Roman throne of a Christian emperor in the early fourth century A.D. This meant not only the assurance of Christian triumph among the competing religions of the Mediterranean world but also the use of state power, at the behest of the Christian clergy, against Jewish freedom and well-being. By the end of the fourth century A.D. the long and bloody record of Christian persecution of Jews with state support was well under way.

In this context of war, persecution, cultural conflict, and state oppression, the deteriorating social and economic position of the Jews led to a sharp decline in the size of the Jewish population in the Mediterranean world. The size of the Jewish population was probably also adversely affected by the general demographic decline of the Roman Empire in late antiquity for biomedical reasons of plague and other disease. In A.D. 500 the Jewish population was less than half of what it had been at the beginning of the Common Era. Both demographically and culturally the Jews experienced a long period of struggle for survival and anxious self-defense. If the redemptive factor that emerged from this period, Talmudic religious culture, had intellectual limitations as well as social effectiveness, it must be viewed in this context.

The five-stage process of Jewish decline was paralleled and significantly countervailed by a panoply of writings second in importance only to Tanach itself. These consist first of the judicial and sociological works the Mishnah (A.D. 200) and the Palestinian Talmud (A.D. 400). They were accompanied by Midrash and Haggada, which involve scriptural exegesis, narrative legend, medical advice, folklore, and imaginative storytelling intended to instruct as well as entertain. Elaboration of law, commentary, social coding, and imaginative narrative culminated in the sixth century A.D. in the Bavli, the six thousand large-sized pages of the Babylonian Talmud, constructed in the still prosperous old Mesopotamian communities under the rule of the successive Iranian Parthean and Sasanian empires.

The Talmud is not a book. It is a library of judicial reasoning, ethical rules, social imaginings, and psychological modification generally formulated as a commentary on the Bible and ostensibly to clarify the Mishnah and adapt its teachings for contemporary (sixth-century) society. Bavli is a very thick culture, an elaborate compilation whose intensive study prepares leadership for judicial decision making, political guidance, and family, moral, and psychological counseling.

The conventional view that the Talmud provided the Jewish masses, the Am haarez, with a "hedge around the Law" to preserve their faith and lifestyle in dark and difficult times is not untrue, but it is a limited perception. The Bavli provided the training ground for thirteen hundred years of a learned rabbinical elite (associated with a high bourgeoisie) to govern and preserve Jewish communities under pressure and duress and occasional prosperity. The age of the making of the Talmud also confirms the dominance of Jewish life by the rabbis. Written down, after centuries of preparatory study and discussion, the Babylonian Talmud sustained Jewish courage and promoted Jewish consciousness while reflecting an ambience of social anxiety and intellectual withdrawal.

The further development of liberal and apocalyptic forms of Judaism was suspended while the Pharisaic tradition blossomed into a distinctive hegemonic rabbinical culture that in its full articulated texture, sensibility, and sociological superstructure exhibits some similarities to Indian Brahmin culture, as Columbia's Alan F. Segal has suggested. There are some similarities also to the cultural situation formulated by the Roman Catholic hierarchy in Western Europe. By the sixth century A.D. the foundations of the Jewish Middle Ages, which endured into the seventeenth century, had been set down.

At the beginning of the fourth century A.D. Jewish destiny in the ancient world was running its course, and the outlines of the medieval world were fast emerging. Two communities—or as they said in the Roman Empire, two cities—that both traced their origins to Abraham and the Hebrew prophets stood against each other: the Jewish community, increasingly dominated in the Diaspora as well as in Palestine by what we call Talmudic Judaism; and the Christian Church.

There were similarities in the governance of the two communities. Jewish life centered on the town synagogue; the Christian culture focused on the city cathedral. In both communities religious authorities above this level made ambitious claims. In the case of the Jews there was a Nasi (prince), who for long periods held a mandate from the Roman authorities to exercise law and collect taxes from the Palestinian Jews, and a hereditary prince called the exilarch, who had pretentious claims, with the approval of the Iranian ruler, over the Babylonian Jewish community. The exilarch also enjoyed economic privileges such as a special role in the lucrative silk trade with the Orient, foreshadowing the long relationship between religious authority and capitalism in Jewish life. The synagogues were not eager to accept close control by the exilarchs. The Nasis in Palestine were more popular because of their rabbinical learning. One of them, Judah the Prince, about A.D. 200, defined the authoritative text of the Mishnah.

Similarly in the Christian community the great archbishops—and patriarchs in the East and the pope in Rome—claimed high authority and intermittently exercised it.

Commentators on Jewish history often claim a profound difference between the Talmudic rabbis and the Christian clergy. The latter were not only teachers, preachers, missionaries, and community leaders, they point out, but also priests whose sacerdotal powers gave them, and particularly the bishops, the keys to the kingdom of heaven. The rabbis were not priests and did not claim the extravagant sacerdotal powers of the Christian clergy. This is an important formal distinction, but in social practice within their respective communities the difference was not great. In times and places where the Jewish masses were regular conformists to Talmudic Judaism, the rabbis' domination of people's public and private lives was almost as substantial as that of the Christian clergy in their sphere. As Jacob Neusner has remarked:

> Judaism as we have known it for nearly two millennia, was born. When Jews reached the conviction that the figure of the rabbi encompassed all three—the learning, the doing, the hope— Judaism had come to full and enduring experience . . . So Judaism became *rabbinic* . . . Judaism as we know it . . . by 600 C.E. was fully worked out.

Both the Jewish rabbis and the Christian patriarchs talked about the coming of the Messiah, but neither group acted as though that event was imminent. Apocalyptic and eschatological visions governed their behavior and shaped their sensibilities, but only at the margin, not at the core of their daily experience. The Jews believed that the Messiah would come eventually, but the rabbis were meanwhile concerned to govern their communities in accordance with Talmudic codes. They were present-minded and socially directed; eschatology, keen anticipation of the Messiah's early arrival, was not within their emotional horizon.

The Christians believed that the Messiah in the person of the god-man savior Jesus Christ had already come once, a doctrine that was anathema to the Jews, and that the Christian savior son would come again and the world would end. But that too was not existentially imminent to the Christian bishops. They were content to build up their authority in the cities and acquire property, possibilities that were immensely enhanced when the superstitious and violent emperor Constantine in A.D. 312 gained the Roman throne and professed his faith in the Christian god (whom he frequently confused with the pagan sun god).

The series of events that led to the two cities, Jewish and Christian, of A.D. 300 was inaugurated by the great Jewish rebellion against Rome in A.D. 66. How and why did it happen? A participant, Josephus, wrote a lengthy account of it in Rome around A.D. 80. Josephus was on his mother's side a descendant of the royal Hasmonean line; he belonged to the high Jewish aristocracy. At the beginning of the war, he was commissioned to head the Jewish forces in the north, the Galilee. He had always been uncomfortable with the Zealots, and when his forces suffered an early defeat by Roman arms, he went over to the Roman side, became an adviser to the Roman commander at the siege of Jerusalem, then a client of the Roman imperial family, and wrote *The Jewish Wars* in a comfortable villa near Rome. Obviously, one of his prime purposes in writing the book was to make himself look good to his imperial patron and explain away his treason to the Jewish cause, but his work is sufficiently circumstantial to indicate essentially what happened.

There were two main causes for the great rebellion. On the one side, political nationalists, the Zealot party, had since the early years of the first century A.D. been conducting propaganda and guerrilla warfare leading to a full-scale rebellion. Even given that Josephus the aristocrat and the Zealots, who were supporters of the exploited and distressed tenant farmers, were bitter enemies, his assessment of them is persuasive:

> All sorts of misfortunes sprang from these men, and the nation was infected with this doctrine [of rebellion] to an incredible degree. One violent war came upon us after another [so that] the very Temple of God was burned down by the enemy's fire.

The government in Rome also played into the Jewish radicals' hands by sending to Judea a series of inept and frequently mean-spirited governors who oppressed the Jews by heavy taxation and corruption and sometimes insulted their religion as well. This brought the mass of the population, including the aristocratic Sadducees but not most of the Pharisaic leadership, into a confrontational mood.

The bad quality of Roman officials in Judea over seven decades can be gauged from the failure of all but one of them to get another government post when they left Judea, often in disgrace. The Roman governors of Judea for more than half a century were so consistently bad that Hyam Maccoby has proposed a conspiracy theory. People high up in the government in Rome kept sending out these losers to goad the Jews into rebellion and create a pretext to smash the Jewish population.

The situation was exacerbated by the normal absence of the Roman army from Jerusalem, leaving the city open to radicalization and conspiracy most of the year. The center of Roman power was in Caesarea on the coastline, memorialized today by the well-preserved ruins of an outdoor Roman theater, now the site of upscale summer concerts. Only three times a year, on important religious festivals (when the Jews from the countryside flocked to the animal sacrifices at the Temple), did the Roman governor go up to Jerusalem with large forces. It was pleasant along the coast (Caesarea is today a favorite place for the villas of Israeli cabinet ministers and business executives) and the governor and his troops also wanted to protect the string of urban Greek-speaking Gentile enclaves that the government had established in the coastal plain. Jerusalem was a distant, crowded, dry, hot, uncomfortable city (it still is); no place for a Roman aristocrat to take his ease.

The Jews lost the war, after two years of initial standoffs against the Romans, for two good reasons. One was obvious; they were outnumbered when huge Roman reserves were brought in from Syria and Egypt. The Judean rebels probably hoped for a Jewish rising in the Diaspora, but that did not occur. The other reason was the very deep divisions among the Jews. They were murderously fractionalized along economic class and sectarian lines. Even when Jerusalem was under siege in A.D. 69–70, armed conflicts occurred among contending groups in the city. One Zealot faction burned much of the city's grain supply to keep it from the others. Those among the Jewish masses in the city who belonged to no faction were trapped there, and tens of thousands were massacred after the Romans broke through the walls.

Whether the Roman commander Titus, the son of the emperor

and later emperor himself, intended to burn down the Temple is uncertain. Possibly the destruction was the result of spontaneous pillage by his troops. But the triumphal arch in Rome commemorating Titus's victory depicts his army carrying off the holy candelabra from the Temple; his intentions were far from moderate.

Even after the destruction in Jerusalem, Jewish resistance continued. Finally in A.D. 73 the last Jewish freedom fighters and their wives and children—nine hundred of them—in the desert hill fortress of Masada, forty miles south of Jerusalem, the site of King Herod's winter palace, committed mass suicide as the Roman armies penetrated their defenses.

Masada has a special connotation for Israelis today, symbolizing unflagging national resistance to hated enemies. At the end of their basic training, Israeli conscripts camp out there overnight and at sunrise take a fiery oath of allegiance to the state and people.

Less is known about the cause of the second rebellion against Rome of A.D. 132–35 led by the posthumously glamorous but historically vague figure of Bar Cocheba, who has fired the modern Zionist imagination much more than he did his contemporaries. He was supported by the venerable rabbinical scholar Rabbi Akiba, who accorded him messianic dignity, and hence his name was changed from the original Bar Koseba to Bar Cocheba, Son of the Star, in accordance with the injunction in the Torah, "A star rises from Jacob." Most of the rabbis were unimpressed. One of them remarked to Akiba, "Sooner grass will grow out of your cheeks than the Son of David [the Messiah] come" in the person of Bar Cocheba.

Israeli archaeologists have discovered a letter from Bar Cocheba to his supporters in the north. It is exhibited today, along with some of the Dead Sea Scrolls, in a shrine located across the street from the Israeli parliament building in Jerusalem.

The Roman punishment of the rebellious Jews was savage in the extreme. Close to half of the remaining 1.3 million Jews in Palestine were killed. Jerusalem was given a Roman name and settled with Gentiles. Any circumcised person henceforth caught within its walls was to be executed. The remaining impoverished Jewish population, when they did not go into exile, were driven northward into the hills of the Galilee. There the rabbis moved their school from Jabneh south of Jaffa on the coast. There in the north the Mishnah was completed.

The rabbinical redactors of the Mishnah, about A.D. 200, said little about the course of Bar Cocheba's war against Rome fought two generations earlier, but they did preserve this record of its consequence:

> For seven years the people of the world [the Gentiles in Palestine] harvested their vineyards without manure as fertilizers but with Jewish blood . . . They [the Romans] killed until the blood flowed out of the doorways . . . until the horses waded in blood up to the nostrils . . .

The most insightful book on the Jewish rebellions after Josephus, *The Bar Kokhba Syndrome,* was published in 1983 by Yehosafat Harkabi, a former general in Israeli intelligence. The syndrome, in his view, is a reckless militant nationalism that assumes that Jewish will can overcome insuperable military odds and work miracles. This induces delusions of grandeur and cataclysmic adventurism. Obviously Harkabi had the ill-fated Lebanese imbroglio of 1982 in mind when he rendered his negative judgment on Bar Cocheba, noting the second-century rabbi's judgment that the Son of Star's conduct was "self-aggrandizement against God." Harkabi's book caused a storm of controversy in Israel.

The Bar Cocheba rebellion could only have made things worse for the Jewish community in Palestine. It was doomed to miserable failure and its importance as a turning point is therefore inferior to what happened in Alexandria shortly before, in A.D. 115. Partly a civil war between Jews and Jew-hating Gentiles, partly a rebellion against Rome in sympathy with events in Palestine, the Alexandrian disaster led to the deaths of many thousands of Jews, placed the once confident and wealthy Alexandrian Jewish community on the defensive, and began a long series of persecutions and pogroms that by A.D. 300 made the Alexandrian Jewry a poor shadow of itself in its days of glory in Philo's time.

The decline of Hellenistic Jewry, which the disaster of A.D. 115 signified and precipitated, came in the context of rising Judeo-phobia among the Roman aristocracy as well as among the pogromist Gentile masses in the eastern Mediterranean. Writing about the same time as the conflict in Alexandria, the aristocratic Roman spokesman and historian Tacitus condemned the Jews for their "wickedness...

wretches of the most abandoned kind . . . a most lascivious people . . . among themselves nothing is barred." These violent remarks come in a section of Tacitus's history in which he discussed the rebellion of A.D. 66–70. One can see at work a cyclic phenomena, to be repeated many times until our own day. Hatred and jealousy of the Jews inspired mean and hurtful conduct against them, and when they rose to defend themselves, the hatred became even more violent. We may call this the UN syndrome.

The destruction of Herod's Temple in A.D. 70 and the Roman terror that followed rationalized the sectarian makeup of the Jews in their homeland. The Sadducees' strength had lain in their association with the aristocratic Temple priesthood. When the Temple was destroyed, many priests perished with it, and without the existence of the Temple the raison d'être of the Sadducee party was gone, and they quickly disappeared from the scene.

A Roman army marching into the Negev Desert along the Dead Sea to attack the last Zealot outpost at Masada eliminated the nearby Qumran community. Fortunately the Qumran sectarians concealed their vast library of apocalyptic and other writings going back more than two centuries in large jars and buried them in caves overlooking the Dead Sea. There the scrolls were accidentally discovered by Bedouins in 1948, and further searches by Bedouins and Israeli archaeologists in the following three years turned up a vast compendium of religious literature, although unfortunately one-third of the Dead Sea Scrolls fell into the hands of Jew-hating and lazy Belgian and French monks working under the patronage of the anti-Zionist Rockefeller Museum in East Jerusalem, Jordanian territory until 1967. Qumran and the Essenes thus also disappeared under the Roman sword.

This left in existence only two active sects in Jewish Palestine: the dominant Pharisees and the recently founded splinter group called the Nazarenes and a little later the Christians. Now began in earnest the struggle between the rabbis and the leaders of Jewish Christianity that were to become the two cities, the two communities that comprised the religious legacy of the Roman Empire to the Middle Ages and beyond.

Not inappropriately, since the emergence of historical science in the early nineteenth century, no subject has received closer attention than the life of the Jew Jesus Christ (meaning the Messiah, the King), the Nazarene, and the origins of the Christian Church. Until the 1930s scholars believed that a historical account of the life of Jesus could be written and tried to do so. From about 1935 to 1965 the skeptical view of the German New Testament scholar Rudolf Bultmann was dominant. He said that the four Gospels ("good news") account of Jesus' life, almost the only existing sources, were midrash, a pastiche of Jewish legends applied to a holy man, and no verifiable circumstantial historical account could be constructed of the course of Jesus' life, although, as a devout Lutheran, Bultmann did not doubt the actual existence of Jesus.

The past quarter-century has seen a general move back to trying to write the life of Jesus, "the marginal Jew," as a recent liberal Catholic scholar, John Meier, called him.

Bultmann had a point. Jesus died in or around the year A.D. 30, at the age of thirty-three. The four Gospels of Mark, Luke, Matthew, and John appear to have been written between A.D. 70 and 100. They all almost certainly were written outside Palestine, in such places as Antioch, Alexandria, and Rome. Luke makes elementary errors in Palestinian geography and likely never visited the country, although he ended up as a traveling companion and secretary to Saint Paul. Mark and Luke were very likely Gentiles, and John, writing around A.D. 100 in a discourse heavily conditioned by Neoplatonic philosophy, certainly was. Matthew probably was too, although because of his circumstantial familiarity with Jewish law, some critics think he may have been a Jewish Christian. That Matthew hates the Pharisees and the Jewish populace in general so vehemently can support either ethnic ascription of him.

These characteristics of the Christian Gospels are not strongly conducive to belief in their historicity. Nineteenth-century scholars tried to countervail this implausibility by claiming that the so-called synoptic Gospels—Mark, Luke, and Matthew—all drew from a more contemporary now vanished source, coded Q (for Quelle, source in German). This is mere speculation. More important is that we have here four accounts of Jesus' life written not only at least one generation removed from him and written in the Diaspora and probably by Gentiles, but written after two events that affected the later Christian view of Jesus were known: The Temple was destroyed and the minuscule Nazarene community was left as the only competitor with the Pharisees in the Jewish community; and the rabbis had not responded in any positive way to Jesus. They simply ignored claims that he was somehow the Messiah and regarded his followers as minim (heretics).

Contemporary Pharisaic disdain for the Christian sect accounts for the ferocity with which the Gospels, especially Matthew, the longest and most circumstantial life, turn upon the Pharisees and make them—and through them the whole Jewish community—responsible for Jesus' death: His "blood," says Matthew, is on their hands. Nearly all Christian writers today, even officially the Catholic Church since 1965, believe this accusation to be wrong. The Gospels' ascriptions of guilt for Jesus' death to the Pharisees are either due to a misunderstanding or are more likely libels concocted for later first-century purposes during Christian competition with the rabbinical successors of the Pharisees.

The Gospels were written in the last three decades of the first century, when rabbinical Judaism was the only competitor in the Jewish world against the ambitious new Christian Church. It was evident at that time that the rabbis would make no concessions to the Christians or recognize the existence of Jesus as even a latter-day prophet. The authors of the Gospels took their revenge on the implacably hostile rabbis by portraying their Pharisaic predecessors in the time of Jesus as primarily responsible for his death. The Pharisees were held to be the primary Christ killers. The blood of the Lord was on their hands.

It is a common literary device to rewrite history and make your current opponents responsible for earlier alleged crimes. The consequences for Jewish history of this particular retroactive literary campaign, however, were not merely intellectual. The Gospels became the central texts in the Christian New Testament—their new Bible, with the authority of divine inspiration.

The Gospel picture of the Pharisees' responsibility for Jesus' death was taken up into Catholic teaching and was in itself responsible for the death and persecution of millions of Jews in the next two millennia. Repudiated by the reforming Vatican Council II in 1965 at the urging of liberal Catholic biblical scholars and theologians such as Father Hans Küng, it is no longer the official teaching of the Roman Church. But it still lingers in the Christian popular culture in places like Poland, the Ukraine, and the American Midwest and South. Would the authors of the Gospels have been appalled by the holocaust consequences of their literary device of Pharisees as villains? Probably not. They were very angry and hateful toward the implacable rabbis.

If any group of Jews was in part actually responsible for Jesus' death, it would be the Sadducees. They would have been most disturbed by his criticism of the Temple priests and they, not the Pharisees, controlled the Sanhedrin, the Jewish high court, which—or a subcommittee of which (the accounts are confused)—turned Jesus over to the Roman authorities as a subversive. But as even Catholic scholars acknowledge today, crucifixion was a dreaded Roman punishment for enemies of the state, certainly not a Jewish punishment for blasphemy. If Jesus had been condemned by the Sanhedrin or members thereof, it could only have been for blasphemy, not subversion, which was a Roman crime, and the execution would have been by stoning, not crucifixion.

The Gospels go to dramatic lengths to blame the Jews and let the Romans off the hook—an obvious public relations ploy in the late first century A.D. when the Christian Church had been rejected by the Jewish community and had to seek its future exclusively among the Gentiles, and needed tolerance from the Roman authorities. The inept and cruel Roman governor Pontius Pilate (so condemned even by a contemporary, Philo of Alexandria) is whitewashed in the Gospel story. He doesn't want to condemn and execute Jesus, they say. He mysteriously offers a Jewish crowd a choice unknown to Roman law. They can free either Jesus or another condemned prisoner, Barabbas, "a robber." The Jews say, "Give us Barabbas." Efforts have been made to give plausibility to this fanciful story by suggesting that Barabbas was a member of the Zealot underground, sometimes called robbers in contemporary accounts.

If there is history rather than a series of romantic screenplays in the Gospels (everyone interested in the life of Jesus should see the film of Matthew's Gospel made by the Italian Communist director, Pier Pasolini—the only good film ever made about a Jewish religious leader), the substratum of truth comes down to this.

Jesus the Jew was born the son of a carpenter, Joseph, in Nazareth, a small hill town in Galilee (it is still there) about twenty miles west of Lake Kinneret, or the Sea of Galilee. His mother Miriam (Mary), of like humble stock, had several other children, including James, an elder brother. Jesus inherited his popular mission from a cousin, John the Baptist. John was an itinerant preacher and holy man affiliated with the Essenes and the Qumran community who specialized in the ancient Hebrew cleansing rite of immersion in water. He somehow annoyed King Herod, who executed him. Jesus simply took up John's mission—it ran in the family—widened John's message, and did more faith healing. Jesus grew up a charismatic preacher and faith healer. He gained a handful of local disciples, especially from among the poor fishermen on Lake Kinneret.

The leader of this small group was the fisherman Simon Bar Yonah, whom Jesus later rewarded with the nickname (in Aramaic) Cephas (steadfast, "rock," in Greek, Peter). If you go now to dine at one of the splendid resort hotels in Tiberias on Lake Kinneret, the menu will appropriately feature Saint Peter's fish, a kind of scrawny sea bass.

Jesus never separated himself from the Jewish community or rejected the Law. To the end of his life, he was an observant Jew. At times he may have criticized the priests as too formalistic and materialistic, but so did many other Jews. He saw himself giving the Law a deeper ethical content, making it more meaningful in the lives of ordinary people, not disavowing it in any way:

> Do not suppose that I have come to abolish the Law and the Prophets: I did not come to abolish but to complete . . . Anyone who keeps the Law and teaches others so will stand high in the Kingdom of Heaven.

Jesus began to refer to himself as the Son of Man, an obscure term mentioned in the Book of Daniel, which may have come to signify the Messiah. Jesus was an observant Jew but preached a radical ethic in which material wealth was held to threaten morality, in which the poor and wretched would inherit the earth. It was a kind of extreme backwater amplification of the voluntarist ethics taught in Jerusalem by the liberal Pharisaic school of Hillel. Many other such backwoods oddball preachers and faith healers wandered around in Judea. Jesus was far from singular.

The messianic motif began to affect Jesus under pressure from his disciples. He may have had conversations with his doting mother that led him to fancy she was descended from the line of David— given David's popularity and the king's sexual activity, such fancy was not uncommon among ordinary people.

Jesus' little mission reached a point of such local celebrity that he felt impelled to try it out in the big league of Jerusalem and went there with his disciples for the Passover festival. He made two grave tactical errors. First, he entered the holy city in noisy, triumphal fashion and gained the attention of the authorities. Then he went to the outer courtyard of the Temple where moneychangers (necessary for the country people who had come to purchase sacrifices by the Temple priesthood) were located and made a disturbance and denounced them for materialism. This brought him to the further attention of the Roman authorities and generated complaints by the Sadducee priests. Under the pressure of a threatening situation, Jesus revealed himself to Peter as the "Christ, the Son of God," but told Peter to keep the news to himself.

Rumors spread that the Roman soldiers were looking for Jesus and that he had been targeted as a subversive. Either at the Passover Seder or at a prequel sitting one evening before Passover (the Gospel accounts vary), Jesus presided over a Passover meal. Afterward he said that he expected to be arrested soon and, holding up a cup of wine and a piece of matzo, told his disciples to remember these as symbols of his blood and body.

He also said that his disciples would deny and betray him, which indeed they proceeded to do when he was arrested and brought before the governor, Pilate, who pressured the exhausted and frightened Jesus into admitting that he had called himself king of the Jews. He was forthwith crucified for treason by the Roman governor.

Jesus had always been on good terms with two despised elements of the population—tax collectors and prostitutes. Three days after his death some of the latter went to the place where his body was laid out (now allegedly in the Church of the Holy Sepulchre) and found that the body was gone. His disciples came out of hiding, professed that the savior and Messiah had been among them, and that Jesus had been divinely privileged by bodily resurrection as in the legend of the prophet Elijah. The Nazarenes formed a little community who met together and celebrated Jesus' memory in thanksgiving (Eucharist) and taught his ultraliberal Pharisaic ethic.

The fact is that Jesus was a sweet soul and not a political revolutionary. In the final days of his life, he must have come to personalize Deutero-Isaiah's description of the "suffering servant" and to begin to think it applied not so much to the people of Israel as a whole but to himself as an individual. He himself was the "lamb of

God" who had by divine will to suffer and die so that mankind might be somehow cleansed. If he saw this only murkily, it immediately became a fixation with his followers after his passion. They applied the 118th Psalm to Jesus, and he became not just a branch of the Tree of Jesse (House of David) but some kind of metaphysical savior: "I shall not die, but I shall live, and recount the deeds of the Lord. The Lord has chastised me sorely but he has not given me over to death."

The rabbis received the Nazarene brotherhood's perception of the meaning of the life, death, and resurrection of Jesus with silent contempt. But there is something very Pharisaic about Jesus, and not just his echoing of Hillel's golden rule. The existential pessimism, the noble fatalism, the unflinching conviction that the mighty goyim will fall down and the meek Jews be lifted up ("the first shall be the last"; "blessed are they who are persecuted for righteousness' sake for theirs is the kingdom of heaven"; "a little child shall lead them")—this downside/upside conviction lies at the center of the rabbinical-shaped Jewish temperament, and it is there with Jesus on the Cross.

His response to Pilate was at the same time evasive and provocative, bringing on the terrible punishment of ignominious crucifixion. Jesus radiated the masochistic temperament that lies at the heart of Pharisaic consciousness: "Lord, why has thy forsaken me?," *Lamah sabachthani,* the Job-like cry of Jewish martyrs at the hands of the pogromists through the centuries—this too was Jesus' cry on the Cross.

When Jesus told his audience that he was bringing not peace but a sword he was speaking metaphorically; he meant he was shaking things up culturally. Left alone, Jesus would have come down clearly on the side of pacifism. But he was not left alone; he was swept up in events in a politically charged atmosphere. He was compelled to make provocative statements and perform symbolic acts, and the result was a tragedy. Such is an interpretation derived from a hundred and fifty years of intense scholarship and debate.

In the disturbed times running up to the rebellion of A.D. 66 any radical charismatic group was likely to gain some adherents, and so it was with the Nazarenes, but Church membership remained very small in number. Things changed radically when Rabbi Saul of Tarsus came to study in Jerusalem some fifteen years after Jesus' death. He was "a Pharisee," "a Hebrew born of the Hebrews," in his own words, who came from a solid middle-class, possibly affluent family in Tarsus in eastern Asia Minor, not far from today's Turkish border with Lebanon and Syria.

In Jerusalem Rabbi Saul encountered the Nazarenes and became paranoid about them, seeing them as a big threat to traditional Judaism. He heard the Nazarenes were preaching in the synagogues of the large Jewish community in Damascus and got a commission from the rabbinical council to head there and verbally attack the Christians. On the road to Damascus Saul experienced one of his epileptic fits, in the course of which the return of the repressed occurred. He had a vision of Jesus, who told him to stop persecuting his followers and to become an apostle preaching Jesus' divine and messianic role.

Paul, to use his Greek name, returned to Jerusalem and joined the Nazarene community headed by Peter and James, "the brother of the Lord." There were tensions from the beginning. This gloomy obsessive, ascetic (Paul never married, almost unheard of for a Pharisaic rabbi), outspoken, intellectual, learned rabbi fit in poorly with the little group of lower middle-class, uneducated, pious, humble people.

They were not sorry to see him leave to preach the Christian message in the synagogues of the Diaspora and convert Jews there. A decade or so later, however, there was a huge blowup when Paul returned to Jerusalem and told Peter he wanted to preach to the Gentiles and accept uncircumcised men into the Christian community. Paul inevitably had received rough treatment in the synagogues from devout Jews of the Diaspora. He discovered, however, a potentially large clientele—the uncircumcised "God-fearers" or righteous Gentiles who were adherents but not members of the Greek-speaking Jewish communities. He wanted to offer these Gentiles, now Greek-speaking second-class citizens among the Jews, full membership in the Christian Church without circumcision. In the end Paul as always got his way, but the deep bitterness between him and Peter and the Jewish Christians remained.

Christian tradition has them both ending up in Rome, Peter as first bishop, and both martyred there. This end is much more plausible for Paul than for the cautious Peter, who with his hostility to the Gentiles was an unlikely candidate to lead the Church in Rome, even though a substantial Jewish community lived there. Paul appears to have been denounced to the Roman authorities by the Sadducees for "preaching contrary to Caesar." The priests found his successful mission and conversion of the uncircumcised disturbing. Paul insisted that as a Roman citizen he should be tried in Rome and was sent there. What happened to him is unknown. He probably died just before the great rebellion of A.D. 66 began.

According to Roman Catholic tradition, both Peter and Paul were martyred in the Eternal City by bad Roman emperors, and the Church of Rome is officially dedicated to Peter and Paul—two good Jewish boys, Simon Rocky and Saul of Tarsus. This should make the papacy today either a devout supporter or a bitter enemy of the state of Israel. Until 1993 it chose to be the latter, after doing nothing to try to stop the Holocaust in the early 1940s.

In the Christian New Testament six letters are attributed to Paul that scholars believe to be authentic although they may have undergone editing by later hands. In addition a lengthy and circumstantial account of Paul's missions is offered by his faithful companion, Luke. There are problems in using Paul's letters to understand his teaching. They are relatively short and are addressed to various Christian communities in Asia Minor, Greece, and Rome itself, and deal usually with ad hoc matters. Paul often assumes that his readers already know his general message because, with the exception of the one letter to the Romans, he has already preached there.

Even when he tries to articulate his general principles, Paul frequently seems awkward and conflicted. Indeed a leading New Testament scholar, Paula Frederikson, after many years studying Paul's slim body of writings, concluded in 1988 in exasperation: "Paul is extremely difficult to understand . . . Paul was more successful at communicating excitement and conviction than clarity. He confused his own congregations."

This judgment is not unwarranted but is a bit harsh. The essentials of what Paul was feeling and saying are clear enough. Pauline teaching remains one of the important chapters in Jewish history because, as David Fussler of the Hebrew University has said, Christianity was a Jewish creation. And it was Rabbi Paul more than the simple good man of Galilee who founded the Christian Church. Paul was greatly admired by and profoundly influenced leading Christian thinkers in all ages. Saint Augustine in the fifth century, Martin Luther in the sixteenth, and Karl Barth in the twentieth, formidable names, were all his straight-line disciples. We ought to try to understand what this intense, obsessive Pharisee is saying. It is an important chapter in the intellectual history of the Jews.

To the end of his life Paul the Pharisee remained an observant Jew. He also did not disparage Judaism in the interest of the Gentiles. He said the Christian message was equally a challenge to both: "a stumbling block to Jews and a folly to Gentiles." "Has God rejected his people? By no means." So what was the nature of his teaching that was so troublesome for his colleagues among the Pharisaic rabbinate?

At the simplest and perhaps most existentially disturbing level, he removed the barriers of circumcision and allowed any who converted their will and mind to the Christian faith to enter the new community. Similarly he allowed Jew and Gentile to eat together, and though he did not deny the value of kashruth and apparently personally continued to observe the dietary laws, this comingling of Jew and Gentile at mealtimes effectively terminated the Jewish character of Christianity as much as the lifting of the circumcision barrier. By these actions, Paul was creating an international multicultural community of faith that did not tell a Jew to give up the Halakah but made it a mere personal choice, an idiosyncrasy, and not part of the nature of the Christian community. Jewish Christians could not but be deeply disturbed, and the Pharisees regarded him as a traitor to the Law.

Paul then turned around and, while not advocating the dissolution of the Law and its abandonment, called it a psychological impediment and ultimately a moral "curse." Why? Because it led the Jewish Christian to focus on the distinctions stipulated by the Law; by its existence it induced negative thinking rather than the positive ones arising from Jesus' life and death. It is easy to believe that Paul expected that, among Jewish Christians, the Law would soon wither away from its power to shape religious feeling and constrain individual and group behavior, and he welcomed this early occurrence. If you take a critical attitude to the Law, you have assaulted the essentials of Pharisaism. He knew that.

The third theme in Paul's thinking was the doctrine of justification by faith. He thought deeply about the significance of Adam and Eve's expulsion from Eden, which came to him to symbolize the fall of man, the innate corruption in human nature. By ourselves we can never justify God's love; we are rooted in sin, in rebellion against God. So God sent His son to be incarnated in human form, and in his life and death he earned such merit that mankind could vicariously through Jesus Christ merit salvation—but only if God chooses us individually: We cannot love God until He loves us, until He justifies us, makes us personally just, embraces us individually.

In the letter to the Christian Romans Paul set forth this key and troublesome doctrine in all subsequent Christian theology:

> For there is no distinction, since all have sinned and fall short of the glory of God, they are justified by his grace as a gift, through redemption which is in Christ Jesus, whom God has put forward as an expiation by his blood, to be received by faith.

Paul's salvation theology is grounded in disillusionment with the Jews' historic role as the "man of sorrows" by whose suffering mankind is supposed to be redeemed. That had not happened. Paul turns then to Christ, who saves mankind by the expiation of his blood.

Paul's political doctrine was founded in eschatalogical sociology. The world is coming to an end soon. It makes no sense now to draft constitutions or to change governments. So stay in subjection to the current "governing authorities" and cultivate instead one's personal relationship with God. Internally we are all free, whether slave or citizen, Jew or Greek. Externally we should accept where God has called us to be in society, whose days are in any case running out. This is a doctrine of extreme acceptance of the status quo, and we can see a touch of Pharisaic political passivity in it.

The rabbis turned their backs on Jerusalem when it was doomed and cut a deal with Roman power so that Torah study could endure. Similarly Rabbi Saul wanted his Christian communities to keep quiet and not arouse the attention of the authorities. In both instances the life of quiet learning and prayer is valorized and the life of political activism proscribed.

Paul's view on sex and marriage is very different from the traditional Jewish one, although it probably was close to that held by some of the Essenes who remained celibate. Paul's teaching on sexuality and the association between John the Baptist and the Essenes are the strongest arguments for those today who see a connection between the Qumran community and the early Christian Church.

Paul told the Christians that it is best to stay in the celibate condition and not to marry. Marriage is only for those who burn with desire and cannot control themselves. Sex inside marriage is only for purposes of procreation of children. The rabbis permitted sex only in marriage too, but they accepted a man's carnal "knowledge" (the biblical term) of a woman as a natural thing. They had no admiration for celibacy. It is God's will that Jews marry, and enjoyment of the sexual act inside marriage is commendable. In accordance with Pharisaic tradition, the Talmud describes the union of husband and wife as a "sanctification" and declares that "a Jew who has no wife is not a man."

Where did the provincial rabbi Saul get these radical ideas that exploded the framework of traditional Judaism at the same time that he skillfully drew on much of its rhetoric? First there were strong influences from Hellenistic culture, especially from Platonic and Stoic philosophy and also from dualistic Gnosticism. Paul was an exact contemporary of Philo, living in pretty much the same intellectual and social milieu. This generation of Diaspora Jews were searching to restructure the Jewish religion in terms of vanguard Hellenistic thinking.

Philo had his version. Paul had his, which at the margin overlapped with Philo's but at its core was more radical, darker, foreboding. In both the writings of Philo and Paul there is a Greek-derived dualist tendency, but in Paul it comes wrapped in a brooding pessimistic sensibility. That may be a product of his Pharisee background. It may also be the result of an eschatalogical conviction that the last days were at hand.

This kind of pessimistic dualism was central to Gnosticism, and the heretical Christian Gnostic church of the second century regarded Paul's letters as the authoritative part of the New Testament. Therefore, when Gnosticism embedded itself in mainstream late medieval Jewish culture through the Cabala, it was ultimately the long shadow of enigmatic Rabbi Saul projecting itself on the Jews again.

In Asia Minor where Paul was brought up and received his education, the Greek mystery religions, such as Isis and Great Mother, were very active, and this background too may be reflected in his teaching. In the mystery religions a savior-god in human form dies, is reborn, and carries those of mankind who have fastened themselves to the reborn deity by some sacramental rite (eating or washing or both) to safety and immortality. Paul's theology combined a historical human messiah in the Jewish mode with the sacramental savior-god of a mystery religion. But assuredly there were dozens, indeed hundreds of rabbis in Diaspora cities who encountered Platonism, Stoicism, Gnosticism, and Isis. They did not turn into Saint Paul.

The ultimate explanation for this great Jewish thinker and visionary was psychological. He wanted activity; he wanted turmoil; he wanted to create a revolution in faith; he wanted to found a new international community of true believers. That is where his satisfaction lay, not in leading a traditional synagogue community, not in marriage and family, not in private wealth, not in political activity and public power. He was a Pharisee, but he did not have the restrained, reticent rabbinical temperament. He went his own way and created his own destiny and absorbed thousands into it—not unheard of as the radical kind of life experience among the Jews. He was, like Marx, Freud, Einstein, Herzl, and Trotsky, a breaker of the molds of the past. Although the rabbis insisted that prophecy in Israel was long over with, Paul knew better.

Paul offered one kind of redemption to the Jews, a kind taken up and used in the Gospel of John, about A.D. 100, to reinterpret the life of Jesus: In the beginning was the Word; we preach Christ crucified. Pauline Christianity offered to the Jews a redemption through a savior religion and international multicultural congregation. Jews did not have to give up the Law, but there was no need and some disadvantage to maintaining it, in the Pauline projection. So most circumcised Jews rejected the Pauline message just as thousands of uncircumcised hangers-on to the synagogues relished it, and slowly the Gentile world was converted to it.

Paul's background in the Diaspora gave him a perception of developing religious crisis in the Roman Empire. Old Greco-Roman paganism was losing its appeal for the teeming masses of the Mediterranean world. They wanted religion in which a savior-god gave them security in this life and eternal bliss after death. The mystery religions such as Isis offered that, but Paul must have noticed how popular Judaism was, with its holy scriptures, its historical myth, and its puritan ethics. That was what attracted all these "God-fearing" uncircumcised Gentiles to attend the synagogue services offered in Greek. If Judaism would offer a dying and reborn savior-god incarnated in human form, and if it dropped the severe requirement of circumcision, it could gain vast numbers of new members from among the Gentiles and possibly become the dominant religion of the Roman world.

But the rabbis would not do this and the Jewish Christians would not give up circumcision and the dietary laws. They, like the rabbis, were missing a unique opportunity that Paul had seized upon. He had the mind of a media entrepreneur who assesses the market and gives the people what they want, just like those Jewish movie magnates in Hollywood today who know that what moviegoers want is violence and sex and give them these thrills irrespective of their own well-educated and sometimes refined sensibility. Paul was one of the all-time entrepreneurial magnates in religious experience and popular culture.

Only a small number of circumcised Jews bought into Pauline Christianity. They found it personally repugnant to take baths with the uncircumcised and share food with them. To do so was to become impure oneself, to lose caste.

The ethnic, circumcised Jews shunned Christianity for additional reasons. Until the mid-second century A.D. the Jews were more wealthy as a group than the Christians. Only after about A.D. 200 were there probably more Christians than Jews in the Roman world. Furthermore, Judaism was an officially tolerated religion, Christianity was not, there were local persecutions of Christians, and in the late third century a protracted and harsh imperial one.

Even in A.D. 300, when Christians were a quarter of the population of the Roman Empire and the Jewish segment of the population had shrunk to less than five percent, a Jew might still feel that his was a more privileged religion. Why join the Church? Indeed, all through the second and third centuries A.D. there were Christian conversions to Judaism, probably more than those who went the other way. The millions of ethnic Jews who drifted away from their faith conveniently disappeared normally into the mass of the pagan population and much more rarely into the Christian Church before it became a state-privileged entity in the fourth century.

So the Jews stayed with the rabbinical code and generally rejected the teachings of Rabbi Saul. They sought redemption in the way of the Mishnah and the Babylonian Talmud. The rabbis in the first three centuries of the Common Era almost totally ignored Christianity, pretended it didn't exist, gave it no religious legitimacy. If they ever mentioned Jesus and Mary it was to make sarcastic, impolite remarks, such as that Mary was a harlot and an unwed mother.

It is not for us to criticize the rabbis for their totally negative attitude to Christianity except perhaps to reflect wistfully how much tragedy and suffering for generations of Jews might have been moderated if the rabbis had been a little less unyielding, if they had made some gesture of conciliation. Yet if they had done so, they might have opened the door further to intermarriage and apostasy.

The reputation of the Talmud among liberal and secular Jews, especially in the United States, has undergone a big change in the direction of a highly favorable attitude in the past quarter-century. In the first half of the century, or at least until 1940, the Talmud was commonly identified by liberal and secular Jews with the narrow and retrograde culture of the Eastern European ghetto and shtetl that most American Jews, or their parents, had fled and wanted to forget. It was associated with a narrow, obsolete, suffocating, repressive culture and the domination of public and private life in the impoverished Russian and Polish communities by obscurantist and intolerant rabbis, gaunt old men with long beards, bad eyesight, and thin, unsmiling lips.

The Talmud had almost as doubtful a reputation among the majority of secularized Western Jews in the first half of this century as it had among Christians since the thirteenth century when it first became identified with a devious conspiracy of anti-Christian rabbis against known European civilization. Some prominent medieval Jewish apostates, usually former rabbinical scholars turned Christian friars, often took the lead in blackening the reputation of the Talmud as reeking with social and moral evil.

The grief produced by the Holocaust and the extinction of Eastern European culture with which the Talmud had been so closely associated effected the beginning of a change in attitude. By the 1970s the Talmud was nostalgically seen by many secular Jews as belonging to the mainstream of what was good in the Jewish tradition. An Israeli Talmudic scholar, Aldin Steinsaltz, published a short, enthusiastic book called *The Essential Talmud.* An American paperback translation of it appeared in 1976 and has since gone through eleven printings.

Even more impressive was the publication of the first volume of

a sumptuously printed English translation of the Talmud, with attendant classic commentaries, in 1990 by the same Rabbi Steinsaltz. This
volume, issued by Alfred A. Knopf, one the most distinguished of
American publishers, was a main publishing event of the season and
sold extremely well. It received highly laudatory if incomprehensible
reviews in the upscale media.

The Talmud had become a coffee-table book for suburban Jewish America! And perhaps a few hundred of such bourgeois pur-
chasers may have perused a few of its difficult talismanic pages.
Meanwhile the proliferation of Judaic studies programs on American
campuses disseminated well-informed overviews of the Talmud
among thousands of American Jews of the younger generation. The
Talmud, rescued from forgetfulness and Nazi horror, was back in
prominence. God had not forsaken the old rabbis after all.

On top of all this, Isaac Bashevis Singer, whose novels about the
immigrant community in New York before 1940 are poignantly realistic, began to turn out a series of sentimental accounts of the doings
in his father's rabbinical court in the old shtetl that were featured in
the upscale *New Yorker*, put together in best-selling books, and honored with the Nobel Prize for literature. One wonders what "Mendele
the Bookseller," the realist novelist of the late nineteenth century
who wrote mordantly bitter novels about this same rabbinically dominated world as a sinkhole of ignorance, superstition, and social
pathology, would have thought of Singer's imaginative reversal.

The Mishnah was put together in Palestine at the end of the second century A.D. in the rabbinical schools now located in the north.
It was a law book, for the most part narrowly focused on a series of
quite technical problems in religious, family, business, and civil law.
For instance, there is close and very intelligent attention to the problems of personal liability for injury. The Mishnah was intended as a
judicial guide for rabbinical courts. The Talmud, whether in its Palestinian (A.D. 400) or Babylonian (A.D. 600) version, was a series of
extended commentaries on the Mishnah and the passages in the
Torah on which the Mishnah legislation was based but often not
specifically cited.

The Talmud, in its Babylonian form, is the most famous work of
Jewish religious law after the Torah, but it is discursive and dialogic,
not legislative in style. The Bavli provides lengthy transcripts of
debates among rabbis about the meaning and implications of the

Mishnaic laws and the passages in the Torah or traditions of the oral law (upon which the Mishnah legislation is in turn based, ultimately but often not explicitly) by the way of explanation, amplification, and derivation.

Some of the judicial debates in the Talmud are closely edited and come to a decisive point. Others seem almost raw transcript in which the discussion meanders on and on, sometimes straying pretty far from the ostensible issue, and the judicial point is not very clear and has to be inferred—which necessitated yet further commentaries over the centuries on the Talmud itself.

The Talmud is best perceived as not so much imparting information as training the minds of rabbis who will have to make decisions on various matters of civil and religious law in their own courts. The Talmud is therefore much like a first-rate American law school today: It is more interested in getting its readers to think like judges than in giving them easy lists of legislation and clear-cut decisions to memorize.

The authors of the Talmud were writing not just for their own times or their own communities but for the long future and for communities all over the Near East and Western Europe, wherever the Jews lived in exile. They wanted to train the mind, to immerse the students of these many volumes in ways of thinking, to educate them for leadership within the context of a well-defined rabbinical culture. The Talmud is a school, a training ground, an immersion process.

Think of the Talmud as a very long and perpetually renewed TV series in which week after week rabbis sit around and leisurely discuss another point of civil law within the context of Torah and Mishnaic legislation. After a little while we enjoy the rabbinical insights and sharp repartee and idiosyncratic remarks. We identify the participating rabbis as individuals (the composition of the panels changes from time to time), some more obviously learned than the others, some right on target, others out in left field somewhere but amusing and occasionally offering special insights. We get drawn into this distinctive world. We cannot miss our hour or two of weekly Talmud.

We can feel how the study of the Talmud became itself a life's calling for a small elite through the centuries. Yes, most of the time they were more or less preparing themselves to sit on rabbinical courts, but the study of the Talmud became itself their main occupation, their cultural home, their passion, so much so that in the ghettos and shtetlach of Eastern Europe in the modern era the rabbis sometimes sent their wives to work and bring in money for the family while they sat, self-indulgent rabbinical saints, in the academy or synagogue day and night and with other privileged males studied the Talmud.

There are a handful of streets in Brooklyn and the older section of Jerusalem where this kind of Talmudic obsession is still going on, and perhaps we shall see more of it. It should be noted, however, that the medieval Talmudic tradition was that the rabbis not be supported by their wives or even by salaries from community funds. Rather the Talmudic rabbi was supposed to learn a craft or enter a profession—being jewelers, goldsmiths, or physicians were favorite occupations—and support themselves by their own labor.

Historically, the Talmud stood at the end of a long tradition of religious literature with social focus that began with King Josiah and the discovery of the Book of Deuteronomy before the first exile and Ezra and redactors of the Bible after it. Sociologically the Talmud was the prime vehicle for entrenchment and perpetuation of the leadership role of the educated, often hereditary elite in Jewish society at the beginning of the Middle Ages.

From the point of view of literary theory, the Talmud was the formulation in canonical structure of a hermeneutic intellectual tradition in which written interpretation and commentary were identified with socially recognized authoritative Jewish culture. In that sense the Talmud represented a departure from and defeat for the alternative Jewish cultures, philosophical and apocalyptic, outside the rabbinical mainstream, that had for a time flourished in the Jewish ancient world.

The Talmudic mind is a very practical and quite earthy one. It dislikes extremism and high hopes and visionary programs. The rabbis tell us that interpreting the oral law is more important than interpreting the prophets and that the age of Jewish prophecy is long gone. Quoting the prophets is not their favorite occupation; they were not comfortable with the more extreme statements of Isaiah and the other prophets. They did not burn with messianic zeal. The rabbis say that if you are plowing a field and someone tells you that the Messiah has come, "finish plowing and then go see if the Messiah has come."

This kind of pragmatism is common in the Talmud. Sexual passion is a good thing, "because without it no one would build a house, nor take a wife and beget children [nor engage in business]." "He who reaches the age of twenty and has not married spends all his days in sin or thoughts of sin," says the Bavli. The three things that will be asked of a man in the world to come are whether he bought and sold in good faith, whether he set a time for studying the Law, and whether he procreated.

In reaction to the social conflicts that preceded the destruction of the Second Temple, class conflict is condemned in the Talmud—"you shall not divide yourself into separate groups"—but the gathering of wealth in agriculture and fair business dealings is endorsed. There is the traditional responsibility of the rich to help the poor through charitable institutions and practices, but no socialism or criticism of affluence is in the Talmud. It assumes and legitimates a landlord and mercantile society. The Talmud is intelligently and humanly conformist to the prevailing economic and class system. It is in no way oppositional.

The rabbis in the Palestinian Talmud, about A.D. 400, go so far as to say: "The words of the scribes are more beloved than the words of the Torah and more cherished than the words of the Torah." The Bavli rabbis do not contradict this view. What they are saying is that the oral law as interpreted by the rabbis is more beloved and cherished than the words of the Torah themselves.

This view seems arrogant and self-serving. It has been condemned by Christian writers from the Middle Ages to the twentieth century. But look at it another way: The Talmudic rabbis are opposing scriptural fundamentalism and asserting their freedom to counsel and legislate in the context of their own day. Considered from this point of view, they turn out to be not privileged reactionaries but pragmatic progressives, and this can plausibly be regarded as the intrinsic practical and rational spirit of the Talmud.

Yet their general pragmatism does not extend to relations between Jews and Gentiles. The Talmudic mind is hostile to ethnic equality and to universalism. It is very anxious to enforce an ideal of communal purity. All possible contact with the Gentile untouchables is to be avoided. Jewish bathing is to be segregated in the mikvah, the community-sponsored bathhouse.

Greater purity is stressed in the dietary laws. You can no longer mix meat and dairy products in the same meal. The resulting austerity in preparing food and awkwardness in the kitchen, with two mandatory completely separate sets of dishes, will make you concentrate all the more intensely on the quality of what you eat, and make Jewish eating even more different in its manner.

The rabbis have also improved the reward system. They no longer tell you, Job-like, to rely on God's goodwill, even if you haven't recently experienced it. "All Israelites have a share in the world to come," says the Mishnah—all, that is, except heretics, apostates, and those who say there is no resurrection of the dead. Conformity to the teachings and authority of the rabbis assures your resurrection. This is very similar to the promises made by Catholic clerics.

The Talmudic culture finds nothing persuasive in Saint Paul's universalist proposition that there should be neither Jew nor Greek, neither slave nor free, neither male nor female. The Talmudic way preserves and stresses categories; it makes discriminations. The Jews are very different from the Greeks, and only the Jews are able to follow the laws fostering purity, the rabbis believed. Intermarriage with Gentiles was, of course anathema. But even among Jews, a kind of eugenics prevailed. Rabbinical families took great care to maintain records of family lineage, and marriage among such elite families was the rule. Occasionally marriage between an established rabbinical family and a wealthy family that was not composed of scholars occurred, and the unscholarly high bourgeoisie were expected to feel greatly honored by such unions.

The Talmudic way was that of elitism, but it was more of an intellectual and educated than blood or moneyed elite, although over time these categories of superiority tended to blend together. "Under all circumstances," says the Talmud, "should a man sell everything he possesses in order to marry the daughter of a scholar, as well as to give his daughter to a scholar in marriage." The rabbis were not embarrassed by this blatant self-promotion.

It is curious today to sit in a Reform or so-called Conservative American congregation and listen to the rabbi sermonize about the equality between Jew and Christian, black and white. This is actually the universalizing message not of the Talmudic rabbis but of Rabbi Saul, who was beaten up and driven from the Diaspora synagogues when he preached this leveling message.

The Talmudic rabbis believed that in the eyes of God, Jew and

Gentile were not equal. Yes, indeed there were righteous Gentiles who looked good in God's eyes. They were like Noah—a good man before Yahweh's covenant with Abraham, which changed everything. The Jews were henceforth the chosen people, a nation of priests, to be separated as much as possible from the contaminating Gentiles. Righteous Gentiles have a place in the world to come; they are latter-day Noahs. But the Talmud does not want Jews to socialize with Gentiles, and eating with them is particularly taboo, a contamination of kashruth.

The Talmud conceives of observant Jews of all social classes as a Brahmin-type caste, the refined purity of whose lives is to be maintained, as is fitting for a chosen people of priests, by as much separation as possible from other people, no matter how learned or moral. Ironically, American black nationalists have come up with a somewhat similar view of themselves, stimulated by the Black Muslim faith.

At the level of theory, Pauline doctrine was universalist and much more liberal than rabbinical Talmudic culture, which looks comparatively conservative, defensive, and segregationist. In practice, in terms of actual social experiences, the difference was not great between the rabbinical and Christian clerical ways. The Church was eager to assert the authority of the clergy over moral and social life, just like the rabbis, and the Church too in its canon law developed an elaborate judicial code. The Christian clergy claimed much more wealth and social privilege for themselves than the rabbis did.

The difference between the Church of late antiquity and the Talmudic way (A.D. 300–600) lay not so much in the intrinsic doctrines of the two systems, although there were some, but in the social context in which they functioned. The Church operated within a relatively open and pluralistic society, and furthermore emperors and kings placed limits on its authority. The Jews living in the Christian empire after Constantine's conversion in 312, and in the Germanic successor kingdoms to the western half of the empire that developed in the late fifth and sixth centuries, were constantly under pressure and endured circumscribed conditions of deterioration and disability as Church and Christian state punished and segregated them.

At the accession of Constantine in 312 only a quarter of the population of the empire was Christian. When word got out that conversion to the Church would bring government jobs and other imperial patronage, the result was wholesale pagan conversion to the Church, which furthermore was richly endowed by the imperial family and immediately went on an intensive building program, much celebrated in Ivy League art history departments today.

Constantine's sons and immediate successors were also Christian, but in 361 the imperial throne was inherited by his nephew Julian, who renounced his family's Christian faith and proposed to turn back the religious clock. He went so far as to propose rebuilding the Jewish Temple. To the delight of the Christian clergy, and with their gratitude for divine intervention, Julian the Apostate died suddenly in 363 before his anti-Christian policy had any practical effect.

All subsequent emperors were Christian, and a strenuous campaign was begun to close the pagan temples, or convert them to serve as Christian churches (as in the case of the Pantheon in Rome), and to force the whole remaining pagan population into the Church. Some members of the Roman aristocracy for a short time resisted and argued eloquently for freedom of religion and liberty of conscience, but the emperor rebuffed them, at the insistence of the Italian bishops, and the aristocracy gave up the fight and entered the Church, and forthwith the ranks of the episcopate were graced by names from old families who had been governing the empire for centuries. By the early fifth century all inhabitants of the empire, except the two million or so Jews, were members of the Church, which had become truly catholic, that is, universal.

The Christian view was that Jews had rejected the special opportunity given them to recognize Jesus as the Messiah and had thereby segregated themselves from the Catholic community. Their "Old Testament" had itself prophesied the coming of the "suffering servant," the "lamb of God," it was claimed, but when Jesus the savior appeared they had turned against him. So they were guilty people who in a stiff-necked manner persisted in their loyalty to the old witness of the covenant that had been superseded by Jesus.

Constantine's chief minister for Church affairs, Eusebius, bishop of Caesarea in Palestine, set the tone for the Christian empire's policy toward the Jews by denouncing them as Christ killers. The only question then was: How should the Jews be treated?

Church theorists divided on this issue: Some said punish the Jews physically now. The majority said let Christ do it at his Second Coming, but meanwhile do not let the Jews prosper and feel secure.

Do not physically assault the Jews but make them feel miserable. Therefore, the Jews suffered a myriad of legal and social disabilities, were subject to extraordinary taxation, experienced limitations on where they could live and build their synagogues and what they could wear, were absolutely forbidden to proselytize. They were excluded from officeholding, a great disadvantage when government jobs were the main expanding employment sector in the economically declining later empire. They could not hold Christian slaves, which made intensive agriculture of large holdings in Christian countries difficult for them.

The prejudicial legislation forcing social disabilities on the Jews was written into the great codes of Roman law—the Theodosian Code of 425 and the definitive Justinian Code of the 570s. The high prestige that these impressive legal texts enjoyed in the Middle Ages helped to perpetuate the sharp reduction in status the Jews experienced in the fifth and sixth centuries in Christian lands.

Besides these official policies of Christian state and Church, Jews faced the frequent menace of individual bishops or groups of monks taking it upon themselves to lead popular pogroms in the streets, to murder Jews and burn down their synagogues. These combustions were only restrained to the extent that a Christian emperor might fear their spreading into more widespread civil disorders.

When the Germanic kings, newly converted to Christianity, took over from the disintegrated empire in Western Europe and North Africa around A.D. 500, the Jews found the situation could occasionally be better for a while. In a rapidly deteriorating economy, Jewish mercantile and banking capabilities could be useful to kings and lords and even bishops. But the rule of these violent Germanic kings could suddenly turn into a reign of terror. In Spain in the sixth and seventh centuries, the new Visigothic rulers came under the influence of a particularly fanatical Judeo-phobic group of bishops, and the result was extended persecution and efforts at forced conversion.

The authors of the Mishnah and the two Talmuds perceived these sad events all over the known world as repetitions of the tyrannical acts against the Jewish people familiar to them from the Bible. History is virtually absent from the Mishnah and the Talmuds. That was relegated to the exegetical and anecdotal Midrash, written at the same time. This Midrashic history is extremely typological, that is, romantically conventional. It consists of anecdotal lists of heroes and villains drawn from the Bible. The result is mythologizing of the past and dehistoricization within a romanticized and simple mythological paradigm. The Midrashic approach to early Jewish history consists essentially of further vulgarization and romanticization of the biblical account. It has had a long run of popularity.

The biblical era in Jewish history is still preached in the synagogues and taught in Jewish parochial schools in the Midrashic mode. And major American publishers still churn out for the "religious market" accounts of Jewish history or works promoting "Jewish literacy" that are heavily tilted the Midrashic way.

The secular-minded, politically liberal New York publishers who would not for a moment tolerate American history told in this legendary way think it fine for the Jewish religious market, although two hours in the library would indicate that such books should not be called histories of the Jews, but the Midrashic legends of the Jews for the uncritically pious or the sentimentally ignorant.

The genre of Midrashic history was foreshadowed in one of the last books of the Bible itself, the romantic Book of Esther with its entirely fictional account of the triumph of the good Jewish hero Mordecai and his sister, the beautiful and virtuous Queen Esther (married to a Gentile monarch!), over the evil Haman, persecutor of the Jews, and set as an entirely musical comedy in Persia. This book slipped into the biblical canon around 200 B.C., and its immense popularity continues to the present day, when it is the pseudo-historical pretext for the festival of Purim. The Midrashic approach to Jewish history consists of proliferating sentimental fantasizing of the Esther genre, retelling more simply already legendary stories from the Bible or inventing new ones.

This kind of mythological heroic history gave Jews comfort in the era of decline in their political and economic status that followed the Christianization of the Roman Empire, those same three centuries in which the Talmudic text was defined. The completion of the Talmud around A.D. 500 came at a gloomy time for the Jews. They appeared to be living in dark and difficult times from which no full surcease was promised until the Messiah came, and that was not imminently anticipated.

Therefore Salo Baron was enthusiastic when he wrote in 1952 that the social function of the Talmud was "building a fence around the people of Israel against all the storms from without." The Bavli was "a much-needed, tremendously effective and in many ways unique bulwark."

Writing in 1990 Jacob Neusner presented a more essentialist, more triumphalist, and less instrumental judgment on the Babylonian Talmud:

> The Bavli has formed the definitive statement of Judaism from the time of its closure to the present day. The excellence of its composition, the mastery and authority of those who every- where studied it and advocated its law, the sharpness of its exe- gesis and discussion, the harmonious and proportionate presen- tation of all details, these virtues of taste and intellect may well have secured for the document its paramount position . . . The Bavli served from its closure as an encyclopedia of knowledge and as a summa of the theology and law of Judaism. The com- prehensive character of the Bavli, in form and in substance, and its dependence upon the Scripture's and the Mishnah's redac- tional framework, gained for it the priority it would enjoy . . . The Torah was now complete.

A more realistic and sociological assessment of the Talmud than the views of Baron or Neusner would run as follows: The Bavli was the product of a skillfully advocated, traditionally grounded main- stream Jewish culture going back a thousand years, and gathering momentum and consistency over time. The Talmud was a distinctive way of looking at the world and of trying to secure group and per- sonal stability within that world. Its final form took shape under the pressure of an adverse social context for Jewish communities, and lit- tle or no prospect for early melioration of that context.

The Bavli legitimizes a particular kind of relatively complex insti- tutional structure, dominated by a self-perpetuating learned elite and the behavioral code, at once humane and repressive, that this elite elucidated and enforced.

The response of alternative Judaisms, Philonic culture, or Qum- ran's confrontational apocalypticism to the deepening Jewish crisis of the fifth or sixth century would each in its own way have been dif- ferent from the Talmudic rabbinical response. There is no way of knowing what the alternative outcomes would have been. It is plau- sible to argue that the relatively passive, socially inner-directed Talmudic program was the only viable one under the circumstances. It avoided critical confrontations with strong and hostile forces, and it did achieve communal survival, although not without adverse consequences for Jewish culture and society, particularly intellectual stagnation and increased hierarchic stratification.

In any case, the alternative options for praxis were largely forgone well before the sixth century with the decline or elimination of these alternative Judaisms. Rabbinical Judaism so dominated intellectually the defensive and deteriorating Jewish world of A.D. 600 that the only road forward appeared to be further cultivation of the mainstream way of the Torah and the Pharisees as interpreted and codified by the empowered rabbinical elite.

The Mediterranean world in A.D. 600 was about to undergo a monumental sudden upheaval that would halt and in some important respects reverse the centuries of Jewish decline. The situation even in Christian Europe would in a century or so begin to improve for the Jews. Yet the strong, thick, and confident Talmudic culture was already in place and fully capable of perpetuating itself in changing social contexts. The Talmud endures today, although fewer than ten percent of the Jews in the world are committed to a life mainly within its scope and mission.

Whether or not the Talmud merited Baron's pragmatically based enthusiasm or Neusner's essentialist and triumphalist celebration, it had come to occupy the central point in Jewish life in the dark times of the sixth century A.D. The historical issue was whether it would continue this role in a context of significant improvement in the Jews' situation in the Mediterranean, the Near East, and Western Europe in the seventh and eighth centuries A.D. The other issue that arose from the better environment in which Jews then found themselves was whether alternative forms of Judaism, beyond the rabbinical mainstream represented in the Talmud, would recover some of their former vibrancy.

The eclipse of the Palestinian version of the Talmud by the later Babylonian version confirmed in the intellectual sphere what demographic destiny had already indicated, with ninety percent of the two million Jews in the world by A.D. 600 living in the Diaspora. The overwhelming predominance of forces in Jewish history had shifted to the Galuth. It was the Diaspora that for the next thirteen centuries would be the almost exclusive theater of Jewish history.

In 1936 Fritz (later Yitshak) Baer, who in 1945 as a professor in Jerusalem wrote the standard work on the Jews in medieval Christian Spain, published in his native German language a short and deeply thoughtful book entitled *Galut*, reflections on the historical meaning of the Diaspora. By 1947 Shocken Books, the publisher of Baer's *Galut*, had relocated from Berlin to New York (where it is today a subsidiary of Random House) and issued an English translation of the book. It was republished in 1988 in *Brown Classics in Judaica*, with a laudatory introduction by the series editor, Jacob Neusner.

This is Baer's assessment in the 1947 version of the book on the significance of Diaspora history:

> We went among the nations neither to exploit them nor to help them build their civilizations. All that we did on foreign soil was a betrayal of our own spirit . . . Our place in the world is not to be measured by the measure of this world. Our history follows its own laws, maintaining its innermost tendencies in the face of the outward dangers of dispersal, disintegration, secularization, and moral and religious petrification.

In the immediate aftermath of the Hitlerian destruction, it is understandable that Baer would write these bitter words about the Galuth. Yet in 1988 Neusner endorsed them and agreed with Baer "how and why Zionism in its time and place could make better sense of the world than any other Judaism."

It is explicable that the hurt of the Holocaust should inspire Baer's polemic. Yet everything he said in 1947 can be challenged. For whatever reasons Jews went among the nations in the Diaspora—and there were many—unquestionably the Jews helped to build those civilizations. Jews have every right to regard those civilizations as their own—as do the Hebrew and Tel Aviv universities today by the nature of their curricula. Jews' sweat, blood, and intelligence helped build Western civilization, and they have every right to insist on their equity in its structure. They have purchased their freehold condominium in the West. What the Jews did on foreign soil, for the most part in fulfillment of their better natures, was the outcome rather than the betrayal of the Jewish spirit.

There is no other way to measure the Jews' place in the world except by measure of the world. Otherwise the Jews will be destroyed by the world. Since the Jewish people are part of humanity, their history has followed the patterns known to historical and social science and is to be understood in the language and paradigms of these sciences. It is not midrash, to be conceptualized as rote projections of mantra imagery.

The innermost tendencies of the Jewish people, at least since the destruction of the Second Temple, and to some degree long before that, have been shaped interactively with the Diaspora environment. This record has produced its disappointments, defeats, and terrors and has not indeed been free from some moral and religious petrification. But it is also a record of change, creativity, and moral inspiration in many facets of life.

The Diaspora has entered into the innermost sensibility and the deepest consciousness of the Jews. The waters of Babylon, the cities of Spain, the plains of Germany, the forests of Poland, the steppes of the Ukraine, and, yes, the suburbs of America have been the locus of Jewish destiny as well as Jerusalem, Galilee, and the Negev Desert.

Turning hurtfully to rail against the value of the Diaspora, expressing anger and contempt for the whole Galuth experience, this comes naturally to Jews at those times and places they have suffered injustice, terror, and Shoah. But that does not efface the way in which the Diaspora shaped the Jewish experience and affected integrally the Jewish mind, and it appears to be a never-ending story.

The smells, sights, and sounds of the Canaanite homeland fasten upon Jewish consciousness. No doubt they are familiar enough, these high historical icons: the smell of the burning flesh of the sacrificial animals that once wafted over the walls of the Old City of Jerusalem from Herod's Temple, now memorialized by the exhaust fumes rising from the lined-up tour buses across from David's Tower outside the gates of the Old City. The searing desert haze rising at midmorning on the Negev horizon. The salt wet air blowing harshly upon Caesarea during a winter squall. The fragrance of fresh bread blending with the scraping of hundreds of cobbled feet on the rough stone streets of the open air-markets on Israeli Friday mornings.

The Galuth has its signifiers too. The long shadows falling on the former Sephardi synagogues and courtyards of Andalusian cities, emptied of their prayer books and mezuzahs by the Inquisition; the immaculate angles of the central market against the gingerbread houses of a north German town on crisp fall afternoons, the scowling Christian burghers hustling past the anxious offerings of Jewish *handel*; the sweet black earth of the Ukrainian soil turning to the plow on a wet spring morning; the air-conditioned chill neutralizing the smell of the huge bouquet on the platform of a suburban New York synagogue.

Shall the former memorial endure and not the latter? Thin and deteriorated it would be to limit the whole Jewish experience to sites between Golan and Beersheba, between the Mediterranean and the Jordan, and turn off at last the millennia between Rome and Odessa, and the decades between Brooklyn and Los Angeles.

Down through the American dreamland of Appalachia and the rivers west, you will find in city and town, Binghamton, Louisville, Nashville, the clothing stores with the proud names of Jewish proprietors who came first by boat and then by cinder-sputtering railroads in the nineteenth century and lifted themselves from peddler's pack to ambitious family establishment still selling ladies' dresses and men's suits to the goyim on a Saturday bargain afternoon.

And will the Hebrew University archaeologists turning over stones in Ashqelon or Ramallah say that these distant things are not also monuments still of a living Jewish past, drops of national experience that ingrained itself forever in Jewish being?

Pity for that, poorer for that to forget the Diaspora and the Hasidim dancing in frenzied circles under the green Polish poplars or confident doctors stroking the stiff lapels of their morning coats in the consulting rooms of fin-de-siècle Vienna and Budapest, or professors peering from the podiums of Paris and Berlin, in the glory days, or high-domed bankers filling the ledgers in the leathered offices of London banks, or uncredentialed intelligentsia plotting the revolution, dirty shirt collars askew, over glasses of tea and blintzes at Rattner's on the Lower East Side. This too will not pass away into nothingness.

Images of the Galuth experience, the mundane as well as the spectacular, take their valued place in Jewish historical memory along with those derived from events that occurred in the homeland of the Jews. The claim that Zionism is the best standpoint from which to view Jewish history threatens the valorization of the Diaspora experience.

The understanding of Jewish history in the postantique and pre-Zionist era, the period of the Middle Ages as well as the modern era, will be more fully gained when events and personalities of Diaspora times are intrinsically scrutinized and not assigned to way stations on an instrumental bridge between the ancient Judean and the contemporary Israeli state.

Whatever judgments may be made on Galuth history from the point of view of political Zionism, these millennia were the time of a distinctive Jewish culture that remains intriguing and, in terms of literary, intellectual, and religious legacies, an extremely creative episode not only in the history of the Jews but in the general history of Europe and the Mediterranean world.

The suffering, persecutions, terror, exiles, flights, and migrations, they were certainly central to Diaspora history, right down to 1945, and possibly have not ceased. But there were moments also of peace, prosperity, intellectual and artistic grandeur, and spiritual exaltation. And always there was the peculiar quality, many-faceted in its content and implications, of Jewish psychological and sociological interaction with the surrounding world.

The taste and style of the Jewish Galuth were unique in the history of mankind.

CHAPTER FIVE

Mediterranean Renaissance

In the year A.D. 1003 in the city of Cordoba in Muslim Spain, a couple dozen elders of the main Jewish synagogue sat quietly after late afternoon prayers, waiting for a messenger who was on his way from the Maghreb, from North Africa across the Straits of Gibraltar. These sober-looking men, well-dressed in flowing white robes and turbaned in the Arab manner, sat quietly, only a few engaging in whispered conversation. They were wealthy, most of them, and all were well-acquainted with the Halakah, the Jewish law as set down in the Torah and explicated endlessly in the Talmud and then by later commentators from the Muslim era, particularly Saadia Goan around A.D. 900.

They were patient, grave, dry, responsible men who carried on their solid shoulders the burdens of commercial banking, industrial enterprise, and communal relations with the Muslim princely rulers of Spain, as well as the normal cares of patriarchally shaped family life.

As the synagogue candles burned down and darkness fell, only two or three of the assembled elders began to exhibit restlessness and anxiety. The others sat quietly, almost motionless in the falling gloom, their eyes fixed on the entrance door of the assembly hall.

Finally there was a rustle of activity outside, the sound of a horse-man arriving, muffled conversation between the rider and a groom. The messenger from the Maghreb entered, walked straight up the central aisle of the synagogue, and went directly to the table in front of the ark, where the Torah scroll was laid and read every Sabbath morning.

The newcomer put a leather sack on the table and carefully extracted a small parchment scroll protected by another piece of leather, the whole bound up with scarlet ribbons.

"My lords," said the messenger, "Here at last is the response to your questions from the great rabbis, the learned scholars, the Gaonim of Babylonia. Yes, it has taken a long time since the rabbis of the East sent you their manuscript containing their legal responses to your pressing questions. Four months this packet has been en route, first to Egypt, then shipped on to the Maghreb, and now I have brought it personally to you."

The head of the synagogue community thanked the messenger, passed him a small bag of gold coins as payment for his services, and dismissed him. Then the two dozen elders of the synagogue gathered around the table, jostling to look upon the text of the judicial response of the Babylonian Gaonim. The ribbons were cut, the leather wrapping carefully unfolded, and finally the small scroll unrolled, and at last the sharp black letters of the rabbinical text set out on pumiced vellum in compelling Hebrew characters was revealed.

At the beginning of the eleventh century the wealthy and normally safe and comfortable Jewish communities in the eighty percent of Spain that lay under the rule of Muslim Arabs, including the wealthy cities of the plain, were still not confident enough in their own mastery of religious law, of Halakic learning, to make final determinations of some difficult, obscure, or highly controversial points of religiously ordained, morally prescribed group and individual behavior.

Fifty years later they would have more confidence in the learned authority of their own rabbis. A century later they would rarely feel need to turn to the East, to the two great academies of Gaonim, experts in religious law, that still flourished in Mesopotamia, in now Muslim Arab-speaking Iraq.

These Gaonic academics traced their origins back to the final redactors of the Babylonian Talmud in the sixth century A.D. The heads of these academies a century earlier had come to replace the exilarch, the holder of inherited dynastic office, as spokesmen for the Babylonian Jewish community to the Arabic ruler in Damascus.

Saadia Gaon, an Egyptian Jew who first studied in the Palestinian schools and then spent his mature years as head of one of the Mesopotamian Talmudic academies, finalized this change in formal as well as intellectual leadership by his refusal to accept any other legal authority over him in the Jewish world. Antique survival of the rule of the scions of aristocratic dynasties had to give way to the dominance in the Jewish community of the merited legitimacy of the Gaonim, who earned respect by their mastery of the ancient written and oral law and of the complex Talmudic text that interpreted it.

In far-off Spain the rising Jewish communities were still prepared to turn eastward to seek rabbinical response on matters arising from rabbinical law, even though the Jewish community in Spain in A.D. 1000 was entering a time of renaissance, an era of economic, political, and intellectual vitality not seen among the Jews anywhere since the downfall of Alexandrian Jewry in the second century A.D.

By the time the Spanish renaissance, the golden moment of Sepharad, as the Jews called Spain, had reached its too short-lived peak in the early twelfth century, the vitality and creativity of the Babylonian rabbis was in decline. Yet in the twelfth century a visiting teacher from the East, or even an instructive written communication, while no longer intrinsically authoritative, would still be received with respect in Cordoba or Toledo and the other great centers of Jewry in Muslim Spain.

Halakic learning purchased solid respect among the Sephardi Jews. A man from the East learned in Talmudic tradition was always welcome among the Jews in Muslim Spain. In the eleventh century the merchants and scholars who headed the Jewish communities in Sepharad were normally on good terms with the Muslim rulers. Yet the Jews' ease and prosperity, their developing mastery of Arabic language, literature, philosophy, and science, did not detract from their devotion to ancient Jewish law and Talmudic lore. They were keen to preserve Halakic culture at the same time that they enjoyed, in the eleventh century, the benefits of Arab government and economy.

The symbiotic relationship, the mutually beneficial interaction of Jews with the Muslim Arab rulers of Spain around A.D. 1000, was in stark contrast to the beginning of Jewish and Muslim engagement in Saudi Arabia in the early seventh century A.D. during the lifetime of Muhammad, the founder of the religion and the international community of Islam (a word meaning submission to Allah, God).

Muhammad came from a prominent clan in one of the two leading commercial cities of Arabia, but he was poor and obscure. He began his rise by marriage to a wealthy widow, for whom he had worked as a camel driver. There were that time at least two large Jewish tribal groups in Arabia. These Jews played a great role in the international commerce that stretched not only across the then less desiccated peninsula but also beyond across the Indian Ocean to East Asia, the source of the spices and perfumes greatly prized in the Mediterranean world and in primitive Germanic Europe as well.

Inevitably Muhammad's representation of his wife's trading interests brought him into contact with the Jewish merchants, and from them he learned the rudiments of Jewish history in the standard rabbinical-mythological model. Muhammad came to see himself and his initially tiny group of followers as direct descendants from Abraham, like the Jews, but through Esau, the rejected son of the patriarch Isaac and the half-brother of Jacob.

The essentials of the faith that Muhammad set down in the Koran may, as Muslims believe, have been dictated to him by an archangel. If this dictation occurred, the angel spoke with a Jewish accent, because the theology and ethics and to some extent the dietary laws of Islam presented in the Koran are more than an echo of the Jewish Bible. Islam is rather a simplification, a vulgarization of biblical Judaism.

Yet there was an obstacle to Muhammad's good relations with the Jews in Arabia. Muhammad saw himself as not only the heir of the patriarch Abraham but also as the "seal of the prophets," the last and greatest prophet, whereas the rabbis in Judea as long ago as the third century B.C. had stipulated that there were no more prophets.

Because he took so much from Judaism for Islam, Muhammad expected or at least hoped that these two Jewish-Arabian tribes would follow him as he built up his political and military power over the Arabic people. But he and his religion were rejected by the Jews, and Muhammad took a terrible vengeance on the Jewish tribes. He warred against them, defeating and subjugating both of them, in one instance putting all the adult males (perhaps close to a thousand people) to death and committing their wives and children to slavery.

The Koran is harsh in speaking of the Jews, sounding much like Christian bishops: "Humiliation and wretchedness were stamped upon them [the Jews] and they were visited with wrath from God."

Maimonides, the greatest Jewish rabbi and thinker of the medieval era, who personally suffered from Muslim intolerance in the later twelfth century, has a gloomy and bitter view of the Arabs, even though when he wrote his condemnation he was personal physician to the chief minister of the sultan of Egypt:

> You know, my brethren, that on account of our sins God has cast us in the midst of this [Muslim] people, the nation of Ishmael, who persecute us severely, and who devise ways to harm us and to debase us . . . No nation has ever done more [harm] to Israel. None has matched it in debasing and humiliating us. None has been able to reduce us as they have. [transl. Bernard Lewis]

So much for ethnic brotherhood and religious ecumenism. Yet this is only one side of a sharply two-sided story.

This was a bad beginning. But after Muhammad's death, as the newly united and aggressively conditioned Arabs strove to break out of their drying out peninsula and penetrate the eastern end of the Mediterranean and beyond, Jewish-Islamic relations rapidly improved. First, the Jews living under persecuting Christian rulers in the Byzantine empire and in Spain could help the Arab invasion, and they probably did, especially in Egypt and Spain. Second, the Jews could serve the new Islamic states with their commercial, political, and administrative know-how.

After opening the gates of Christian cities to the Arab armies, Jews served the newly established Muslim princes as government officials, bankers, and especially leaders in international commerce, stretching from Western Europe to India. Officially the Jews, like Christians, were dhimmis, second-class citizens, a designated subordinate minority in the Arab states. They had to pay a poll tax, the law stipulated, and wear special insignia or clothing to show their inferior status. But in practice, in substantial stretches of the Muslim Mediterranean world and especially in Spain before the mid-twelfth century, these restrictions against the Jews were often lightly enforced.

The Jews were not the threat that the Christians posed as the shrunken Byzantine empire yearned to strike back from Constantinople against the Arabs, and the papal-affiliated kings of Italy and France sought to become potential military rivals to the Arab states.

Good Arab treatment of the Jews between A.D. 900 and 1150, the Jews never attaining equality but frequently not far from it, resulted in fervent devotion to Arab rule from the Jewish communities, growing again in size as well as wealth. After all, there was a kinship between the Jews and the Arabs—they were cousins, both putatively direct descendants of the patriarch Abraham; the Jews also were a People of the Book; and long stretches of the Bible and the Koran were fully compatible, or even similar in teachings.

When in the mid-nineteenth century Jewish scholars in Central Europe first brought the research instruments of modern secular scholarship to determine the course of medieval Jewish history, they were quick to discover what Heinrich Graetz designated as the golden age of Muslim Spain from about A.D. 900 to 1150. The frequent haughty personal disdain among the Muslim ruling class for the Jews was underplayed, and the importance of the Jews in Arab government and the remarkable intellectual accomplishments of the Arab-speaking Jews were stressed and perhaps exaggerated.

Graetz's model of benign Arab treatment of the Jews and the Jewish response with cultural glory as well as political skill and commercial acumen remains a central image in Jewish historiography, elaborated circumstantially in a three-volume work on the Jews in Muslim Spain by the Israeli Eliyahu Ashtor, published in the 1950s and then republished by the establishmentarian Jewish Publication Society in Philadelphia in 1992.

If Diaspora Jewish history in Christian lands is generally seen as fifteen hundred years of fear and gloom, these two centuries of happy times under Islam, especially in golden medieval Spain, became the contrasting other way against which Christian oppression, pogromism, and ghettoization looked even worse.

From celebrating the favorable lot of the Jews in Muslim Spain, the privileged few Jewish professors in the German-speaking universities around 1900 went on to inaugurate the first scientific studies of the life of Muhammad and the rise of Islam. The founder of medieval Arabic studies from about 1890 to 1920 was Ignaz Goldziher, who inaugurated and presided over the great school of Arabic and Muslim history in Berlin and Vienna, with Jews playing a large role among his disciples.

Jews in the eleventh century served Islam by their role in commerce, government, and science. German Jewish scholars in the early twentieth century served Islam by opening up the study of the medieval Arabic world to modern research. Certainly the Arab world before the 1920s, perhaps before the 1940s, had no capability for this kind of historical research. The Arab scholars of the day could read the Koran and the Traditions of the Prophet but they could not analyze and interpret these texts according to the methods and terminology of Western scholarship. It was mainly German Jewish scholars, with some help from Englishmen and Frenchmen, who inaugurated the modern scientific study of medieval Islam.

After Arab nationalism developed in the 1920s, this Jewish contribution was resented rather than rewarded. In the world of humanistic scholarship no good deed goes unpunished, especially if Jews are doing the good deed.

In the universities of the West in the 1950s, Jews were still holders of many important chairs of Islamic studies, whereas at that time only one ethnic Arab, Philip Hitti, a Lebanese Christian teaching at Princeton, enjoyed a major reputation. In the 1970s at the Princeton department of Near Eastern studies, a department Hitti founded around 1950 with funds from the Arabian-American Oil Company, the three leading historians were all Jews, one originally from Canada, another from New York City, and the most eminent of all, Bernard Lewis from London.

Lewis was a confirmed Zionist and perhaps because of what happened in Palestine and Israel in his lifetime he backed off somewhat from the traditional heaping of praise upon the Muslims to which Jewish historians in the Graetz tradition were prone. He stressed that medieval Jews even in the glorious era of Sepharad were second-class citizens, subservient to the Arabs, and he sharply criticized Muslim behavior, with its violence, anti-intellectuality, greed, waste, mismanagement, and outbursts of chauvinism and fanaticism, particularly in recent centuries.

This inspired Edward Said, a Christian Arab born in Palestine, expensively educated in Egypt and England, who had come to be regarded as a world-class literary critic and who held the senior chair of humanities at Columbia University (to which Jewish philanthropists like Lawrence Wein had lavishly contributed in the 1960s and 1970s) to lash out against the Jewish overrepresentation—in Said's bitterly hostile eyes—in Islamic and Arabic studies.

Said's celebrated *Orientalism* (1978) sounded a clarion call to ethnic Arabs to liberate their historiography from Jewish imperialists. Said, a member of the Palestine Liberation Organization governing council, cleverly incorporated the concept of the social "other" from French radical social thinking to conflate Jewish involvement in Arabic historiography with nineteenth- and early twentieth-century Western imperialism in the Near East.

The doctrine of the social other that Said used so effectively in *Orientalism* and then in many later writings, runs like this. The world is divided into two groups. The bad are the old-line hegemonists—Western imperialists, white colonialists like the Zionists, and Jewish Orientalists who sought to divest the Arabs of their cultural patrimony. The good are the other—Arabs, especially Palestinians ill-treated by the Zionists, and all other groups that have been victims of Western white male imperialists, including women (Jewish women belong to the other if they oppose Zionism and express contempt for Orthodox rabbis).

Although hurtful to Zionists, and to Jewish Orientalists, and to Jews in general, the radical doctrine of the social other appealed also to many Jewish academics and intellectuals. The first clear formulation of the doctrine of the social other occurs in the celebrated 1955 book, *Tristes Tropiques,* by the Parisian cultural anthropologist, Claude Lévi-Strauss, who was the son of a Belgian rabbi. Almost as effective in American academia as Said in the 1970s in using the social other polemically was Immanuel Wallerstein, a prominent New Left ethnically Jewish sociologist.

But Edward Said built his career and his lifework on this doctrine, applying it once again in 1992 in a study of imperialism and literature. Not only was Said the most important Arab humanist of the twentieth century, but he was also a literary critic and cultural theorist of the first rank. His disputes with Bernard Lewis constituted a clash of academic titans. His identification of Orientalism with cultural imperialism penetrated centrally into humanistic culture in the 1970s and 1980s.

At Columbia University Said never lacked for Jewish graduate students ready to salute his doctrine, even though for him it meant driving Jews out of the field of Arabic history that they in effect had founded. As a Britisher, a Zionist Jew, and an Orientalist who expressed mixed judgments on the character of Arabic culture and society, Bernard Lewis was the ultimate devil in Said's personal Orientalist hell.

Lewis in Said's view was identified with British exploitation and manipulation of the Arabs for their oil, with European and especially Jewish chauvinism toward the Arabs, and with Zionist mistreatment of the Palestinians, including Said's own family, who longed to get back the patrimonial lands they lost in the late 1940s. In Said's view, Lewis as an Islamic historian is fundamentally corrupt, or to use a favorite Said term, "cavalier." Said comes to this conclusion: "To look for a . . . fair . . . judgment by Lewis on Islam . . . is to look in vain." Said was endorsed by a leftward radicalized academic profession for whom the doctrine of the social other and condemnation of Western cultural imperialism had by 1980 become a litanized dogma.

Yet Lewis stood his ground, and with very little support in the media and from Jewish organizations he fought back valiantly against Said's critique and his desire to deport Jewish Orientalists to academic oblivion. Only in 1993, in the august pages of the (London) *Times Literary Supplement,* did a distinguished Jewish anthropologist at the University of London, Ernest Gellner, dare to make a devastating attack upon academia's sultan, Edward Said.

Said's scorn and contempt for Lewis was expressed in the face of Lewis's effort to give the medieval Arabs their full due: "In literature and the arts, the Muslim influence on the Jews is enormous, and it is almost entirely one way." "The Judeo-Islamic symbiosis . . . was a long, rich, and vital chapter in Jewish history."

In religious thought and practice, Lewis stressed Jewish adaptation from Muslim culture: "Parallels and resemblances between Jewish and Muslim beliefs and practices may well be due to Muslim influences on Judaism and not merely—as earlier scholars believed—to Jewish influence on Islam."

Yet Lewis rejected the nineteenth-century overdrawn view of how good it was for the Jews under Muslim rule and how bad under Christian rule: "The simplified and idealized nineteenth century accounts of the history of the Jews in Spain present a black and white picture of Christian intolerance and Muslim tolerance . . . It was not always so."

Lewis takes a dark view of modern Arabic history and especially of treatment of the Jews. He stresses how in the nineteenth and twentieth centuries, Christians, such as Armenians, came to displace privileged Jews in the Muslim lands, and "the nastiest inventions of European anti-Semitism have been endorsed in Arab countries at the highest political and academic levels."

Never as tolerant and favorable to the Jews as widely supposed, Lewis claimed, the Muslim Arabs have in modern times treated Jews very badly and the rise of Christians (such as Said's family) to prominence in the Near East during the late nineteenth and twentieth centuries in place of Jews was part of this downward trend into Oriental Jewish ambience.

As a Palestinian Arab, Said must have felt the sting of these remarks by Lewis, coming not from a contemptible Israeli scholar but from a Princeton professor. They would hurt regardless of Said's boiling irredentism and his dreams of his ancestral lands on the West Bank and the cool family villa in East Jerusalem lost to alleged Zionist chicanery.

The greatest of the Jewish Arabists (and one whom Said in his racist polemics against Jewish Orientalists shrewdly ignored) was not Bernard Lewis, but someone working at the other end of Princeton town from the university in the 1970s at the Institute for Advanced Study, a research institute founded in the 1930s with Jewish department store money as a place of refuge for German Jewish physicists, mathematicians, and humanists. By the 1970s this service to Jewish learning had eroded, but the Institute—and jointly the University of Pennsylvania—provided a haven and optimum working conditions in his later years for Solomon Goitein.

Goitein came out of the Goldziher school of Jewish-dominated German Orientalists and was for thirty years a leading member of the Jerusalem Hebrew University faculty, matched for the grandeur of his productive scholarship only by another German Jew, Gershom Scholem. It does not say much for Israeli support for humanistic learning, even when it centrally involved Jewish history, that to complete his lifework in five magisterial volumes, Goitein eventually had to move to the United States.

The work is the two-thousand-page *A Mediterranean Society*, the most important presentation by far on medieval Jewish history ever written, and a major contribution as well to the general economic and social history of the Muslim Mediterranean world. It is a leisurely, immensely detailed, idiosyncratic, perpetually fascinating account of the life and times of affluent Jewish, mostly commercial families between A.D. 1000 and 1300, based on the genizah archive from the synagogue of medieval Cairo (a few miles from modern Cairo and now called Fustat).

Around 1890 a small number of fascinating manuscripts—merchant letters and family records in Arabic and Hebrew—from medieval Cairo began to turn up for sale in Egypt and drifted to the centers of Jewish and Orientalist academic learning in Western Europe, principally to Cambridge University. From there the newly appointed research professor of Jewish studies, a young rabbi named Solomon Schechter, went out to Cairo, with the encouragement of the British government (then in the hands of the upper-class Conservatives personally on good terms with rich London Jews). Schechter discovered a large synagogue storeroom, or genizah, packed to the rafters with medieval documents.

Observant Jews are never supposed to destroy a document with God's name (or initials) on it, so prominent Jewish families in Cairo followed a common practice of giving dead contracts and old letters in which God's name is mentioned to their synagogue for perpetual storage. After a while the genizah, this synagogue depository, received family records of all kinds, such as would now be deeded by heirs to a university or state archive. This practice continued in Cairo down to the eighteenth century. Schechter arranged the purchase of most (but not all) of the genizah records for the library of Cambridge University for a modest price, but he himself made only a brief foray into studying this medieval treasure trove, since he soon accepted the position of founding head of the Jewish Theological Seminary in New York.

It was only in the 1930s and 1940s and then for another three decades of study, analysis, and historical extrapolation that Goitein made the first elaborate and systematic use of these genizah records to lay out the functioning of Jewish high bourgeois society in the Mediterranean Muslim world. This required not only infinite time and strenuous zeal and patience, but extraordinary linguistic and paleographical (handwriting decipherment) capability.

Goitein's *Mediterranean Society* stands alongside Graetz's pioneering multivolume history of the Jews written between 1850 and

1875, and Scholem's small library of volumes, published from the 1950s into the 1970s on Jewish mysticism and messianism from 1200 to 1800, as the greatest work ever written on Jewish history. Goitein's work is still almost unknown to the general public. There is a downside to it—its leisurely discursiveness, detail, and length make it all but inaccessible to the lay reader.

Goitein's method of work on the genizah materials should have been first to go through all the records; and then to publish a two-volume translated anthology from them; and then to produce preferably in one volume a sociology of the Jewish-Arabic upper middle-class society, referring to the published anthologized material.

Instead Goitein combined the publication of documents with lengthy, discursive expositions of their significance. Although the five volumes are supposedly divided topically ("the family," "the individual," etc.), this does not hold fast in practice. One has the impression that Goitein for the most part writes about what came to hand as he burrowed his way through the material. Furthermore, the final volume, published in 1990 shortly before his death, is much more critical of the behavior pattern of these Jews than the earlier volumes and portrays their lifestyles as being much closer to those of the Arab ruling class than the earlier volumes would indicate.

In other words, the sociology is not consistent and thoroughly worked out. Goiten is capable of brilliant insights and some very fine writing. He is also highly verbose, unsystematic, and lacking in conceptual rigor. The job will someday have to be done again, but based principally on his research and his editing of the genizah documents.

Professors of Judaic studies have suggested that Goitein's work should be rated as equal to Ferdnand Braudel's famous two-volume analysis of the end of the sixteenth century, *The Mediterranean World in the Time of Philip II,* published in 1952. Unfortunately, the comparison is not favorable to Goitein. Braudel has sociological mastery of his material, a systemic approach buttressed by quantification, that Goitein's leisurely five volumes lack. Nevertheless, Goitein's work is a monumental contribution to understanding the Jewish Middle Ages.

That at the beginning of the eleventh century the synagogue community in Spain would still seek a legal decision from Gaonim in Iraq indicates the enormous distances that lay within the practical purview of the Jewish merchant class in the Arabic Mediterranean world. They similarly conducted business at great distances, going well beyond even the lengthy Mediterranean littoral to connect with the caravan routes across Arabia, which in turn led to commercial enterprise in India.

The reach of Jewish commercial life in A.D. 1100 extended from Portugal to the west coast of India. This required fortitude, patience, and the capacity to leave one's family for months or even years at a time. It would not have been possible without the embedding of long-distance trade in an extended family business structure. These commercial firms employed and trusted people not related by kinship, but the structure of Jewish commercial life was held together and functioned through family connections.

The ventures in which these commercial families were engaged always involved risk—bad weather anywhere between Portugal and India could suddenly deplete family fortunes with the sinking of a ship carrying the goods in which much of the family capital was invested. All these characteristics were prevalent in the commercial capitalism of England or Holland in the seventeenth century, but that same structure and behavior pattern had already shaped Jewish commercial capitalism in the eleventh century.

These Jewish international merchants were highly rational people who made careful calculations while engaging in high-risk enterprise. They knew what the odds were and what the probable margin of survival in the face of a singular disaster was likely to be. They supervised their operations closely, kept careful records, and engaged in an endless stream of commercial correspondence over enormous distances. The turnaround time on even their correspondence could be many months. It might be as long as five years before they found out whether a heavily capitalized commercial venture toward East Asia brought fortune or disaster.

They had to be patient, confident people. They were austere, stoical in their mentality. They had to maintain their faith in divine will, but not assume God's intervention on their behalf. God was a distant, benign, but self-contained and unpredictable entity.

The Jewish commercial family lived comfortably in a large establishment, a function of a society with a ready supply of cheap labor. They were interested in cuisine and ate substantial meals. But they were not profligate. They lived well within their means because of

the high risk of the failure of a trading venture and the sudden drastic depletion of their capital.

Only moderately learned themselves, the Jewish merchant class
respected traditional learning and purchased religious commentaries
and homiletic works. A great rabbinical authority on Talmudic law, a
man of profound learning, was still the most admired and respected
person in society; to him they readily married a favorite daughter.
The profession of medicine, a personally valuable one and also an
enterprise that, like commercial capitalism, was readily portable, was
also highly regarded.

It is hard to know how observant they were of traditional Halakic rules. They observed the Sabbath and main holy days. They belonged to and supported the synagogue and its attendant schools.
They preferred to settle all disputes in the traditional manner within
the community in a rabbinical court, but that was sometimes not
possible. They were charitable and believed the community had a
responsibility to support the indigent and the orphaned. How closely
they observed the dietary laws is uncertain. But since quality vegetar-
ian cuisine was well known in the climes in which they traveled,
observing kashruth may not have been as great problem as it was in
the more carnivorous society of Western Europe.

In the final volume of his masterwork, Goitein reports with a
heavy heart that by 1100 the merchant-class Jewish males were
assuming the sexual promiscuity common to Arabic society, with
concubinage, sexual exploitation of slave women, and homoerotic
relationships with boys and young men common practices. Promiscuity among married women also seems to have been quite prevalent. Sexually the Jews became Arabized.

The parallel to the third or fourth generations of immigrant Jewish families in later twentieth-century New York is striking. Sexual
acculturation paralleled the linguistic, literary, and artistic assimilation
to the dominant Arabic culture. The educated Jews were thoroughly
bilingual in the two Semitic languages, but Arabic was the common
vehicle of literary expression even for Jews. The most important
works of Jewish philosophy and much of the poetry written by Jews
were rendered in Arabic. The Jews frequently wrote Arabic in
Hebrew characters, but Arabic it was. Furthermore, Hebrew poetry,
especially on erotic or other more or less secular subjects, was written in verse form heavily imitative of Arabic poetry. The parallel to

American Jews is striking—after two or three generations the language of Jewish literary expression in America is nearly always English.

After a half-millennium of static Jewish population, there was likely some increase in the eleventh century. Probably one percent of the Arabic Mediterranean world was Jewish (compared to at least five percent in the first century A.D. under the Romans), but the Jewish presence in the large cities on the coastline made their demographic impact greater than one percent would indicate. Still, they were a small group. In the whole world in 1100, there were not more than two million Jews, and the total may have been closer to 1.5 million. The Jews were not going to scare anyone by their demographic impact.

Yet they played a prominent and dynamic role in the extended mercantile reach of medieval Mediterranean society. Since the writings of Graetz in the nineteenth century it has been conventional to stress the intellectual and literary accomplishments of the Jews under Muslim Arabic rule. The significance of Goitein's work is to show that an equal, or perhaps even greater, importance lies in the way in which the Jewish family enterprises spanned half the civilized world, from Portugal to India from the late tenth to the mid-thirteenth century and anticipated the mentality and behavior patterns of Dutch and English commercial capitalism of the seventeenth century.

The Jews were not the only groups engaged in this international trade. The Arabic world was a mosaic of many peoples, and other ethnic groups were also participants in this vibrant commercial life. But Jewish prominence in international trade there certainly was, and the genizah archive that Goitein's lifework opened and communicated to us throws the historical spotlight on the Jews in a way that is not fortuitous, but is fully merited.

Goitein has allowed us to reach across the centuries and encounter intimately these wonderful men whose strength, rationality, and determination makes them a Jewish society deserving of our highest esteem. There has been a tendency in recent years to celebrate medieval Halakic scholars and thinkers alongside ancient putative military heroes and sentimentally drawn Hasidic rabbis of the nineteenth and early twentieth centuries. Unquestionably Goitein's complement of mercantile capitalists from 1000 to 1200 belongs in this honored company.

From the small, highly specialized, almost exotic population of medieval Mediterranean Jews there emerged, especially in Spain and Egypt, not only strong communal leadership but also a handful of wealthy, educated, dynamic Jews who gained high preferment in the Arabic governments and themselves became renowned for their princely qualities of power, show, and influence. Now the biggest Jew was not Somebody the Gaon but Somebody the Prince who was establishing or perpetuating an aristocratic dynasty while serving as the Arabic ruler's chief minister.

It was risky business. Arabic governments were not known for their long-term stability, or Muslim dynasties for their longevity. A reversal of political fortune could be catastrophic for these politically high-flying Jews. Not only they but their immediate family and all kin within reach could lose their lives after a palace revolution or some other political upheaval. A whole community of several thousands would be deprived suddenly of their security and comfort. Hundreds would have to flee to find refuge under another despotic Arabic ruler—perhaps only a few miles distant but possibly far away. And the beautiful synagogue and comfortable homes of the fleeing Jews would stand empty and desolate.

Politics in the Arabic world was a dangerous game. Yet there were ambitious Jews who wanted to get on the political high wire.

When the Muslim armies pressed northward out of the Arabian desert in the middle of the seventh century, they gained quick and overwhelming victories because their prime opponents, the Byzantine Greeks and the Persians, were exhausted after fighting each other to a standstill in long, ruinous wars. With the aid of dissident Mediterranean groups like the Jews and Christian heretics, the Arabs established by the late seventh century a vast political entity, with its capital Damascus in Syria, that stretched from Iran to Spain and was ruled by a despotic monarchy in the hands of a dynasty from Arabia that had been an early supporter of Muhammad.

This unified world-Islamic state did not last long, as the Persians, now converted to Islam, overthrew the representatives of the Damascus monarchy and set up an independent Iranian state centered on Tehran. This upheaval in the middle of the eighth century was a signal for the decomposition of the original world-Islamic state and the setting up of independent dynastic despotisms all over the Muslim Mediterranean world.

The subsequent political history of medieval Islamic society was marked by a further series of political upheavals. One ruling family was replaced by another in a palace revolution or military revolt or foreign invasion. This political instability provided an opportunity for ambitious Jews, who could provide valuable assistance to the new ruling family that was inexperienced in administration and tax collection.

Politically dangerous and personally risky as it was for a Jew to serve as a prominent minister of an Arabic ruler, whose apparent strong grip on power could be loosened overnight, some Jewish families turned from trade and banking and leadership of their own ethnic communities to royal service, and some achieved for a time high posts near the throne. If they gained this preferment, they usually tried to establish ministerial families and pass on their favored position to a son or nephew.

The rulers of Islamic states in the East were normally too intransigent to permit Jews a significant role in government. But in the more tolerant atmosphere of Andalusia, Muslim Spain, in the tenth and eleventh centuries there were at least two instances of Jewish political advancement. Hasdai ibn-Shaprut, a physician and writer, rose to high position in the government of Cordoba in the mid-tenth century. His Jewish contemporaries stood in awe of this court Jew and called him a Nasi (prince).

In the early eleventh century Samuel ibn-Nagdela served the ruler of Granada, a small principality in the south of the peninsula, not only as a high-level administrator but also as a successful general. Samuel ibn-Nagdela, like Hasdai ibn-Shaprut, was an important writer and he was called nagid (big shot). His son Joseph inherited his father's ministerial position, but he was overthrown and most of the other Jews in Granada were killed after a change in rulership and anti-Jewish riots that followed.

A figure thus made its appearance in Andalusia that loomed large in Jewish history down into the eighteenth century: that of the court Jew, a person of learning and private wealth, much esteemed in the Jewish community, who brought his linguistic skills, learned intelligence, and fiscal competence to the service of a Gentile ruler. Usually the court Jew helped his coreligionists by securing royal protection and particular concessions for them. Usually he was also a patron of literature and art in the Jewish world, and frequently was himself an important writer. Of course his position was a difficult and problematic one.

When after the middle of the twelfth century a new intransigence among Muslim ruling groups, coming over to Spain from North Africa, made it much more difficult for Jews to serve in Andalusian governments, Jews crossed the line northward into steadily expanding Christian Spain and served Christian rulers, who often valued their administrative experience and capabilities, especially in fiscal matters. This activity of the court Jew in Christian Spain continued until, at the end of the fifteenth century, there were officially no more Jews in the Iberian peninsula. Thereafter Jewish converts to Christianity continued the tradition of Jewish service at royal courts.

It was neither for governmental service nor for commercial achievement that the founders of modern Jewish historiography like Graetz labeled the Jewish experience in Muslim Spain from 900 to 1250 the golden age of medieval Jewry. The term seems a bit naive today but is substantially justified by the corpus of Andalusian Jewish writing—the most important collection of Hebrew poetry between the Bible and the late nineteenth century and the greatest achievements in Jewish philosophy between Philo and the seventeenth century.

Although the Spanish locus predominated in this Judeo-Arabic renaissance, it was a trans-Mediterranean cultural movement, with Egypt, Iraq, and Iran also flourishing centers of Jewish learning and intellectual creativity. What needs to be understood most of all with respect to this upsurge in Jewish intellectuality, learning, and literature is that the Jews were not drawing only from Arabic sources to buttress their own traditions. Most of the new Jewish writing was in the Arabic language, but the intellectual foundations were primarily Greek and Hellenistic. What the Arabs did was to inherit, cultivate, and perpetuate Greek and Hellenistic philosophy and science, and literary and art forms.

The cultural and intellectual history of the Mediterranean and Near Eastern world in the medieval Muslim era is a postantique chapter in the development of Greek and Hellenistic thought, which the Arabs readily absorbed. For the Jewish intellectuals, this Greco-Hellenistic cultural heritage, communicated through the Arab language, was a powerful stimulant to their own thinking and writing, and along with the relative prosperity, peace, and security that the Jews enjoyed, was the most important factor in stimulating a extremely productive and complex era of Jewish intellectual development, roughly from 900 to 1200.

There is no definitive study of this Judeo-Arabic renaissance, although it has been much written about, and useful insights have been provided by Goitein and Salo Baron, among others. But what we have now is mainly a highlight film focusing on particular authors. Structural sensibility has not been clearly mapped out.

Goitein's effort to provide a key to this development is intriguing and thought provoking but ultimately unconvincing:

> Islam . . . is from the very flesh and bone of Judaism. It is to say, a recast, an enlargement of the latter, just as Arabic is closely related to Hebrew. Therefore, Judaism could draw freely and copiously from Muslim civilization and, at the same time, preserve its independence and integrity far more completely than it was able to do in the modern world or in the Hellenistic society of Alexandria.

What actually happened in the cultural history of Mediterranean Jewry from the tenth to the thirteenth century seems quite different from this generalization of Goitein's. The course of development was more dialectical and ideological.

The wealth, comfort, and security that the Jewish bourgeoisie enjoyed and their intensive absorption of philosophy and literature available to them through the medium of the Arabic language conditioned them to move toward the formulation of a new Jewish culture. It would be bilingual in Arabic and Hebrew, but nearly all important Jewish prose writing, whether philosophy or imaginative literature or private correspondence and business letters, was written in Arabic. And even Hebrew poetry showed the strong influence of Arabic models and motifs, and the Hebrew language itself was given new clarity and rigor by application of Arabic linguistics.

From all this came the incipient crystallization of a new secular Jewish culture, drawing on both Greek philosophy and science and its Hellenistic and Arabic continuations, and Arabic mysticism and eroticism, while still maintaining largely intact a Halakic tradition founded on the Bible and the Talmud. A liberal secular culture that was keyed to Jewish cultural Arabization and Mediterranean lifestyle would synthesize with Jewish theology and ethics.

There was something of this trend in Philo's Hellenistic Judaism of the first century A.D., but the effort now was more strenuous and much more broadly based, both in terms of numbers of intellectuals involved and the diverse strands of secular culture to be incorporated in the Jewish framework. We would have to go to the Science of Judaism movement in nineteenth-century Germany and to Reform and Reconstructionist Judaism in America in its flourishing era of the 1930s and 1940s to find parallels to the Jewish cultural movement in the medieval Mediterranean world, and even then the comparisons may not be very close.

Saadia Gaon, Bahya ibn-Paquda, Solomon ibn-Gabirol, Judah Halevi, and Moses Maimonides were the great names in this movement.

The new culture, however, had too many contradictions and polarities within itself to become integrated in definitive form. It turned out to be very difficult to synthesize it with unyielding traditional Judaism, even in the hands of Maimonides, who was a master of both liberal rationalism and Halakic Judaism. The deterioration of tolerance within the surrounding Islamic world in the late twelfth century strengthened the neoconservative position that Judah Halevi adopted in his later years, and this reaction in effect stemmed the drive to a new Jewish culture based on a sincere effort to incorporate the main facets of the Greek, Hellenistic, and Arabic intellectual and literary systems.

In the thirteenth century Halakic Judaism was reasserted, intellectual narrowness sanctified, and holistic meaning buttressed with an astrological, demonological, and mystical pastiche. This cultural alteration and reaction after 1200 stopped the effort at a new Jewish culture, but at a heavy price. When Jewish thought was rigidified and vulgarized and intellectual freedom and sensibility were repressed, the way was left open to justify conversion to other faiths, particularly Christianity, as an avenue for personal intellectual growth. Many powerful minds and fine temperaments were driven out of the Jewish community by the conservative reaction after 1200. In the long-run perspective, the theme of the golden age was both triumph and tragedy, both epiphany and failure.

Jewish Mediterranean society with all its economic and political advantages and its access to a thriving diversified culture through the medium of Arabic could not sustain its intellectual progress indefinitely or develop a post-Talmudic Jewish culture that gained general consensus and served as the foundation for subsequent thought and belief in the Jewish world. The golden age culture was marked by internal ideological contradiction. Its main thinkers and writers merit celebration, but as a group they failed to achieve an integrated secular culture that was considered compatible with traditional Judaism received from the past.

Saadia Gaon (Saadia ben Joseph, 882–942), the head of the Babylonian school in Sura, set the pattern for all subsequent Judeo-Arabic thought. He was well-read in Arabic philosophy. He translated the Bible into Arabic; he wrote his most important work in that language; and he legitimized the adaptation of Greek philosophy and Arab commentators on Greek philosophy to support Jewish revelation.

But the purpose of reason in Saadia's view is simply to sustain revelation. There is no doubt about the literal truth of the Bible. Philosophical speculation is another avenue to the same doctrines that the Bible presents, and there is no challenge to the divine truth presented in the Bible, which is furthermore sustained through the senses experientially, by miracles.

Saadia accepts the Bible's miracles, for example, Moses' parting of the Red Sea, as unquestionably occurring and as being demonstrations of the truth of revelation:

> Our Lord . . . has informed us through the words of His prophets that He is One, Living, Powerful, and Wise, and that nothing can be compared unto Him or unto His works. They established this by signs and miracles, and we accepted it immediately. Later, speculation [reason] led us to the same result. [transl. A. Altmann]

Here is Saadia's whole theory.

Much in Saadia's doctrine found its way not only into the mainstream of later Jewish philosophy but ultimately into Christian scholasticism, particularly as propounded by Thomas Aquinas in the thirteenth century.

In epistemology, Saadia is a Platonist:

> When the idea is clarified by speculation, Reason comprehends it, accepts it, and makes it penetrate the soul, and become

absorbed into it; then man believes the idea which he has
attained, and he preserves it in his soul for another time. [transl.
A. Altmann]

Saadia is a cultural chauvinist. Other revelations—Christian, Muslim—are merely human. Only the Jewish revelation is divine and
must be absolutely believed, reason and experience sustaining it
because there is only one truth.

God is a good pedagogue. He makes his revelation known in
stages, proceeding from the easy to the difficult: "When He wanted to
make his voice heard by Moses, He was careful to treat his sight gen-
tly, taking into account its degree and strength." [transl. Colette Surat]

Saadia's doctrine still prevails in the better educated Orthodox
culture of today, such as that cultivated at Yeshiva University in New
York. The writings of its learned president, Rabbi Norman Lamm, are
completely in the Saadia Gaon tradition. This allows for serious study
of philosophy and science, with complete faith that this learning and
speculation will sustain, and in no way erode, the truths of the
Torah. It produces well-educated, confident, and happy, if intellectually limited, people.

Bahya ibn-Paquda (c. 1050–1120) was a rabbinical judge in Muslim Spain, known for one work, *The Duties of the Heart*. Written originally in eloquent Arabic, it received at least two different Hebrew
translations during the Middle Ages and was immensely popular. It is
still recommended today in Orthodox circles.

Bahya is a disciple of Saadia and writes within the parameters of
Saadia's theology. But *The Duties of the Heart* is not a work of theology; it is an essay of ethical homiletics—he tells us how to live the
good life, within the context of Halakic Judaism, with a modicum of
Aristotelian ethics thrown in. Thus the Law provides the way to the
middle ground between the extreme no-no's of ascetic abstinence
and selfish indulgence.

On the whole, this much-praised book is a collection of rabbinical bromides in artificially exalted language. It contains two interesting ideas. One is an encouragement to attain a Neoplatonic kind of
mystical love of God; someone who attains this exalted condition has
passed beyond the need to bear constantly in mind the six hundred
thirteen mitzvoth, virtuous commandments prescribed by the Torah.
They will be fulfilled anyway by the mystical God-lover.

This sounds much like the twelfth-century Christian homilist and mystic Saint Bernard of Clairvaux. Bahya's view does raise the question of whether the God-lover might not be troublesome for religious authority and community, but for Bahya as for Bernard, this sociopolitical observation is an nonissue. The God-lover will automatically observe the mitzvoth and then some. As with Christian mystics, so among the Jews, it didn't always turn out that easy and smooth way.

Even more interesting is Bahya's almost Freudian sense of the power of sexual lust in human life, although, not to worry, the Torah will restrain the erotic appetite. The Talmudic tradition had always been much more realistic than Christian teaching on sexuality (hence the advice to marry early and have spousal sexual relations weekly).

But Bahya's discussion of sexuality offers a keen personal insight that is generally absent from the rest of his platitudinous homily:

> Sensual lust in man is the product of natural forces and of a combination of his physical elements. Its foundation and root are in this world. Food gives it strength. Physical pleasures add to its vigor, while the intellect, because it is a stranger here, stands without support or ally . . . Hence it follows that the intellect must become weak and that it needs an external means to repel the mighty power of lust and overcome it. The Torah is the remedy for such spiritual maladies and moral diseases. The Torah therefore prohibits many kinds of food, apparel, sexual relations, certain acquisitions and practices, all of which strengthen sensual lust, it also exhorts us to use those means which will resist lust and are its opposites. [transl. M. Hyamson]

Bahya's view on sexuality accords with Greek moral philosophy. Both partly anticipate Freud's triad of the id, the superego, and the ego. The critical difference is that Bahya has no sense of a subconsciousness that will absorb the effect of the Halakic repression and return it, possibly, as dysfunction to consciousness. But then trying to find an Orthodox Jewish Freudian psychiatrist today would also be a long quest.

Solomon ibn-Gabirol (1021–58) was not a member of the rabbinate. He was a poet and lived off wealthy courtier patrons. He described himself as small, ugly, sickly, and arrogant. As a philosopher he is a pure Neoplatonist. As expressed in the title of one of his works, God is *The Fountain of Life*. Through intellectual and spiritual exercises our role is to return the soul to God. There is nothing original about this idea. It was fully propounded by the Alexandrian philosopher Plotinus in the second century A.D. and by and large by Plato himself.

What is remarkable about ibn-Gabirol (known in Christian Europe, in Latin translation, as Avicebron) is his capacity as a Hebrew poet (he also wrote prose works in Arabic). He is regarded as the greatest Hebrew poet of medieval Sepharad, and his poems entered the Sephardic liturgy:

> *I have sought Thee daily at dawn and twilight*
> *I have stretched my hands to Thee, turned my face,*
> *Now the cry of a heart athirst I will utter,*
> *Like the beggar who cries at my door for grace.*
> *How long, O my God shall I wait Thee in vain?*
> *How long shall Thy people in exile remain?*
> *We wander ever to and fro,*
> *Or sit in chains in exile drear,*
> *Yet still proclaim where'er we go,*
> *The splendor of our Lord is here.*
>
> [transl. Israel Zangwill]

The prophetic vein is pronounced in these poems. They have a personal, human touch and a strong note of proto-Zionism. Ibn-Gabirol's most ambitious work was the lengthy religious poem *The Kingly Crown*, in which the traditional Jewish view of the relationship between God and man is set austerely within the context of Neoplatonic philosophy:

> *In the midst of my days do not take me away and do not hide*
> *Thy face from me.*
> *Cleanse me of my sins, and do not cast me from Thy Countenance,*
> *Let me live with honor, and after that with honor take me.*
> *And when Thou shall take me out of this world, bring me in peace to the life of the world to come.*

Summon me on high, and let me dwell among the saints,
Number me among those who have a potion in eternal life.

[transl. B. Lewis]

Of the Jewish religious writers of the Middle Ages, ibn-Gabirol is the most ecumenical. His poems fit as well into a Christian as into a Jewish ambience. Indeed the twelfth-century Christians who read his Latin translation did not know that Avicebron was Jewish.

Judah Halevi (1075–1140) was like ibn-Gabirol a proto-Zionist but a more outspoken and vehement one, and twentieth-century Zionists regard him as a great medieval forerunner and frequently quote his nationalist poems, especially this one:

My heart is the east, and I in the uttermost west—
How can I find savor in food? How shall it be sweet to me?
How shall I render my vows and my bonds, while yet
Zion lieth beneath the fetter of Edom, and I in Arab chains?

[transl. Nina Sakaman]

Halevi was a poet, physician, rabbi, communal leader, and social commentator. He was highly visible in the Mediterranean Jewish society of his day and revered afterward. In the last months of his life Halevi went on a pilgrimage to Jerusalem. He stopped in Cairo, and genizah records show he was treated as a celebrity. Whether he ever made it to the Holy Land is uncertain. There was a legend that he was killed by an Arab horseman as he lay prostrate on Zion's shore and kissed the ground. But he may never have gotten beyond the round of Jewish welcoming parties in Alexandria.

Halevi lived in unsettled times in Sepharad. The first wave of Muslim fundamentalists had crossed over from North Africa and gained political power, making life less secure for the Jews. Indeed, Halevi spent part of his career as a physician at the more friendly court of the Christian king of Castile, returning to Muslim territory when his court patron was murdered.

Halevi was immensely learned, with a thorough knowledge of the sciences, philosophy, and medicine of his day. He also reflected deeply on history and ethnography. Halevi especially in his later years had an impact on his contemporaries and future generations.

He turned with anger and contempt against "Greek" (i.e., all secular) learning:

> *Let not Greek wisdom seduce you:*
> *it has no fruit, only blossoms . . .*
> *The words of its wise men are confused,*
> *built on vain foundations and plastered over.*
> *You will come back from them with*
> *a heart stripped empty and with a mouth full of dross and*
>   *idle talk.*
> *Why, then, should I seek my crooked paths*
> *and forsake the straight road.*
>
>   [transl. S. D. Goitein]

This poetical polemic was not sufficient for him. Halevi set out to write a definitive neoconservative treatise, putting into it all his substantial learning and his literary skill (smaller however, in prose than in poetry). The result was the work that made him famous, the *Kuzari,* or to give it its original title (so he said in a letter), *The Book of Refutation and Proof in Defence of the Despised Faith.*

The *Kuzari* was written in Arabic. It has been much praised by modern Jewish historians, which is a wonder because it is an extremely reactionary, anti-intellectual work, verbose and not at all well written (there are at least two English translations).

The book is written in a common genre of religious literature in the High Middle Ages, that of a disputation among spokesmen for different faiths, in this case a rabbi, a Christian, and a Muslim, each trying to persuade the king of Khazars to accept his religion for himself and his people.

While Halevi's text is fictional, this dramatic dialogue had a historical base. In the tenth century the Khazars, an obscure Asiatic people living north of the Crimea, embraced Judaism, or so Hasdai ibn-Shaprut, the Sephardic court Jew, heard via the Byzantine empire. The Khazars probably were converted by Jewish merchants or missionaries from Constantinople. Hasdai ibn-Shaprut made strenuous efforts to contact the king of Khazars but failed; perhaps by that time their kingdom had already been destroyed by the Slavs.

Halevi used this well-known story only as a dramatic setting for expounding his views. He rejected philosophic reason in favor of revelation as the source of truth. Since philosophers cannot agree, the intellect cannot lead to God. The knowledge offered by Aristotle should not be regarded as true. The only principle that counts is belief in "the existence of the Creator and His power to do what He wishes when He wishes."

Knowledge of this principle comes through God's revelation to the people of Israel, who are ethically superior to all other people. Even a converted Gentile is not the equal of a born Jew.

Halevi presents a kind of proto–Social Darwinism argument that the Jewish "perfect fruit" developed organically through the patriarchs and reached perfection in Moses: "At that time, they [the Jews] merited the appearance of light upon them and that lordly providence." [transl. L. V. Berman] Corresponding to the superiority of the Jewish people is their language, which is superior to all others: "It is the language in which revelation was made to Adam and Eve." The Jews in the Holy Land will prevail over all people: "On account of the dwelling of the presence of God among you, the fertility of your land and the proper ordering of your rain."

It is not hard to see why modern Zionists love Halevi. What is surprising is to find him hailed as a powerful mind, an important thinker. There is nothing in the *Kuzari* except neoprophetic nationalist racism. What is most disturbing about the later Halevi is that he wants to deprive the younger generation of Jewish intellectuals of access to that Greek and Arabic philosophic thought that he himself had once cultivated. He is an advocate of Orthodox censorship and thought control.

Moses Maimonides (Rabbi Moses ben Maimon, Rambam, 1135–1204) was the most ambitious theorist by far that the Mediterranean Judeo-Arabic renaissance produced. He is regarded as belonging in the world pantheon of Jewish leaders, in company with the biblical patriarchs and prophets. "From Moses unto Moses there was none like Moses." This reputation, however, was based on his codification of Talmudic Law, the *Misneh Torah* and his enunciation of what became the canonical *Thirteen Principles* of the Jewish faith, not on his philosophical work, which was extremely controversial in his time.

Maimonides aroused bitter opposition for excessive rationalism, especially among the mystically inclined rabbis of Provence in southern France. Maimonides's main philosophical work was suppressed in rabbinical circles in the late thirteenth century and was not studied again until the nineteenth century.

Meanwhile Maimonides had gained a substantial reputation in the Christian world. His main philosophic work, the *Guide of the Perplexed*, was translated into Latin and carefully studied by, among others, Saint Thomas Aquinas, the Dominican scholastic at the University of Paris in the mid-thirteenth century. Aquinas believed he was trying to do for Christian thought what Maimonides did for Jewish thought, namely, to achieve a synthesis or at least integration and reconciliation of revealed faith and the best science known at the time, the Aristotelian system that had just become available through translation in the mid-twelfth century.

Maimonides believed that philosophical and scientific speculation was for a very small privileged elite. The mass of the Jewish populace should accept and act upon revealed truth in the Torah and the oral law propounded in the Talmud and its commentaries. This faith he summed up in the *Thirteen Principles* of the Jewish faith. After Maimonides innocuously propounded the majesty, providence, and incorporeality of God, its twelfth principle stated somewhat more provocatively: "I believe with complete faith in the coming of the Messiah, and even though he should tarry, nevertheless I shall wait for his coming every day."

The thirteenth principle is the resurrection of the dead. It is not explained. While the resurrection of the dead had been part of Jewish belief since late Pharisaic times, adapted from Mesopotamia, this was the first time it was enunciated as an explicit article of faith.

Goodness and membership in the Jewish community require only adherence to these principles and acting upon them: "When a man has accepted these principles and truly believes in them, he forms part of the community of Israel; and it is incumbent upon us to love him, to care for him" (transl. Colette Surat).

The Orthodox devout, Maimonides is saying, have a prescriptive right to communal distribution of welfare. From one point of view, this is an eminently humanitarian doctrine. From another, it discourages enterprise and legitimizes dependency. Traditional devoutness assures communal charity. Especially in Eastern Europe in the nineteenth century, Maimonides's doctrine of care had adverse social consequences.

Maimonides was a generous and warmhearted person who cared

for people. He was born in Cordoba, the son of a prominent rabbinical judge. When Maimonides was thirteen, the family fled because of the bleak ambience imposed by the new Muslim fundamentalist rulers from the Maghreb. After some time in Morocco, where they may have pretended to be Muslims, the family ended up in Fustat (Old Cairo) in Egypt. There Maimonides became at first a merchant in cooperation with his brother. His brother's death in a shipwreck on a trade voyage to India eliminated the family's commercial capital.

Maimonides then became a prominent physician, serving both the chief minister of the sultan and his own community. He reports his exhaustion when after a long day at court he would come home to find a lineup of sick people at his door. But he took care of them. On top of these responsibilities, Maimonides served for long stretches as the head of the Jewish community in his town and yet found time to master the whole Aristotelian corpus and many of the Arabic commentaries on it. He was a man of prodigious industry. And also a man of deep feeling, as he revealed in a letter he wrote to the persecuted Jews of Yemen, in which he indiscreetly expressed his contempt and hatred for both the Christian and Muslim religions.

Some rabbis felt that Maimonides's religious law-code had undercut them and were jealous. But his effort to resolve tensions between faith and reason, between Jewish belief and Aristotelian science in the *Guide of the Perplexed* produced a firestorm of debate shortly after his death. Either his opponents in France had waited until the great man died before attacking him or it took time to translate (it was written in Arabic), copy, circulate, and study the *Guide of the Perplexed.*

The book is disarming from its preface onward. At the beginning Maimonides only posits two kinds of faith—the simple credulity of the masses and the rationalizing faith of the philosophically sufficiently trained. He makes clear that the latter is superior. Also, many intricacies of the Law, such as dietary provisions, turn out to be historically and socially conditioned, not divine mandates. Maimonides sounds at times like a social and moral relativist.

In the body of the work, there were at least two propositions of Aristotle that Maimonides could not reconcile with Jewish faith: Aristotle's belief that the world was eternal, not created, and his view of a collective rather than an individual immortality.

Ironically, on one of these issues, whether the world was created or existed though infinite time eternally, astrophysics today leans toward the biblical view that the world was created—what is known as the big bang theory. Yet the important point is that Aristotle in the High Middle Ages was generally considered the source of scientific truth in such matters, and the issue of whether the world was created, as the Bible says in contrast to Aristotle, was extremely troubling to Maimonides, as it was to Thomas Aquinas, who was faced with the same conundrum.

The issue of personal immortality arose from Aristotle's view that mental energy on the death of the individual returned to the intellectual force in the universe. This apparently ruled out personal immortality and the resurrection of the dead. Maimonides had made the resurrection of the dead his thirteenth principle of faith. Aristotelian science seemed to conflict with that proposition.

Maimonides's efforts to resolve these contradictions between revelation and science are extremely labored and awkward. It is not easy to read these passages. The ambiguous language either suggests that the conflict cannot be resolved or that Maimonides sides with Aristotle. In the latter instance he is transgressing his own *Thirteen Principles*.

In the end he comes close to the double-truth doctrine of his contemporary, the radical Spanish Arabic philosopher Averroës, that there is a divine truth and a human, scientific truth, and there is no way to bridge them. In the *Guide of the Perplexed* this made for highly provocative reading:

> We know all that we know only through looking at the beings; therefore our knowledge does not grasp the future or the infinite. Our insights are renewed and multiplied according to the things from which we acquire the knowledge of them. He, may He be exalted, is not like that . . . With regard to Him, may He be exalted, there is no multiplicity of insights and renewal and change of knowledge. [transl. Colette Surat]

Maimonides ran up against a conundrum that lies at the center of Jewish religious and intellectual history to the present day. A very old and thick religious culture was expressed in every aspect of Jewish life—the Bible, the Talmud, personal and behavior, and not least the synagogue liturgy. This ethos was centered on a view of divinity as transcendent and omnipotent and omniscient. Aristotle represented a discourse that was very different—the rationalistic, scientific frame of mind that envisaged a universal force that was immanent not transcendent, mechanical not personal, a prime mover that started the world but interfered little or not all in the world's operation and humanity's destiny.

Maimonides thought that somehow he could demonstrate that intellectual and highly educated Jews could live simultaneously in both intellectual worlds—he himself did, so he tried to show others how they might emulate him. He failed, and the central problem that challenged and defeated him—making Judaism compatible with science—remains unresolved. He failed principally because he either would not or could not face the radical significance of the problem.

To make the Jewish heritage compatible with science would demand a massive overhauling of that tradition, not a guidebook through intellectual thickets. It would require reconsideration of the attributes of God and his relationship to humanity. It would require recognition of the distinctiveness and legitimacy of the scientific as opposed to the humanistic mind. It would require a very different-sounding liturgy.

Maimonides was not prepared to purchase intellectual harmony by such a massive expenditure of time and talent. There the issue still lies and powerfully contributes to the erosion of the very existence of the Jews as a distinct group.

What especially appeals in Maimonides is his unyielding integrity and intellectual honesty. While Thomas Aquinas, as a university professor of philosophy and theology, was compelled to confront Aristotle—it was a text in the curriculum; the problems that Aristotle raised were being debated in academia and Aquinas had to rise to the challenge—Maimonides was under no professional compulsion to raise these difficult issues. He himself undertook to study Aristotle because he thought it was marvelous science, to comment on it, and to try to resolve the disparity between the principles of Judaism that he himself had codified and summarized and these scientific propositions.

We do not know whether he was satisfied with his own work, but the rabbinate, especially in Europe, turned strongly against his philosophical efforts. There is a story, possibly true, that the Provençal rabbis influenced the papal Inquisition to burn the *Guide of the Perplexed.*

Indirectly, Maimonides achieved just the opposite of what he intended. Instead of making Jewish culture more rationalistic and scientific, he seemed to demonstrate the futility and danger of bridging secular culture with traditional Judaism, and thereby he helped to propel traditional Judaism into its quasi-mystical, astrological course called the Cabala, a theosophical, antiscientific pastiche. It too offered a special higher learning for the rabbinate, but it was an esoteric learning that was antiscientific, not the higher learning of science.

There is an ironic and strange postscript to Maimonides's life and work. His only son, Abraham Maimonides, who replaced him as head of the Jewish community in Old Cairo, attempted to reform the Jewish synagogue liturgy along Muslim lines—to make it more similar to the Muslim form of prayer. His community rose in wrath and ejected him. Apparently Abraham Maimonides was trying, like his father, for a kind of cultural synthesis, but the form that he proposed was no more acceptable than the one that Maimonides presented.

To assess the cultural and intellectual achievements of a particular society in the past, critical judgment must be exercised to evaluate the quality of its most famous writings relative to literature and theory in other times and places. Enthusiastic partisanship is not the same thing as criticism.

This exercise leads to the conclusion that the image of an intellectual golden age among the Jews in the medieval Arabic world is overdrawn compared to the highlighting of their achievements in commerce that were revealed in the genizah archive as adumbrated by Goitein in his immensely interesting if verbose and messy work.

It was indeed a golden age in terms of Jewish freedom for two centuries or so to act to near full potential in a market economy engaged in the nexus of commercial capitalism. Jewish performance in this economic context was remarkable and forecasted the impressive record that some Jewish entrepreneurs were allowed to build up during the sixteenth and seventeenth centuries in Western Europe and much more broadly in the nineteenth century and thereafter.

With regard to intellectual achievement, the record of the Judeo-Arab renaissance leads to a more circumscribed judgment. Saadia Gaon's achievement was principally pedagogic, to update Talmudic Judaism so as to bring it minimally within the literary and philosophical Arab discourse of his time. Ibn-Gabirol was a superior Hebrew poet, as was Halevi, and some other poets of distinction were stimulated by Arabic literary accomplishment.

But when it comes to theoretical, philosophical work, the Jewish Mediterranean renaissance gained only partial victories. To read its three most celebrated books is disappointing. *The Duties of the Heart* is a work of formalist ethics that only occasionally confronts the complex behavioral problems and agonizing marginal choices, such as those rising from sexuality, of real life.

The *Kuzari* is written with passion and a certain clever subtlety, but it amounts to a neoconservative anti-intellectual diatribe along the lines of nationalist racism. This point of view is tenable. It is Halevi's presentation of it that is faulty. Whatever translation you choose, the *Kuzari* is mostly unreadable today, and perhaps was not much more readable in the era when it was written.

The *Guide of the Perplexed* is admirable for its reflection of both Halakic and Aristotelian learning and for its intellectual courage in confronting the immense problems in defining the difficult junctures of Judaism with the more problematic propositions of Greek philosophy. It is this honesty that attracted Thomas Aquinas to it and led him to praise Maimonides, no easy concession by a Dominican friar whose colleagues in his religious order were at the time of his writing making life very hard for the rabbis of southern France.

But Aquinas's own way of encountering the tension between the Bible and Aristotle was on a scale of ambition and accomplishment much beyond Maimonides's *Guide*. Aquinas created a vast philosophical edifice that tried to resolve the tensions between the Judeo-Christian and Greek scientific traditions down to the smallest detail, then raised up an elaborately structured intellectual synthesis that became a culture of its own and still has plenty of adherents both within Catholicism and without. Maimonides's *Guide* is simply not comparable as an intellectual achievement with Aquinas's *Summa Theologica*.

The *Guide* is only a rough pass at the problem of Jewish and Greek disjuncture, leaving the issues unresolved, or resolved in a way that neither satisfied (to put it mildly) his rabbinical colleagues nor inaugurated, as did Benedict Spinoza (another admirer of the *Guide*) in the seventeenth century, a new rationalist, posttranscendental trend in philosophy. The *Guide* has the tone and structure of personal advice, as its title implies, and is not the comprehensive treatise that Aquinas provided.

This sounds cruel and ungrateful to Maimonides. He was a community leader, a practicing, busy rabbi as well as a hard-pressed physician with a huge practice. He did not have anywhere the leisure and opportunity that Aquinas and Spinoza had to develop the elaborate responses that they offered, each in his own way, to the intellectual problem generated by the incompatibility of transcendental providential monotheism and scientific, naturalistic immanence. But Maimonides's work demonstrates the intellectual limitations of the Jewish Mediterranean renaissance. It reached the borders of modern thought, but was unable to provide the social and institutional context for entering that Promised Land.

Maimonides was a genius who exhibited incredible learning, extraordinary intelligence, and unusual courage, but he failed in his highest ambition—to found a new rationalizing Jewish culture that would at the same time leave undisturbed the Talmudic tradition. Perhaps he did not fully realize the difficulty and complexity of the task he was facing. That no one has had much success in this effort since his time possibly indicates that it cannot be done.

A half-century after Maimonides in effect brought the Mediterranean Judeo-Arab renaissance into intellectual crisis, its general vitality, already threatened by the triumph of fundamentalist Muslims in Spain, was shaken by adverse events at the eastern end of the Mediterranean. Political upheavals in Egypt also brought less tolerant rulers to power there. Meanwhile the whole Arab world began to slide into economic depression caused by the interruption of major trade routes to Asia and the decline of agricultural productivity. The agricultural difficulties were due to deterioration of the irrigation system of the Near East in the wake of political instability and possibly also a climatic change, namely a decline in annual rainfall, and increased desiccation of the land.

The economic prosperity of the Mediterranean Jews slowly and steadily worsened. There was a momentary upturn in the sixteenth century under powerful and intelligent Ottoman Turkish rulers after they captured Constantinople in 1453 and with the immigration of Spanish Jews to the Ottoman empire with ready capital after their expulsion from Spain in or around 1492. But after 1600, with the opening of new transoceanic routes to East Asia by the Iberian Christian powers, the whole economy of the Mediterranean went into a decline from which it still has not recovered, taking down with it the last vestiges of Jewish prosperity.

By 1700 the Arab-speaking Jews were poor farmers and small artisans, which they remained until their forced migration to Israel around 1950. Although close to half the population of the Jewish state, there too the Oriental Jews, as the Westernized Israelis called them, remained undereducated, powerless, and proletarized.

CHAPTER SIX

Ashkenaz and Sepharad

Like a dark, poisonous cloud that blotted out the sun, covered the landscape, and penetrated with its dark vapors into every core of social life, the conversion of the Constantinian dynasty to Christianity in the fourth century brought misery to the Jews.

It is possible that Helena, the mother of Constantine I, who gained the imperial throne in the West in A.D. 312 and all of the Roman Empire in 324, was herself Jewish. She came from among the teeming urban masses in Asia Minor, where she had been a serving maid in a tavern. Constantine was the product of her union, as concubine, with a Roman officer who rose to be assistant emperor. That his mother may have been Jewish did not affect Constantine's religious policies, except perhaps in a negative way from a Jewish point of view.

The emperor hated Jews so much that he joined the Christian bishops in rescheduling the date of Easter so that Easter was kept from being celebrated on the same day as Passover, even though Jesus' Last Supper with his disciples was a Passover Seder. Perhaps Constantine thought that the Jews had never treated his mother Helena rightly and this resentment heightened his hostility toward the Jews.

It would not have been such a dire decline of fortune, this political triumph of the Christian Church, with bishops now surrounding the imperial throne and advising the receptive emperor on the implementation of anti-Jewish policy, if at the birth of the Church and during its early struggling century or two, the then much more numerous and politically influential Jewish community had treated the Christians more tolerantly. But what was Christianity to start with in the era of the Pharisees and rabbis during the first century A.D. but an obscure sect devoted to the memory of a Galilean preacher remote from the centers of Jewish learning and power, his initial disciples only poor, ignorant fishermen from Lake Kinneret?

And how would this trivial sect have become a religious movement, gaining adherents and turning into a fractious community, if it had not been for the querulous, irresponsible, traitorous Pharisee from Asia Minor, Saul of Tarsus—Saint Paul, the Christians now called him. The subtle way Paul combined the fifty-third chapter of the Book of Isaiah about the "man of sorrows" and the "suffering servant" with the sacramental idea of a dying and rising God—an old theory that had circulated in the eastern Mediterranean among Greek-speaking people for centuries—was anathema to the rabbis.

Insofar as they thought about the Christians in the first seven or eight decades after the Nazarene's death, the rabbis considered them only as desperate underclass heretics, at best pathetic, more evidently contemptible and damnable. They made jokes about Mary. She was a whore, they cackled, and Jesus was the offspring of one of her sloppy unions.

The Church, thanks initially to Paul's relentless, self-sacrificing missionary travels, his incessant preaching in hostile synagogues and in more receptive market squares and in front of pagan temples—as often as not abused and whipped out of town—and his stream of wise, comforting, and advising letters to Christian communities, began to gain in numbers. Some were Jewish converts but more readily and soon overwhelmingly they were Gentiles, at first mostly from among the "God-fearers" who had long stood at the backs of the synagogues but were not admitted to the Jewish communities because they shrank from the immolating act of circumcision.

As Jewish reaction to the growth of the Church varied only from cold indifference to furious contempt and active condemnation, the Christians responded with the malice and hatred of an outcast minority against a self-satisfied, hegemonic majority. In A.D. 100 this was the relative position of the Christians and the Jews.

In the new holy books they were creating, the New Testament to the life and death of Jesus Christ and the earliest history of the Church, the Christians—either Gentiles or angry converts from Judaism—inserted malicious stories about the Jews, designed to enclose the Jews in implacable Christian hatred for the intervening historical time—short, it was expected—until Jesus would come again in the flesh and human history would terminate.

Jesus had been an observant Jew preaching Jewish ethics of only a more radical tinge. His disciples were all Jews. Paul was a Pharisee and a rabbi. Yet the Church was viewed in the New Testament as subtly an anti-Jewish phenomenon from the beginning because the Sanhedrin, the leaders of the Jerusalem community, the Gospels alleged, had arrested and indicted Jesus and handed him over to a weak and confused Roman governor for condemnation and crucifixion.

By the end of its first century the Church had become intrinsically more Greek in its doctrine, absorbing full force Alexandrian Platonism, which had been largely developed by Philo the Jew. But Philo's prominent intellectual disciples were all Gentiles, and now through the voice of Christian preachers in accordance with Philonic theory, Jesus became the saving Logos, the Word that cast the saving divine shadow in the world.

That was not the only critical modification the early Christians achieved. The Alexandrian Christians, by A.D. 150 replacing completely the original Judean leadership of the Church, brought into the Church the terrible Judeo-phobia endemic to Alexandrian culture. It had risen from the bitter competition and street fighting between the pagan Greeks and the wealthy and large Jewish community of the eastern metropolis. Between A.D. 115 and 117 the Alexandrian Jews and the Gentiles, the latter backed by Roman power, had engaged in a protracted and cruel civil war. This not only catastrophically diminished Jewish wealth and numbers and political influence, but also left a dark legacy of rancor toward the Jews, which in turn was a conduit for anti-Semitic labels that had circulated in the jealous bazaars of the Hellenistic world for two or three centuries.

All this Jew-hating ethos was now imported into the basic culture of the Church and given authenticity by the already rancorous view of the Jews in the Gospels. The Jews! The Jews! Untrustworthy merchants. Exploiters of the poor and innocent. Traitorous rebels. Secretive operators of a tribal cult. Killers of Christ. Enemies of the Church. Vermin loosed on the fair land of the Roman Empire. Horned instruments of Satan. The fateful liturgy of Jew hatred had now congealed and the lethal litany was sounded, to be evoked and broadcast down the unyielding centuries to Auschwitz and beyond.

The Christian bishops could have countered this Jew hatred and stemmed its impact if they had taken a generous and loving attitude toward the Jewish community, if they had stressed the Jewishness of Jesus and Paul and the positive role of many Jews in the early Church, if they had emphasized to the Christian masses how Christianity was unthinkable without Judaism, how the New Testament was founded on the Old Testament, which in its basic monotheistic theology and its ethical principles was fully in force in Christian teaching.

But generosity, loving care, and forgiveness were not common in the ethos of the Christian episcopate in those times. The bishops did not choose to take a positive attitude toward the Jews. Inflaming the endemic anti-Semitism of the masses, they stressed instead the negative.

Until the third century Judaism was still a realistic competitor with the Church for the conversion of the souls. The hard-pressed bishops could not afford a benign attitude toward the Jews. In Roman law the Church was still technically an illegal community, whereas the Jews were a privileged group. The masses the bishops were trying to convert and then educate were suffused with dark Hellenistic anti-Semitism, and instructing the populace was hard enough for the bishops without going against the grain of mass prejudice.

The kind of men who became bishops, drawn from the literate middle class before Constantine and after he ascended the throne as the first Christian emperor in 312, from the opportunist now converted Roman aristocracy itself, were by their family interests, education, and class ideology not prone to be charitable to the Jews. As bourgeoisie they had imbibed the image of the Jewish merchant, farmer, and artisan as a tough competitor, now to be brought down by partisan sectarian instruments. As senatorial aristocracy, they inherited a long tradition of regarding the Jews as aliens, interlopers, obscurantists, and traitors—they only had to read the archaristocratic historian Tacitus to know that.

In the first quarter of the fifth century the Church's policy toward the Jews was set down in canonical form and not really changed officially until the Second Vatican Council of 1965, backed by the Vatican's full recognition of the state of Israel in 1994.

Saint Augustine of Hippo in North Africa, the theoretical voice of the Church then and for many centuries thereafter, made the decisive canonical statement about the Jews. The Theodosian Code of Roman law, the first comprehensive collection of Latin jurisprudence, which had great impact on European royal policy in social matters in subsequent centuries, as well as on the formulation of the Church's own canon law, shortly thereafter put the Augustinian doctrine into practical terms, although possibly more severely in the application than Augustine envisioned.

Augustine stressed that the Jews should not be subject to physical violence. They should not be assaulted, nor should force be used to effect their conversion. This was the charitable side of Augustine's view of the Jew. He himself favored use of force to compel Christian heretics back into the Church. But the Jews were different; they were a special case, not to be subject to the violent power that Augustine felt the state should use against heretics. Leave the Jews alone, said Augustine. But he stressed "alone" as much as "leave."

The Jews should be segregated from Christian society, with just enough economic opportunity to survive. In the Augustinian doctrine, they were not to prosper, not to have fine houses and elegant synagogues to insult the eyes of faithful Christians. For the Jews were indeed spiritual criminals. They of all peoples had first been offered the grace of salvation by Christ. But they had rejected Jesus, these stiff-necked, foolish, bad people. But they, the Jews, were after all kinsmen of the Lord in his human form. Jesus, Mary, Peter and the other Apostles, Paul—they were all Jews. It was to be left to Jesus Christ at his Second Coming to deal with the Jews.

It was he who would decide what to do with them, what punishment to mete out to them. Presumably the Jews would be cast eternally into hell. But who knows? Perhaps Jesus, the fount of love and mercy, would forgive his earthly kinsmen for their ultimate wrong in rejecting him and conspiring against him.

Meanwhile the Jews were to be segregated from Christian society to survive economically and wait out the coming of the Lord in constrained and humiliating circumstances. Not until 1965 did the Catholic Church repudiate Augustine's teaching on the Jews, not entirely but substantially.

The Theodosian Code put the Augustinian doctrine into the perspective of law. The Jews were not to own slaves or have Christian servants. In a society organized along strong hierarchic lines, this provision made it very difficult for Jews to be substantial landowners or industrial entrepreneurs beyond small operations. The authors of the Code knew that; they wanted to prevent the Jews from being prosperous.

The Jews were to live in segregated quarters. They were to wear distinctive clothing. They were to build synagogues only with the permission of the imperial government and the municipal authorities. There were to have no sexual relationship with Christians. For a Jew to marry a Christian was forbidden; for a Jew to have a Christian concubine was death for both. The image in antique literature of the Jews' avarice extending into sexual aggression was thereby recognized.

There was nothing now, if there had ever been, for the rabbis to use countervailing the Augustinian doctrines and the Theodosian regulations. The last few pagan temples had closed. Since A.D. 395 paganism had been a proscribed religion in the Christian Roman Empire. Only the Jews, whose numbers had shrunk from five million in the first century A.D. to only a million, remained as a licit but severely circumscribed religious minority.

A fanatical belief in religious uniformity gripped the Church's leadership and gained support from the imperial government. From the perspective of the bishops and the state lawyers, the Jews were getting off lightly. They alone were receiving special treatment as a permitted religious minority. They were lucky. They had nothing to complain about.

There is no evidence that the rabbis did complain, except in some Job-like muted dialogue with Yahweh: Why has Thou forsaken us? The Talmudic culture molded dry, silent men who took the blows of life and endured as best they could, and women who had no voice and no choice whatsoever, even with their husbands. The Jews suffered in silence, suffered mutely further diminution of their once prosperous economic endeavors, confined themselves to small farms they could work themselves with their families (or, in remote areas when no one was looking, perhaps with a handful of prohibited slaves) or to small artisan businesses.

Wine production became a favorite Jewish occupation; it could be a family operation leading to a small store in a back alley of a town. Carpentry was another trade for penurious Jews. Jewish capitalism was in remission. The Jews were poor now; humble, silent, hidden people, waiting quietly in the obscurity of the late Roman twilight for a change of fortune.

Not all Jews were prepared to wait out the Christian terror. Escape from ignominy and poverty was possible through conversion to the Church. No doubt the Jewish population remained low and static, despite the fecundity of Jewish families following the Halakic injunction to be fruitful and to multiply, because of a significant number of Jewish conversions to Christianity.

A Jewish convert was welcomed and rewarded by the Church. It was not easy to resist the opportunity to escape from poverty, segregation, and moral condemnation that was now imposed on the Jews by state and Church. It was a tribute to the strength of the Jewish family and the impact of early education, for males, in Jewish religion and lore that the conversion remained idiosyncratic and individually determined, and did not become a mass phenomenon.

For the majority of Jews who remained loyal to their religion and community in the face of hard times imposed by the Christian Church and the Roman Empire, a new dawn eventually rose.

It came with the German invasions of the Roman Empire in Western Europe in the fifth and sixth centuries and the Arab conquest of eighty percent of the Mediterranean coastline in the seventh century. Now the Jews could look up from their hovels, their ghettos, and become entrepreneurs, capitalists, wealthy and influential people once more. As far as Europe was concerned, by A.D. 750 not only in Muslim-ruled Sepharad (Spain), "the East," but also in the rest of Western Europe, Ashkenaz ("the West"), there developed an enormous difference in the status and condition of the Jews in comparison with what it had been in the early fifth century, the age of Augustine and the Theodosian Code.

The Messiah had not come to answer to the Jews' prayers during the miserable centuries from 400 to 600. Instead the German kings had come (the barbarians, the Romans called them), had led their peoples across the devastated Rhine and Danube defenses of the Roman Empire, and during three centuries of wars, upheaval, and constant violence had replaced the Roman Empire in Western Europe with the Germanic successor states. The largest and most important of the Germanic kingdoms was France.

The eastern Roman Empire, centered on Constantinople, Christian Byzantium, survived the Germanic invasions easily, and there the Church's Judeo-phobia and the draconian Jewish laws of late antiquity endured full force. The definitive codification of Roman law made by the Emperor Justinian I in the sixth century repeated the deprivations of the Jews legislated in the earlier Theodosian Code.

The Byzantine Emperor Heraclius I in the early seventh century, with the encouragement of the aggressive Greek bishops, violated Augustine's teaching on the Jews and undertook active physical persecution of them, trying to force their conversion. From this oppression the Jews were rescued in much of the Near East by the Arab conquests of the eastern Mediterranean.

In the West by the middle of the eighth century, especially in the huge Frankish kingdom, called the Carolingian empire after its greatest ruler, Charlemagne, who ruled for nearly four decades around the year 800, the condition of the Jews also significantly improved.

Things did not start out well for the Jews under Germanic rule. In Visigothic Spain in the seventh century, the bishops persuaded weak Gothic kings to use violence against the Jews, and the clergy constantly pressured the Jews to accept the Christian faith. But in 711, with help from the persecuted Jewish minority, an army of Arabs and Berbers crossed the Strait of Gibraltar and easily eliminated the Visigothic monarchy, driving the surviving Christian nobility into the northern foothills of the Pyrenees, where they remained in timid isolation for three centuries.

North of the Pyrenees in the great land between the Atlantic and the Rhine, which the Romans had called Gaul, the Visigoths were first crushed by the Franks. Then in the eighth century a new ruling Frankish family, the Carolingian family, rose to power, and came to dominate this favored wealthy land for the next three centuries. Charlemagne—the most ambitious of the Carolingian rulers—bestrode Europe like a colossus at the end of the eighth century, incorporating most of western Germany, northern Italy, and even a slice of Spain into his vast French realm. It was a realm in which the Jews could travel freely; engage in both local and international commerce, including the slave trade; serve profitably as moneylenders to Christian lords, bishops, and monasteries; and hold extensive estates in the wine-growing regions of the south.

Already in the sixth century, just after the Frankish invasions, there were "Levantine" or "Syrian" merchants at work in France. Most of them were actually Jews. The sight of renewed Jewish prosperity deeply offended the bishop who wrote the history of the Franks, his ideological heritage of fifth-century Judeo-phobia conflicting with the sudden resurgence of the Jews.

It speaks to innate Jewish rationality and racial energy that two centuries of repression and impoverishment, when they were constrained to being small farmers and homely artisans, did not efface their ambition to be international merchants and major capitalists in the backward, underdeveloped, but potentially rich society of Ashkenaz, or apparently blunt their capabilities. Well into the tenth century, Jewish trade and moneylending almost uniquely served the economic needs and satisfied the tastes of the great noble families of feudal France, a land bereft of a bourgeoisie and whose social structure was almost entirely one of lords and peasants, plus the Jews.

The Jewish merchants exported to the Mediterranean world not only furs, timber, and swords, but also slaves. Blond Germanic slaves brought to the markets and Arab Mediterranean cities by Jewish merchants were much in demand, especially if they were young boys or adolescent, nubile women.

The Jewish merchants crossed the line between the religious blocs, establishing contact with Jewish trading families in Spain, North Africa, and Egypt. From their Mediterranean Jewish suppliers the Jewish merchants brought to Ashkenaz the spices, perfumes, jewels, and silks that in many instances had originated in the Jewish trade with East Asia. There was a steady market for these Jewish imports among the French lords.

The Christian bishops were not happy to see the Jews raise their heads again, to find them engaged in large-scale trade, to see them taking Christian slaves to Arab cities, to watch them leading their caravans across the landscape, to learn of their influence at the Carolingian court at Aachen and at the residences of other dynasties of the feudal world. They were dismayed to see Jews emerge as powerful landlords in southern France. Rumor had it that one such Jewish lord had married a Carolingian princess.

In the middle of the ninth century the prominent archbishop of

Lyons preached against the Jews and called for enforcement of Augustine's repressive policy and the social strictures set down in the Theodosian Code. The Carolingians and other magnates ignored him. They needed the Jews, gave them the freedom of their empire, and protected and favored them politically. To the indignation of the clergy, Charlemagne did not bother to punish a Christian bishop at the southern extremity of France, whose diocese spanned the mountains into northern Spain, when, to please the numerous and influential Jewish population in the southland, this bishop preached the "adoptionist heresy"—that Christ was only adopted, not begotten of the Father. Charlemagne accepted clerical condemnation of this pro-Jewish heresy but did not remove or restrain the bishop who was then appeasing the Jews.

Slowly Ashkenaz broadened out beyond the borders of even the gigantic Carolingian realm. In the tenth century Carolingian power waned. The northeastern part of the kingdom was invaded and settled by Danish Viking freebooters, and out of this Scandinavian plantation the powerful feudal duchy of Normandy, in practice independent of and in conflict with Paris, developed in the late tenth and eleventh centuries.

The chief city of the feudal duchy of Normandy, Rouen, became a prime settlement for Jewish merchants in northern Europe. The Jewish capitalists there served the Norman dynasty well and were imported into England in the late eleventh century after that wealthy but politically impotent country was conquered by the Norman dukes. By 1125 the Jewish merchants and moneylenders were hard at work in the streets of the London Jewry and spread out inland from there to other cities.

The Carolingians lost their royal title to the duke of Paris in the late tenth century. But it made no difference to the Jews. Western Germany had become an independent kingdom in the early tenth century, and the Jews by the Christian year 1000 were well settled in hilltop towns along the Rhine, which they used as a conduit to trade in the Low Countries, northern Germany, and Scandinavia. The size and prosperity of the slave trade with the Mediterranean increased.

In the Rhineland's oldest city, Mainz, there developed the first important center of rabbinical learning in Ashkenaz north of Italy. It was from Italy that Talmudic learning came, imported and disseminated particularly by the Kolymonos family of rabbis, who had relocated in Mainz. The Ashkenazi Jews, except those in southern France in touch with the Jewish centers in Muslim Spain, had been deficient in knowledge of Hebrew, the Bible, the Talmud, and Halakic lore.

There was probably no close observance of the dietary laws in the carnivorous region of Europe, where the nobility ate venison steaks three times a day and the peasants devoured the meat of the wild boar. Probably the Jewish merchant capitalists, who for three centuries had so ably served the underdeveloped economy of feudal Europe and catered to the demands of the high nobility, were not even assiduous observers of the Sabbath.

But in the early eleventh century, at Mainz in Germany and at Troyes in northern France, major centers of Halakic learning were put into operation. A new generation of well-trained rabbis spread out across Ashkenaz, reinforced by learned emigrants from the schools of northern Italy and Muslim Spain.

Ashkenazi culture did not pursue the deep philosophy and theology or the elegant Hebrew poetry of Sepharad. It was a society committed to economic practice, to trade and banking, backed up by farming and craftsmanship. But by the middle of the eleventh century Ashkenaz had been regained for rabbinical Judaism, and the lifestyle of its bourgeois class was now conditioned by traditional religious law.

The greatest of the Ashkenaz scholars, Rashi (Rabbi Solomon ben Isaac, 1040–1105) headed the school at Troyes in the early twelfth century. His commentary on the Torah is practical, commonsensical, pithy, realistic. He sought to clarify the plain textual meaning of the Bible. His commentary was so attuned to the tastes and needs of the ordinary educated Jew that it became the favorite marginal gloss located alongside the Hebrew text of the Torah into the twentieth century. In the 1940s a twelve-year-old Jewish child in Minneapolis or Winnipeg was still reading the text of the Pentateuch with Rashi's commentary printed in antique script below. Such is the wonderful timelessness of Halakic continuity.

Perhaps it was the tendency of Graetz and other German founders of Jewish historiography in the nineteenth century to admire the golden age of Sepharad with its elaborate literature, or perhaps it is just a natural inclination to fasten on the works of glamorous writers. For whatever reason, the greatness of Jewish accomplishment in Ashkenaz in the tenth and eleventh centuries (precisely also the happiest years of Sepharad) has not always been given its due. It took Salo Baron, a tough-minded Viennese who worked on Jewish history at Columbia for forty years, to bring out the attractiveness of Ashkenaz. He particularly liked its strong communal structure.

The capitalist and rabbinical families intermarried and comprised a dynastic oligarchy in Ashkenazi cities. They provided all necessary communal services in the way of synagogue, school, ritual slaughterhouses, and charity for the indigent. At the same time they conducted their business enterprises and negotiated skillfully with the kings and dukes for whatever was needed for their own families and the communities they ruled and represented.

They did this in an environment of Christian clerical intolerance. For the bishops knew in A.D. 1000 that what had happened was not right according to Augustinian doctrine or Roman-canonical law, that the Jews should not thrive so freely, should not practice their religion so boldly, should not wield so much influence at royal and ducal courts.

The Jews prospered, but their position in medieval society was parlous and at bottom fragile. It depended on the goodwill of the magnates, and while the Jewish trade continued and their social and legal privileges were confirmed, by the end of the eleventh century the Jews were everywhere the close dependents of the exchequer, the fisc, the chancery—organs of royal and local government. These administrative systems issued the documents that protected the Jews, but at the same time became more and more demanding of the taxes, gifts, and forced loans that the Jewish merchants and bankers were required to offer up annually, even monthly, to the irresistible power and insatiable maw of the mature, expanding feudal state.

We only have reliable statistical information from England in the second half of the twelfth century on Jewish transfer payments to the feudal state. There and then the taxation of the Jews was so profitable to the crown that a separate branch of the exchequer, the accounting division of the royal treasury, was set up to deal with them and extract an increasing flow of tax money from them. By 1175 the Jews were providing at least a quarter of the annual income of the English crown, and the Jews were paying taxes at a rate five times heavier than any other group in society.

To protect this revenue source, the English crown refused to issue licenses for serious moneylending (at the usurious but legal fifty- to three-hundred-percent rate) to Christians with liquid capital, such as the abbots of the larger monasteries, who wanted to get into the credit business. The Jews alone could be moneylenders because the crown in turn got most (but not all—there was a small number of Jewish millionaires in England) of the money that the Jews generated as profits on loans. The theory was that the Bible prohibited money-lending to the disadvantage of kinsmen. Jews were outside the Christian kinship community, so loans across the two religious communities, but not within them, were permitted. This was just a subterfuge to protect the Jews' crown-stipulated near-monopoly in moneylending because it provided so much income for the crown.

How long could this situation prevail? It raised bitter, partisan criticism from bishops; it stirred the envy of an emerging Christian bourgeoisie; it enraged the jealous masses; it depended solely on the willingness of the kings to go on protecting the Jews. By the 1170s Ashkenaz was already into a century of threats to the Jewish position in society. England was a late holdout against the tide of anti-Jewish activity simply because the king there was so powerful and found the Jews so lucrative a source of revenue.

The traditional date for the beginning of the decline of Ashkenaz is 1096. In that year Christian crusaders, an army of French knights led by a few great lords, after papal inducement on the way to the Holy Land through the Balkans and Constantinople, came upon the Jewish quarters in the Rhineland cities. As preparation for killing Muslims in the Near East, the French crusaders inflicted terrible pogroms upon the Rhenish Jews, who were totally unprepared for this catastrophe. It was a rupture with several centuries of Jewish peace, prosperity, and privilege in Ashkenaz, the dawn of a new era of destruction and deprivation. The attacks were a terrible shock to Jewish sensibility, only explicable as the evil days that were alleged to precede immediately the coming of the Messiah.

The Rhineland pogroms committed by the French crusaders in 1096 brought home to the Jews that their world was adversely changing. These changes, which had begun in the middle years of the eleventh century, severely boded ill for the Jews because they were the product of developments in at least four recognizably distinct spheres of European life: economic, legal, political, and religious.

The changes in the economic sphere involved modifications in the method of landholding and in the organization of urban economy. In many parts of Europe, all land, from a duchy to a pigsty, came under the iron structure of feudal relationships. In practice, this meant, among other things, that to hold land one had to swear an oath of loyalty to some kind of overlord. Because the oath was a Christian one, observant Jews could not meet this requirement to become landholders.

In the towns, both industry and commerce were beginning to be vested in regulatory corporations called guilds—craft guilds for industry and merchant guilds for trade. They excluded Jews. Indeed, one of the main reasons for the guilds' existence, particularly in the case of the merchant guilds, was to squeeze out Jewish entrepreneurs.

In law, a large-scale revival of Roman law was occurring. This affected both the law of the feudal states everywhere except England and the Church's canon law, which drew upon Roman law for its principles and procedures. Law schools were founded for the study of Roman law in the textual form of the Justinian Code. All the old Roman disabilities against Jews were now closely studied in a revered juristic text. This conditioned graduates of these law schools, who went on to important jobs in state and Church, to claim that the Jews had gotten away from the controls that the Code prescribed, that the Jews had had it easy for too long, and that it was time to crack down on them as Roman law dictated.

The legal revival contributed to the third development that worked against the Jews. Feudal monarchies began to turn themselves into absolutist states. In addition to the Roman law revival, which inspired royal governments to make themselves over in the authoritarian Roman image, other causes contributed to this political shift, including the simple ambitions of energetic rulers. What was significant for the Jews was that the medieval state in its newer absolutist mode was intolerant of privileged corporations within its borders.

Feudal monarchy had tolerated, even encouraged, a plurality of corporations within its jurisdiction. Now the fashion, carried out often by the new breed of Roman lawyers, was to level all corporations, remove their privileges, and bring all groups, agencies, and institutions equally before the power of the king. Autonomous cities thereby suffered; many aristocrats suffered. The Jews suffered too from this political shift toward absolutist leveling.

By the late twelfth century it was hard to get a royal councilor or judge to listen to a Jewish petition for special status. Privileging of a minority was no longer within the dominant political ethos. The Jews in the early Middle Ages had lived off the recognition of their special status by royal governments. They often paid cold cash for this, but they usually got what they wanted. Now their petitions for autonomy ran against the grain of political thinking and administrative practice. Their vulnerability greatly increased as a result.

The fourth change that worked against the Jews' security and status in the High Middle Ages was in the religious sphere, and it was the most deleterious and corrosive of all because it directly inspired attacks on the Jews from all groups in medieval Christian society.

Historians have called the alteration in European religious sensibility in the eleventh and twelfth centuries the New Piety. Its leaders were Pope Gregory VII (1073–85) and Cardinal Peter Damiani, one of his main associates; Saint Anselm of Canterbury, (d. 1109) a theologian and monastic leader who moved Catholic thought in new directions; and Saint Bernard of Clairvaux (d. 1154), a theologian, preacher, and mystic of enormous influence.

These spiritual leaders and their thousands of followers turned medieval Christianity away from concentration on external rituals toward a much more personal, experiential religion. They effected a shift in focus from the Old Testament to the New Testament. They concentrated on the humanity of Jesus, his personal sacrifice for mankind, and his relationship with his loving mother. In the hands of the fomenters of the New Piety, the Virgin Mary was virtually elevated to a place in the Christian Godhead. The mode of religious feeling was shifted to Jesus the man from Christ the emperor.

Along with many fine things that came out of the New Piety—the Virgin cult, which feminized and democratized Christian theology, Gothic architecture, religious poetry and music of great power— there was almost bound to be a wave of revived Judeo-phobia. The more Christian people thought about Jesus' humanity, the more they thought about his death, and the more they were directed to the Gospels' blame of the Jews for his death. The humanization of Catholic theology in the High Middle Ages is one of the monumental and generally admirable chapters in the history of the Catholic

Church. Its downside was the stimulation of renewed hostility to Jews among all levels in European society.

Hatred of the Jews, denunciation of their heretofore special and protected position in society, and renewed pressure to secure their conversion was an attitude that prevailed at the center of religious leadership. Pope Gregory VII wrote letters to the Christian kings in Spain warning them against employing Jewish administrative officials, who were moving over from the Muslim territory to the Christian side. Cardinal Peter Damiani was the author of vehement anti-Semitic pamphlets, as was one of the prime members of the circle of Saint Anselm of Canterbury. Saint Bernard of Clairvaux preached against the Jews, stressing their guilt and blame for Jesus' death and their privileged position in the economy. It is true that he reaffirmed Augustine's injunction against forced conversion (and this restraint is often cited by historians), but Bernard's fiery, extremely hostile sermons on the Jewish problem were bound to stir popular hatred and physical violence against the Jews.

It is possible, as his political enemies claimed, that Gregory VII came from a family of Jewish converts to Christianity. Certainly his family were close associates of a prominent Roman family of converted Jews, the Pierleonis. But being a Jewish convert would not make a medieval cleric more tolerant of the Jews. Quite the contrary, he would be at the forefront of the clamor against the Jews. Any feelings of remorse or guilt on the part of the Jewish convert to the Church would be repressed by a demand that all Jews go down the same path of apostasy.

Clerical anti-Semitism in the Catholic Church of the High Middle Ages should not be viewed as the work of marginal fanatics. It stemmed rather from the very center of Christian spirituality and was enunciated by the most creative minds the Church had to offer in the eleventh and twelfth centuries. This is a troubling fact that raises uncomfortable issues in the ecumenical context of the later twentieth century, but it must be stressed if the causes of the downfall of Ashkenaz are to be understood. Gregory VII, Peter Damiani, Anselm of Canterbury, Bernard of Clairvaux—these ecclesiastics stood at the pinnacle of power in the Western Church of their day and were the re-creators of medieval Christianity along the lines of a deeper and more personal sensibility. They also hated Jews and spewed hostility toward them that was bound to echo through all the ranks of the hierarchy, down to the level of parish priest and simplest monk.

For fifteen years in the second quarter of the eleventh century, Bernard of Clairvaux, the most influential preacher of his day, extruded his venom on the Jews to multitudes gathered in churches and market squares:

> What is there in that [Jewish] people which is not crude and coarse, whether we consider their actions, their inclinations, their understanding, or even the rites with which they worship God? For their actions carried them [of old] into many wars, their inclinations are all devoted to the pursuit of gain, their intelligence stopped short in the thick husk of the letter of their Law, and their worship consists in shedding the blood of sheep and cattle . . . Not the flight of demons, not the obedience of the elements, nor life restored to the dead, was able to expel from their minds that bestial stupidity, and more than bestial, which caused them, by a blindness as marvelous as it was miserable, to rush headlong into that crime, so enormous and so horrible, of laying impious hands upon the Lord of Glory . . .

For a peasant, an artisan, or even a literate knight or fancy nobleman hearing these venomous words, what could possibly be his reaction, other than to want to bring harm to the Jews? In the revered Bernard's preaching on the Jewish question is the central and authentic voice of the Catholic Church. Nothing changed fundamentally in the Catholic Church's hatred for the Jews and the teaching of contempt and fury against them between the twelfth century and the Second Vatican Council of 1965. In all that time the Catholic Church was the most persistent fount of anti-Semitism in the world. Things are different now, but the truth about the old days, these long dark centuries of Jew hatred, must not be forgotten.

Yet this is not the voice of the Nazi Holocaust, we are required to remember, because the Nazis would give the Jews no escape from their doom, but the Catholic Church always left the door open to Jewish conversion and escape. Indeed the converted Jew would be celebrated and rewarded. But this possible transformation does not seem to restrain Bernard. He does not make the distinction between the Jews as a people and as the members of a superseded and mistaken religion. He talks of the damned, bestial Jewish people. His sermon breathes with racism. The Jews were not in his view the alternative and less correct community that sprang from events in the

Holy Land long ago. They are the terrible other, the ugly, the evil, the damnable.

A leading characteristic of the medieval Catholic New Piety was its mass popularity, its address to the laity. When the anti-Semitism taught by the leaders of the New Piety reached down to the level of knights, peasants, and artisans, the results were only the first of a very long series of popular assaults on Jews in Western European cities in the next three centuries. Sometimes the Jews were given protection by a local magnate, sometimes they were not. Sometimes a bishop or an abbot led the pogromist mob. Sometimes Jews congregated in their synagogue and were burned alive together as the mob torched it.

The glorious painting and sculpture of high medieval Europe, so rightly treasured today by museums, publishers, universities, and art collectors, portrayed the synagogue always as blind and the Jews as minions of Satan, as warlocks and witches, as beasts of prey, the blood of Christian children drooling from their sharp teeth and fat lips.

Beginning in England in the mid-twelfth century and then moving across Europe eastward (in France by 1180, in Rhineland by 1200) was the motif that became the most incendiary form of mass hysteria against the Jews—the blood libel. It is still popular in the Ukraine today.

The blood libel was the claim that at Passover the Jews engaged in the ritual murder of Christian children, whose blood allegedly became the ingredient in Passover matzos. In the disordered and violent society of Europe, children, not greatly prized and watched in an era of a runaway population boom, easily fell prey to death by misadventure or disappearance. The Jews were blamed for these misfortunes.

The Catholic officials never made up their minds whether to endorse or condemn the blood libels. There were Popes and bishops who uttered cautionary, even negative pronouncements. But these had little effect on the populace. And some bishops, abbots, and licensed preachers were at the head of the pogromist mobs.

It is a curious and disconcerting fact of cultural history that the blood libel appeared and moved simultaneously eastward alongside the Arthurian theme in medieval literature.

The genre of Arthurian romantic literature appeared first at

Oxford University around 1140, written there by a Welsh graduate student working under the patronage of the bishop of Lincoln, in whose diocese Oxford lay. The blood libels erupted in the city of Lincoln in the 1150s, and the bishop of Lincoln gave them authenticity. The blood libels appeared in Troyes in northern France (Rashi's town and a commercial center with a substantial Jewish population) around 1180, at the same time that the greatest of the Arthurian poems in the French language were written there by a court clergyman. The blood libels appeared in the Rhineland shortly after 1200 at the same time and at the same location that the best Arthurian literature in the German language was being composed there.

What is the significance of this dissemination of the blood libel in the same place and at the same pace as the Arthurian literature, the finest body of medieval vernacular literature in the twelfth and thirteenth centuries? The conclusion must be that the Jew-hating blood libel was centrally integrated in the most creative side of medieval literary culture, the first wave of romanticism in Western civilization.

This would again negate the modern liberal rationalist hope that Catholic anti-Semitism was something marginal, extraneous, disseminated by unruly and underliterate people. No, anti-Semitism lay at the center of medieval Christian sensibility. It was at the core of medieval spirituality and the vanguard literary culture of that day. Blood libel, King Arthur and the Round Table: They were jointly integral to the medieval ethos, inseparably bound together in the structure of the medieval imagination. The child-killing Jew and Sir Lancelot were equally fixtures of the medieval mind and embedded inextricably in the same romantic culture.

Another prime facet of high medieval religious sensibility and ecclesiastical policy that contributed to the marginalization and miseration of the Jews was the rise of the crusading ideal. Harking back to Saint Augustine's justification of the use of force on behalf of the Church, and influenced not a little by the mirror image of the Muslim idea of holy war, jihad, Pope Gregory VII around 1080 called for a two-front war against the Muslims—in northern Spain and to rescue the Holy Land.

The latter call resulted in the First Crusade of 1095–96, the only really successful attack upon the Muslims in the Near East among seven such costly Latin Christian ventures in the next two centuries.

Aided by temporary disunity among the Arabs, the French crusaders were remarkably successful, taking Jerusalem and slaughtering hundreds of pious Jews living there. A hundred years later Jerusalem was regained by Arabs, and two hundred years later the crusaders abandoned their last outpost in the Holy Land, the great fortress port of Acre on the Mediterranean (it has recently been dug up by Israeli archaeologists and is a prominent feature of today's tours of Israel).

The drive against the Muslims in Spain was much more successful because in the Christian Spanish nobility of the north, the papacy had an integrated and determined army. The *reconquista* of Spain for the Cross moved steadily forward after 1100, and by the middle of the thirteenth century three-quarters of the peninsula had been recovered from the Muslim princes by the Christian Spanish kings.

Fighting for the Cross, the papacy decreed, earned a medieval soldier full forgiveness for his sins. The crusading ideal became a popular fixture of medieval religious culture and central to the ethos of the feudal nobility. Although only a tiny minority of medieval Christian warriors ever fought in an actual battle against Muslims, their pent-up crusading ardor could be loosed upon the defenseless Jews at home if they found it inconvenient and too dangerous to encounter the Muslim armies in Iberia or the Near East. Jewish suffering from the crusading movement was initially demonstrated in the Rhineland pogroms of 1096 and was repeated several times. Every time the papacy launched an official call for a crusade or an inflammatory preacher like Bernard of Clairvaux toured town and country arousing militant passions, the local Jewish community was very likely to be assaulted.

Beating up and killing Jews was not sufficient virtue in the Christian mentality of the twelfth and thirteenth centuries. Out of the New Piety at the end of the twelfth century came a new conviction—that the conversion of the Jews should be ardently pursued because it would accelerate the Second Coming of Christ. The idea spread among academic theologians as well as popular preachers that Jesus was waiting until the whole world was converted to Christianity. In Western Europe the Jews were the obstacle to the apocalypse. They had to be brought within the Church before Jesus would return to judge and bless mankind.

As a result, rewards for Jews who converted became more elaborate. If the convert was highly literate—a rabbi or a rabbinical student—he could move (as soon as he mastered a bit of Latin) into an ecclesiastical office. But those Jews, still the great majority, who would not accept conversion were to be subject to more pressure, to be threatened, abused, segregated, and vilified until they came to the baptismal font.

This was a significant departure from Saint Augustine. It was a vast departure from the world of Charlemagne, when Jews were prized and protected because of their economic value to society.

Herein lies an important key to the steady and bloody decline of Ashkenaz in the twelfth and thirteenth centuries. The Jews were no longer needed in the European economy. The Jews had brought capitalism—long-distance trade and banking—to the underdeveloped society of the early Middle Ages. But the European economy in the High Middle Ages was rapidly being converted to a market economy. There were now ample numbers of Christian merchants and bankers who were jealous of vestiges of Jewish privilege (such as the Jews' patent on moneylending in England to about 1200) and wanted them out of the way.

In northern Italy particularly by the late twelfth century great entrepreneurial Christian families who could provide all that Europe needed in the way of capitalist functions were on the rise. And there were other such families in southern France and the Low Countries.

The Jews were no longer needed; indeed, their competition stood in the way of the advancement of Christian entrepreneurs. So by the early thirteenth century no economic reason existed for the Jewish well-being in Europe, while the religious culture of Europe banged a steady drumbeat of hatred against them.

The outcasting of the Jews from European society was formalized by the Fourth Lateran Council of the Church, presided over by the most powerful of the medieval popes, Innocent III, in 1215. This is one of the four most influential general councils of the Catholic Church in its long history. It was ordained that the Jews were to live in segregated quarters (around 1500 the term "ghetto," from the Jews' quarter near the iron foundry in Venice, came into wide use for such quarters). They were to wear distinctive clothing (a yellow star, a funny hat). In general they were to be treated as pariahs in society. After this blow, it was just a matter of time before the Jews would be massacred or expelled.

Writing around 1130, Peter Abelard, the radical Parisian philosopher, already perceived that the Jews of Ashkenaz were doomed:

> No other people has borne so much for God's sake as the Jews. Dispersed among strangers, without king or prince, the Jews are oppressed with the heaviest taxes . . . The lives of the Jews are in the hands of their deadliest enemies . . . Jews cannot own fields or vineyards . . . So the only profession open to them is that of usury, which only increases the Christians' hatred of them. [trans. Friedrich Heer]

Ashkenazic misery increased in the thirteenth century, leading to the extinction of the venerable Jewish community in France and its offshoot, the smaller but once very prosperous Jewish population in England, because of three developments: the policy and attitude of King Louis IX (Saint Louis) of France; the formation of the new orders of friars; and the rise of Christian heresy and the effort of the papal inquisition to combat it.

Louis IX ruled France for almost five decades in the thirteenth century. Although his canonization as a saint was a political ploy developed by his grandson's government, he was indeed formally conscientious and pious, a brave (if militarily unsuccessful) crusader. He became the ideal monarch in the eyes of European society. But he was a vitriolic hater of the Jews, intent on humiliating them and removing whatever shred of dignity, prosperity, and protection remained from the glorious days of Charlemagne.

Saint Louis set the style for European kingship in the thirteenth century. He was the most admired, glamorous, and fabled king since Charlemagne. Louis provided a desirable image for all other kings, to many of whom he was related by marriage. He therefore legitimized persecution of the Jews for any king or lord who might be wavering on the Jewish question.

Thus the history of Ashkenaz can be set almost perfectly to open and close with a great French king: Charlemagne elevated the Jews; Louis devastated them. The prophet Samuel was right when he warned the Jews of his time not to put their trust in kings.

The New Piety was institutionalized in the early thirteenth century with the creation of two new religious orders of friars, the Dominicans and Franciscans. They were to be monastic service orders working in the world, not cloistered. The friars loomed large on the religious and cultural horizon of the thirteenth and later centuries. They devoted themselves to providing education, medical facilities, care for the homeless and poor, and other human services, especially in the burgeoning European cities.

In their service work in the cities the friars were bound to encounter the Jewish populations. Conversion of the Jews became one of their favorite projects. To achieve this purpose, they got kings to command rabbis to engage in public disputations with them before huge crowds. The expectation was that the friars would win the disputation (it did not always work out that way) and the Jews would flock to conversion. The main impact of these disputations was to stir up the populace against the Jews.

The papacy faced a real crisis in the early thirteenth century—the emergence in southern France of widely supported Albigensian (named after the town of Albi) Catharist (named after the Cathari, pure ones, the leaders of the separated community) heresy. Catharism revived the old Manichean dualist doctrine. There were two gods, one of light and one of darkness, struggling for the soul of mankind. Probably a quarter of the population of southern France by the second decade of the thirteenth century subscribed to this dualist theology and this counterchurch.

The papacy unleashed all its weapons to extirpate the Albigensian heresy: the friars' preaching, a crusade of northern French knights, and the papal inquisitions—special courts presided over usually by friars trained in canon law and theology to repress and condemn the heretics.

The courts of the inquisition used the characteristic features of Roman criminal law—secret informers and torture against suspected heretics. The inquisitions were not eager to use capital punishment but rather to persuade and frighten suspected deviants back into the Church. The defendant had to be recalcitrant or a triple recidivist to end up being "turned over to the secular arm," that is, the state, for burning.

The inquisitorial friars were mandated to pursue Christian heretics—which they did successfully—not Jews. But in Provence, which had a large, learned, and still wealthy Jewish community, Jews were swept up in the inquisitors' dragnet and were persecuted, pressured, and condemned by the inquisitorial courts.

This did not occur on a large scale, but it occurred. It is usually seen as an excess of prosecutorial zeal, attributed to an illicit blending of all possible enemies of the Church in a paranoid mania of persecuting fervor. Heretics, Jews, witches (old women or unmarried young women unwanted by their families), lepers (a catchall for any kind of social deviant, not just people with skin disease) were all confronted by the inquisitional courts and at the judgment of friar-judges removed from society by imprisonment or death.

This view of how the Jews became caught up in the inquisitorial net is substantially true, but it is only one side of the story. The Jews were not entirely innocent victims within the religious structure of southern France, nor was the inquisitorial friars' attack on them idiosyncratic and fortuitous.

The Jewish community of Provence was the place where the Cabala started. The rabbis of Provence vehemently rejected Maimonides's rationalism. Instead they supplemented traditional Halakic, Talmudic learning with a pastiche of mysticism, demonology, and astrology that came eventually to be called the Cabala. It moved to the Jewish community in northern Spain in the fourteenth century and there produced its definitive text, the *Zohar,* but its origins lie in Provence in the early thirteenth century, precisely at the same time as the flourishing of the Catharist heresy.

Gershom Scholem showed that the Cabala was a late continuation or revival of ancient Jewish Gnosticism of the first century A.D. or earlier. Gnosticism's roots lie probably in the ancient dualistic religion of Zoroastrianism or later Manicheanism in Iran, and the Jews may have brought it back with them from their exile in Mesopotamia and perpetuated it as an esoteric, hermetic set of doctrines. It was a powerful subversive religion that flourished among the early Christians as well as the Jews. The Gnostic community was the greatest internal threat that Christianity faced in the first two centuries of its existence.

Gnosticism is a pastiche of Persian dualism, Hellenistic astrology, and Neoplatonism mysticism. In the early thirteenth century it surfaced at the same time and in the same place, southern France, among both Christians and Jews. In the case of the Christians it takes the form of Catharism; among the Jews, of Cabalism.

The extensive overlap of the two religious cultures, hermetic among the Jews, but blatantly separatist among the Christians, is shown not only by the common dualist theology of God versus Satan but also by the belief of both religious movements in metempsychosis, or transmigration of souls.

It is likely therefore that the intellectual roots of the Albigensian heresy lie in Jewish neo-Gnosticism, the early phase of Cabalism in southern France. The attack upon the Jews by the papal inquisitors—and Pope Innocent III's determination at the Fourth Lateran Council of 1215 to segregate the Jews from Christian society—was due not only to general cultural and social developments but also specifically to the Jewish Gnostic involvement in the rise of Catharism. The Jews were therefore not entirely passive victims. When the inquisitorial friars went after them, there was an immediate cause.

The Jews were not just passive victims of the Church's onslaught but contributed to their own demise in another way. Among the first generation or two of Dominican friars—and the Dominicans staffed most of the posts in the inquisitorial courts—were a remarkable number of Jewish converts. The reason that the friars, Franciscans as well as Dominicans, could engage in lengthy debate with the rabbis in their public disputations in France and Spain was that these debating friars were almost invariably former rabbis or rabbinical students, or sons of rabbis.

We do not know the extent of conversion of Jews to Christianity in the High Middle Ages, but the rewards for a Jewish scholar making the great leap were high, and apparently some did, and became learned and polemical spokesmen for the Church against the Jews.

To a degree, therefore, the friars' attack on the Jews, pursued with frequent and learned use of Talmudic citations, constituted a split within the ruling elite of the Jewish people. A small but significant minority of the rabbinate went over to the Christian side for either idealist or opportunist reasons. A cultural civil war was being fought among the Jews in thirteenth-century France and later also in Iberia. We will probably never know what happened in detail, but it happened, that is for sure.

The public disputes between the reluctant rabbis, forced into these uncomfortable confrontations by a king whose assistance the bishops had solicited, and the friars, normally apostate rabbis or rabbinical students, have, at least from our point of view, their sardonically amusing sides. The friars pointed out that in ancient texts of the Talmud Jesus and Mary are mentioned, and this was supposed to provide the foundation for the decisive argument that the ancient rabbis knew about the life and death of Jesus and now the Jews should recognize the historicity of the Incarnation and convert en masse to the Church. The rabbis responded: Jesus and Mary, Yehoshua and Miriam? Just common Hebrew names. Yes, the old rabbis knew about a Jesus and Mary, but not *that* Jesus and Mary! Jewish humor was born. If the debating rabbis escaped with their lives from this encounter, they immediately set about excising all mention of Jesus and Mary from the Talmudic text so another apostate rabbi or delinquent rabbinical student turned friar couldn't throw it in their faces.

The Ashkenazic Jews were certainly victimized by the Catholic Church and its members. They were overwhelmed by a culture suffused with anti-Semitism. But the Jews were not entirely just the victims of Christian fervor and prejudice. They contributed to their own demise in two ways: the Cabalistic stimulation or at the very least compatibility with the Catharist heresy, and the turning of Jewish converts become prominent friars against their own families and former communities. It is a sad story, but it must be told. Detailed study of the period readily reveals this aberrative Jewish behavior, but it is normally ignored in general history of the Jews, presumably because it does not fit into the standard model of Jews as invariably passive victims.

By the second quarter of the thirteenth century the days of Ashkenaz were numbered. Anyone could see the future was gloomy, indeed hopeless. When Maimonides in later twelfth-century Spain encountered the lash of Muslim fundamentalism, he escaped with his family, going first to Morocco and then to a more benign atmosphere in Egypt. But Maimonides was a rationalist. The Ashkenazi rabbinate did nothing. They believed that the terrible deterioration of the status and security of the Jews in their charge was a sign of the coming of the Messiah. This was a characteristic figment of the medieval mind; the Christians were prone to it too. The worse things are, the better they will soon become. Salvation is imminent and will pierce the darkness by divine intervention.

In the Jewish context it is the syndrome of waiting quietly for the holocaust. Thus the Orthodox rabbinate failed to exercise leadership on behalf of the Jews in thirteenth-century Ashkenaz as they were to do again in twentieth-century Poland. Meanwhile the rabbinate drugged itself into comfort with the narcotic of the Cabala, an otherworldly withdrawal into astrology and demonology, considered fit only for those who had mastered traditional Talmudic learning. The Cabalistic hermetic pursuits of the rabbinate were an evasion of reality.

The reality was a grim one indeed. By the last decade of the thirteenth century the Jews were no longer useful to the English monarchy. They had lost their important position in moneylending. The crown had already bled them dry, and the Jews, after suffering several waves of pogroms, were no longer in a position to generate profits that the crown could tax heavily. King Edward I, Saint Louis's nephew, expelled them from his realm in the 1290s to create an excuse for one last Jewish payday, so that the royal treasury could seize most of their diminished capital before they left. The Jews were not readmitted to England until the middle of the seventeenth century.

In 1306 Saint Louis's grandson, Philip IV the Fair, expelled the Jews from France, effectively terminating the great community, renowned for business enterprise and Halakic learning from the time of Charlemagne to Rashi. Now this was all gone, and the Jews were to hit the road, again leaving behind most of their capital for the benefit of the crown. A few years later came a partial remission of the Jewish expulsion, and a sizable community developed in Alsace, on the border with Germany, which flourished until the twentieth century and the coming of the Nazis.

It was to Germany, across the Rhine, that most of the exiled Jews headed. Germany at the end of the thirteenth century was a country in name only. It consisted of some three hundred different political entities. The Jews expected they could always find at least a temporary home with one or another margrave, count, or prince-bishop. Either he would be enlightened enough to take pity on them, or he would need them for a while to pump up the economy of his principality. Or they could simply bribe him into offering them a refuge.

The first half of the fourteenth century was a flourishing era for the German Jews. They learned to speak a late medieval German dialect that with accretion of Hebrew words became their Yiddish vernacular. But disaster struck the German Jews as well.

In the middle of the fourteenth century the bubonic plague, the Black Death, decimated Western Europe, including western Germany. Between a quarter and a third of the population died painful and quick deaths. Contemporary medicine could not devise a remedy or even point accurately to the cause of the bubonic plague. The physicians thought it was spread through the air and advised people to shutter their windows and cover them with heavy tapestries. They advised against taking baths because opening the body's pores in a bath would let in the airborne particles that allegedly caused the plague. Not until the eighteenth century did Europeans again let fresh air into their houses and take baths instead of drenching their bodies in cologne and perfume to stifle the unwashed smell. (Only in the nineteenth century was it discovered that bubonic plague is spread by parasites that live on the skin of a certain species of rat.)

Anti-Semitism assigned the blame for the Black Death naturally to the Jews. If they could perform ritual murder on children, the Jews could also believably aim to kill the adult population by poisoning wells—that was held to be a source of the plague. Widespread pogroms in western Germany were the result.

The Jews pushed into eastern Germany where economic development lagged behind the principalities closer to the Rhine and powerful princes establishing centralized states could give the Jews some security if they could be persuaded to do so for idiosyncratic or socially advantageous reasons.

As eastern Germany developed economically in the late fifteenth century, however, the Jews were less welcome. Consequently they turned eastward to Poland. The Polish king and nobility held vast lands and ruled millions of newly enserfed peasants and could make varied use of the Jews. Hence the Jews were welcomed into Poland in the sixteenth century from Germany and Western Europe. Even Jews exiled from Spain in 1492 and those tired of the ghettos of northern Italy under the oppressive eye of the papacy found their way to Poland. Its green, fruitful, and underpopulated land seemed wonderful to the Jews.

By the end of the sixteenth century Poland was being hailed as the new golden land of the Jews, a salutation that one reads with eerie discomfort today, when the ashes of three million Polish Jews lie under its verdant soil, dumped there by the Nazis and their many Catholic Polish collaborators.

The Jews in sixteenth-century Poland repeated the previous economic and social history of Ashkenaz. They brought international trade and banking to a backward economy. But they also provided a special new service to the Polish ruling class, unique in the history of European Jews. They were made estate agents, sent out to the outlying properties of the nobility to govern the serfs and produce revenue for the lords. This the Jews did so well that when the Polish and Lithuanian crowns were joined in the mid-sixteenth century, the Jews moved into Lithuania and provided the same services there.

The Jews reached their zenith of wealth and social importance when around 1600 the Polish nobility opened up the frontier region of the Ukraine. The Jewish estate agents developed these potentially rich agricultural lands for their Polish lords, ruling over thousands of serfs, turning the virgin soil into marvelously wealthy grain-growing regions and returning immense profits to the absentee Polish and Lithuanian landlords.

The Jews were rewarded in various ways, but one benefit stands out. The Jews were given a monopoly on the liquor trade in rural Poland and the Ukraine. Only they had a license from the nobility for retail liquor sales, and they held long-term leases on the taverns in the peasant villages. Whenever a Polish or Ukrainian peasant wanted his necessary shot of vodka, he had to buy it from the Jewish tavern owner, whose markup in this monopoly situation was lucrative. The Jews had brought their Yiddish language with them from Germany, and they sang, "Shicker is a goy . . . trinker muss er" (The Gentile is a drunkard; he has to drink.)

More intellectual aspects of Askhenaz were transplanted in the Slavic lands. First Krakow, then Vilnius became great centers of Talmudic learning. The printing presses that in sixteenth-century Italy had begun to produce Hebrew prayer books, the multivolume editions of the Talmud, and the Torah with commentaries by Rashi and other sages, now appeared also in Krakow, Vilnius, and other Eastern European centers. Great yeshivas, schools of rabbinical learning, dotted the cold landscape of Poland and Lithuania.

As before the wealthy capitalists married their daughters to the most promising rabbinical students. Something was even done for Jewish daughters: They were taught to read Yiddish, and the printing presses produced biblical storybooks for them in that language.

The format of a strong Jewish communal organization was imported from Germany and further embellished. There was not only a kahal, an oligarchic council of capitalists and rabbis, for every Jewish community, but also two regional councils, one for Poland and the Ukraine, the other for Lithuania. They negotiated effectively with kings, nobility, and bishops. The Church in Poland, completely subservient to the aristocracy, left the Jews alone. The Jews were never happier.

By 1650, in a world Jewish population of not more than 1.5 million, close to two hundred thousand were already in Poland. But as early as 1560 a Jewish writer in Poland had warned that the Jews had to be careful: "The Jews in this time must not prosper too well in order to avoid becoming too proud, nor must they suffer too much punishment or they will vanish." In the middle of the seventeenth century severe punishment began.

Ashkenazic history had turned out beautifully. Then, overnight, disaster struck in 1648, another year of terror like 1096. One of many rebellions of Cossacks, a group of military freebooters, overcame weak resistance in the Ukraine and stirred up the repressed and exploited peasants against their lords. In practice this meant massacre of Jews who were the prime representatives of the absentee landlords on the Ukrainian frontier. The Ukrainian peasants were fired by the fierce anti-Semitism of their Greek Orthodox priests, a Judeo-phobia that goes directly back to the Greek Church of the early Middle Ages, which sent missionaries to convert them.

But the Ukrainians had a right to resent the Jews, if not to kill them. The Jews were the immediate instrument of the Ukrainians' subjection and degradation. The Halakic rabbis never considered the Jewish role in oppression of the Ukrainian peasants in relationship to the Hebrew prophets' ideas of social justice. Isaiah and Amos were dead texts from the past in rabbinical mentality.

Or perhaps the Jews were so moved by racist contempt for the Ukrainian and Polish peasantry as to regard them as subhuman and unworthy of consideration under biblical categories of justice and humanity. There is a parallel with the recent attitude of the West Bank Orthodox and ultra-Orthodox toward the Palestinians. Judaism can be in its Halakic form an extremely restrictive and blinding faith.

The Cossack rebellion under the formidable Bogdan Chmielnicki (still a great hero in the Ukraine) gathered force and swept into the heart of Poland itself before it was finally stemmed. Thousands of Jews were massacred, their homes destroyed, their communities dispersed, their imposing wooden synagogues burned to the ground.

Polish Jewry never recovered from this blow. They never regained their security, their self-confidence, their prosperity. By 1700 Poland's agricultural expansion had stopped and the Polish state also began to disintegrate, pulled apart by selfish, quarreling nobility. The Jews would sink with their Polish masters.

At the other end of Europe, in Christian Spain, Sepharad, another drama of rise and fall was playing itself out in the later Middle Ages.

The decline of a distinct Jewish community in Spain in the later Middle Ages generally paralleled the downfall of Ashkenaz, but its outcomes were more complex. Most of the Sepharad Jews remained in Spain and converted to Christianity instead of going into exile.

The story of the demise of Sepharad was much in the public mind in 1992 because of the many discussions of the significance of 1492 in the media and among academicians.

Three important events happened in 1492 in Iberia: the fall of Granada, the last Muslim territory in the Iberian peninsula, to the Spanish Latin Christian monarchy; the expulsion of the professing members of the Jewish religious community; and the first transatlantic voyage of Christopher Columbus. The deadline for exodus of the Jews and the beginning of the Columbian voyage occurred only one day apart. Granada fell half a year earlier. Five hundred years later it is worth contemplating the historical significance of these events and their possible meaning to us.

We have seen that the Muslims—an ethnically mixed group of Arabs, various Near Eastern peoples, and North African Berbers—conquered most of Iberia in 711 with help from the Jewish population, who for half a century had been experiencing severe persecution by the Spanish Visigothic kings at the behest of Catholic bishops. Between 900 and about 1140 Muslim Spain, an extremely diversified society ethnically and religiously, but under firm control of Arabic princes and united culturally by Arabic language and philosophic and scientific learning, flourished intellectually and economically, perhaps more remarkably than any other segment of the vast Muslim world that stretched from the Atlantic to India. Then after the renewed invasion of the Iberian peninsula by Berber tribes from the North African Maghreb, who were fundamentalist in religion and race conscious, internal deterioration of Muslim Spain set in during the late twelfth century.

The Christian princes in the north of the peninsula had been pursuing a *reconquista,* a military crusade to push the Muslims back, since the early eleventh century. In 1212 the Arab armies suffered as decisive a defeat as the Visigothic Christians had experienced in 711, and by 1265, of fabled Andalusia, only Granada, in the deep south, remained in Muslim hands, to fall to the Spanish monarchy of Ferdinand and Isabella in 1492. The conquest of Granada was the first important event of 1492.

We have seen that the Jewish population of Sepharad (Iberia) had flourished culturally under Muslim rule until the fundamentalist Muslim reaction after 1140. The greatest works of Jewish philosophy and theology produced in the Jewish Diaspora since Alexandria in the first century A.D., and the most impressive corpus of Jewish poetry, some written in Arabic and some in Hebrew, between the Bible and the late nineteenth century, were the products of Muslim Spain. Jews became important ministers of finance and ambassadors for Muslim rulers.

But even before the decisive Christian victory in 1212 there had been a northward movement of the Jews into the expanding Christian kingdoms. The Muslims under Maghreb rulers had become intolerant and their kingdoms unstable. The Christian rulers, despite contrary advice from the clergy, were highly tolerant of the Jews because they wanted their capital investment, their banking and commercial skills, and like the Muslim rulers before 1100 they employed aristocratic and learned Jews in high administrative positions.

This situation changed in the fourteenth century, leading up to the second great event of 1492, the expulsion of the Jews. The Jews of Spain and Portugal in the late fourteenth century—characteristically in the medieval world—were polarized into a mass of artisans and small shopkeepers on the one side, and an elite of wealthy businessmen, courtiers, scholars, and rabbis who married within these prominent families to form a closed caste on the other side. Increasingly, the rich Jews lost enthusiasm for traditional doctrines and observances, even among the scholars.

Rabbinical court records of the fourteenth century show a Jewish propensity to adapt to the lifestyle of Muslim society. Among the Sephardim, polygamy, concubinage, adultery, and wife-beating were common. Disenchanted by rationalistic philosophy and science after 1250, the Sephardic elite were intellectually attracted to the Cabala, which is usually defined as Jewish mysticism but which more accurately can be said to comprise Gnostic dualism, astrology, magic, and demonology. Between 1391 and 1420 there were repeated physical attacks by Christians on Jews on religious grounds, some of them spontaneous mob assaults, some organized attacks led by popular Church leaders such as Saint Vincent Ferrer.

As a result of these persecutions as well as a decline of enthusiasm for traditional (Talmudic) Judaism, by the second quarter of the fifteenth century more than half the Jewish elite and an unknown proportion of the Jewish masses—at least one hundred thousand people—had converted to Christianity. These included great merchants, government officials, and rabbinical scholars. Some of the scholars advanced to prominent roles in the clergy. A prominent fifteenth-century bishop of Burgos in Castile was a former rabbi, and his son became a bishop.

The Spanish laity who had been jealous of the Jews because of their favorable economic and political positions were anguished to see the Jews now prospering even more as New Christians, with their civil disabilities alleviated. The response was twofold: First, the idea was advanced that membership in the leadership rung of the Iberian community demanded "purity of blood" as well as religious correctness. Second, the New Christians were charged with being crypto Jews (Marranos, pigs) who were secretly practicing their religion (e.g., observing the Sabbath) and were therefore the worst kinds of heretics and betrayers of Christ who ought to be pursued by the religious court of the Spanish Inquisition.

In 1480 the pope reluctantly authorized the establishment of an inquisition—a special ecclesiastical court directed against heresy—in Spain to be directly under the control of the Spanish crown. Two special motives were involved in establishing the Spanish Inquisition. First, it was an instrument of centralizing royal power against the nobility, of whom the New Christian (converted Jewish) elite was an important segment. The state-controlled inquisition was a way of attacking the wealth, autonomy, and self-confidence of the nobility, among whom, by the sixteenth century, due to conversion and intermarriage, about a third was at least in part ethnically Jewish.

Second, the inquisition in Spain in the late fifteenth century, like the inquisitions in southern France in the thirteenth century, involved a fratricidal conflict within the Jewish population itself—between the

Jewish converts to Christianity and those who had remained loyal to the old faith. Again Jewish converts to Christianity condemned their former faith in public disputations with rabbis. After 1480 clergy from New Christian families were prominent among the inquisitors in the first generation of the inquisition (as they had also been, though proportionately and numerically less so, among the inquisitors in France in the early thirteenth century). Again the Jews had split and were devouring each other while the Christian state and the Gentile clergy urged them on. King Ferdinand, the most determined advocate of the inquisition, had a Jewish grandmother.

The number of people actually executed by the Spanish Inquisition in its whole history down to 1700 was relatively modest. We are not dealing with a Nazi Holocaust. After all, the inquisitors in theory did not want to kill anyone who sincerely confessed to being a crypto-Jew, accepted a punishment that could be light (public confession) or heavy (confiscation of property), and was not again convicted of being a Marrano.

No one would claim that the Spanish Inquisition was distinguished by sensitivity to civil liberties. It used torture to obtain evidence and it did not reveal to defendants the names of their accusers or allow the defendants to confront their accusers in open court. But use of torture to obtain evidence was standard procedure in all continental (civil as well as ecclesiastical) courts until the eighteenth century. And the defendants could give the inquisitors a list of their known enemies who were supposed to be removed from among their accusers. As for the use of the death penalty, that was common in the Middle Ages for the crime of heresy, and was used by Jews as well as Christians. The Jewish community in Cordoba and Seville in the eleventh century had also executed heretics with permission of the Muslim ruler.

The Marranos after 1480 only suffered execution by burning if they persisted in being loyal to Judaism or were repeatedly convicted of secretly being Jews. Probably half of these condemned Marranos were strangled before being burned.

The inquisitorial records are fragmentary, but historians estimate between two thousand and four thousand crypto-Jews were executed by the Spanish Inquisition between 1480 and 1520, and very few thereafter. As these figures indicate, most of the New Christians were sincere converts or at least behaved as conventional Christians, and both the paranoid claims of some inquisitors and the myths propagated by modern Jewish historians that most Jewish converts were actually Marranos (crypto-Jews) are fanciful.

Whether because of conviction or fear, the great majority of New Christians were unquestionably apostates, and within a generation or two rarely different in their religious commitments than the rest of the Christian population. Indeed not only were the great majority of Jewish converts sincere, but from among learned and aristocratic New Christian families came some of the greatest names in early sixteenth-century Spanish ecclesiastical and cultural history: Juan Luis Vives, the Erasmian humanist; Bartolomé de Las Casas, the apostle to the Native Americans and nemesis of the reckless conquistadors; Saint Teresa of Avila, reformer of the Carmelite order, the first female Doctor of the Church, and the teacher of Saint John of the Cross; as well as some leading bishops of the time, such as Hernando de Talavaro, the first bishop of Granada, formerly Queen Isabella's confessor.

It is not an exaggeration to see the role of scions of converted Jewish families as central to the Spanish Renaissance of the early sixteenth century, as were Jews in the modernist cultural revolution of the early twentieth century. In both cases complete access to general culture induced an explosion of intellectual creativity. The Jewish New Christians and their children in the early sixteenth century embraced Christian thought and learning with the same kind of creative enthusiasm as assimilated Jews contributed to modernism in literature and theory between 1900 and 1940.

The demand for expulsion of the Jews in the 1490s was justified on the grounds that as long as there were observant Jews in Spain, the converts would be tempted to return secretly to their religion, would be corrupted in their faith to betray Christ. Seizure of Jewish property by the crown was also a motive—as it had been in the expulsion of the Jews from England and France around 1300.

Here again we run into conventional myth—about the vast numbers of Jews who supposedly departed rather than undergo Christian baptism in 1492. Some prominent ones did depart, particularly Don Isaac Abrabanel, one of the two leading Jewish ministers of the crown. The other, Abraham Seneor, who helped finance Columbus's first voyage, converted. The number of Jews who departed in 1492 probably was only around forty thousand, about half the practicing

Jews left in the country in 1492. And the great majority of them initially didn't go far; they crossed over into Portugal. Although an expulsion or conversion order was issued by the Portuguese crown in 1497, it was loosely enforced until the mid-sixteenth century.

In the later sixteenth century Portuguese Jews moved in large numbers to Protestant Amsterdam (and from there a handful went to England, to which Jews were readmitted in 1653). The Spanish Jews who suffered the 1492 exodus if they did not go with the majority to Portugal went to Italy, particularly to Venice, Leghorn, and of all places Rome (the pope usually protected them—an old tradition on the Tiber and still in effect in the 1940s), and to Turkey.

The Ottoman sultan was eager to import Jews to boost the economy of his empire, and a significant number of the Jews who left Portugal in the sixteenth century found comfortable refuge in Turkish domains, particularly in Greece. The Salonika community, which the Nazis eliminated in the early 1940s, were descendants of these Sephardim.

The Sephardic Jews who left after 1492 for other Mediterranean countries took with them Ladino, a Castilian patois written in Hebrew letters, the equivalent of Yiddish for the Polish Jews, a German dialect written in Hebrew letters. There are still a very small number of Jews in Israel who can speak Ladino.

Of the descendants of the hundred and fifty thousand to two hundred thousand Jews who had lived in the Iberian peninsula in 1390, eighty percent were still in Sepharad in 1520, but they were now Christians. If Spain declined economically in the sixteenth century—a controversial proposition—it was not because of the exodus of the Jews, since the exodus was relatively marginal in dimension. There is no more prominent and persistent myth about 1492 than that the expulsion of the Jews ruined the Spanish economy, and thus retribution fell upon the Catholic monarchy. This is fiction, even if some Marranos, fleeing from the inquisition, continued to trickle out after 1500.

> Many of the Sefarad felt themselves to be more Catalan or Iberian than Jewish . . . They simply could not imagine leaving Spain. Their families had been [in Spain] too long, many of them for more than twenty generations, partaking in one of the world's most vibrant centers of Jewish culture, where their fore-

fathers had lived total, fulfilled lives. They had lost any sense of the Diaspora, of being outcast, wandering Jews. [Richard Schweid]

The small number of Jews who did flee Sepharad appear to have done as well, or better, abroad. Jewish capitalists, usually of Sephardic origin, became extremely important in northern Italian, Turkish, and Balkan commerce and industrial development after 1550. The Hapsburg Austrian cousins of the Spanish rulers in the seventeenth century made great use of these Jewish capitalists to finance the Thirty Years' War against Protestants in Central Europe and to supply the Hapsburg armies.

Jewish businessmen played a major role in the rise of the international mercantilist (state-controlled) form of capitalism in the early modern period. There is a definite Sephardic or Marrano ingredient in the rise of mercantilist-type capitalism, especially in Central Europe and the Adriatic region. This view of the role of the Marranos in early modern economic development was propounded by Ellis Rivkin in the 1960s and demonstrated in detail by Jonathan Israel in the 1980s.

The third great event of 1492 was the Columbian enterprise. It was, first of all, a direct outcome of the other two changes, the Muslim and Jewish ones. The Portuguese had already tried to undermine Arab wealth and power in the eastern Mediterranean by opening up a route around South Africa to India, the source of the silks, spices, and jewels that the Turks imported from East Asia and sold at great markups to the Western European nobility. The Portuguese were also trying to tap into the Arab dominance of the black African slave trade. They had success in the slave trade, and five years after Columbus's first voyage they rounded South Africa and opened the sea route to India and later established a great commercial center in the Goa, which they held until recent times.

Columbus offered to the Spanish crown another route to India across the Atlantic. He too was trying to override Muslim commercial wealth. The outcome of the Portuguese and Spanish seafaring was the decline of the Arabic Mediterranean world by the early seventeenth century. The Catholic powers were, however, in the seventeenth century forced to share the wealth of India and the African slave trade with the rising Protestant powers of Holland and England.

Whether Portuguese or Dutch, Jewish merchants played a visible although secondary role in the black slave trade, just as in early medieval Europe Jews had been prominent traffickers in white flesh.

Columbus's voyages were related also to the Jewish experience in Spain. He was descended, as he indicated in his will, from a Jewish convert family. He was, however, not trying to find a home for exiled Jews. He was trying to bring all history to a conclusion. There was a powerful messianic movement in the Spanish Church at the end of the fifteenth century. The old idea was that history would end and Christ would return only when the Church was fully triumphant in the world. Conversion of the Jews was one important sign of that totalization of Christianity. Another was the conversion of the peoples in the East, for which Columbus's voyages were intended to establish the basis. He took with him on his first voyage an Arabic-speaking Jewish New Christian to spread the faith in the Orient.

The Marranos suffered from the Christian idealism that Columbus exhibited. They were buffeted about between Judaism and Catholicism. Their families in many instances were disgraced and suffered loss of status and properties. The great majority of the Marranos stayed in Iberia and accommodated themselves to Catholicism, some with such zeal and capability that they emerged as leaders of the renaissance in Spanish Christian humanism in the early sixteenth century. But others resented what had happened and developed a new critical rationalism and skepticism.

A rationalist, scientific, antitraditional frame of mind, skeptical about the core of religious culture, arose among some Marrano families in the sixteenth and seventeenth centuries. The emergence of a post-Christian commonwealth secular mentality can be traced to a handful of Marrano families who found themselves caught between Judaism and Christianity, bouncing back and forth between the two faiths and cultures, until they became disoriented and disenchanted equally with priests and rabbis.

We can see this secularization with the Spanish New Christian Fernando de Rojas, the creator of the subversive picaresque novel (*La Celestina*) in the early sixteenth century, and the forerunner of Cervantes's critique of decaying medieval culture. We can see it in the skeptical humanism of the French humanist Montaigne, who was also of Marrano lineage. We can see it in the writings of two Dutch Jews of Portuguese extraction in the third quarter of the seventeenth century—Uriel da Costa, who condemned rabbinical Judaism and was excommunicated by the Jewish community of Amsterdam, and Baruch (Benedict) Spinoza, who turned away from the whole theistic tradition toward a new kind of scientific naturalism and universalism and was also excommunicated from the Jewish community.

The Marrano descendants who were buffeted about in the sixteenth century from one religion to another became alienated from both, and turned first to money-making in international mercantilist capitalism and then secular, scientific rationalism. They were immensely successful in these endeavors. A parallel can be drawn with the Jewish immigrants to America after 1890 from the traditionalist and Hasidic communities of Eastern Europe. They too abandoned devotion to their old faith and did extremely well in business and science and embraced doctrines of radical secularism.

The great weakness of late medieval Judaism was its finite, static quality. Its only innovative wing was in hazardous theosophic irrationalism. It could not offer a durable response to persecution and discomfort or a comprehensive social theory. At the same time those many Sephardic Jewish intellectuals who, after 1390, for whatever initial motive, proceeded to cross over into Christianity, found in Latin Christian culture a much more complex and vibrant culture that they eagerly embraced and pushed in obsessive eschatalogical directions. But this high idealism soon ran into the realities of sixteenth-century politics and economics. The reach of the Spanish state toward world power, abetted by the intensely exploited wealth of America, made the heavily conversos-shaped humanistic Iberian Christianity of around 1500 incapable of practical realization.

The Jewish New Christians in Spain committed themselves to a late medieval flowering of Christian idealism precisely at the time when it was being countervailed by the expansion of commercial capitalism, the rise of overseas empires, and the further social realities of the absolutist state and international power politics. To some descendants of Marrano families who had left Sepharad, especially those who had become disillusioned with both rabbinic Judaism and medieval Catholicism, the changed environment that prevailed in Western Europe by 1600 signified a paradigmatic cultural shift that groped its way to a new, much more secular and rationalist ethos.

Roots of cultural modernity lie in the Marrano culture of the seventeenth century. This came about because of the disillusionment with both Judaism and Catholicism that had sought to envelop them, and because the Marrano families were affluent, resourceful, well-educated, and cosmopolitan in their outlook.

Uriel da Costa's critique of rabbinical Judaism looks back to medieval Jewish sectarian opposition to the rule of the Talmudic rabbis, and forward to the reform and liberal Judaism of the nineteenth and twentieth centuries. Baruch Spinoza (1632–77) went further than da Costa, his fellow excommunicate from the Jewish community of Amsterdam. Spinoza developed the first historical critique of the Bible and brought into question the veracity of its claim to be a credible account of Jewish origins in the second millennium B.C. Spinoza anticipated the higher criticism of the Bible that developed in the nineteenth century and all the modern biblical analysis that communal Jewish culture, even in its more liberal form, still finds difficult to accept.

In this philosophical work Spinoza established the intellectual foundations of the eighteenth-century Enlightenment by advancing a pantheistic view of divinity as immanent in nature and an ethics derived from pure logic and not revelation.

Spinoza replaces Jewish transcendence of God with the principle that "God is in the world and the world is in God." Nature "is a particular way in which God himself exists," and human consciousness "is a particular way in which God himself thinks" [Hans Küng].

What was important was not so much Spinoza's particular arguments but the severely rationalistic and scientific tone of his writing. This scientific rationalism was not unknown in his day but he propounded it with singular clarity and eloquence and can therefore be regarded as the great forerunner of the eighteenth-century Enlightenment and beyond, the liberal rationalist proponent of scientific culture in the modern world.

> Spinoza . . . became the first European of importance who transcended the universe of revealed religion while presenting it with a powerful systematic alternative. His move encapsulated the principle of modernity in a most radical form. [Yirmayahu Yovel]

The Amsterdam rabbis, whether justified or not in their draconian action against Spinoza, were right to see in his work a cultural revolution that constituted a fundamental threat to traditional Judaism, ultimately more perilous than the conventional Christian anti-Semitism, which was waning in the Protestant, in some ways philo-Semitic, atmosphere of capitalist Holland.

Pressured intellectually and emotionally between Judaism and Christianity, a segment of expatriate Marranos endured such shock to their intellectual system that they went beyond the medieval veil and emerged into modernity. This is the meaning in historical perspective of Spinoza's philosophy.

It was a turning point in Jewish history that was only marginally glimpsed at that time. Two hundred years later it would be seen as the central issue in the cultural ambience of the Jews, and that view still exists today. The fundamental question that Spinoza—and to a somewhat lesser extent Uriel da Costa—raised was: How can Judaism be rethought and restructured in the context of modern science and rationalist ethos?

Only in Western Europe were these critical issues addressed to the foundations of Judaism broached. Only in Western Europe did Jewish culture significantly develop beyond a Halakic and Talmudic phase and encounter the rationalism and science of modernity, forcing a reconsideration of that cultural structure that late antique and medieval rabbinical Judaism had established.

It was not simply that in the eighteenth and nineteenth centuries Jews came to live in Western Europe in an increasingly secular culture and felt compelled to respond to it. The development of later Sepharad and Marrano culture already stimulated a transvaluation in the Jewish mentality.

The Iberian Jews who became Christians contributed powerfully to the Catholic humanism of the late fifteenth and sixteenth centuries. Those who departed for Protestant Holland developed in a few generations an anticipatory liberal Judaism (da Costa) and a radical scientific rationalism (Spinoza). In terms of intellectual advancement of the Jews, if not often their personal security and comfort, the European environment was beneficial in forcing their intellect to focus on the leading edge of Western culture. This was a development to be writ large in the late nineteenth and twentieth centuries when Jews stood at the forefront of creativity in science and the arts.

What was there in the Western European ambience that induced this intellectual vitality in the Jews? Three factors were at work. First, in one way or another the Jews were forced out of the intellectually suffocating encasement in Halakic culture that, whatever its virtues in terms of communal solidarity and personal satisfaction, had become a conservative, anti-intellectual ethos looking to preservation and continuity rather than innovation and intellectual creativity. Maimonides's failure to achieve a socially approved synthesis of science and Halakic Judaism proved that, and the Orthodox rabbis never made another attempt at this intellectual level, turning instead to the soft theosophy of the Cabala.

Secondly, the presence of missionary and militant Christianity where the Jews of Western Europe lived forced them to engage in fundamental intellectual inquiry and speculative reconsideration of their value system. As the social other in the Christian world, the Jews had to examine dialectically their relationship to the dominant religious culture. In this regard, the more hospitable ambience of Protestant Holland was only marginally different from the hostile ambience of Catholic Iberia.

Finally, the corrosive impact of commercial capitalism developed in early modern Europe to the takeoff point that its ethical and behavioral implications could no longer be insulated from traditional Judaism. This insulation had been possible in the Muslim Mediterranean society between 900 and 1250. The Jews then, in the Goitein-genizah world, separated their economic lives from their religious and moral ones, living calmly as bifurcated beings. But the European commercial capitalism of the sixteenth and seventeenth centuries, powered by the mercantilist state, a vast influx of overseas capital, and significant urbanization, entered that dynamic phase when the mobility of wealth breaks all barriers that communal institutions and family boundaries can erect and demands that the individual reconstruct his assumptions about the world relative to the domineering secular market and the liberal, scientific, and material conditions that the market fosters.

This transformation was beginning among the Jews of Amsterdam in the mid-seventeenth century. There occurred the staging ground, the forecast of Jewish modernity. It continued among the capitalist court Jews of Germany in the seventeenth and early eighteenth centuries. It developed into the German Jewish Enlightenment of the late eighteenth century, the inauguration of modern Jewish culture.

The conventional talk about the golden age of Spain is therefore vulnerable from a sociological viewpoint. Whatever their literary accomplishments, the Mediterranean Jews of the Goitein-genizah world did not break out of the cultural mold of Talmudic times. It is only in Christian Western Europe between the fifteenth and seventeenth centuries that the breakout began, first in Iberian Jewish Christian humanism, and perhaps more important in the long run, in post-Christian, post-Halakic, Marrano culture.

That the turning point in Jewish cultural history away from a medieval Talmudic, Halakic, rabbinically based culture to a modern secular one makes its appearance among Marrano descendants in Calvinist Amsterdam raises the question of the impact of the Protestant Reformation in Jewish history. In the sixteenth century about a third of the population in Christian Western Europe separated itself from the Roman Catholic Church, the old enemy of the Jews, and set up their own diverse religious communities.

Was this a meliorative development for the Jews? Not necessarily. Marrano families, including those professing Judaism or thinly hiding it under a veil of Catholic conversion, rose to prosperity in the seventeenth century in service to the devoutly Catholic Hapsburg Austrian dynasty as it struggled to recover territory in Central Europe from the Protestants, and did so successfully in the case of Prague, thereby setting off the international conflict called the Thirty Years' War.

The Jewish capitalists not only served as bankers to the Hapsburgs, but also made fortunes as contractors or suppliers of material to the Hapsburg armies, one of whose main efforts earlier was directed largely unsuccessfully—against Protestant Holland. Therefore the Jews did not necessarily suffer at the hands of the intransigent Catholics in the Counter-Reformation.

Nor did they necessarily fare well in treatment by Protestants. Martin Luther, who started the break with Rome in northern and eastern Germany in the second decade of the sixteenth century, appeared at first friendly toward Jews, but that was because this volatile ex-monk and theology professor expected the Jews would convert to the Lutheran church. When this did not happen, Luther summoned out of his cultural background the vestigial anti-Semitism of the German bourgeoisie. He unleashed a torrent of abuse and hatred on the Jews that equaled anything produced in the Catholic Middle Ages. Luther's anti-Semitic pamphlets left a heritage of Judeo-phobia in the German national church he founded and were effectively cited by the Nazis in the 1930s.

The Anglican (Episcopalian) attitude toward the Jews was more humane and understanding than Luther's attitude but also hostile to the Jews at the bottom line. The Anglican attitude was enshrined for all time in William Shakespeare's *The Merchant of Venice* (c. 1600). Shakespeare dramatized the Anglican view of the Jews at a time when very few Jews lived in England. Hence the play is set in Italy. Shakespeare brilliantly articulates that Shylock, the Jewish usurer, is a human being and has the feelings of a human being. If you cut him, he bleeds too. But Shylock cannot escape the behavior pattern of the mischievous, domineering Jewish capitalist when he can put someone at a disadvantage. The Jews are not organically devils, as many late medieval Catholics thought, but their behavior pattern is unacceptable within the confines of Christian society.

Drawing upon the neoclassical culture of the Renaissance and serving the interests of the princely state that protected them, the early Protestant groups, the Lutherans and Episcopalians, focused on the ideal of normalization in society. Against the vestiges of medieval pluralism, they wanted a systematic, controlled cultural uniformity imposed on society at all class levels. Their Protestantism was the social policy of the centralizing, culturally normalizing Leviathan state.

In this context the Jews were an archaic anomaly both socially and religiously and could not be tolerated. They had to be converted and their behavior pattern normalized. This is the idea that lies behind Shakespeare's subtle and provocative Jewish drama.

The Jews were a sore point in the Lutheran and Anglican state not only because of their faith and behavior, but because they represented for the Protestant ideologists all that was wrong in loose, disorganized medieval pluralism.

But the Calvinist reformed churches emerging in the late sixteenth century, especially in Holland and England, were different in their Jewish policy. The Calvinists were close readers of the Old Testament and taught a bleak image of a wrathful, judging, and omniscient and omnipotent God that accorded well with Jewish tradition. Calvinist societies were sympathetic to market capitalism as a sign of God's grace working in the world.

There was a millennial fervor among the latter-day Calvinists, a sense of the coming end of time. These qualities did not necessarily lead to a more favorable attitude toward the Jews; theoretically it could have gone the other way. But shaped by a Calvinist elite that favored an ethic of hard work, rational application of communal standards to individual behavior, and postponed gratification, a comity of attitude emerged in the early seventeenth century between the ruling capitalist oligarchy in Amsterdam and the rabbinical-capitalist oligarchy that controlled power in the Jewish community. Not only did the Jews of Amsterdam prosper, but Calvinist England readmitted them in 1653, for the first time officially since the 1290s.

The initial settlement in London was that of Marrano families from Holland. In the eighteenth century, as Protestantism in every denomination became more tolerant and more rationalistic in viewing the divinity, there was an opportunity for close contact between the Jews in Western Europe and the Protestant groups. This was not a matter of theology; it was more a meeting of the two groups in a common personal lifestyle and mentality, that of the proto-modern liberal bourgeoisie.

Everywhere that Calvinism spread after 1600—Holland, England, Scotland, and overseas to the United States, English-speaking parts of Canada, and South Africa (a Dutch colony until 1815, and British thereafter)—the Jews prospered in business and were given the opportunity in the nineteenth century to enter the learned professions. The Calvinists were too Christian to regard the Jews as fully their equals. But they showed the Jews more than tolerance; they accorded them a dignified respect. This was because of Calvinist inclination to the Old Testament literary text in its covenant theology; because the Calvinists and the Jews agreed that business success was a blessing from God and a sign of the worth of the entrepreneur in God's eyes; and because both religious groups admired the patriarchal family, hard work, social intelligence, rational calculations, and puritanical postponed gratification.

While this Jewish/Calvinist ethos is no longer fashionable and receives heavy (and on the whole accurate) condemnation as the mentality conducive to market competition and nineteenth-century imperialism, it did have a long and influential run. It is the juncture at which the Protestant Reformation and the heritage of medieval Ashkenaz and Sepharad came together. Someone growing up in the English-speaking part of Canada in the 1940s would have encountered the Scots Presbyterian Sunday, when by law there were no movie houses or football games to attend. Sunday was supposed to be, in the good old Edinburgh Calvinist tradition, a day of prayer, study, and meditation. No Jew could find this strange or objectionable: It was just the Jewish Sabbath idea, except they had gotten the day of the week wrong.

CHAPTER SEVEN

The Jewish Reformation

Both Jewish and Christian societies experienced a long series of religious upheavals over many centuries before the emergence of the modern secular technological and democratic worlds in the later eighteenth century. We may call these waves of spiritual quests and doctrinal controversies reformations.

A series of disruptive efforts aimed to restructure religious beliefs and communities among both Jews and Christians, so as to "reform" the prevailing thought-world and social institutions that served them. Without abandoning the fundamental precepts of the traditional religious systems, parallel reformations in Jewish and Christian societies sought to make these received cultures and their systemic expressions more responsive to the needs and modified aspirations of the populace.

In premodern society, religious reformation is the most convenient way of legitimating rebellion against autocracy and oligarchy. The proponents of reformation make a claim to superior moral value and fresh divine inspiration for a radical, popular movement against traditional systems and old dominant elites.

Religious reformation is therefore the normal avenue for group and class rebellion in the old regime of premodern society, a way by which a group of discontented intellectuals, who feel displaced from power, asserts its claim to a share of power and attempts to gain suitable recognition of the group's conceptual capability.

Through religious reformation an emerging and discontented social group gives itself a sense of identity and moral purpose and confronts governmental institutions and an older, now mature and oligarchic elite.

Reformation is the vehicle by which dissident and novice professionals, fearing their incapacity to meet rigid conventional standards for job entry, alter the admission standards to a set that they can meet, since the standards are rewritten to stress what they do well and easily.

The Christian Reformation is conventionally identified with the Protestant churches and sects of the sixteenth and seventeenth centuries. But the Christian Reformation extended for six centuries, beginning with Catharist and other heretical movements in the late twelfth century and concluding only with Methodism, German Pietism, and the American Great Awakening in the late eighteenth century. The Christian Reformation also embraced movements of reform within the Catholic Church during the late sixteenth and seventeenth centuries, especially related to the rise of the Jesuit order and the papacy.

The Jewish Reformation was a series of religious movements within, on the margin of, or self-consciously critical of but still closely related to Halakic (traditional-rabbinical-Orthodox) Judaism. The Jewish Reformation stretches from Karaism in the tenth century to Hasidism in the eighteenth century. Each phase of the Jewish Reformation was marked by efforts to modify in some significant way Halakic Judaism, just as the Christian Reformation offered modifications of medieval Christianity.

In both religious cultures, Jewish and Christian, the reforming movements and groups were not calling into question the essentials of the old faith. They were trying to amend or supplement some of its secondary characteristics and claimed to make it thereby more vital, meaningful, and authentic. They claimed to be rescuing a more inspirational and pristine spiritual force, now overlaid by alleged improper accretions, from fossilizing and entropic characteristics of recent development. The old religion, Judaism or Christianity, would be reborn and returned to the rightful path of fulfilling its original mission, they asserted.

This was the essential motif in all movements of both series of reformations. The Jewish Reformation shared this sociological identity with the Christian Reformation and ran chronologically alongside it for many centuries. Now and again they impinged on each other, but for the most part the two reformations were autonomously parallel and categorically similar rather than empirically interactive.

The Christian and Jewish reformations arose from a similar set of social, political, and cultural conditions. The European Christian world was controlled by kings, lords, and clergymen. Jewish society was under the tight control of rabbis, capitalists, and court Jews. In both Christian and Jewish societies, intellectuals, if they wanted to secure power, prosperity, or even significant visibility, had to accommodate themselves to these dominant groups and satisfy their stiff entry requirements.

In both societies ordinary people lived in the tight encasement of a local community—what the Jews called the kehillah or kahal—that were protective and stable but were also oligarchic engines of repression, overtaxation, and thought control.

What the reformations, both Jewish and Christian, sought to do was to legitimate and elaborate alternate circuits of expression and claims to power based on novel or modified religious doctrines. A religious movement sought to destabilize the ruling oligarchy and displace or at least loosen up its institutional system by offering an alternative value system, based, however, on familiar religious assumptions.

Using religious claims in this way made it more difficult for the oligarchies of the old social regime to dismiss as alien or unacceptably revolutionary the demands and ambitions of the reforming group. The trend was usually to deal, to negotiate, with the reformers and co-opt them into the prevailing system, now loosened only slightly at the perimeter. The reformers had the problem that their constituencies could not see significant advantage for themselves in these sidebar negotiations, and pressed for more fundamental change.

Another function of the reformation was to break down the local encasement in corporate communities and transfer issues and action to a more regional or national or even international level, where change might be more rapid and reward for repressed groups more readily decided upon.

Ideologically, it could be said that all the waves and segments of both the Christian and Jewish reformations had two aims perpetually in common: first, to reconstruct and revitalize old faiths to make them more credible, authentic, and dramatically responsive in the face of rising capitalist materialism and a developing market economy that would corrode traditional values and familiar lifestyles; and second, to find a way by which individual consciousness and personal sensibility might be more immediately expressed and legitimized while integrating this individuality within a close-knit spiritual community fastened together by loyalty to a text or a charismatic spiritual teacher.

The Jewish and Christian reformations could not come very close to meeting these ambitious and ambiguous goals, and hence the heritages of the reformations were heavily eroded by manifestations of secular, democratic, and technological modernity in the nineteenth century.

But in the meantime the reformations threw off important cultural forms and phenomena that had long-term currency. Some of the textual and charismatic communities sufficiently embedded themselves in society and culture by the intrinsic strength of their discourse and the subtlety of their dealing with the old oligarchies so that they managed to survive, normally in attenuated form, to the present day.

The first movement of reformation in Judaism was Karaism, which emerged in ninth-century Mesopotamia and within a century had became a great force in the Near East, threatening the authority of the rabbinates, the supporters of the Talmudic rabbis. Saadia Gaon devoted a great deal of his time to combating the Karaites. They were heavily influenced by Arabic thought and developed a doctrine of rejecting the oral law and the Talmud, and accepting only the Tanach, the Bible, as their authority, which was furthermore to be normally interpreted literally.

Along with attacking the rabbis, the Karaites assailed the "rich of the Diaspora" and "the merchants of the Diaspora," who were the oligarchic allies of the rabbis. The Karaites were fervent Zionists. Emerging originally in Iraq, then gaining strength in Persia, they developed initially through immigration a large community in Palestine.

The Karaites suffered a crippling blow from the victory of the French crusaders in Jerusalem in 1096. The majority of the Jews slaughtered by the crusaders when they took the city were probably

Karaites. Subsequently they developed strength in the Crimean and Black Sea regions of Russia, and Karaites survived in Russia into the twentieth century. After the founding of the state of Israel in 1948 a group of Karaites, continuously in Egypt since medieval times, migrated to Israel, where they have lived quietly.

The story is that the Karaite sect was founded by a certain Anan after a dispute over succession to titular leadership of the Mesopotamian community. However it was started, the Karaites' point of view—the Bible as the sole inspired text; literal reading of it; and opposition to the established clerisy—closely parallels the views of early sixteenth-century Protestantism, and their proclivity also to rationalism and science looks like later Protestantism. Obviously the main cause of Karaism was restless opposition to the rabbis and their rabbinate supporters.

The Karaite movement may indeed have originated in a personal struggle over communal leadership, but it soon developed an ideology to counter the rabbis' authority by denying the canonical force of the Talmud, whose interpretation gave the rabbis much of their power.

Goitein thinks the Karaite schism was "a great rejuvenating force in Judaism" by forcing the rabbis to become more learned and literate. In that regard an exact parallel exists between the impact of Karaism and the impact of Protestantism on the sixteenth-century Catholic Church. The Protestant schism forced the Counter-Reformation Church to improve delivery of its religious services, as Karaism did among the Jews in the eastern Mediterranean in the tenth and eleventh centuries.

By the eleventh century a degree of accommodation had developed between the two groups, the rabbinates and the Karaites. The latter persisted theoretically in their biblical fundamentalism, but in practice they accepted, in their words, "the burden of inheritance" of rabbinical Judaism and its customary law. This eventual accommodation between the Orthodox rabbis and the Karaite reformers is a common development in religious reformations. The two groups stop fighting each other and learn to live together and accept each other, as was the case of Catholics and Protestants after 1650.

The second segment of the Jewish Reformation was the rise and dissemination of the Cabala between 1200 and 1600. The Cabala is often called Jewish mysticism, and that designation is not wrong if it is simply intended to mean a religious trend toward the irrational and one that employs inspirational feeling to compound tradition and law. But mysticism in the Christian tradition was an outgrowth of Neoplatonism, and this signified the effacing the material world and personal consciousness, and the ascent of the individual to the divine, purely spiritual godhead.

This kind of mystical theology did exist in Judaism. It can be found in the Alexandrian Philo in the first century A.D. and the Sephardi Solomon ibn-Gabirol in the eleventh century. The Cabala was so syncretic, it absorbed such a variety of religious and intellectual traditions as it developed, like some megaton electromagnet rolling across the cultural landscape, that it cannot be said that such a negativist, self-effacing mysticism is entirely absent from the parameters of this demonological and theosophical pastiche.

But the essence of the Cabala was different from Neoplatonic mysticism. It focused not on ethereal realms but on reconstruction of this world. It looked downward as much as upward, perhaps more downward than upward, while Neoplatonic mysticism was directed only upward.

The roots of the Cabala lie not in Platonism but in ancient Gnosticism, the dualist religion perceiving the world as a struggle between the god of light and the god of darkness. By whatever means, perhaps as an esoteric theosophy preserved through late antiquity and the early Middle Ages by the more cerebral rabbis, it surfaced in the Jewish community in Provence in southern France around 1200. The struggle of the rabbis there against Maimonides's rationalism brought this neo-Gnosticism much more into the open. The French rabbis asserted that if a supplement was needed to the traditional Halakic faith, it should not be perilous scientific rationalism but the theosophy of the Cabala. They preserved it still as a special study only for the most learned and devout, but they developed there the first texts of the new culture.

The Cabala posited the world as the scene of a cosmological struggle between Yahweh and Satan, contending—in sexual imagery—for the feminine Shekinah, God's shadow in the world that makes for good and evil in human lives. At a certain point God partly withdraws from the world. There is a condition of *tzimtzum,* divine contraction. Satan then has his moment of damaging triumph, and the breaking of the vessels—the constitutive structure of the world—occurs. But as the vessels rain down in shattered pieces, the *kellipot*—the shells—are conjoined to particles of light from the now restored or reinvigorated God.

A process of *tikkun,* or healing, occurs, by which the world is slowly brought back to the triumph of divine order. This struggle between good and evil goes on in each individual; man is a microcosmic replication of the cosmological drama.

All sorts of variants can be worked on this mythology, but that is the essence of it. It is an attractive drama, intended to be infinitely more personally meaningful and persuasive than Aristotle's mechanistic naturalism.

One of the most insightful explanations of the Cabala was offered by the American abstract expressionist painter Barnett Newman in the 1950s and 1960s. He perceived that the spirit of Cabalism involved not expansion and thinning out of spirit, but enclosure, compaction, the drawing inward of spirit into the thickest texture imaginable, and it is therefore amenable to communication in painting of an abstract kind. Cabalism in Newman's perception is represented by the kind of thick color field that he painted. Cabalism represents spiritual implosion, not explosion, the concentration of sensibility and intelligence into the tightest of packages.

The spread of the Cabala was given a big boost in the midthirteenth century when it was endorsed by Nachmanides, the renowned rabbinical leader of the Jews in Aragon, the expanding and powerful Christian kingdom in northern Spain. In the mid-fourteenth century in Sepharad, the canonical text of the Cabala, the *Zohar,* was put together by Moses de Leon. It is full of complex imagery, subtle distinctions, and elaborate metaphors.

The *Zohar* takes the form of conversations of Rabbi Simeon ben Yohai, who established the great school of rabbinical learning in Judea after the destruction of the Second Temple in A.D. 70, and his entourage. Modern scholars like Gershom Scholem and Yitshak Baer have no doubt that this is a work of the theosophical imagination and historically has nothing to do with Rabbi Simeon. They also suggest influence upon Moses de Leon of the Spiritual Franciscans, the radical, hypermystical wing of the Catholic Franciscan order.

The essential theosophical Gnostic dualism in the universe and microcosmically within man comes through clearly enough in the *Zohar:*

The Shekinah being thrust out, another Spirit comes and hovers over the world, bringing with it corruption . . . The flesh reminds us of the evil side of the universe . . . The deep mystery of Celestial Man is within . . . When the righteous are affected by illness or sufferings, it is that all the sinners of their generation may receive redemption.

This is not a departure from traditional Judaism. It is a reinterpretation of it, a particular reading of it. The rhetoric and imagery are reminiscent of Christian Gnosticism and medieval Catharism—not surprising, because the Cabala and these Christian heresies have common, interactive derivations.

What made the Cabala persuasive in a prescientific, pretechnological society (and why comparable New Age theosophists remain popular today) is that it offered explanations for observed experience at both cosmological and anthropological levels. The persistent evil in the world, the imminence of climatic, economic, and other disasters could be ascribed to a time of the breaking of the structural vessels of the universe and the intrusion of satanic force. At the human level, the duality of personality between the flesh and the spirit, especially as exhibited in sexual behavior, could be seen as the cementing together of the mean shells with the redeeming points of light. The libido could be assigned to material shells—in Yiddish vernacular *kellipah* came to be a synonym for evil in human nature.

Or, more boldly, the sex drive could be attributed to the redeeming light, and promiscuity, in challenge to Halakic strictures, could thereby be justified. Copulation was doing God's work, was part of the healing of the world. Cabalism, anticipating Freud, was used to justify a liberated libido.

The shock of the disappearance of Sepharad at the end of the fifteenth century through mass apostasy and exile gave additional impetus to the popularity of Cabalistic doctrine among learned Jews. Along with its cosmological and personal planes, the Cabalistic idea was now historicized. What had happened in Spain was viewed as a kind of breaking of the vessels and the onset of the temporary rule of Satan. God's providence in history had suffered *tzimtzum*, contraction, to be rectified by an imminent messianic reversal of fortune. Messianic, apocalyptic, and millennial speculation increased in the sixteenth century and frequently was expressed in dramatic Cabalistic imagery.

In response to apparent Cabalistic popularization, its moving out of esoteric study and into more common discourse, traditional orthodoxy more vigorously stressed Halakic behavior. The new instrument of dissemination of religious information was the printing press, which Jews in northern Italy took up early in the sixteenth century. It was used by Jews in Holland and Poland by the early seventeenth century and was skillfully applied by the upholders of the Orthodox mainstream (although it was also possible to hold fast to this mainstream and also be a Cabalist).

The printing presses not only issued the Talmudic text (with some excision of anti-Christian passages) but also Joseph Caro's mid-sixteenth-century textbook of personal, family, and communal behavior along traditional lines—the *Shulchan Orach* (the well-prepared table). This neoconservative book is still canonical in Orthodox circles today.

But the *Zohar*, the classic Cabalistic text, was also issued by the Jewish printing presses and thereby made much more easily available. Given the tumultuous circumstances of the times, with Sepharad having disappeared and Marranos relocating themselves in Turkey, Greece, Italy, and Holland, and finding new capitalistic opportunity as suppliers and bankers to Catholic as well as Protestant sides in the Christian wars of religion, the Cabala continued to gain adherents and move to a central place in Jewish culture.

It was a time when the synagogue liturgy, a lengthy pastiche of biblical quotations and medieval prayers, austere and repetitive, interspersed with cantorial chants similar to Catholic Gregorian chant, became canonically fixed. It is the same liturgy that is still used in Orthodox and Conservative synagogues and in mercifully abbreviated form in Reform communities. With this liturgical rigidification, the reading and discussion of the more provocative and glamorous Cabala received an increased impetus.

At the same time that Caro was preparing his jejune guidebook to Halakic behavior, in northern Palestine, on the edge or the Golan, in Safed—an old center of rabbinical culture, and still one today— a new formulation of Cabalistic theosophy and astrological and demonological mysticism was devised by Isaac Luria. By the early seventeenth century the Lurian text had penetrated to Jewish communities all over Europe and the Mediterranean.

The Cabala in the Lurian formulation was less restricted to a learned and elite audience. It filtered down to more common levels of literate Jews and became the textual focus of a new phase in the Jewish Reformation.

Indeed the Cabala now received wide distribution and close study in the Christian world by, among others, the English Protestant poet and polemicist John Milton. The popularity of the Cabala in the Christian Reformation helps to explain the peculiar era of philo-Semitism that marks the middle and later decades of the seventeenth century, especially in Protestant England (which readmitted Jews in 1653) and Holland.

It is the much disputed thesis of Gershom Scholem that the wide dissemination of Lurian Cabalism was the main impetus to the messianic movement that roiled the Jewish world from Turkey and Greece to Italy, Holland, Germany, and Poland in the later seventeenth century, its echoes and reverberations continuing beyond that time. In Scholem's view, the most dramatic and influential outbreak of messianism centering on Sabbatai Zebi in 1665–66 was an effort to turn Lurian Cabalism into a movement of activist reformation in Jewish life.

This Cabalistic impetus seems to have been central to the Sabbataian movement, but other causes were also at work. Stephen Sharot has stressed the contextual impact of what historians call "the crisis of the seventeenth century." A half-century of general economic depression began around 1625 and fell very hard upon the Jewish commercial capitalists along with many Christian ones. The distraught Jewish entrepreneurs, important community leaders as they usually were and closely tied to the rabbinate, sought an alternative to fiscal misery in apocalyptic messianism. This explanation seems plausible.

A third explanation for the upsurge of messianism in the form of the Sabbataian movement can be offered by pointing to the most common social groups who adhere to religious reformations: The poor, downtrodden, and socially marginal at one end of the class spectrum are joined by a group at the other, affluent societal pole, the relatively wealthy who are, however, not yet empowered and do not have high status in the community despite their economic success. Either this disfranchised affluent group is too nouveau riche to be absorbed into the circle of oligarchic power or they do not have sufficient education and literacy to be legitimized as communal leaders. The latter type was especially prevalent in the Jewish world, where a high degree of literacy and learning was preferred along with wealth for access to membership in the rabbinical-capitalist oligarchy of the kehillah, the community structure.

From information provided in Scholem's detailed biography of Sabbatai Zebi, this latter group was significantly prevalent among those who hysterically hailed Sabbatai as the messiah. This upscale group was joined by poor people who were desperate and alienated from a Jewish society that charitably assured them of sustenance but deprived them of self-confidence and communal power.

The fourth cause for the rise of Sabbatai Zebi and the messianic movement was the Chmielnicki pogroms in Poland in 1648 that were extremely destructive of the well-being of the Eastern European community that seemed to have found a new golden land for Diaspora Jews. The heavy incidence of fatalities in the Cossack pogroms (forty thousand people, twenty percent of the Jewish population) plus the sudden deflation of high expectations for the continued security and prosperity of Polish Jewry precipitated a spiritual crisis. This malaise led to the conviction that the evil times that were held in both Jewish and Christian religious thought to precede immediately the coming of the Messiah had begun in 1648.

After the disaster of 1492 there had been substantial messianic speculation along these same lines among exiled Sephardi Jews like Don Isaac Abrabanel. As a result, in the early and mid-sixteenth century in the Marrano world there were a couple of small messianic movements. But the Marranos were too prosperous and adjusted too readily and comfortably to their places of refuge for the feeling to cut deep and long that the evil, premessianic times were at hand.

The Polish catastrophe was another story, particularly as the Cossack pogroms were immediately followed by war, invasion, and economic decline in Poland that brought widespread and enduring misery to the Eastern European Jews. Before Scholem published his monumental study on Sabbatai Zebi and his significance, the shock impact of 1648 was a favorite explanation for the Sabbataian messianic movement. Scholem deflated this as a cause by stressing the eastern Mediterranean center of Sabbataian messianism and by his designation of Polish Jewry as reactive, not formative, in the Sabbataian upheaval. Scholem was right, but 1648 still etched like acid, as had 1492, into Jewish consciousness and probably had a role in precipitating what happened.

The Sabbataian messianic phenomenon should be seen as another, although particularly volatile and consequential, stage in the Jewish Reformation. An oligarchic society dominated by a small circle of rabbis, capitalists, and courtiers who excluded from power ninety percent of the population of the communities they ruled were bound to experience periodic challenges to their cultural and political hegemony, and the most feasible form such opposition could take was one of religious reformation.

Rebellion needs moral legitimation, and this pious society had to pay attention to messianic and apocalyptic and millennial claims within a cultural ambience increasingly saturated with volatile Cabalistic theosophy and demonology. Having permitted such provocative theosophic discourse to become widely familiar in its Lurian form, the leaders of Jewish society had to allow an outbreak of messianic hysteria to play itself out now and again. Indeed in the case of Sabbatai Zebi, members of the ruling Jewish oligarchy were in many instances themselves caught up in the fervor of the moment.

Sabbatai Zebi was a young, handsome, manic-depressive drifter who in his manic phase exhibited charismatic qualities. As a young man from Smyrna in Turkey, he encountered in Gaza in Palestine a certain Nathan Ashkenazi, who became Nathan the Prophet. After receiving divine instructions in a trance, Nathan persuaded Sabbatai that Sabbatai was the personification of the Messiah and publicized this millennial and apocalyptic moment to various Jewish communities. Mass hysteria over the breadth of the Jewish communities in Europe and the Mediterranean was a result. Both wealthy and poor families by the thousands prepared for their triumphant return to Zion, taking the exhumed bodies of deceased relatives with them for expected resurrection. Families packed their bags and waited on rooftops for angels to carry them to Jerusalem. Before most of these enthusiasts could complete their travel plans in 1666 (a year that Christian theorists had long predicted as having apocalyptic significance), disaster struck. Sabbatai Zebi was arrested by the Turkish Muslim government and given the choice of death or conversion to Islam. He choose the latter.

The apocalyptic messianism of the majority of Sabbatai Zebi's adherents subsided as quickly as it arose. But a substantial minority, especially in Salonika in Greece and other places in the Balkans, resolved their cognitive dissonance by explaining this disaster through Cabalistic doctrine. Just as the light is temporarily joined to the evil *kellipot* (the shells of darkness), in the process of *tikkun* (cosmic healing), so the Messiah has to undergo an evil phase of humiliation to emerge as the purified redeemer. Even Sabbatai's death in a Turkish fortress in 1676 failed to discourage these true believers.

Many of Sabbatai's loyalists became in the end *doenmeh,* the Turkish word for converts. Marrano-like, they were Muslims externally but Jews privately. In the early twentieth century these Sabbataian survivors were still living in Greece and Turkey. Among them were rich merchants and important intellectuals and politicians.

Another offshoot of the Sabbataian movement was the sect of Jacob Frank (d. 1791) and his followers, first in Poland and then in various places in Central Europe. It remained a small sect that never had more than a few thousand members. Frank was born in Podolia, a backward region in southeastern Poland bordering on the Ukraine, but he accompanied his father, a merchant, to Salonika and there became involved with Sabbataian messianic ideas. A charismatic personality, skillful in dealing with Jews and Christians alike, Frank in the 1750s and 1760s developed a cult of himself as the Messiah. He, his family, and some of his followers went through a nominal conversion to Catholicism to obtain governmental protection against angry Jewish authorities, who rejected his claim that the mantle of Sabbataian messianic authority had passed to him.

Central to Frank's doctrine, and practiced by him and some of his followers, was the legitimacy of sexual promiscuity based on the assumption, from Cabalistic derivation, that sexual activity was a form of cosmic healing, unifying the spiritual and the material realms. This view of sexuality was also prevalent among some radical sects in the Protestant Reformation and some evangelicals and charismatics in nineteenth-century America, and is still popular among New Age West Coast Christians today.

The Frankists as a tiny distinct group survived into the twentieth century in Central Europe and included distinguished businessmen and professionals. There is no mystery why sectarian groups like the Sabbataians and the Frankists produce successful progeny. It is due to extraordinarily careful child care and early childhood education.

Astonishingly, the founder of the last of the most important movements in the Jewish Reformation, Hasidism, also came from the same obscure impoverished Polish-Ukrainian province of Podolia as Frank did. This was Israel ben Eliezer, known as the Ba'al Shem-Tov, the Master of the Good Name, Besht for short (1700–60). At the time of Besht's death his followers were scarcely more numerous than the Frankists. A half-century later, Hasidism was well on its way to embracing the majority of Jews in Eastern Europe, and highly visible groups of the heirs of Besht still live in Brooklyn and Israel, the Holocaust of the 1940s having wiped out millions of them in Europe.

Like the life of Saint Francis of Assisi, the Christian saint whom he resembles in personality and message, the life of Besht, this most influential Jewish religious leader of the past three centuries, is shrouded in hagiographical legend. Hence historians give significantly different interpretations of his biography and the early days of his movement.

We know that as a Ba'al Shem he was a faith healer and a magician. Whether he was an ordained rabbi and reasonably well educated is uncertain. Probably he had some rabbinic schooling but may not have finished the Halakic training program. He was a kind of lay preacher who first attracted attention by his healing and magical services. Then Besht began to propound a religious message to a group of devoted followers among, for the most part, the lower middle class in the Polish villages. The message comes down to us heavily filtered through his disciples of the second and third generation, especially his successor as leader of the Hasidic movement, Dov Baer, "the Great Maggid" (preacher, d. 1772) of Mezhirech in the more central and heavily populated province of Polish Volhynia.

The Hasidic message, drawing heavily from a vulgarized version of the Cabala and reflecting the shock waves of Sabbataian yearning for charismatic leadership, comes down to two words: "devekut" and "zaddik." "Devekut" is a term in the *Zohar* that means cleaving or adherence to God. The Besht and his successors taught that this could be gained not only through fulfillment of the traditional mitzvoth and study of the Torah and the Talmud—the Orthodox way—but through good living. God was immanent in the ordinary and the material.

Hasidism preached the sacring of (finding the holy in) the mundane—eating, drinking, dancing, storytelling, traveling, and, not least, sexual relations. One did not need a sober attitude and a learned background to encounter God. One could do it in the enjoyable and

necessary acts of ordinary life. Happiness and goodness were integrated with each other. Synagogue prayer itself could be an outlet for
joyful personal expression, allowing for exaggerated shaking, dancing, and even turning cartwheels.

God was present always in the universe; the material world was
suffused with divine light. A good heart and a happy countenance
meant that the ordinary man and woman, including children, and the
poor and homeless could encounter the divine immediately. There
are strong similarities between Hasidism's sacring of the mundane
and the expressive joyfulness of early Methodism and African-American Pentecostal religions.

Devekut as interpreted by Besht and his successors aroused the
ire and fear of the Orthodox rabbinate. It undervalued learning,
eroded traditional discipline, and challenged rabbinical authority. It
seemed to the Halakic rabbis to promise a democratic revolution that
would demolish the traditional authority of learned rabbis and
wealthy merchants that had for so long dominated the kehillah, the
Jewish community. The great majority of Orthodox rabbis were
opposed to Hasidism as it spread through Poland and the Ukraine
and even into Lithuania, famed for its great school of Talmudic learning in Vilnius. These opponents, Mitnaggedim, were no more sympathetic to the doctrine of the zaddik than to devekut.

The zaddik was very much like a Christian saint, and some histo
rians have seen a measure of influence from that quarter, but there
did not have to be a Christian derivation. The zaddik was a combined faith healer, spiritual counselor, charismatic preacher, and
sanctified intercessor, who could harrow hell and move the heavens
on behalf of his followers. Whatever your problem—health, money,
marriage, or simply doubt and psychological depression—the zaddik,
the carrier of God's light in the world, would resolve the problem, or
at least make you go away feeling much better after you consulted
him. Again there is a similarity to charismatic Methodist lay preachers
and African-American Pentecostal ministers.

The zaddik was usually learned in rabbinical lore but he did not
make a fuss about it, and his power and prestige did not come from
Halakic learning. He was a saint, an activist, a wonder-worker.
Within two generations of Besht's passing, if not earlier, the zaddik
had become the central force and institution in the Hasidic world.

The community lived in, around, with, and for the zaddik. And the zaddik's charisma was transferred down through his family, normally to his son or son-in-law. Zaddik dynasties became entrenched and endured for decades and beyond. They demanded substantial gifts from their communities and became affluent.

Hasidic treatises are a pastiche of Talmudic and Cabalistic explication and make now, and probably then, for dreary reading. The effective Hasidic genre was the folktale that illustrated the principles of devekut and zaddik in compelling, often lyrical fashion. This large body of folk literature illustrating Hasidic themes began to be published as early as the second decade of the nineteenth century in the Yiddish vernacular. In the late nineteenth century I. L. Peretz, one of the masters of the Yiddish renaissance then flourishing in Russia, retold these stories artfully, and from Peretz they entered permanently into Jewish culture. Martin Buber in the 1920s also published a retelling of Hasidic stories and used them to expound his theology focused on interactive dialogue.

Three stories from Hasidic lore as retold by Peretz communicate better than other presentations what Hasidism represented in its more positive vein. In one story, on Yom Kippur eve the congregation is waiting for the most solemn of liturgical chants, the Kol Nidre, to begin. A little boy in the synagogue starts to whistle, a blatantly sacrilegious act in Jewish lore. As his embarrassed father tries to shut up the boy, the zaddik says: "Leave him alone, he is praying. We each have a right to address God in our own way."

In another story, the congregation is puzzled that the zaddik disappears for hours at a time. Is he seeing a mistress? Someone is assigned to follow him, and discovers that the zaddik anonymously does volunteer menial labor for the poor and the handicapped. The investigator reports to the elders of the synagogue. The zaddik is not seeing a mistress. Is he ascending to heaven when he disappears? "If not higher" is the response.

A third story is "Boynze the Silent," the most admired and anthologized short story in the Yiddish language. Boynze, a simple worker, dies and rises to heaven. He is told that because he was so virtuous he can gain anything he wants as his reward. He asks for a roll with butter. Peretz puts on the story a gloss of his generation's ambivalent feelings about the Hasidic world; the story can be read as the pathetic consciousness of a well-meaning but ignorant man. In its original Hasidic version, devekut was being illustrated: The divine is in the simplest, most naive act. The rabbinical tendency to establish a hierarchy of behavioral patterns is replaced by a egalitarian value system in which ordinary acts of people are touched with the divine.

Of the early Hasidic zaddikim we know most about Rabbi Nachman of Bratislav (1772–1810). Not only have his writings survived in what appears to be reliably authentic form, but care was taken by his prime disciple to gather detailed information on Rabbi Nachman's biography. This material has been put together in a useful biography (1979) by Arthur Green.

These are the most interesting things about this zaddik. He was the grandson of Besht, which confirms the dynastic quality of the Hasidic zaddikim. He was married at age fourteen. He made a trip to Israel at age twenty-six. His religious power was deemed to lie at least in part in his own early struggles common to humanity, presumably sexual. He preached entirely in Yiddish, saying, "In Yiddish . . . it is easier to break one's heart . . . In Yiddish it is possible to pour out your words, speaking everything that is in your heart before the Lord." [transl. Arthur Green]

Nachman was an extreme believer in free will. "Everything depended first and foremost on good deeds, struggle, and worship. He said explicitly that everyone in the world could reach even the highest rung, that everything depended upon human choice." He stressed the charismatic quality of the zaddik. Relying on the zaddik was superior to learning from a book as the way to gain access to goodness: "The wickedness which lies inside of each of those people who hears the teaching [of the zaddik] is vanquished by the goodness which dwells within the sage."

Nachman was prone to depression, self-doubt, and despair. But as he was dying, "He shouted from the very depths of the heart: 'Gevalt! Do not despair.' He went on in these words: 'There is no such thing as despair at all.'" It is easy to see the similarity between Rabbi Nachman of Bratislav and West Coast New Age or Southern evangelical preachers today.

Hasidism's success severely undercut the authority and social influence of Orthodox rabbis and threatened a social transformation of a fundamental sort. The Orthodox opponents of the Hasidim, the so-called Mitnaggedim, led by the Vilna Gaon, a great Talmudic scholar, lashed out at the Hasidic zaddikim and the leveling ideas and practices of devekut at the end of the eighteenth century.

The conservative Mitnaggedim tried to prevent Hasidic writing from being printed and importuned the governmental authorities to suppress the Hasidic movement. These efforts had little success.

The phenomenal spread of Hasidism forced the learned rabbis to try to co-opt rather than eliminate the dynastic zaddikim, and they succeeded in doing so. During the first half of the nineteenth century a slow accommodation between orthodoxy and Hasidism evolved. The Hasidic communities under their zaddikim became more respectful of traditional law and learning and moderated their radical view of prayer. The Orthodox rabbis became more tolerant of the religious consciousness of ordinary people and more capable of and willing to give inspiring and comprehensible sermons in the Yiddish vernacular.

By the third or fourth decade of the nineteenth century the intrusion of modernity into the villages and cities of Eastern Europe was threatening the social and economic foundations of Hasidism and orthodoxy alike. These competing Jewish religious cultures slowly coalesced or at least tolerated each other in the face of political repression and social and economic turmoil.

There are three ways in which Hasidism can be perceived in long-term historical perspective. First, it was the last phase of the Jewish Reformation that had begun with the Karaites in the tenth century, and had proceeded through the Cabala and Sabbataian messiniasm. Like all these previous religious reform movements, Hasidism was an effort to challenge the authority of the traditional oligarchy and to make Judaism a faith more accommodating to personal sensibility.

Secondly, Hasidism was part of the romantic movement of the late eighteenth and early nineteenth centuries, that massive cultural change that shifted temperament and attitude away from law, reason, and tradition to feeling, personal experience, and environmental sensitivity, as demographic and economic transformation established the foundations of modern democratic society.

Besht's behavior and teaching resembles that of his near contemporary, John Wesley, an Anglican priest whose sentimentality led to his being driven from his clerical post in Georgia back to England where he preached to peasants and industrial workers and founded the Methodist church. Wesley's "method," like Besht's devekut, gave ordinary people access to divinity. The people's joy and religious experience improved their self-image. The Methodists too offered the sacring of the mundane.

When the English Romantic poet William Wordsworth in 1798 referred with praise to "the little nameless, unremembered acts of kindness and of love," he was evoking the spirit of both Hasidism and Methodism. Obviously, although Wesley's and Besht's lives overlapped by some three decades, they had no contact with each other. But they were both developing a religious and moral response to the harshness of the decaying old regime of predemocratic Europe and its insensitivity to the feelings of the common man.

The third way to explain the onset of Hasidism in the villages and towns of Eastern Europe, to the point that by the mid-nineteenth century it had millions of adherents, is its social context. Rafael Mahler's studies illuminated the social aspect of Hasidism. The basic fact to be considered is the severe economic deterioration of Polish Jewry in the eighteenth century, following the catastrophic pogroms and wars of the later seventeenth century, and culminating in widespread pauperization in Eastern European Jewish villages and towns during the first half of the nineteenth century.

The main reasons for this economic decline to the point of mass miseration are clear. The Polish Jews had risen during the sixteenth and early seventeenth centuries to prosperity as well as security by their service functions on behalf of the immensely land-rich Polish nobility, especially with regard to estate management for absentee landlords over the Ukrainian peasants. Conducive as this was to instilling endemic hatred among the peasantry toward the Jews as the visible embodiment of their repression and exploitation by the nobility, the Jews for a century and a half enjoyed their profitable preferential status, which was suddenly interrupted by the Cossack pogroms of 1648, followed by less widespread but still lethal and destructive assaults of a similar nature in the following century.

The Jews were never able to regain their previous position in Poland and the Ukraine because of a deterioration in the status of the Polish nobility itself in the eighteenth century. Unable to agree on rational political solutions, the nobility watched in futile disunity as Poland was partitioned during the last three decades of the eighteenth century among its greedy autocratic neighbors, German Prussia, the Hapsburg Austrian-Hungarian empire, and the Romanov czarist Russian empire. About seventy percent of Jews ended up under Russian rule, which was coldly unsympathetic to them from the outset and was conditioned by the traditional anti-Semitism of the Greek Church.

There were still some great noblemen in Poland but many of the Polish landlords generally experienced status and wealth declension, and with that, their Jewish dependents were no longer in a fortunate service position. The Russian government asserted monopoly over alcoholic production and sale, which had previously been the Jewish leaseholders' most lucrative enterprise, in which they had held a virtual patent on sales to the peasants. Insofar as Jews continued in the liquor trade they were now normally sub-leaseholders on much less advantageous terms.

Chronic underemployment among the Jewish petty bourgeoisie in the towns and villages became the central condition of their economic and social life, and continued until the great immigration to America at the end of the nineteenth century.

A significant segment of the Jewish population was by the early nineteenth century living the most marginal existence and many Jews were luftmenschen, "people living on air," perpetual paupers. The situation was exacerbated by the heavy taxation imposed by the Russian government on each Jewish kehillah, the local community government. Many communities became heavily indebted as a result, and their traditional capacity to provide charity to paupers was eroded.

Eastward migration out of Poland, the Ukraine, and Lithuania to the interior of Russia, where there was plenty of open frontier land, was prevented by the czarist regime, which, aside from accommodating a small handful of wealthy Jewish entrepreneurs who purchased special privileges, prohibited Jewish migration eastward. The Jews were frozen into a designated Pale of Settlement in the western segment of the Russian empire.

This draconian policy was inspired by anti-Semitic hatred on the part of the czarist bureaucracy, but it was also the result of the more intelligent of the imperial officials being appalled by the Jewish parasitical petty bourgeois lifestyle and their propensity to exploit the peasantry. Until the Jewish problem could be resolved, and the Jews somehow assimilated into Russian culture and made more productive, the Jews were to remain in the Pale of Settlement.

Historians often write about the Pale as if it were some Nazi-like Warsaw Ghetto. But a look at the map will show that it was a vast territory, about as large as the mid-Atlantic and New England states of the United States. The problem was that along with a general deterioration of economic opportunity, the Jews were experiencing a population explosion that unquestionably was a critical factor in their pauperization and misery. By 1750 their numbers in Poland and the Ukraine had risen to half a million from two hundred thousand in 1700. By 1800 the Jewish population was approaching a million, to more than double again in the next half century without any significant improvement in their economic circumstances.

The Jews were breeding themselves into penury, as for the first time since A.D. 200, the Jewish population—in Eastern Europe for the most part—rose dramatically. With the rabbis, whether traditionally Orthodox or Hasidic, opposed to family limitation of any kind, with the Talmudic injunction to be fruitful and multiply, with a propensity to marry very young to mitigate the stresses of libido, with good child-rearing practices, and with a general abstinence from alcohol abuse, all conditions were right for a Jewish population explosion, but their economic nexus was incapable of responding to this demographic bulge. The result, along with social pathologies of widespread petty criminality and bitter class polarization, was an economic disaster. It is easy enough in retrospect to blame the Russian government for this dreadful situation. And they were to blame, although historians are more prone now to point to ineptitude, inexperience, and general befuddlement along with sheer racist and religious rancor, as impelling the czarist government's Jewish policy.

Yet the leaders of the Jewish community were also responsible, because they never considered either of the two meliorative measures: family planning and limitation, and mass migration to the vast empty lands in North and South America. A few pious Jews now and again went to study and die in the Holy Land, but the economic decline of the Near East and Turkish hostility to significant Jewish immigration put a proto-Zionist resolution out of the question.

It was in this calamitous economic and social situation in Eastern Europe that Hasidism rapidly expanded. Despite Mahler's predisposition to a Marxist interpretation, he could not demonstrate that Hasidism constituted a class revolution. The great majority of the followers of the zaddikim were petty bourgeoisie, but then the great majority of the Jews were petty bourgeoisie. Some rich people—usually those seeking enhanced status recognition—also participated in the Hasidic communities. Hasidism was not a class revolution because it had no class ideology. Indeed, like contemporary English

Methodism, it softened the edges of class conflict by teaching personal satisfaction in the very modest pleasures of diurnal underclass life.

Hasidism can be viewed as a response to the miserable economic ambience of the late eighteenth and nineteenth centuries in Eastern Europe because in the pathetic Jewish villages and drab, insalubrious urban enclaves, it brought hope, joy, and comfort to increasingly impoverished and bewildered masses of people.

This situation also helps to explain why Hasidism became in effect a religion of the saints, why it focused on the zaddik dynasties. The systemic realities of Jewish life were so discouraging that ordinary people could only find solace in the wonder-working skills of a shaman—a saintly leader and magician. All the magic, demonology, and superstition that had circulated for centuries in the Jewish cultural underworld, some but by not means all of it articulated and given special legitimacy in the Cabala, plus folk cults dredged up from the Catholic and Greek peasantry, became focused on the Hasidic zaddikim.

The argument can be made—and it was certainly articulated by Jewish secularists, socialists, and the more radical Zionists at the end of the nineteenth century and down into the 1930s—that Hasidism was a disaster in Jewish life and became an even greater disaster when the Orthodox rabbis by 1850 stopped combating it and to some extent collaborated with it.

The indictment is that the principle of devekut, finding God's light in the trivia of pauperized everyday life, was a narcotic administered to the Jewish masses that prevented them from attaining a consciousness that would realistically address the hopelessness of their prevailing situation. It would have required strong communal efforts and a high degree of applied rationality to rectify the economic downturn, to organize immigration, and possibly to engage in effective political protests. All these meliorative efforts, of course, looked much more possible in 1910 than in 1840.

Another charge against Hasidism, less easy to dismiss, was that it debased Jewish culture, that it glamorized ignorance and superstition, that it allowed the mass of the Jewish population to wallow without pity in the cultural and physical slime of an unpromising and backward existence, while the zaddik dynasties joined the Orthodox rabbinate and a handful of wealthy merchants in an affluent and selfish existence.

After the Holocaust wiped out in the most violent and sudden of circumstances the thousands of surviving Hasidic communities in Eastern Europe, less was heard of this indictment of Hasidic life. What Martin Buber, the German philosopher and mystic, had already begun to do in the 1920s became fashionable by 1970, which was to sentimentalize the Hasidic world of the nineteenth century and to highlight its positive side and say little about its adverse consequence for the destiny of the Jews.

Writing humorous newspaper columns from his home in the Bronx in the early years of the second decade of the twentieth century, a Jewish journalist named Sholem Rabinowitz imaginatively depicted the world of the shtetl, the small town or village in Jewish Eastern Europe, already being transformed by economic and technological change. Sholem Aleichem, as we know him, amused his readers by creating the character of Tevye the milkman as symbolic of this already vanishing world.

In the 1960s and 1970s Jews on several continents were delighted by the musical comedy derived from Sholem Aleichem's Tevye stories. What was already filtered romanticization in the stories became further simplified and sentimentalized through the medium of American musical comedy in *Fiddler on the Roof.*

Some of the desperation and poverty of the shtetl world comes through in the musical comedy, as do the tense relations with the peasants and the harsh and idiosyncratic treatment meted out by the czarist government. What also stands out in the stereotyped image imparted to the comfortable Jewish audiences in New York, Tel Aviv, Toronto, and London is the dignity, courage, and good humor of the poor Jews in Eastern Europe, and the warmth and beauty of family life.

All these things existed. But what is excluded is the ignorance and superstition of the Jewish masses in the shtetl, the hopeless marginality of their economic conditions, the disease and the criminality that affected their lives, and the tyranny exercised over them by traditional religion and the rabbis and zaddikim who maintained this culture and operated it in their own interests and for the comfort of their own families.

From *Fiddler on the Roof* the audience gets no sense of the downside of the Jewish Reformation as it left its impress on Jewish life in the Pale in the nineteenth century.

The Jews had their Torah to comfort them, although women

were rarely taught Hebrew so as to be able to read it. They had their Talmud to guide them, although only a small minority of males and no women had the privilege of Talmudic study. They had rabbis and zaddikim to turn to for inspiration and personal counseling, but frequently these leaders were indifferent to the miserable conditions of the ordinary Jewish men and women, and were more concerned with their own power and affluence than with the physical and moral needs of their followers. What you do not learn from Sholem Aleichem is the superstition and the ignorance and the general ambience of cruelty and deprivation, of fatalism and magic, and of comatose squalor that characterized the culture of the shtetl.

In the perspective and judgment of history, the Jewish Reformation by the middle of the nineteenth century had exhausted its capacity to improve any aspect of Jewish life and meliorate either the physical or the moral conditions of the Jewish masses.

The Cabala, the messianic movements, and the Hasidic movement had congealed into a suffocating, conservative detritus that shut the Jews off from the technological and intellectual prospects of the modern world. Religion was adversely affecting the possibility of challenging the difficult circumstances in which the Eastern European Jews found themselves. They had to break out of their repressive shtetl existence one way or another, or die. But it was in the interests of the zaddikim and rabbis to keep them where they were, physically and mentally, shut out of access to change and progress.

The same judgment can be made of the Christian Reformation's heritage to the nineteenth century. Whether in Protestant or Catholic communities, the religious movements of the period 1500 to 1800 had also by the nineteenth century engendered more obstacles than avenues to the betterment of the lives of ordinary people.

The greatest dramatist of the early twentieth century, Henrik Ibsen, made this failing of the Christian Reformation a central theme in his plays. It also comes through with respect to the Jewish Reformation in the novels of the late nineteenth-century Yiddish writer Mendele Mocher Sforim (Sholem Abramovich). There has been no attempt to make a musical comedy out of one of Mendele's dark portrayals of life in the shtetl.

The world of the shtetl whose culture and behavior patterns were so heavily shaped by the heritage of the Jewish Reformation is presented in a highly favorable light in some of the writings of the

Nobel prize–winning writer Isaac Bashevis Singer, especially *In My Father's House*. The world of rabbi- and zaddik-dominated villages and small towns of Eastern Europe early in this century are here presented through a sentimental scrim, so different from Singer's highly realistic and deeply psychological accounts of immigrant life in New York. Singer presumably knows what his readers want to think about when they focus on the pre-Holocaust world of the shtetl. To be severely critical as Mendele was, writing in the late nineteenth century, would be too painful after this world and its pathetic people were devoured in the Nazi death camps.

In the 1950s and 1960s, Rabbi Abraham Joshua Heschel, the much revered spiritual teacher at the Jewish Theological Seminary in New York, presented a passionate defense of Eastern European Ashkenazic Jewish religious culture under Cabalistic and Hasidic influence. Heschel was himself descended from a distinguished Hasidic lineage.

The best book on Heschel's thought is, perhaps not surprisingly, by a Jesuit priest, Donald J. Moore (1989), who summarizes Heschel's view of Ashkenazic culture under the influence of Cabalistic and Hasidic traditions in this way:

> While the Sephardic Jews of the Iberian Peninsula tended to blend their Jewish culture with that of their neighbors, the Ashkenazi Jews lived in an isolated manner from their European neighbors and hence tended to emphasize much more their own Jewish roots and tradition. In contrast to the Sephardic ideal of prudence and practicality . . . the Ashkenazic approach was much more fervent and personal, "praying and learning without limit or end." Under the influence of the mystical teachings of the Kabbalah, the Ashkenazis stressed attachment to the "hidden worlds," those spiritual worlds built by power of devotion invested in deeds.

In Heschel's view, which has gained a wide measure of assent in Jewish circles, the outcome of the Jewish Reformation in Eastern Europe should be seen as producing both a distinctive and a thoroughly admirable culture. Living in isolation from one's non-Jewish neighbor, investing Jewish society's wealth, literacy, and energy in limitless prayer and religious learning, its finest spiritual intellects searching constantly for hidden, internal worlds: These qualities seem in the Heschel perspective not only innocent but admirable, to be recalled with nostalgia and praise.

Yet Heschel was describing the core of society generated by the Jewish Reformation, not some remote sect or separated community. That is the problem. Can a society involving millions of people commit itself so intensively to such otherworldliness, piety, and disregard of the general forces of politics, technology, and economy of the world in which these Ashkenazic Jews lived? Could they behave this way in the short run without bringing misery and penury and in the long run without risking an implacable disaster?

The neoromantic nostalgia of the secular American Jews plus their prejudice against the Christian Slavic world make Heschel's view of Ashkenazic culture shaped by the Cabala and Hasidism immediately poignant and persuasive. But placed within a broader frame of historical and social thinking, it is a view that is vulnerable to criticism.

Two specific reflections on this Jewish Reformation–dominated Ashkenazic society are worth pondering. The first is the tremendous waste of literate intelligence that occurred there. Perhaps as many as three percent of the adult males in this society in the nineteenth and early twentieth centuries did nothing in their adult lives except study the Talmud and the Cabala and related religious writings. They were supported by wives who operated stores and took care of all family responsibilities—and a new sentimentality has recently enshrined these burdened woman as proto-feminists in babushkas. Or the Talmudic scholar was supported by a wealthy father-in-law, honored to have a man of learning in the family.

Some of these scholars were practicing rabbis, communal leaders who conducted services, gave sermons, counseled, and made judgments. But most played no social role whatsoever. They just sat immersed in two millennia of religious tradition. In retrospect, it would have been better for their families, their communities, and perhaps themselves if they had devoted their finely honed intellects to alleviation of the poverty and social pathology of the villages and towns in which they lived. Here was a sad waste of human resources, a misapplication of learned intelligence. Superior human stock, highly selective blood lines, were applied to very modest social purpose.

The other illuminating perspective on the world the Jewish Reformation generated comes from considering what happened to these people when three million of them moved to the United States between 1880 and 1920. A lot of different things occurred, as in any mass migration, but one fact stands out—the general loss of leadership by rabbis and zaddikim in the new environment of Manhattan's Lower East Side and Brooklyn and the Bronx, where most of them had settled by 1920.

The domination over Jewish communities, the loyalty exhibited perpetually through family lineage to the religious leader, famous for his learning or his sanctity or both, disappeared somewhere in mid-Atlantic. By the time these people had settled in their new, usually humble abodes, and had begun the struggle to make a living and raise families in a demanding environment, the intellectual domination and religious charisma of these spiritual leaders had declined to insignificance.

In the great majority of cases the immigrants went their own way and their children and grandchildren even more emphatically worked out their private destinies with little or no reference to religious leadership.

This tells us that the hold over the people of the shtetl was more a matter of a culture of poverty than merited charisma. Religious leadership played an important part in the lives of people who grew up in the old world because they had no alternative other than to accept this authority in an enclosed and impoverished space. Once they got to America, the more economically secure and physically and socially mobile they became, the less of a role in their lives did the rabbi and zaddik play, and by the time the second and third generation of American Jewish immigrant families appeared on the scene in the 1920s, the rabbi and zaddik usually had no role at all except on sparse formal occasions.

By the end of the 1920s among the ten percent of American Jews who remained Orthodox or fully observant, there was still respect for men of deep learning, and sometimes a traditional rabbi would exercise considerable prestige and influence. Sometimes among more reformed and liberal congregations a charismatic preacher would achieve a significant moral impact.

But these were highly exceptional instances of rabbinical leadership even among active synagogue attendants. For the two-thirds or more of American Jews who attended synagogue only on the High Holidays or never, even this marginal rabbinical impress on their lives had become nonexistent by 1930. Only among a few ultra-Orthodox and Hasidic communities (and some of these did not coalesce in America until after 1945, as in the case of the followers of the Lubavitcher rabbi in Brooklyn) was there a holdover of the old rabbinical power.

The Jewish Reformation, its impress eroded by social and economic change in Eastern Europe in the late nineteenth century, suffered a massive deterioration in the course of the Jewish migration westward. Drawn in upon itself culturally and institutionally, Jewish religious leadership that was the product of the Jewish Reformation had become rigidified, conservative, and incapable of adjusting to rapid and profound change.

There is no more essential fact in Jewish history of the past century than this one, and it is remarkably underemphasized in standard histories, written as they are either by rabbis or by their admirers.

This loosening of the mold of the Jewish Reformation was already evident at the turn of the century in the large cities in Eastern Europe, such as Odessa, Kiev, and Warsaw. Many business entrepreneurs and literary intellectuals were operating outside the orbit of rabbi and zaddik. Labor union leaders and socialist and Zionist activists were trying to create new secular societies. A great transformation in Jewish life was under way, the most fundamental since the time of the Pharisees and their Talmudic successors.

CHAPTER EIGHT

Modernity and Jewish Emancipation

The fulcrum upon which Western and eventually world history turns from the time of the democratic, industrial, and demographic revolutions of the late eighteenth century until the First World War is signified in two conceptual terms, modernity and modernism. These words represent forces that finally terminated the medieval world and created, for the most part, the society, economy, and consciousness we experience today.

Modernity refers to the process of alteration of the old regime and society to the one that exists in the twentieth century. It was a shift from a world still dominated by lords, priests, and peasants—the social framework since the ancient world—to one of the democratic, high-tech, heavily populated and high-consumption urban mass society we recognize.

The modern world is almost as class-ridden as the old regime was, but the individual seeking economic success has much greater freedom of mobility. The durable caste systems of the old society were broken. Humanity is still divided into the privileged and the affluent as against the poor and the deprived, but not in the long-term predictably inherited way that characterized the premodern situation.

Violence and conflict exist in the modern world, but they are much less endemic and idiosyncratic and much more collective, systemic, and deliberate. While before 1914 many people thought that general peace was a fundamental ingredient of modernity, they were soon to learn that it is a peace interrupted by an unprecedented degree of carnage.

A distinguishing feature of modernity everywhere was population boom, rapid and extensive urbanization, and communication and transportation that was unimaginably faster than the old world could provide even to the most powerful and affluent people.

This change in the transportation network and the communication grid had major social consequences. It allowed for the drawing of large areas of the globe into one economic distribution system. It made feasible rapid migration and resettlement of millions of people. And it facilitated the diffusion of a secular culture from metropolitan centers to the interiors of nations and then of continents and finally, in our day, along information highways, through the whole world.

Provincialism was threatened with being stigmatized as backward. All religious groups faced the tremendous challenge of a secular mass culture. Ideas were disseminated much more rapidly, particularly as universal elementary education became the European and American norm in the late nineteenth century. The shell of textual and charismatic religious communities was difficult to protect from severe erosion and fragmentation in these modern circumstances.

Modernism is a cultural movement that emerged at the end of the nineteenth century and ran out of its main impetus by 1940. But its imprint on our culture, especially in its academic, scientific, artistic, philosophical, and literary—the more elite—aspects still remains a very powerful conditioning agent in our lives and perceptions.

Modernism was so overwhelming in its impact upon the psyche, the moral sense, and the perception of reality that we are still not sure how fully and in what ways we have recently entered a new cultural era. We can therefore only refer to the current situation as postmodernism.

Modernism is related to modernity in that it was an effort, successful in many ways, to come to intellectual terms with the consequences of social and economic modernity and to develop a cultural perception and a justificatory (or condemnatory) ideology along with it. Modernism put forth judgments on science, literature, and art that related to the nexus of social and technological modernity and proposed new ways of thinking and feeling within that framework. Modernism essentially was a rejection of the nineteenth-century emphasis on the big, the general, and the simplified in favor of the twentieth-century focus on the small, the particular, and the difficult.

Modernism replaced the Victorian propensity to moralizing, democratizing, and synthesizing of intellectuality and art with a propensity to close, technical analysis of a specific facet of human culture by an enclosed professional elite group.

In the longer run, although modernism articulated the way we still think of ourselves and the universe, we are no longer fully satisfied with the modernist culture and its corrosive ideology. But only in a marginal and fragmented way do we recognize the contours of a postmodernist alternative, which in many instances looks at least superficially like a cultural pastiche that involves aspects of reactionary premodernism.

The only way to understand Jewish history since the late eighteenth century and particularly in the transformative era 1780–1910 is in terms of this historical model of modernity and modernism. If we do not place Jewish history within the modernity/modernism model, we will be left, as surveys of Jewish history normally are, with data about this and that but with very little meaning, with particular chapters but no overall understanding.

We can turn Jewish history since 1780 into provincial chronicles, sentimental tableaus, lachrymose dirges, heroic friezes, or even entertaining musical comedies. Any good university library will provide plenty of such volumes, and on certain occasions and for special purposes they are useful, even admirable.

But for understanding what happened to the Jews from the late eighteenth century until the early twentieth century, and beyond, Jewish history has to be perceived within the framework of the modernity/modernism model or we shall have only pieces of information but not the confident and inclusive imaging of the past that provides for group resolve and personal illumination.

By 1910 we have reached the world of our grandparents and great grandparents. Some of us are old enough to remember the faces of Jews who were children or young adults in 1910. To understand what'lies behind these remembered faces, we have to understand Jewish history within the framework of modernity and modernism.

The period from about 1780 to 1910 witnessed the greatest transformation in Jewish life since 1500, perhaps since the Roman Empire. In 1780 the world population of the Jews was 2.5 million people. In 1910 it was eleven million and climbing. In 1780 the bulk of the Jewish population lived in Eastern Europe, mostly under Russian rule, with another substantial community under Austrian rule. The next largest Jewish community lay in the Mediterranean under the rule of the Ottoman Turks. In the West the largest Jewish community was in Germany.

By 1910 a new Diaspora had occurred, as millions of Jews fled westward from the Russian empire and significant numbers also fled from Austrian rule. There was a much enhanced Jewish community in Germany and a substantial number of Jews in France and England. But the monumental transformation was the immigration of three million Eastern European Jews to the United States, with Canada and Argentina also gaining Jewish population in this rise of the American continent's presence in Jewish world history. In the Holy Land, the customary tiny numbers of pensioner rabbis and mystical saints was in 1910 being augmented by a group of young people of socialist commitment intent on building a new democratic and secular Zion. Though they were still very small in numbers, their intellectual and moral impact on world Jewry was on the rise.

This upheaval and westward migration of the Jews (still leaving five million in Eastern Europe, however) was accompanied by two major changes in their occupations and well-being. The Jews in the Americas and Western Europe entered more freely into the nexus of market capitalism not only as petty bourgeoisie but as industrial workers and corporate owners. Although millions of Jews had carried their Eastern European impoverishment with them to the West, their literacy, native intelligence, religion-conditioned moral discipline, and superior genetic quality made them excellent prospects for upward mobility in Western society.

This social mobility occurred so rapidly and visibly as to instill fear and hatred among the Christian petty bourgeoisie and working class. At the same time, despite all kinds of obstacles and screening devices, the Jews gained access to the learned professions, the writing crafts, and the entertainment industries at a volume of penetration not seen since the Mediterranean Renaissance in Arab lands almost a thousand years earlier. This penetration into the preserve of the Christian elite in the West aroused fear and hatred among the upper middle class as well as among the other classes.

This revolution in the social circumstances of the Jews, particularly among those escaping from their miserable condition in Eastern Europe, meant essentially that the Jews experienced, particularly between about 1880 and the First World War, a rapid absorption into modernity—an intensely secularized world of social mobility, individual opportunity, mass consumption, and centrality of the learned professions.

Because of economic and political change in Eastern Europe, this transformation would have occurred on a visible scale had the Jews all stayed where they were. Large numbers of Jews, especially those in Russia and the Austro-Hungarian empire, much less so in Poland, made the transition to modernity, especially after 1900. But those Jews who migrated westward to Western Europe and the Americas after 1880 made the most rapid alteration in their way of life and their mentality and did it on a demographic scale unparalleled for rapid change in Jewish history, and rarely seen among other peoples. The Jewish rabbinate as a group never really adjusted to the upheaval and suffered almost total loss of their communal leadership.

This adjustment would have required a fundamental reordering of theological expression, liturgical service, and ethical discourse in terms compatible with modern science, technology, high art, and mass culture. With only marginal and historically unimportant exceptions, the rabbinate exerted no substantial effort to make this adjustment and lost their option to maintain a high degree of leadership in modern Jewish society.

It would have required a cohort of dozens of religious intellects of the caliber of Maimonides even to begin meeting the challenge of modernity. The Orthodox had no Maimonidean exemplars; in the words of the Psalmist, there were no more prophets in Israel. More Reform and liberal congregations generated an occasional rabbi who made a gesture at relating Judaism to modernity, but it was a feeble and inconsequential effort.

The judgment of history cannot lie too harshly on the rabbinate.

Among Christian churches, particularly the Protestant ones, there was a parallel enfeeblement and loss of empowered social leadership in the late nineteenth and early twentieth centuries under the impress of modernity. Yet in the long perspective, looking at the century after 1860, perhaps only among Anglicans and Episcopalians was there such drastic deflation of traditional religious leadership within the communities of the hitherto faithful as occurred among the Jews under the impact of secularizing, materialistic, and democratizing modernity.

Broadly speaking, the dynamic transition of the Jews to modernity in the past two centuries, and with it large-scale advancement in market capitalism's network and the learned professions, was heavily impelled by far-reaching contextual change in government and economy wherever Jews lived that pulled them along into its creative orbit amid destruction of the vestiges of the medieval world.

But the Jews were not just passive material in the transformative mechanism of modernity's technology, secularism, consumerism, and democracy. The Jews developed internally in the late eighteenth century within their own society, before the impact of modernization was much in play, an ideology of self-improvement, drawing upon the reforming and secularizing doctrines of the European Enlightenment.

The Jewish Enlightenment—Haskalah—was an identifiable internal movement for Jewish auto-emancipation, of particular importance in Germany, but also influential on pockets of Eastern European and American Jewry. It is probably the most undervalued intellectual movement in Jewish history.

As Jews in the West in the late nineteenth century gained remarkable success within the structure of liberal capitalism, an ideological commitment to the politics and culture of the market society took hold, and this attitude joined with the heritage of the German-French Enlightenment to create the drive for a drastically different kind of reformed or liberalized Judaism.

In the late nineteenth century Jews became prominent in the socialist movements and labor organizations from Russia all the way to the United States, and this comprised not only a prime form of Jewish involvement in world society, but constituted an ideology for transformation of specifically Jewish life as well.

Between 1800 and 1910 a vibrant Yiddish-speaking culture,

mostly secular in orientation, was created in Odessa, Warsaw, other Eastern European centers, and New York City. By 1920, however, Yiddish language and literature were being swept aside by the commitment of American Jews to English, and Palestinian Jews to Hebrew.

The emergence of Zionism, in three or four distinct ideological forms in the late nineteenth and early twentieth centuries, was the most important cultural ideology within Jewish society and aiming directly at its reform and reconstruction since the rise of Hasidism in the eighteenth century.

At the end of the nineteenth century the Jews went on the cultural offensive in a creative and aggressive manner and on a broad front that was unprecedented since the Mediterranean renaissance of eleventh- and twelfth-century Muslim Spain and the involvement around 1500 of Jewish converts in the renaissance of Iberian Christian humanism, with its offshoot in the Marrano culture of seventeenth-century Amsterdam.

The Jews individually, and to a debatable extent as a cultural and racial group, moved by 1910 from absorption into modernity and translation of Jewish values in response to modernity, to take leading roles on many fronts in the natural and behavioral sciences, the humanities, and the arts within the nexus of the devastating cultural revolution called modernism. The Jews, seeing no residual obligations to Victorian Christianity, imperialism, historicism, and Gentile racism, stood in the first three or four decades of this century at the leading edge of cultural modernism, the complex and immensely creative cultural revolution that permanently altered the human consciousness just as the deconstructive waves of political, social, and technological modernity had transformed behavior and well-being.

The details of Jewish history during the age of the impact of modernity upon Jewish society in Europe and America, roughly from about 1780 to 1910, have been well established. There is abundant information on the fate of the Jews in particular countries at specific times. There are valuable biographies of major Jewish figures. There are monographs analyzing important events and institutions.

The historigraphical issue is: How can all this information be brought together and organized in a meaningful way so that the pattern of Jewish destiny in the context of modernity can be perceived? This has not been well done in the surveys of Jewish history. The approach adopted here is that of structural-cultural analysis, or historical sociology. It should be stressed that the sociology of the Jews from the late eighteenth century into the early twentieth century does not refer to that ten percent of the Jewish population who still lived in Near Eastern and Mediterranean Arab lands. Since the Muslim Arab world was itself very little affected by modernity in this period, the Jewish communities there, impoverished and marginalized, were not caught up in the dynamic nexus of modernity and were totally unaffected by modernism. They remained in a placid medieval social and intellectual condition until the middle of the twentieth century, when they were abruptly expelled, departing mostly to Israel, but some to France and the United States. Nor does this sociological model refer to the idiosyncratic slivers of Jewish population in East Asia and black Africa.

The pattern of historical sociology we are using does embrace ninety percent of the world's Jewish population, stretching by 1900 from Moscow to San Francisco.

Jewish emancipation from the vestiges of medieval ghettoization, the removal of legal and political disabilities, and the awarding to Jews of their full rights of citizenship in the state, is often viewed as a process of diffusion. Mostly from progressive revolutionary France of the 1790s, the ideas of Jewish emancipation and equality are held to have radiated out to the rest of Europe, carried physically to many places by the armies of Napoleon Bonaparte, the dictatorial heir of the French Revolution, between 1796 and 1815. In surveys of modern Jewish history, we are often treated to an opening sunlit scene in the French National Assembly in the mid-1790s as fiery orators in knee-breeches deliberated on the fate of French Jews—who numbered some fifty thousand at the time, mostly in the postmedieval enclave of Alsace along the German border.

The French revolutionary government and legislature offered the Jews a kind of Faustian bargain—the ambivalent contract popular as a motif in the literature of the day, as in Goethe's *Faust.* Just as Faust received wisdom and knowledge but had to sell his soul to the devil, the Jews individually received full rights as citizens but were supposed to give up their medieval ways of thinking and behaving, particularly their communal separatism, clannishness, and unmodish way of talking and dressing. From now on, they were to look and act like middle-class Frenchmen—to be assimilated in the national bourgeoisie.

Emancipation signified assimilation into French liberal culture, asserted the ideologues of the French Revolution. The Jews could keep their peculiar religion, but that was a private affair. Otherwise, they were to be full-fledged Frenchmen, culturally as well as politically, behaviorally as well as legally.

And that is pretty well what happened to French Jews over the next century, even as they were joined by many thousands of immigrants from at first Germany and then, after 1880, Poland, leading to a community of three hundred thousand French Jews, prosperous, well educated, and nearly all thoroughly assimilated to French national culture by 1900.

The Parisian debate on the Jewish question in the 1790s and the subsequent history of French Jews can be taken as a kind of foreshadowing, prototype, or abstract paradigm of the process and character of Jewish emancipation. By 1870 Jewish emancipation had been achieved everywhere west of the Russian empire.

The Jews had the full right to live where they wanted, and indeed not only to remain within a state, but to migrate across the wide-open borders of the time. They were free to pursue the business or craft they preferred and, increasingly, despite restrictive quotas and other obstacles, to enter a learned profession. They were free to take advantage of state-supported educational facilities where such schools increasingly operated, and west of Poland they overwhelmingly did so. They had equal legal rights—to hold property, to litigate, and to sit on juries where they existed.

With some pockets of resistance, the Jews could participate in political life not only by voting, but by standing for election to legislatures. Rarely did they hold high political office, but that was not unknown—a British prime minister in the 1860s and 1870s was a Jewish convert to Christianity who nevertheless flaunted his Jewish ethnicity, and the finance minister in the government of the Southern Confederacy during the American Civil War was a Jew.

Between the heated debates on the future of the Jews in the French revolutionary assembly in the 1790s and 1870, the states in the European and Atlantic world west of Russia thus moved somewhat unevenly but over time consistently toward the full civil and political emancipation of the Jews.

It would, however, be very one-sided to regard the process of Jewish emancipation as radiating diffusion outward from Paris of the liberal democratic ideals of the French Revolution. That played a part, especially down to 1815. But the emancipation of the Jews was more a functional than an ideological matter, more calculating governmental policy than moral fervor. It was due more to the operational aims and needs of the nineteenth-century state, whatever its ideological profile on the long scale between liberal democracy and conservative oligarchy, than to the impact of political theory.

In Britain, the great and ultimately victorious opponent of revolutionary and Napoleonic France between 1793 and 1815, the small Jewish community, mostly Sephardim from Italy and other Mediterranean places and numbering around thirty thousand in 1800, had by 1750 all civil and legal rights except the privilege of sitting in Parliament. You had to take a Christian oath to do that. This obstacle was overcome in the 1850s when a member of the Rothschild banking family was finally seated in the House of Commons after being elected several times by a London constituency (he did not have to take the archaic oath).

The nearly complete emancipation of the Jews in eighteenth-century England, well before the beginning of the French Revolution, was a product of many causes. One was the legacy of Calvinist philo-Semitism. Another was regard for the Sephardic Jews as a kind of exotic Mediterranean breed, reminiscent of those delightful Italians the English lords encountered when they made the Grand Tour to examine classical monuments in Italy.

Perhaps more important was the nationalizing and leveling tendencies of the English common law system that systemically sought to eliminate all peculiar jurisdictions, whether privileged or underprivileged, and to bring every subject of the crown judicially before the royal courts on a litigiously equal basis. This led in 1829 to restoration of full civil and political rights to Roman Catholics, discriminated against since the late seventeenth century. It had also led to Jewish emancipation even earlier. It was a dysfunctional nuisance, a bad legacy of the Middle Ages not to treat Jews equally in the courts of the common law. In England, legal ideas and practice tended to purchase political outcomes. The juristic equality of the Jews in the eighteenth century led naturally to their full political liberties in the nineteenth century.

The final and probably most important cause of Jewish emancipation in England—a country from which Jews were proscribed officially between the 1290s and the 1650s—was the functional need of the imperial British state. Gearing up its fiscal and human resources to contend against France for world hegemony between the 1790s and 1815—a world conflict in which the British triumphed even though the population of France was three times that of Britain and its gross domestic product was probably twice as great—the landed aristocrats and millionaire merchants who dominated the British political ruling class had to maximize their resources. In these circumstances it made no sense not to use fully the fabled intelligence, industry, and fiscal acumen of the innocuous Jewish minority.

It actually didn't make much difference before 1815 because the Sephardic English Jews were a plebeian lot. But in the next phase of British imperialism in the nineteenth century, equal treatment of the Jews paid off well for the imperial governing group. New Jewish immigrants coming from France and Germany, like the Rothschilds, who brought with them capital and international banking operations, were highly beneficial in providing liquid capital and international fiscal operations that a world empire readily put to maximum use.

Historians disagree on whether the French doctrines of republicanism and the universal rights of man played an important role in shaping the ideas of the American Revolution of 1776, the Constitution of 1787, and the Bill of Rights (the first ten amendments to the U.S. Constitution) of 1791, or whether the American political culture was a direct offshoot of English law and politics. However derived, the American idea was that of a "New Order of the World" in which the privileges, discriminations, and prejudices of Europe were to be superseded, so said the American Revolution of 1776, by a new era of freedom in human history. This does sound like English common law filtered through the prism of French ideological enthusiasm.

What was important for the small number of Jews in the United States of 1790—mostly of Marrano and other Sephardic descent, as symbolized by the oldest American Jewish synagogue, a Sephardic one, in Newport, Rhode Island—was a political and judicial system that gave them from the outset full political as well as civil rights. These rights were immeasurably strengthened by the radical innovation of the First Amendment, prohibiting Congress from making a law for "establishment of religion" (i.e., a state religion). (However, this ban applied only to the federal government; not until 1925 did the U.S. Supreme Court begin to decide it applied to state and municipal governments as well, and this was not widely implemented until the 1960s, with the effect of wiping out partisan Christmas displays without a balancing Hanukkah show.)

The United States was the first government in the history of the world thereby to separate itself absolutely from endorsing any religion, a step not yet taken by the state of Israel.

Yet these intellectual and judicial contexts were no more important in determining the Jewish situation in the United States than the fundamental material fact in American history—a vast continent fabulously rich in agricultural and mineral resources (the aborigines having been killed or shunted away) and marvelously accessible by a network of rivers supplemented after 1825 by canals and then, beginning in the 1850s, by a railway network. The country was ready for exploitation, the greatest land grab in history.

What was needed was people with the energy, intelligence, courage, and capital to exploit this limitless opportunity. The tiny and placid American Jewish population made no significant contribution until the new wave of Jewish emigration from Germany in the 1840s and 1850s. That made an enormous difference.

From Cincinnati as their religious and cultural center and their takeoff point the Jewish peddlers, sutlers, traders, and eventually entrepreneurial magnates fanned out down the vast interior funnel of the American continent, the Ohio river system, into the upper South of Kentucky and Tennessee, and then farther south and west. Then they swung over around 1860 into the Mississippi valley and did the same thing all over again, from St. Paul to St. Louis to New Orleans. And they also got in on the opening of California in the gold rush of 1848, contributing among other things Levi-Strauss blue jeans to American Western culture spreading out from San Francisco.

Often we read today historians' complaints that Hollywood Westerns (made mostly by Jewish-dominated film companies) falsified the picture of the True West by not revealing the large minority of black cowboys. But these classic Westerns, from Tom Mix to Gary Cooper to Clint Eastwood, similarly filtered out the truth of how much Jewish tradesmen contributed to the American West as well as to the upper South. Whenever the hero rides into a Western town to be supplied at a general store, historical accuracy requires a distinctly Jewish name for the store proprietor at least half the time.

The Jews felt at home in America by 1860 not only because of the Constitution and the First Amendment but also because of the integral role they played in the commercial development of the continent as well as some of its important mining. When the head of the Union Army in 1864, Ulysses S. Grant, evicted Jewish tradesman from occupied Southern territory on the grounds that the unscrupulous Jews were exploiting soldiers and the civilian population, President Abraham Lincoln immediately overruled his favorite general.

As a former railroad lawyer from Illinois, Abe Lincoln knew firsthand how much the Jews had contributed to the development of the American interior, and how much their commercial and fiscal resources were needed for the big boom over which his Republican party was prepared to preside once the war ended and the building of transcontinental railroad resumed—a boom that like an megaton vacuum cleaner was to suck millions of pauperized Jews out of Eastern Europe in the late nineteenth century.

In the Central European countries—Italy, the united German empire (both which came into existence in 1870–71) and the Hapsburg Austro-Hungarian empire—functional need and the service that Jews could provide to government and economy counted much more than liberal ideology for Jewish emancipation. Here the Faustian bargain was visibly, harshly articulated—Jewish civil and political liberties in return for Jewish assimilation to the general culture's behavioral patterns and demonstrable loyalty to the state and Christian society. This was the social contract offered to the Jews, and they eagerly accepted it to the mutual benefit of both parties.

French egalitarianism and secularism entered Italy with the armies of Napoleon Bonaparte in 1798 and shook up the archaic, Catholic-drenched, papal-driven political culture of northern Italy, where, from Venice to Rome, Jewish communities had lived quietly ghettoized since the sixteenth century. Catholic reaction followed Napoleon's defeat in 1815, but Italy had been affected by the starting up of nationalism and middle-class liberalism, and the next six decades were a time of complicated struggle over political ideas.

The debate on both sides was somewhat romantically naive, because what the various Italian states needed most of all was industrialization to raise the peninsula out of the chronic economic depression Italy had endured since the shifting of overseas trade to the Atlantic axis in the sixteenth century. Much of the push for a national liberal state in Italy had an operatic flavor. But out of this confusion, the House of Savoy in the far north of Italy and its skillful chief minister Count Cavour created a united Italian kingdom in 1870, with French and German acquiescence.

For the Italian Jews in the northern cities it was a springtime of raised expectations and belated recognition of their citizenship. The new Italian state, after 1870, ramshackle and poverty-wrenched as it was, put the papacy at arm's length and shrank the papal state that had dominated central Italy to a few square miles of the Vatican. The Italian Jews in the previous three centuries had lived in an ambiguous medieval situation of ghettoization combined with security. Now they were free to move about and fully use their intelligence, business skills, and rationality.

The House of Savoy and Cavour had always been open to Jewish support and assistance, and now from the ranks of the grand old Italian Jewish families, many of Marrano descent, some indeed going back to the time of the Caesars, came two generations of business entrepreneurs, lawyers, doctors, professors, government officials, and generals. These affluent families fully assimilated themselves to the lifestyle of the urban bourgeoisie, focused on the town house and the country villa, and lived until the late 1930s a life of unusual ease and refinement. This is beautifully captured in Vittorio De Sica's great film, *The Garden of the Finzi-Continis,* a loving memorial to the patrician Italian Jewish families of the early twentieth century.

The Jewish population in nineteenth-century Germany steadily grew to half a million from internal growth and emigration from Poland and Bohemia (Czechoslovakia). A distinctive symbiosis developed by the middle of the nineteenth century between the Jews and German society and especially in the united German empire and the conservative Hohenzollern state under Otto von Bismarck in the 1870s and 1880s. Under the impress of the cultural movement of the Haskalah (Jewish Enlightenment) of the late eighteenth and early nineteenth centuries, Jewish leaders, sometimes rabbis but more often gentlemen scholars and professionals, advertised Jewish readiness to engage in an intensive assimilation to German culture.

The excellent German state-supported school (the gymnasium) and the state universities afforded the Jews the opportunity for deep immersion in German language, literature, philosophy, and science. Of course there were tensions, particularly in the universities, where Jews were excluded from most fraternities. But that was of little social consequence. A greater obstacle was the quotas against Jewish entry to the professional schools and to academic appointments.

Yet the Jews persevered and fully internalized German literate culture. Its deep learning and rigorous academic discipline—*Wissenschaft*—appealed to Jews. It was an objective body of knowledge that they could master and thereby demonstrate that they belonged as physicians, lawyers, professors, civil servants, applied scientists, and poets; and it was reminiscent of the dry, systemic rationality of the Talmud. For German Jews, secular learning was pursued with vestigial and vicarious religious fervor.

Some German Jews remained observant. Others tried to develop a reformed, edited, up-to-date Judaism that coalesced with their learning and bourgeois lifestyle. Others fully assimilated themselves into German society and quietly abandoned all affiliation with their ethnic and religious past. Still others, seeing residual blockage and deprivation in their nominal Jewish status, underwent formal conversion, normally to the Lutheran church, which made little demand on them personally.

The pattern in this regard was set in the 1830s by Heinrich Heine, Germany's greatest lyric poet of the first half of the nineteenth century. A well-educated, Francophile, thoroughly secularized Romantic intellectual, Heine converted to bring himself fully into German literary circles, and his conversion achieved its purpose. He worried about the significance of his conversion; it was something that bothered him a bit. A half century later someone of his culture and literary ambition took conversion as a matter of course and rarely let it become something to mull over.

By 1900 the conversion and intermarriage rate among German born Jews was approaching fifty percent. If Hitler had not intervened, Jewish identity in Germany could very well have lapsed by the middle of the twentieth century.

In the fierce political struggles within Germany in the first seven decades of the nineteenth century between the French- and English-influenced liberals and the aristocratic-led conservatives, the issue of democracy—to Germany's and mankind's ultimate misfortune—was never clearly resolved. In the united German empire that was proclaimed in 1871 in the French Royal Palace of Versailles after the German army crushed France in the Franco-Prussian War and temporarily occupied Paris, the legislature was dominated by liberals, and by 1900 by socialists (among whom Jewish leadership was highly visible), while the imperial executive, not responsible to the legislature, and appointed by a reactionary, militarist emperor, was staffed by old-line Prussian (northeast German) landlords and their conservative followers.

Germany had by 1890 eclipsed Britain as the most advanced industrial power in Europe, its only world competitor being the United States. Yet the German empire was flawed by an incapacity to turn itself into a modern democratic state. The imperial government remained a vestige of eighteenth-century despotism and oligarchy, frequently at loggerheads with the liberal and socialist majority in the legislature.

Yet the Jewish capitalists did very well under the rule of Otto von Bismarck as imperial chancellor and his conservative successors. Bismarck's favorite banker was Jewish. The Rothschilds, who had originated in the Rhineland before spreading their banking network to Paris and London; the Warburgs, a new millionaire family of fiscal titans from Hamburg; and other Jewish financiers played a central role in providing the investment capital for Germany's frenetic industrial expansion in the late nineteenth century. Jews were prominent in the shipping industry, in chemical production, in transportation and communication, and in ownership of department stores, and they dominated the book publishing and newspaper business.

By 1900 two representative types of German Jews loomed large on the Central European horizon and signaled that the German Jews as a group were perhaps the most fully integrated into society of any in Europe. One was the figure of the financier and industrialist, with his private bank on an elegant Berlin or Hamburg street or his thriving publishing house or his smoke-belching steel mill, supplemented by an imposing town house and baronial country estate. Was the family still Jewish in a formal sense? It was impossible to tell from their lifestyle. Often some members of the family were still nominally Jewish, and some were Lutheran converts, which meant the children in any case would be raised as Christians. Some of the Rothschild and Warburg children remained Jewish; some were Christian. Intermarriage was common.

Another representative German Jewish figure by 1900 was the Jewish academic, the scholar or scientist, editing classical manuscripts, writing treatises on medieval monasteries, expounding on Roman law, developing distinctive German traditions in philosophy, and even opening up Islamic history for inquiry. Although in the first half of the nineteenth century German Jewish scholars had begun a systematic study of Jewish history, and again in the 1920s Jewish studies won some young adherents among Jewish academics, between 1870 and 1920 the German Jewish scholars turned their attention productively to other fields.

Jewish academic prominence occurred despite severe quotas limiting the percentage of Jews at the University of Berlin who could be tenured professors to five percent of the faculty. In the more provincial universities, especially in departments of physics, mathematics, and philosophy, the percentage of Jewish representation was higher. A member of the Warburg banking family single-handedly started up the field of art history. His family's money funded an institute independent of the university.

The Jewish contribution to German academia in its golden age far exceeded the celebrated Jewish role in the higher culture of the medieval Arabic world. It was unprecedented. One has to turn to the United States in the 1970s and 1980s for comparable statistics about Jewish prominence in academia and the close fit of Jewish scholars and scientists into university culture.

To speak of the emancipation of the German Jews is to belittle their accomplishment. The economic and intellectual triumph of the German Jews would be a much more accurate rubric.

An informed observer of German Jewry in 1910 would make only three cautionary, downside observations. One was that the Jews were much more at home in the Protestant world of the north than in the Catholic culture of southern Germany. Prussian Berlin was a Jewish city; Bavarian Munich, Germany's second city, with its spectral memories of the Catholic Middle Ages, definitely was not. Second, while Jews were fully at home in the plutocracy and there was as yet no great resentment against them by the working class, the petty bourgeoisie—lower civil servants, small tradesman, schoolteachers, skilled workers in heavy industry—resented the Jewish triumph and felt severely the pressure of Jewish competition.

Third, the Jewish emigration from Poland after 1880 not only further inflamed petty bourgeois resentment and inspired some hostility in the working class but more immediately marred the perfect picture of Jewish assimilation that had previously existed. By 1900 the influx of the more visibly alien Polish Jews, slower to dispense with

the signs of traditional Judaism, was raising concerns among assimilated Jews and Gentiles alike. How fast would the acculturation of
the Eastern Jews occur? And as their scions progressed in business
and the learned professions, had they truly internalized German
Protestant culture, or were they merely paying lip service to it while
they advanced their private interests? These could be troublesome
issues in a less comfortable and prosperous era.

But in 1910 it seemed certain that the twentieth century would
be Germany's century and recent Jewish arrivals would be absorbed
into the dynamic force field of German culture.

The clearest instance of Jewish emancipation following from the
immediate needs of the nineteenth-century state and calculated political decisions rather than from liberal ideology is the example of the
Hapsburg Austro-Hungarian empire. The old Catholic dynasty and its
chief officials were extremely conservative politically and hostile to
liberal ideas. Its greatest ruler in the eighteenth century, Joseph II,
renowned as an enlightened despot, was keenly aware of the disparate minorities in his multinational empire. After the partitions of
Poland, the southeastern province of Galicia with a large Jewish population came under Hapsburg rule.

The backwardness and separatism of the Jewish population worried Joseph II, and he tried to bring the Jews into closer conformity
with the dominant German culture by forcing public schools on the
Jews. This was bitterly resisted by the rabbis, whose communal leadership was threatened by any departure from the Halakic-Hasidic
culture. Yet Joseph II pointed the way for the Jews to become integrated into the dominant culture and society.

Austria's political elite until the 1860s was persistently reactionary. The Catholic Hapsburg rulers fought hard (and usually lost)
against revolutionary and Napoleonic France. The emperor in 1848
resisted liberal reform and called in the Russian army to help him put
down the liberal movement by force. The big shift in Hapsburg policy came from military defeat at Prussian (northern German) hands
in 1866. It was a shock to the old system and forced the emperor
and his ministers to reconsider what it would take to bring stability,
prosperity, and a modicum of modernity to the huge, ramsackle,
multinational empire. They became much more generous in responding to the demands of non-Austrians such as the Hungarians for a
high degree of autonomy and self-government. In general, the impe-

rial regime in Vienna acceded to greater recognition of minority rights.

As a German-speaking group tied by culture to the Austrians within foreign enclaves in Budapest and Prague in the closing decades of the century, the Jewish middle class in these cities prospered in business and the learned professions. By 1920 half the lawyers of Budapest were Jews, and Jews were also prominent in science, literature, and the arts. Large numbers of Jews moved from the outlying ethnically Polish and Romanian provinces to Vienna in the late nineteenth century and sought to play a role in Viennese intellectual, professional, and academic life similar to what they were gaining in Berlin.

Vienna was not Berlin. In a Catholic ambience charged with tensions among competing and conflicting racial groups, there was more outspoken resistance among the elite to Jewish advancement in Vienna than in Berlin, and in the racially charged atmosphere, the Viennese working class was persistently anti-Semitic and resistant to Jewish inroads into employment. There is truth in the characterization of turn-of-the century Vienna as "the staging-ground of the world's destruction," for there lay one of the prime breeding pools of Nazism; a prominent mayor of Vienna in 1900 won election on an anti-Semitic platform. Nevertheless, the emperor and his government remained friendly toward the educated Jewish middle class, whom they saw as productive and contributing to the economic development of a country much less affected by modernity than Germany.

In the vibrant intellectual and artistic life of Vienna, Jews played a significant role, and Jews also were industrial and commercial magnates in Austria. The largest steel company belonged to a converted Jewish family. Jews were prominent as well in the leadership of the Austrian labor unions, as they were in Germany at that time.

We may sum up this account of Jewish upward social mobility, leaving Russia aside for the moment, by saying that the nineteenth-century state not only allowed but welcomed the emancipation of the Jews, less out of liberal doctrine than out of national self-interest. Whether the ruling group was committed Catholics or Protestants or relaxed secularists, they need to marshal and organize the human resources within their boundaries if they were to respond effectively to the challenge of modernity.

By this criterion, the Jewish position in Christian Western society was bound to improve substantially. The loyalty of the Jews had to be gained and retained, and maximum use of their rationalizing intelligence, fiscal experience, and investment capital had to be purchased, whatever Catholic, Anglican, Lutheran, or other prejudice against them existed. The Jews were imagined—perhaps to the point of fantasy—to have unusual economic capability, and this is what the nineteenth-century state wanted to recruit for its own purpose.

Rational policy therefore dictated Jewish emancipation and the moving of Jews from the margin to the center of the national society. Only a nineteenth-century state governed by religious fanatics and rabid racists would have wished it any other way. The challenge of modernity and the need to adjust politically to the onset of economic and technological change worked against adherence to old-fashioned prejudices.

The Jews in turn had to stop being isolated, standoffish, and medieval in dress and deportment and assimilate fully into Western society and culture at large. West of Poland the great majority of Jews were eager and willing to transform themselves—shave their beards, wear up-to-date clothes, give their sons and usually their daughters a secular education, and be of immediate service to the government and society. This Faustian bargain, this social contract, appealed to Jews everywhere from Berlin to San Francisco. Some Jews assimilated to the dominant culture yet remained fully observant. Some loosely retained their Jewish identity while integrating with the majority culture in dress, behavior, and discourse. Some converted officially to Christianity because of ambition for advancement, or because of intermarriage, or simply because they lost interest in Jewish traditions as they became immersed in modernity.

Of course, the more Jews converted, the more Jews became assimilated, the happier were the governments with their generous Jewish policies. They appeared to be gaining not only Jewish capabilities for the state's national purposes in the short run, but the prospect of the disappearance of the Jews as a distinct minority in the long run. This might have happened by the middle of the twentieth century if not for the anti-Semitic reaction and Hitler.

But in any case there was a formidable obstacle to gaining this fortunate denouement of Jewish cultural extinction. East of Germany there remained a huge mass of underassimilated Jews who threatened to turn around and move westward. The Russian empire, with by far the largest Jewish population, failed to develop a consistent and successful emancipation policy, partly because of indecision and ineptitude in its government over time, and partly because of the enormous demographic and cultural impediments to Jewish assimilation in Eastern Europe.

It is conventional in histories of the Jews to blame the czarist governments and portray them as monsters of reaction and prejudice. Some officials were despicable indeed, but what happened in Eastern Europe, as more research is done and less ideological hostility is vented on the czarist government, appears to be an unfortunate but understandable failure in social engineering, comparable to what Gunnar Myrdal called the American black "dilemma" before the 1960s or even now.

The history of the Jews under czarist rule is customarily written as though the only good policy for the government in St. Petersburg, facing millions of Jews in the western parts of its territory gained after the partition of Poland concluded in 1791, was to do everything it could to maintain Jewish life in villages and towns in the nexus of rabbinical and Hasidic culture. The argument is that the Russian government should have realized what it was getting into when it expropriated the vast Polish territory and should then have done the liberal thing and minimally left the Jews alone, or, since they were already in descent to pauperization, improved their economic base.

Applying the mentality of today's welfare and liberal multicultural state is not helpful, however, in understanding the Eastern European situation of the nineteenth century. The nineteenth-century state anywhere was not tolerant of large separatist minorities. The existence of such groups violated its centralizing political and cultural assumptions and precluded the maximal organization of the country's human resources to face the challenges of modernity.

The failure of the Jewish policy of the nineteenth-century Russian imperial government, considered in terms of the political assumptions of that era, was not its lack of sympathy for traditional Jewish culture and rabbinically dominated Jewish society. It was its inability clearly to articulate a policy of getting the Jews out of this deteriorating medieval world and assimilating them into the mainstream of Russian culture. It was a failure to identify clearly and execute the Faustian bargain, the social contract, that worked so well elsewhere—worked well, that is, from the point of view of national interests and the personal happiness of Jews who accepted assimilation, if not well from the partisan expectation of Jewish historians today.

To understand the Jewish policy of the Russian government in the nineteenth century one can accept as a given that the czar and his ministers in the best of times had little tolerance for the Jewish religion and the Jewish way of life in rabbinical-Hasidic culture. Between the 1820s and the 1860s czarist officials continued to confine ninety-five percent of the Jews to the Pale of Settlement in Poland, the Ukraine, Belarus, and Lithuania. The czar's men exercised draconian means to erode Jewish separatism in their thickly settled villages, towns, and city wards and to wean the Jews away from the culture and behavior they had inherited from the prosperous days of the sixteenth century and held on to in the face of extreme economic deterioration.

Before we unequivocally condemn the czarist officials for trying to force change upon the Jews, we should bear in mind two things. First, the aim of the Russian government's policy was essentially that of other governments of the time—to maximize the Jews' service to state and society. Second, as severe as the czarist measures were, when we look at the other side of the ledger and see what the rabbis and zaddikim were doing (aside from distributing charity) to get the Jews out of their stinking impoverished domiciles and into an improved systemic situation, the answer has to be—nothing.

The czarist regime in the years from the 1820s to the 1860s had two strategies for Jewish assimilation. The first was trying to force thousands of Jewish children into state-supported schools where they would receive some secular education. This was done in imitation of Joseph II of Austria's program in the late eighteenth century. Despite bitter rabbinical opposition and endless noisy disputes, the czarist educational program relative to the Jews did go forward and was a qualified success. By the 1870s a new generation of Russian Jews, after imbibing secular education in the state-supported schools, sought to continue on to universities and train for the learned professions. Many Jewish writers of the 1880s had been educated in the state-supported schools. It was a limited but important program, and it laid the foundations for new kinds of Russian Jewish intellectuality in the late nineteenth century.

Second, for a quarter-century after 1825, the czarist regime imposed quotas for military recruitment on the Jewish communities—Jews were no longer to be exempt from the military draft. To meet the designated quotas each kehillah (council) had to send chappers (grabbers) into the streets and kidnap adolescents for long terms of military service.

The sons of rabbis and the upper middle class never served in the Russian military. It was the Jewish poor who regularly had to provide the conscripts. This practice not only had a military purpose but also served to erode rabbinical control over the next generation. Conscripts inserted by force in this way into the Russian military often lost consciousness of their race and religion and converted. For those who did not, it was a wrenching of their lives from which recovery was slow and difficult.

The practice of using chappers for conscription contributed to an inflammation of hostility between rich and poor in Jewish society. That had the effect of eroding the solidarity of the Jewish community, and it was probably intended to do so.

Forced military recruitment of Jews lapsed in the 1850s, and in the 1860s and 1870s under a more liberal czar, Russian officialdom showed greater tolerance for the Jews. This did not solve the economic and population problems in the Pale, where Jewish numbers continued to rise rapidly, enhancing poverty and misery. But a greater number of Jews by one means or another were able to move eastward to St. Petersburg and Moscow. By 1880 perhaps ten percent of the Jews, mostly affluent businessmen and professionals, had moved to the interior of Russia.

The reforming czarist government, however, created new problems for the ordinary Jews by the emancipation of the serfs in 1861. This overturned the old village economy in which the Jews were still trying to eke out a living by catering to the needs of the peasantry. As the peasants became free and more mobile, they had less need of Jewish small tradesman selling them things, and Jewish underemployment and poverty accelerated.

The one positive development economically was that by 1880 Russia was going through the early stage of industrialization, and the emergence of factory production provided jobs in Warsaw and elsewhere. These factories, usually owned by Jewish entrepreneurs, were highly exploitative and unsalubrious places, as was characteristic of the early Industrial Revolution elsewhere. A Jewish industrial proletariat emerged in the late nineteenth century. Jewish socialists and revolutionaries, already expressing solidarity with the peasants, now could try to organize the Jewish industrial workers.

A more conservative regime followed the liberal czar's assassination in 1881 by anarchist revolutionaries—among whom was a Jewish woman. This inaugurated a long era, lasting until the Russian Revolution in 1917, of the czarist government's renewed hostility to the Jews. Everywhere the officials looked they could find cause to take a negative and critical view of the Jews. Millions still lived in an alien rabbinical culture in poverty and superstition. Middle-class Jews with secular education caused tension by pressing for admission to the universities and entry to the learned professions. In the rising Jewish generation, a visible number of socialists and revolutionaries were prevalent.

The Jews in the Russian Empire "fought back against oppression . . . Jewish terrorists in Russia killed many czarist officials in the decades immediately preceding World War I." [Albert S. Lindemann]

In these difficult and volatile circumstances, the czarist regime lost its never high capacity to articulate a meliorative Jewish policy and sank into resentment and hostility toward the Jews. In early 1880s severe pogroms broke out in Odessa and several other cities, to be repeated in 1903 in Kishinev, in the Russian province of Romania. At the time Jews within Russia and without widely believed that the czarist secret police had generated the pogroms. Recent research seems to disprove this familiar claim that has entered ineradicably into Jewish historians' mythology. But local officials may have been implicated in some cases, and they did not do much to stop the pogroms until the terror threatened to turn into widespread civil disturbances, or to identify and punish the ringleaders.

The czarist regime watched in sullen contempt and inaction as millions of Jews fled westward. This loss of manpower, in a country with an enormous open frontier to the east where settlers were badly needed, indicated a regime totally unable to formulate an effective minority policy in the case of the Jews and then defending itself by venting its frustration.

But not even the massive Jewish emigration resolved the Jewish problem in Russia. Several millions remained in Poland and elsewhere in western Russia, sunk in ignorance, poverty, disease, petty crime, and superstition. The czarist officials, even relatively enlightened and energetic ones, condemned the Jews as a backward and antisocial people, chained to the past and to their unprogressive religious leaders, implacably resistant to modernity. This became a self-fulfilling prophecy of doom, first for czardom, then for the Jews of Eastern Europe. This was a tragedy without heroes, only villains and fools.

It was a harsh irony that the one place the Faustian bargain between the state and the Jews in the nineteenth century did not come into play was the place that needed a radical meliorative social contract the most.

The chorus of Jewish historiography is overwhelming in blaming the czars and sentimentalizing the Jews. But there is plenty of blame to go around.

CHAPTER NINE

The Response to Modernity and Modernism

Jewish emancipation and the context of modernity in which Jews came to live in the nineteenth century and assiduously to cultivate raised for Jewish intellectuals and scholars the challenge of respond ing through theory and expression to this fundamental set of changes. Even in the Russian empire, fragmentary emancipation occurred, and the impress of modernity made itself felt sufficiently in Odessa, Warsaw, and other centers to stimulate responses to modernity.

Jewish interaction with productive, provocative, and powerful secular culture had striking precedents—Hellenistic Alexandria in the first century A.D., Arab Spain in the eleventh century, Calvinist Amsterdam in the seventeenth century. The cultural and intellectual impact of modernity on the Jews, joined with the consequences of emancipation, was much greater than the outcomes of those previous eras of Jewish response to secular culture. Modernity offered ready access to general society's intellectual elite and their cultural institutions for Jews to interact with and distinctively respond to. Modernity represented an all-embracing alteration of ambience and behavior and therefore resonated more broadly and more deeply than those previous Jewish eras of thinking at the leading edge of general culture.

Modernity demanded radical reconstruction of mentalities and moral commitments. Never before had the Jewish intellectuals been immersed in a context of such transformative capability.

There were of course those who shut out the new cultural and social world. In Eastern Europe, millions of such Jewish cultural rejectionists maintained loyalty to rabbinical and Hasidic traditions. West of Poland, the intellectual conservatives were in the minority, compared to those Jews wanting to rethink the old assumptions or move directly into a new intellectual nexus. The responses to modernity the latter came up with, both with respect to the content of Jewishness and toward new intellectual horizons that could rapidly filter or block Judaism from its range of vision, were extremely diverse.

The failure of Halakic rabbinical culture, after two millennia of counseling and controlling Jews, to remain a viable participant in this multidiscourse is in itself highly indicative of the traditional rabbinic mind's incapability of responding effectively or productively on a theoretical level to the dynamics of modernity in the nineteenth century.

The message that Maimonides in the twelfth century had sought to deliver to the rabbinate was that in a relatively open society, the Halakic authorities had to relate Jewish biblical and Talmudic learning to the vanguard sciences and philosophy of the day. If they could not create an integrated culture embracing science and faith, they had at least to encounter frankly perplexities that intellectual disparities engendered. Maimonides's rabbinical colleagues rejected his prescriptive method and instead relied on tight legalism supplemented by various kinds of irrational exercises.

By and large, they were able to take this exclusive approach with impunity, although we do not know how many brilliant young Jews over the centuries were driven to the Christian churches as a result. When Spinoza, who greatly admired Maimonides, tried to engage in philosophical discourse while he was a member of the synagogue community of seventeenth-century Amsterdam, he was expelled.

The coming of Jewish emancipation in the nineteenth century, the open access to secular thought, and the full immersion of the Jews in the West in modernity changed the whole context of religious and moral discourse for the Jews. The traditional, Orthodox rabbinate did not make the necessary radical, Maimonidean adjustment, and hence they defaulted in their opportunity to respond to modernity. It was left to others among the Jews.

Some will claim that the rabbinate has made a substantial recovery in the twentieth century. There have been efforts, but they have not been consequential. Nothing in the internal history of Jewry in the past two centuries has been more important than the traditional rabbis' failure to respond intellectually along Maimonidean lines to the challenge of modernity, and the attendant encounter of Jewish intelligentsia with secular thought. A consequence of the rabbinical failure to respond theoretically to modernity was to leave the way open for a marvelous variety of Jewish responses, which have greatly enriched Western culture.

Some of the responses to modernity occurred within the context of Eastern European Jewry. Rabbinical and Hasidic Judaism was more of a rejection of, rather than a response to, modernity, but there were other voices and other ways of responding in Eastern Europe, interactive ones in the context of Jewish culture and society in the Yiddish world.

In the West, some Jewish respondents to modernity regarded traditional Judaism as narrow and sectarian, and offered other models of Jewish thought and practice for consideration of the cultural marketplace.

Some ethnic Jews did not even consciously relate their mature ideas to their previous adolescent culture, but developed a new set of assumptions and concepts that they shaped into intellectual systems having, at least in its surface textuality, no specifically Jewish content. But because these authors were born as Jews and because their outriding systems were the structural alternatives to their childhood Jewishness fixed in their subconsciousness, the new systems evolved in a dialogic interaction with Judaism on the issues raised by modernity.

No matter how secular Jewish intellectuals' responses to modernity might appear, lurking somewhere beneath the surface texts was a coupling or contrast with Jewish theology and ethics, which had been part of their upbringing and remained as, in Jacques Lacan's term, the Name-of-the-Father to admonish and assure them.

The Haskalah, the Jewish Enlightenment that rose in late eighteenth-century Germany and had a substantial and often underrated impact in the Russian Pale in the first half of the nineteenth century, was a prodigious effort of highly learned men, and some women of the Berlin salon variety, to integrate Judaism with the German philosophic and academic mainstream founded by Immanuel Kant.

Kantian culture stood for two things: a universalist moral command for peace, justice, and friendship among individuals and groups; and heavy scholarship and rational inquiry in an academic setting. This kind of worldview propounded by Immanuel Kant around 1790 appealed not only to the German Maskilim (as the fomentors and followers of the Haskalah were called) from Moses Mendelssohn in the 1770s through Abraham Geiger and Leopold Zunz in the nineteenth century, down to Heinrich Graetz a century after Mendelssohn. It is a mind-set that also appealed to a number of writers and historians in Odessa, Warsaw, and Vilnius in the late nineteenth century. The necessary transposition in language and style having been made, the spirit of the Haskalah endured amomg the prodigious number of Jewish academics in the United States from the 1950s to the present.

This fecundity and durabilty of the Haskalah tradition is due not only to its conversion of biblical and Talmudic teachings to a substratum of peace, justice, harmony, and scientific learning, but also to the essential point made in Kant's theory of knowledge. We know, said Kant, only the world of phenomena; that is, we can explore and rationalize out of our experience and collectible data, but the ultimate realities of God, freedom, and immortality are beyond rational proof. Yet such is the power of our mental categorization that out of sense data, or information networks we would say now, we can construct a highly coherent and stable universe for ourselves.

The Haskalah mind in Judaism, like the Kantian mind in Christianity, like the American Jewish academic mind in the second half of the twentieth century, excluded the mysterious and the irrational, the vulgar and the violent (no small part of human life!) and projected a holograph of rationality, justice, and learning. It asserted its scientific and rationalized character and climbed into this beautiful structure and lived therein.

Not surprisingly, in the first three decades of the twentieth century the more this Kantian culture was threatened by passions of the heart and violence in the streets, the more German Jewry through the neo-Kantian theorists Hermann Cohen and Franz Rosenzweig tried to buttress it and advertise it as the essential philosophy of Judaism.

Cohen sought to distill out of Judaism an ethical sublimity that is identical with Kantian principles of universal rational morality. Everything else in Judaism, its historical and legal tradition, is outside this ethical core and can be abandoned in the modern world to concentrate on the moral essence. Kant posits universal moral principles, identifiable by reason, that transcend animate nature and individual wills. Cohen sees Judaism as arriving at the same frame of mind.

Rosenzweig's neo-Kantianism was more ambitious and more anthropological (or existential) in character. Not just the rationally sustainable ethical principles of Judaism ought to be preserved, he thought, but as far as possible through the medium of a liberal Jewish educational system—Sunday schools and adult education institutes—a substantial part of Jewish law, historical memory, and tradition as a crystallized Jewish culture.

Both Cohen and Rosenzweig found supporters among American Jews, starting in the 1920s. Cohen's philosophical Judaism is perpetuated in the Ethical Culture movement that reduces Judaism to Quaker-like moral principles. Rosenzweig's anthropological or existential Kantianism, in which Jewish morality shines through a cultural prism that pragmatically preserves some of the law, history, and tradition, was echoed in Mordecai Kaplan's Reconstructionist movement.

Ethical Culture and Reconstructionism endure to this day, ultimate derivations of the German Haskalah and its neo-Kantian formulations in the philosophies of Hermann Cohen and Franz Rosenzweig. To highly educated, upper middle-class New York Jews (as was the case with German Jews in the 1920s), these forms of late Enlightenment thought interacting with social modernity were personally meaningful.

The two greatest intellects among German Jewish philosophers in the early twentieth century, Edmund Husserl and the Viennese guru Ludwig Wittgenstein, knew, however, that the game was futile, even when Hitler was still an obnoxious soldier making noise in beer halls.

Husserl doubted that the world built up from phenomenal experience was a rational one. Wittgenstein threw out the whole Kantian program—about the things that are most precious, like ethics and art, language's recalcitrant structure, said Wittgenstein, does "not allow us to speak." For Husserl, human consciousness is embedded in a world of conflicting passion and seductive sensibility. Wittgenstein narrows the scope of rational philosophy to linguistic inquiry.

What Husserl and Wittgenstein did was to destroy Kantian universalist rationalism from inside the parameters of academic philosophy and erode the Kantian tradition's capacity to withstand the onslaught of irrationalist claims to legitimacy and authenticity.

Universal reason was effaced, and the way was open to other claims to truth deriving from personal feeling and group power. Essentially this was the program of Friedrich Nietzsche, writing in the 1870s. His doctrines began to gain attention around 1900. Nietzsche rejected the blatant anti-Semitism of his friend the composer Richard Wagner. But at the same time he castigated the allegedly enervating social and personal outcomes of Jewish prophetic ethics and depicted the Jews of his day as soft and devious.

In the 1920s the worship of Nietzschean unreason ascended in an impoverished and conflicted Germany within both intellectual and popular circles. Cohen and Rosenzweig held on to the Kantian tradition as best they could, sensing the dire consequences of a post-Enlightenment culture. But Husserl and Wittgenstein, Jewish philosophers of much greater influence, gave the intellectual battle away, and the consequences were indeed dire.

From Kantian universalist rational ethics, bonded to Judaism in the eyes of Cohen and Rosenzweig, Husserl excluded rationality and Wittgenstein expelled ethical propositions from the domain of rationally argued philosophy. The German Kantian tradition in Berlin Jewish culture, strong since 1800, quickly disintegrated.

The Haskalah-Kantian stream in German Jewish culture lost its purchasing power in the 1920s. Its two potential heirs in terms of their mental powers, Martin Buber and Gershom Scholem, repudiated the mantle of rationality handed to them by Hermann Cohen and Franz Rosenzweig. Both Buber and Scholem sought to confirm Judaism's integration not with rationality but with Judaism's irrational heritage—Hasidism and the messianic traditions. They also wisely moved to Palestine before the Holocaust descended on them.

If the Haskalah-Kantian Jewish tradition looks tired and shopworn today in the faces of its heirs, defensive Jewish male professors in the age of multicultralism, it was different in the nineteenth century. The Haskalah-Kantian tradition resonated with a certain vibrancy then. Four important legacies came immediately out of the work of Maskilim in the nineteenth century. The first was the so-called Science of Judaism, the application of the tools of German classical and historical scholarship to Jewish history. Graetz's monumental history of the Jews (1850–75) was the summation of this research. Not much work in Jewish scholarship went beyond it until the German émigrés to Palestine—Scholem, Buber, and Yitshak Baer—published in the 1920s and 1930s.

Graetz's eight-volume work reflects the Haskalah's Kantian rationalism. The golden age in Spain is therefore overpraised and the Jewish Reformation, particularly the messianic movement of the seventeenth century, is downgraded.

Graetz is long on heroes and short on social analysis. Graetz did not teach in a university but in a separate Jewish institute. He never had to face a Gentile audience and engage personally in discussion with Christians. His isolation is reflected in his unremitting hostility to Christians and his persistent blaming of them for mistreatment of the Jews, and for all misery in two millennia of the Jewish past. He is insensitive to the Christian side of the story. Notwithstanding these defects, this monument to Haskalah learning is the single greatest achievement in Jewish historiography and places Graetz in the front rank of the impressive array of nineteenth-century European nationalist historians.

The second great service to Jewish culture rendered by the Maskilim is that they provided most of the first generation of teachers in the state-supported secular schools that the czarist regime founded in the 1830s and 1840s to try to shift the Jewish younger generation away from exclusive involvement in the rabbinical-Hasidic tradition. Of course the rabbis and zaddikim of the Pale hated these new teachers of Jewish youth, who provided an alternative curriculum and threatened the hold of superstition, fanaticism, and ignorance over the Eastern European Jewish mind. The Maskilim were denounced then as traitors and fomenters of assimilation. Probably because of this conflict the Haskalah has a doubtful reputation in Jewish historiography to the present day.

The third legacy of the Haskalah is modern Hebrew and the centrality of the Hebrew language among Israelis and committed Zionists in the Diaspora. When you read about the Maskilim you might think they were interested only in imposing a pure German tongue on the speakers of Yiddish patois. Not at all, although the German Maskilim found Yiddish grating in their Goethe-tuned ears, as if we heard the English of the Peasants' Revolt of 1381 all around us. From Moses Mendelssohn onward, the Maskilim, first in Germany, then in Russia, were scholars and advocates of the Hebrew language as the alternative to Yiddish and as a living language. They wanted to modernize the archaic and cumbersome biblical Hebrew and create a renewed written Hebrew.

The Maskilim succeeded in dispatching Eastern European Jews into the late nineteenth-century Hebrew renaissance that enabled the commitment of Russian Jewish immigrants to Palestine in the early twentieth century to make modern Hebrew the popular language of Zion. The form and substance of the modern Hebrew literary journal that flourished in Odessa in 1890 and then in Jerusalem of 1920 had its forerunners among the German Maskilim in the 1840s.

Easy it is to point out that Moses Mendelssohn's grandson, the symphonic composer Felix Mendelssohn, was already a Christian and suggest that the Haskalah led to assimilation and then conversion. Rather, modernity led to assimilation and conversion. The Haskalah led to modern Jewish historiography, to the penetration of secular learning into the Russian towns and villages, and to the making of modern Hebrew and its later identification with Zionism.

The fourth outcome of the Haskalah is socially the most extensive and familiar today—modern Reform Judaism. Confidence in exercising selectivity toward Jewish tradition—derived from historical understanding of its past, a need for middle-class German Jews to practice a religion visibly similar to German Protestantism and Kantian philosophy—impelled the rise of Reform or liberal Judaism in mid-nineteenth-century Germany. It was then brought to the United States by the wave of emigration from Germany and fostered at Hebrew Union College in Cincinnati, the Midwest center of these German Jewish immigrants, as the institutional focus for learned instruction and for the training of American Reform rabbis. Hebrew Union College, founded by Rabbi Isaac Mayer Wise in 1875, continues in its role as the center of Reform Judaism to the present day, with another campus in New York City.

Middle-class German Jews of the nineteenth century wanted to feel that their attendance at synagogue on a Saturday—or better still, on a Friday night, thereby avoiding interference with Saturday business—was no different in essential religious experience and form of worship from what was offered in the Lutheran and Calvinist churches. They were devout and literate and enterprising full-fledged German citizens too, but of the Mosaic rather than the Christian persuasion.

In practice this meant—beyond erosion of Sabbath and kashruth observance (a matter left to family and individual choice)—that the major visible departure from Orthodox Judaism was a drastic editing and downsizing of the liturgy for Sabbath (the siddur) and the High Holidays of Rosh Hashanah and Yom Kippur (the mahzor). The length of the service was cut in half. The agonizing repetitions of prayer in the Orthodox liturgy, pardonable or even desirable in times and places where communal service in a warm synagogue led by admired pentecostal rabbis was an amenity, but now a bore and inconvenience for enlightened and busy people, were eliminated.

The more idiosyncratic and passionate medieval prayers, discordant with enlightened Kantianism, were removed. While the more important prayers were still uttered in Hebrew, a vernacular (German, English) translation was also vocalized by the congregation for everything. Gender segregation was abandoned in the synagogue's seating, although women were still denied ordination to the rabbinate. Prayers and readings were adopted from general literature or closely transliterated from Protestant services.

The effect of the truncation and editing of the liturgy was to make the rabbinical sermon, given in the national vernacular (rather than in Hebrew or Yiddish) much more central to the service. The sermon was freed from windy glossing of the biblical text and usually resembled a university lecture on a moral and spiritual theme. In Reform congregations, skill in sermonizing came to count more than personal sanctity as a criterion for the congregation's selection of a rabbi.

And since affluent and well-educated Jews only rarely needed the ministrations of a rabbi, his sermon on Friday night or on the High Holidays became their main moment of encounter with him. This was about as far as anyone could get from the Hasidic zaddik who was the high-impact center of family and individual lives, more reverently influential than parents or spouses in shaping experience and ideas.

Reform Judaism that came out of the early nineteenth-century

Haskalah and migrated with German immigrants to the United States represented not only a radical reform of synagogue liturgy but also a loosening of the bonds of community and an atomization of Jewish experience within the very loose perimeters of the Reform synagogue community. The synagogue indeed became more a service center, drawn upon by private choice, like a particularly good pastry shop, than a centralized and homogenizing force in the lives of quasi-assimilated European and American Jews.

Orthodoxy still had its adherents, even among the well-educated and affluent. But by 1900 Reform Judaism was an attractive alternative for millions of the Jewish bourgeoisie, who had no time for, patience with, or sympathy with medieval survival and Eastern European conservative practice, but still wanted to retain and secularize an explicit association with open-ended Jewish culture.

The mainline Jewish transcendental view of the deity, going back to the Bible, was given new shape and emphasis by the Kantian-articulated, Haskalah-rooted Reform Judaism. God was the inscrutable noumenon, in Kantian terms—the creator and the cause, but so distant as to be entirely beyond human reason and accessibility. Only God's phenomenal affects were known to mankind, these attributes appearing in nature and history where their movements were discovered and mapped by the liberal intellect.

The problem with this reasonable, further attenuated Jewish transcendentalism was that God was so elevated into an inscrutable and inaccessible Kantian noumenon that it was unclear what could be the purpose of prayer directed to such a remote and self-referential being. Prayer was not a means, in Haskalah-Kantian Reform Judaism, of access to God, of personal communication with an intervening deity. It was a form of cultural affirmation, a formal emblem to identify Germans and later Americans of the Mosaic persuasion. It served this function along with the top hats that Reform men in the nineteenth century (and still so in English synagogues) liked to wear to communal prayer—a gathering of affluent and educated gentlemen to affirm their membership in the Jewish corporation, Yahweh being chairman of the board, a remote figure resident in some other city or distant country.

Whatever its intrinsic intellectual limitations, the Haskalah for close to a century, and its derivation in Reform Judaism, did a great deal of good in Jewish life both on the personal and communal level. It fell short of those radical theological and liturgical changes that would have represented a full encounter between Judaism and modernity, but it made significant gestures in that direction and thereby retained within a Jewish ambience over time millions of highly educated Jews, especially in Germany and the United States, who otherwise would have abandoned completely their Jewish identity.

The tragedy of the Haskalah and Reform Judaism was that it had no way of countering the rise of new barbarism and ethnic cleansing in Central Europe from the 1920s onward. It could only suffer in silence as Jews were bloodied and them massacred by state terrorism.

This breakdown was first graphically and prophetically signaled in Franz Kafka's novels written in the 1920s. Kafka was a health insurance executive in Prague. The same theme provides the focus of the novels of Israeli Aaron Appelfeld appearing since the 1960s. Kafka anticipated and Appelfeld retrospectively depicted the advent of state terrorism in Central Europe. In these persuasive works of fiction, Kafka and Appelfeld show the hopelessness and feebleness, the dumb anxiety and fatal resignation exhibited by the Jewish upper-middle-class Central European enlightment as the remains of the Kantian world were buried under the heels of the monstrous simplifiers of the twentieth century.

A leading manifestation of Jewish immersion in modernity and emancipation in the nineteenth century was the theoretical and moral affinity of Jewish entrepreneurs and members of the professions for the doctrine of the market economy or liberal capitalism. This was a reflection of their personal activity and social success. Market economic theory fit in beautifully with the Kantian-inspired Reform Judaism. God was a distant and inaccessible creator, and the phenomenal world that He had created and set in motion and never seemed to interfere with was the context of human behavior. But this phenomenal world was accessible to rational understanding. It was for the most part a morally defensible world operating according to the laws of nature and history.

For emancipated and well-educated Jews, the market economy was among the most readily identifiable and presently shaping structural segments in this God-created, rationally explicable, phenomenal world they experienced.

The prime theorist of the market economy for the nineteenth

century, whose economic theory is still canonical in most economics departments and all business schools, was a Sephardic English banker, David Ricardo, writing in London in the 1820s. There is a direct line from Ricardo to Milton Friedman, the Chicago Jewish market theorist of the 1980s who was the guru of the Reaganites in the United States and the Thatcherites in Britain.

Ricardo lives. He owed much, of course, to the clever Glasgow moral philosopher Adam Smith, writing in the 1770s. But it was Ricardian economic theory that became and remains the theoretical foundation of that market capitalism in which so many nineteenth- and twentieth-century Jews made their fortune and general fame, or at least found the means for a satisfying private family life. Ricardo was the Moses of Jewish capitalism, who brought down the tables of truth to show to the chosen people and the admiring Gentiles as well.

The main point of Ricardian economics is identical with that of Reform Judaism's Haskalah-Kantian theology. Just as God in the latter is a creator whose majesty is humanly unapproachable, so the market is a universal, rationalizing structure that cannot be modified by human will or sentiment, such as by paying wages beyond the minimum with which the market can operate, or by state interference with the business cycle or capital accumulation. Leave God and the market alone and attend to your personal, family, and communal lives and business interests.

The phenomenological Kantian message parallels Ricardo's demonstration that the market economy must be left alone by ethics and politics to maximize and distribute wealth. Trying for a close encounter with the deity leads to uncouth Hasidic practices and superstition and threatens a return to the ghetto. Trying to rectify the market's distribution of wealth and poverty by government intervention will produce not only social anomalies but also severe economic underdevelopment and therefore much more poverty than the minimally necessary amount that liberal capitalism allots.

Both Ricardian economics and Reform Judaism can be seen as partisan self-promotion for the entrepreneurial and professional classes. Their wealth, ease, learning, and power are allegedly the result of privilege and power rather than divine and scientific revelations of truth in cosmology and sociology. There is inevitably a degree of self-justification involved in the mutually interactive Reform

Judaism Haskalah-Kantian theology and Ricardian economics.

But there is also involved the austerity, the asperity, the social aspiration of the postmedieval Jew who has found stability, comfort, and reason in modernity in its cultural and fiscal aspects, and has no desire or motive for going beyond this resting place in the Jewish historical pilgrimage and wants to make it a permanent home.

Both Reform Judaism and liberal capitalism, whatever their limits intellectually as doctrines, whatever their propensity to cut off spiritual exaltations and impede social revolutions, are quiet havens at last for the Jews where they can be at peace with their Gentile neighbors, within the Christian state, and draw upon their comfortable bank accounts and investments and cultivate the material and behavioral amenities of life. It is a dry, quietly happy world of bourgeois learning, security, and wisdom. There is no need to seek further. Here world history and Jewish history putatively end.

But other Jews would not let history end. They summoned the radical wrath of the prophets to condemn the bourgeois order as unjust and sought a socialist era to supersede the quiet, secure, rich world of Reform Judaism and Ricardian economics. Socialism and the labor movement were, it must be stressed, an asserted opposition, a proposed alternative, not a definitive replacement for the symbiotic juncture of Haskalah-Kantian generated Reform Judaism and market capitalism, which endures fitfully to the present day from Los Angeles and Scarsdale to Herzliah, Toronto, London, and all the other pleasant and salubrious enclaves of market capitalism and liberal enlightenment.

The Red and the Black is Stendhal's great political novel about post-Napoleonic France, the red standing for the revolutionary and Bonapartist tradition, the black for neo-Catholic conservative reaction. The great political novel of Jewry in the nineteenth and twentieth centuries would have to be called *The Black, the Red, and the White*. The black stands for perpetuation of Halakic-rabbinical Judaism. The black kapotes—the long morning coats—and big round felt hats of the Orthodox signify the continuance of the rabbinical-Hasidic world in Eastern Europe and pockets of this persuasion elsewhere, their adherence to once fashionable seventeenth-century clothing styles remarkably similar to the taste of cloistered Catholic nuns who adhered to widow's robes of seventeenth-century France as their habit.

The red stands for three generations of Jewish socialists, communists, and radical labor leaders sprinkled all the way from St. Petersburg to Warsaw to the Rhineland and England, to the New York City sweatshops and Pennsylvania mining regions. The white stands for the scions of Haskalah and market capitalism, bleached of their ghetto and shtetl descent, immersed in a clean Gentile world of starched white collars and crisp silk dresses.

The black tradition of orthodoxy has its recent spokesmen in Israel and the United States—David Hartman, Joseph Soloveichik, Norman Lamm, Irving Greenberg, and in his own raffish, marginal way, Isaac Bashevis Singer—all trying to instill life and find persuasive spirituality in the rabbinical Orthodox tradition. The socialists have plenty of celebrants, since they entered into the mainstream of the radical left tradition and are mourned and glorified today by academic historians, both Jew and Gentile.

The richness and variety of the Haskalah-capitalist heritage is little cultivated and not even identified in its integrity as a Jewish heritage. But it is there, remarkably vital not only in the inspiring and shaping of Reform Judaism, not only in the stories of Jewish business success in the late nineteenth century from Central Europe west to Colorado's mining regions, but in its creative facets. The white force embraced other trends in the nineteenth century and cultivated them within the rubric of liberal capitalism.

The first of these varied expressions of the Jewish white tradition was imperialism, personified in and defined by Benjamin Disraeli, the ethnically Jewish, still self-consciously racially Jewish prime minister of Britain in the 1860s and 1870s. His father was a middle-class Sephardic Londoner whose family had emigrated from Italy in the eighteenth century. After a row with the synagogue elders, Isaac Disraeli, a literary critic of some note, trooped his whole family to the Anglican baptismal font, and that is how little Ben grew up a Christian. He remained one, a formerly pious member of the Church of England and married to a wealthy Gentile widow.

But Disraeli's Jewish consciousness ran deep. In the romantic novels by which he launched his public career, a swarthy, mysterious, Jewish billionaire usually rescues the handsome fair-haired Christian hero-and-heroine couple. Disraeli, with his olive complexion, his Mediterranean ringlets, his foppish clothes and jewelry, thereby released his fantasy triumph as the Jewish wonder-worker set to build the British empire and make Queen Victoria empress of India.

The nineteenth-century upper middle-class Jews liked imperialism because it made for multi-ethnic world entities in which they felt less conscious of their racial separateness. All sorts of races, besides the ruling master race—Anglo-Saxon or whatever—comprised a world empire, and Jews belonged to it without apologizing for their foreign origins and their exotic or marginal character.

They could also lord it over the conquered or submerged peoples—the blacks in the United States and South Africa, the Indians in western Canada—and thereby increase their solidarity with the ruling elite race from the home country. The turn-of-the-century imperialist Cecil Rhodes had a Jewish business partner, and South African Jews came to dominate the diamond mining industry in which the native blacks were remorselessly exploited.

Jews poured into western Canada around 1900 at the invitation of the Canadian railroads seeking to develop this sparsely populated vast land. As small-town storekeepers and cattle dealers, the Jews stood, sometimes with compassion, sometimes with contempt, lording it over the native Canadians, the Metis (the French-Indian "half-breeds"), and the Ukrainian farmers. They made money and their sons became Rhodes scholars, chosen as trainees to rule the empire after an Oxford education where they could sit at college dining tables with sons of home county lords and army officers.

In Argentina, the Jews came in with the British railroad builders and coalesced with German and Italian immigrants in Buenos Aires against the Spanish peasants and cowboys of the rural hinterlands.

In Boston, they sought entry to Harvard in 1910, to solidify their fellowship with the Brahmins against the Irish proletarian immigrants. In New York City, they owned the stores and tenements in Harlem and made the poor black immigrants from the South pay dearly for furniture, clothes, and rental housing.

Imperialism was good for the Jews. It offered the money-making fluidity of aggressive market capitalism combined with a race consciousness in which the Jews could hope to fall on the side of the masters, and often did because of the services they could render—once again as in centuries gone by—and the whitened rationality and behavior they could exhibit.

By the 1880s, in the heyday of imperialism, Jewish lawyers and historians were becoming adept at extracting from behind the hegemonic pomp and circumstance a more durable and liberal entity, the English common law that, with its stress on due process and proclivity to level everyone before the bar of justice, could be a useful barrier against the vestiges of anti-Semitic discrimination or its ferocious ideological revival.

A Jewish historian from a wealthy German family, Felix Liebermann, went to England and in one of the greatest triumphs in medieval scholarship disinterred from moldy archives the whole array of earliest English law, upon which the medieval and modern constitution was thought to have been erected.

A precocious young man from a trading Jewish family of Kentucky, Louis D. Brandeis, turned out to be one of the best students of the common law ever to grace the halls of Harvard Law School. Too poor to be able to live on a professor's salary, Brandeis after graduation went into a law partnership with a classmate from a Boston Brahmin family and made a small fortune practicing corporate law. But at the same time, exhibiting that unexplained and perhaps inexplicable ambivalence that distinguished his whole career and life, Brandeis angered the wealthy people and politicians by his effective representation of incipient labor unions. He became a friend and close adviser to Woodrow Wilson, the mystical son of a Virginia Presbyterian minister who made it to the presidency of Princeton and then by guile and luck to the White House in 1912.

Brandeis showed Wilson how market capitalism could be incorporated into and thereby in the long run protected by the network of the regulatory state. When Wilson in 1916 nominated Brandeis to the U.S. Supreme Court, the first Jew for that exalted bench, anti-Semitic fervor and rightist prejudice enlisted the help of the American Bar Association in fighting the U.S. Senate's confirmation of Brandeis's nomination.

But Wilson persisted, as his forbears among the English Puritans had readmitted the Jews to London in the mid-seventeenth century, and Brandeis served for two decades on the Supreme Court. During that time he did little as a justice. He devoted his time and passionate feelings to Zionism and the raising of another Harvard Jew, Felix Frankfurter, to be his heir and successor.

Withdrawn, remote, never revealing his inner feelings and his ultimate motives, Brandeis was the founder of a major subculture among American Jews. He drew market capitalism and secularized and nationalist Judaism into the archaic textuality of the common law, blew off its dust, revitalized it, and made law the codification of competitive wealth, thereby heightening the legitimacy of capital accumulation. Justice Brandeis was aware of the parallel to the old Talmudic tradition—law as the vehicle of wealth and power, but restrained by codified ethics.

A final example of the way the white component in the Jewish world could be put to novel and creative use was the establishment of the new academic field of art history by Aby Warburg, a scion of the Hamburg banking family around 1900. His private "library" in Hamburg, really a small research institute, funded by his family, moved the study of classical, medieval, and Renaissance and baroque art from sloppy and mischievous connoisseurship (in which the Boston expatriate Jew Bernard Berenson was the luminary) to academic discipline with its own methodology—the relating of picture to text—and its own jargon and ways of presentation.

All the art history departments in the world are direct descendants of Aby Warburg's institute (moved to London in 1932 to escape the Nazis) and his greatest Jewish disciple, Erwin Panofsky. Is it anomalous that a Jew should have been so creative in the study of art that was so little cultivated in Jewish tradition? All the more that a liberated white Jew should pursue art history. But one can also see a Judaizing tendency in Warburg's method of art historical criticism. The picture is studied for its "iconology," its pattern of ideas illustrating a textual passage. Art is thereby approached in hermeneutic fashion, again recalling Talmudic exegis, rather than for its aesthetic content.

Yet the most significant aspect of Warburg's development of art history is the demonstration that market capitalism could embrace and fund a purely cultural and academic operation. The distinctive quality of capital was not its materialism, but its liquidity, the fungible capacity of capital to transform itself into any commodity, including art and humanistic literature, that represented dynamic power in society.

Aby Warburg's historical and critical mastery of art was structurally the same as his brothers' mastery in their international bank of money and its investment potential. The transformative interaction between art and capital is central to the nature of the market economy.

The compatibility of market capitalism and Reform Judaism is paralleled by the capacity of capitalism to include intellectual endeavors like Brandeis's extrapolation of the common law and Warburg's art history within its social network. This conformed to the ideals of the Haskalah-Kantian tradition and in the long perspective represents a continuance into the era of modernity of the medieval symbiosis of Halakic Judaism and commercial capitalism.

Louis Brandeis is a revered name among American Jews. A new Jewish university—one of the only two in the United States, along with Orthodox-committed and supported Yeshiva University—Brandeis University, founded in a suburb of Boston in 1948, along with sundry schools and hospitals, bear his name. This reverent fame is due not only to his becoming the first Jewish Supreme Court justice (and until 1993, there were only four others, one of whom had to resign in disgrace) and the most visible Zionist leader in the United States around 1920. It is because Brandeis offered to American Jews a way of responding to modernity that allowed the thousands who entered the legal profession, and families and admirers of these attorneys, a splendid duality.

They could at the same time be fully committed to market capitalism and yet feel satisfied that they were working within its framework to maximize the justice demanded in the Bible, and especially by the prophets, through the application and refinement of common law tradition of due process and constitutionality.

If there were pockets of injustice in the system of market capitalism that contradicted the pleadings of Isaiah, Amos, and Jeremiah for social justice, an ethos that was particularly stressed in the universalist Kantian ethics propounded by Reform Judaism, these imperfections would in time be resolved, according to Brandeisian doctrine, by application of civil rights litigation and legislation that the Anglo-American judicial tradition afforded.

The Jews who became prominent in American labor unions after 1900 can be viewed as pursuing the same duality as Brandeis's legalism. Through collective bargaining, the condition of industrial workers would painstakingly be improved in terms of wages, benefits, and working conditions, and yet the framework of market capitalism could be assented to and not challenged. This was the line taken around 1910 by Samuel Gompers, the founder of the first national and successful labor union, the American Federation of Labor. Gompers was a product of an old American Sephardi family. He became the leader of an American labor movement that struggled hard through collective bargaining to improve the conditions for skilled labor, yet accepted loyally the overall purposes and institutions of big business. Like Brandeis, Gompers was an admirer of Woodrow Wilson and a supporter of Wilsonian liberal progressivism.

In the 1930s and 1940s two Jews prominent in the leadership of American labor unions, David Dubinsky and Sidney Hillman, while more politically active than Gompers and more demanding of workers' benefits, advocated essentially the same position that Gompers did: improvement in the condition of skilled workers through collective bargaining and firm support for the liberal Democratic party that Wilson had shaped and that was led by Franklin Delano Roosevelt and his New Deal.

Louis Brandeis himself had been a firm supporter of labor unions and had represented unions early in his career when this practice was considered very radical by the bar association. So the careers of Gompers, Dubinsky, and Hillman in the American labor movement can be seen as falling within the Brandeis tradition of integrating market capitalism with secularized Reform Judaism.

These important American Jewish labor union leaders in the first half of the twentieth century can be viewed, however, in another perspective: They were at the most conservative pole within a spectrum of phenomena that signified a rebellion of younger Jews against market capitalism—the international socialist and labor movement. Karl Marx (d. 1884), Rosa Luxemburg (d. 1919), and Leon Trotsky (d. 1940) are the great names at the leftist pole of this Jewish spectrum of socialism and the labor movement. Occupying roughly the center were moderate social democrats in the United States in the 1880s: Daniel de Leon, a Sephardi Jew, and Morris Hillquit, an Eastern European immigrant in the first two decades of the twentieth century; Harold Laski in Britain, for four decades the prime intellectual leader of the Labor party; Léon Blum, the leader of the Socialist party in France in the 1920s and 1930s; and David Lewis, for a half-century a leader of the Canadian Socialist party. Jews such as Viktor Adler also played a major role in the socialist movement and militant labor unions in Austria.

The socialist and labor movements of the late nineteenth century and the first half of the twentieth century were such a hodgepodge of varying aims and methods, and so shaped by personal motivation and specific national circumstances, that is not easy to generalize in this area. But in the context of the response to modernity in Jewish history, it is clear that from the 1840s on, into the 1960s and beyond, while most Jews were enthusiastic or passive supporters of and participants in market capitalism, other Jews did not share this commitment to or acquiescence in capitalism.

They wanted a greater share of wealth for the working class, while still accepting the overall market economy (Gompers, Dubinsky, Hillman); or they wanted anti-Ricardian major state intervention in the economy to modify capitalist operation structurally and assure the working class of a much improved life through systemic reorganization of government and society (Hillquit, Laski, Blum, Lewis); or they wanted the complete overthrow of the capitalist system and its replacement by the authoritarian rule of the Communist party on behalf of the working class (Marx, Luxemburg, Trotsky).

Among Jews there was an important group not satisfied with the Brandeis projection: full acceptance of market capitalism as fully compatible with the prophetic ideal of social justice conditioned by legalism and constitutionalism. They wanted strong collective bargaining to improve the workers' conditions, something of which Brandeis approved. Or they wanted to use parliamentary institutions not merely for public regulation of business, as Brandeis proposed, but to restructure society and mitigate market capitalism, a position to the left of Brandeis, but not incompatible with his position. Or they were communist revolutionaries, the full-fledged reds, who sought by whatever means possible, including organized violence and terror, to achieve the Soviet society.

The latter was the incendiary view that radiated from Russia after the Russian Revolution of October 1917 brought the Bolsheviks to power. Half of the six members of the politburo that was the supreme government of Soviet Russia in 1920 were Jews. The first head of the Soviet secret police was Jewish. Jews were prominent in the leadership of the Communist party in Germany, Hungary, and Austria. In the 1920s close to half the members of the small and politically insignificant American Communist party were Jewish.

There was, therefore, an affinity between the Jews and not only market capitalism but also late nineteenth-century and early twentieth-century communism. Empirical data support the contention of

French and German anti-Semites in the 1920s and 1930s that Jews were both capitalists and communists, and thus doubly anathema to the reactionary racist and religious movements that funneled into Judeo-phobic fascism.

The German cartoonists of the 1920s who depicted Jews as both bloated capitalists swallowing European civilization and nefarious red terrorists plotting to blow up Western civilization were not engaging in absolute fantasy, even though Jewish apologists then and historians now like to make that accusation and try to forget the whole thing.

But we cannot forget it. The Jews were divided in their response to modernity along the lines of three groups: the blacks (Orthodox rabbis), who rejected modernity or at least developed no evident policy of responding to modernity's challenge; the whites, who were fully integrated into market capitalism and applauded it; and the reds, who entirely opposed it and wanted to replace it with the communist system.

Looking at this wide spectrum of Jewish involvement in socialism and the labor movement, from the off-white conservative pole, through the pink center, to the deepest red at the left pole, what factors conducive to this dissent from market capitalism can we perceive? There are two. One is a commitment to social justice that anyone brought up in a Jewish home where there is a modicum of vestigial memory of social justice propounded in the Bible, is liable to have.

The obvious comment on this is: Why just the Jews? Don't they read the Hebrew prophets in Christian homes as well? But in the major Christian denominations—Catholic, Lutheran, Calvinist—there is a central pessimism about human nature that works against egalitarian activism: Humanity is regarded as so corruptly sinful that social reconstruction can do little to remove human misery, which in their view is the consequence of the fall of man and the exile from Eden, rather than due to faulty institutions and class polarization. But as a matter of fact, in Christian congregations where the sense of sin is underplayed, in such Evangelical congregations as Methodism, there is a proclivity to socialist activism and labor union activity that resembles this mainstream in modern Jewish history. The leadership of the Canadian Socialist party in the 1930s and 1940s was an amalgam of Methodists and Jews.

Therefore it can be asserted with confidence that the red/pink code, the impulse to socialist activism and labor union leadership among modern Jews, is derived at least in part from a vestigial memory of biblical prophetic utterances on social justice, communicated through family instruction, the synagogue liturgy, rabbinical sermonizing, and Bible reading. Even in heavily assimilated families a tocsin of prophetic demand for social justice filtered through in one way or another during childhood, even if the mature person was thoroughly alienated from Jewish community and religion.

Memory of the prophetic cry for social justice would remain on the edge of or below consciousness, even among those professedly atheistic communists who grew up to hold Judaism, and all revealed religions, in contempt as the opiate of the masses, a narcotic used by the ruling class to make the workers forget their personal misery and lose their class identity.

It was not just the echoing words of prophetic injunctions, affecting the mind like a mantra to save the poor and the downtrodden, that were psychologically at work on the mentality of Jewish reds and pinks. It was Judaism's intrinsic rationality, its elevation of the deity to such a transcendent position, placing the burden for society upon humanity itself, that had a subtle effect conducive to Jewish leftism.

Mainline Christianity, by positing a deity who assumed human form and walked and worked intimately among mankind, mitigates thereby the burden placed on human agency to eliminate the misery of the poor. Judaism leaves societal justice up to humanity, especially the chosen Jews, the light to the nations. This message was communicated in Jewish homes and in the institutions of childhood maturation. It settled into the subconscious, where it continued to be highly motivational for anyone who had not resolved Oedipal feelings. By this theory, Jewish reds would be people distinguished by unresolved Oedipal feelings.

As adults they subconsciously remain in deep conflict with the parent of the same gender and project outward from there to rebel against and try to punish and overthrow patriarchal and matriarchal institutions of authority in society. The working class becomes sentimentalized as fellow victims and hopefully secret sharers in their post-adolescent rebellions.

This is the psychological explanation for the widespread phenomenon of Jewish reds. There is a sociological explanation as well.

The second factor conducive to Jewish overinvolvement on the left and to the appearance of a hard core of reds among Jews was the inability of modernity and its institutional forms to absorb sufficiently brilliant and active younger Jews seeking a suitable role for themselves in secular society. The Jews innately spawned so many intelligent and ambitious young men and women that not even the vibrant plasticity of the modern market economy and society could satisfy many of them. Once the Jews were emancipated, too many younger Jews of superior capability could not find places in society and economy that were adequate for the exercise of their talents.

The Jews, once emancipated and given opportunity for mobility, were genetically so superior that market capitalism could not accommodate some of this superior species, and inevitably some reacted to this rebuff by becoming not whites but reds.

By this thesis, societies in which Jews were not yet fully emancipated—Germany in the 1840s, Russia in the 1890s—or were legally emancipated but still limited in economic opportunity—Vienna and Budapest around 1910, the United States in the immigrant era from 1890 to 1940—would be especially productive of Jewish reds. This is indeed what happened.

A further empirical check on this sociology of the Jewish left spectrum is illustrated by what happened in the United States in the 1960s, when the Jews were vastly overrepresented in the New Left movement in the college age generation, as they have been among communists and socialists from 1890 to 1940. The main reason for this leftist bulge among younger Jews in the 1960s is that American suburbia of the 1950s could not provide enough interesting and rewarding jobs for a generation of highly educated Jews brought up in suburbs to expect the best of everything. So they proceeded to attack market capitalism itself, using the Vietnam war as a shield for rebellion, just as university-educated young Jews did in Germany in the 1840s and in Russia around 1900, where a similar inelasticity of modernity occurred.

The message can be put very simply. Emancipated Jews are constant in their search for superior access to education and opportunity for social mobility. If the social system is not malleable enough to open up good jobs for all these educated and ambitious young Jews, a significant number of them will become reds instead of whites—

Karl Marx, Rosa Luxemburg, and Leon Trotsky instead of David Ricardo, Louis Brandeis, and Aby Warburg.

In the century and a half after 1800, there were no greater intellectual luminaries of market capitalism than the Jews Ricardo, Brandeis, and Warburg. But also before the Russian Revolution in 1917, of the four communist giants, Marx was a German Jew, Luxemburg a Polish-German Jew, and Trotsky a Russian Jew. Even the fourth, V. I. Lenin, is suspected by some of having had a Jewish grandparent that the Soviet government, anti-Semitic since the mid-1920s, had kept secret.

Karl Marx was the son of a Rhineland lawyer. He studied philosophy under G. W. Hegel, the leading German philosopher after Kant, and became the intellectual leader of the left Hegelians (Hegel's own politics were rightist). Implicated as a revolutionary in the upheavals of 1848, Marx along with his colleague, friend, and many times co-author, Friedrich Engels, fled to England, a haven for all kinds of political refugees in the nineteenth century.

Marx had married a Gentile woman of the petty nobility. Neither had any money. He eked out a living as European correspondent for a New York newspaper, supplemented by incessant handouts from Engels, whose wealthy textile manufacturing family had sent their radical son to Manchester to represent the family business in the heartland of the English Industrial Revolution.

Marx had a miserable life of genteel poverty, sitting day after day in the reading room of the British Museum, working on his immense treatise on the economics and history of capitalism, which he never finished. His wife was a shrew, and his brilliant daughter, after a bad marriage, committed suicide.

This diurnal pain was alleviated for Marx only by meetings of the socialist international organization, usually in Paris. While Marx advertised himself as a "scientific" socialist and poured scorn on the utopian romantics of the early nineteenth century, he was only scientific in his detailed use of economic theory, developed by Ricardo, to support his millennial vision, as sentimental as anything ever conceived by a Cabalistic messiah or zaddik.

The internal contradictions of capitalism (e.g., its inability to find ever-expanding markets) and intense class polarization, would result in an historical apocalypse, in which the proletariat, led by the vanguard communist party, would overthrow the bourgeoisie and inaugurate the classless society. This was Marx's millennial vision. Marx never explained how this heaven on earth would operate. But it is a vision and an expectation that has had greater appeal around the world than any new faith since Christianity and Islam.

Rosa Luxemburg was a well-educated middle-class Jewish woman who joined in the late nineteenth-century Polish Jewish immigration westward into Germany. She always spoke German with a pronounced Polish-Yiddish accent. She became a fiery labor leader, a pioneering feminist, and finally one of the two communist leaders who tried to carry out a red revolution in Berlin in 1919, in the confusion and malaise following the surrender of Germany at the end of World War I. A countercoup by a proto-Nazi rightist group of military officers, the Free Corps, among whom was the later Jewish eminent medievalist Ernst Kantorowicz, put a sudden stop to Luxemburg's communist revolution. Three or four naval officers murdered her in a taxi and threw her body into a canal, from which it was not rescued for several months.

Unlike Marx, Luxemburg knew what a Soviet state would look like; it would be authoritarian and terrorist, but perhaps not as vindictively violent as that envisioned and actually created by Lenin in Moscow. Luxemburg, long forgotten, became an idol of the New Left in the 1960s. Her Jewish background was rarely cited.

Leon Trotsky (Bronstein) was a leader not of the Bolsheviks who seized power in Russia in the October Revolution of 1917, but the other, rival group among the communists, the Mensheviks. This split was mainly a personality dispute, but the Mensheviks may have been a little less authoritarian than Lenin's Bolsheviks. Long a public enemy to the czarist regime, Trotsky at the outbreak of the revolution was living in exile in New York City, where he could join another Russian Jewish émigré, Sholem Aleichem, for blintzes at Ratner's dairy restaurant on the Lower East Side, and listen to Aleichem's endless bittersweet anecdotes about Jewish life in Eastern Europe, for which Trotsky had the utmost contempt as the nadir of the parasitical petty bourgeois.

In 1917 Trotsky took the first boat back to revolutionary Russia, made his peace with Lenin, and was given the seemingly impossible task of organizing the Red Army against the White Ukrainian reactionary pogromists and the invading anti-Bolshevik Allied troops. The indiscriminate massacre of Jews in the Ukraine under White army control from 1918 to 1921 constituted a rehearsal for the first highly organized stage of the Holocaust under German rule there in 1941–42, again with extensive assistance from Ukrainians. Although heretofore Trotsky had not been able to tell one end of a gun from the other, he did a marvelous job as the first head of the Red Army and saved the Bolshevik regime and thereby probably also a million Jewish lives during the Russian Civil War.

Who would have thought that this red Jewish intellectual, sitting around in a cheap cafeteria in New York engaging in hair-splitting ideological disputation, or listening, while he ate his blintzes and sour cream, to Sholem Aleichem fantasize again about Jewish life in the old country, would three years later organize an army that crushed the Ukrainian descendants of those seventeenth-century pogromists who had massacred Polish Jews? Not the Ukrainians and other counterrevolutionaries.

Trotsky was their worst nightmare—the Jew who exercises the awesome power that modernity granted to the state, if the political leaders had the courage to wield it, as Trotsky as well as Lenin and later Stalin did. If the Palestinians and other Arabs who undertook to wipe out a much outnumbered Israel between 1948 and 1967 had read Trotsky's biography carefully, they might have perceived the possibility that the Jews could again, as in the ancient world, become fierce and skillful in war, and the Arabs might have become more guarded in their tactics.

Trotsky was a brilliant writer whose partisan but persuasive memoir and history of the Russian Revolution remains a classic account. He was an internationalist (like Marx) who wanted Soviet Russia to be the pulsating center, a secular Zion, for immediate efforts at world revolution, giving aid and guidance to communists everywhere to overthrow capitalism and the bourgeoisie by all available means. Trotsky's was the mind of an apocalyptic Cabalistic visionary transformed by modernity into a completely secular and materialist millennial prophet.

Soviet Russia had not, however, recovered economically from World War I followed by four years of civil war. Trotsky's policy of giving priority in the commitment of strained Soviet resources to world revolution seemed extremist and perilous in contrast with the apparently more cautious and more rational program advocated by Joseph Stalin, Trotsky's competitor to succeed Lenin in the mid-1920s as head of the Soviet state—the policy of "socialism in one country." (Of course, once in power, Stalin in the 1930s and again after World War II in the late 1940s adopted precisely Trotsky's program of world revolution). The victorious Stalin, gathering to his support most of the other Jews in the Soviet executive, isolated Trotsky, an inept politician, and expelled him from the Soviet Union in 1929.

Trotsky went first to Paris, where he was lionized by leftist intellectuals. He also had a nucleus of fervent admirers among the red and pink Jewish intelligentsia of New York. They were mostly Brooklyn graduates of plebeian, tuition-free City College, who were putting out the *Partisan Review*, a Trotskyite (in its early years) monthly devoted to politics and the arts. Increasingly isolated, Trotsky finally settled in Mexico City, where a Stalinist agent killed him with an icepick in 1940.

In the first half of the twentieth century, Marxist-Leninist communism ran like an electromagnetic lightning flash through Jewish society from Moscow to Western Europe, the United States and Canada, gaining the lifelong adherence of brilliant, passionately dedicated Jewish men and women. It had some of the same affects and motives as the Sabbataian messianic movement in the late seventeenth and eighteenth centuries. In retrospect, Jewish communism looks weird and perhaps pointless, but at the time there was an unquestioning compulsion of many thousands of morally committed, energetic Jews to devote their lives to it and sacrifice their well-being and that of their families for it.

In the 1930s the Asiatic monster Stalin drew to Moscow fervent Jewish communists not only from all over the Soviet Union but from Central and even Western Europe and a few from America; trapped them mercilessly like flies in a bottle; and purged, shot, imprisoned, and tortured them and their families by the dozens. Poland and Czechoslovakia in the late 1940s repeated the process of momentary Jewish ascension to power in Soviet states and then devastating destruction of the Jewish communist leaders by Stalinist police agents and military.

Amazingly, in the United States in the 1980s a peculiar strain of literature appeared, the memoirs of "red diaper babies," nostalgic for the good old days of the fervent communist commitments and activities of their red parents, among these activities being demonstrations against the executions of Julius and Ethel Rosenberg, the pathetic

Brooklyn communist couple, squashed like mosquitoes in the Cold War and executed for atom espionage in 1953.

There were dozens of smaller models of Luxemburg and Trotsky in the first half of the twentieth century all over the world—Jewish communists who hazarded their lives, their security, their spouses and children in pursuit of the millennial dreams of red revolution that would somehow reverse history, or end it, or triumph over it. And like Luxemburg and Trotsky, so many of these Jewish communists came to unhappy and violent ends, or slipped into old age with nothing tangible to rescue from a lifetime of idealism and effort. It was a repetition in the context of modernity of the medieval Sabbataian phenomenon.

Alongside the volatile and poignant, and ultimately futile, drama of Jewish communism, there existed from the 1880s into the 1930s a much more moderate, prosaic, and constructive unit, the Bund, the Yiddish-speaking, left-leaning, but noncommunist labor union. Before the Russian Revolution the Bund was the largest labor union in the czarist empire, and its activities were legal.

The Bund had a profound and beneficial effect on the daily life of working-class Jews in the large cities of western Russia and Poland. It ran schools, clinics, libraries, burial societies, newspapers, theater groups, and adult education facilities. It was liberal, humanitarian, democratic, and peaceful. It was a powerful force for the betterment of Jewish life in the wake of the Industrial Revolution in Eastern Europe.

The Bund stood at the center of the bold and for a time successful effort to create a permanent Yiddish-speaking secular society, an Eastern European Diaspora cultural homeland for the Jews in the context of modernity. The Bund was labor unionism in its most beneficial, progressive, and humanitarian mode.

But the Bund's era of effective operation was a relatively short one—the two decades before and after 1900. The Russian Revolution began a period of rapid deterioration for the Bund. The Soviet government suppressed it and shot and imprisoned many of its leaders—Jewish Bolsheviks eliminating Jewish labor leaders. In the newly independent Poland of the 1920s and 1930s, dominated by Catholic rightists, the Bund struggled to find political allies and could not do so. In 1939 the Nazi and Soviet armies engulfed Poland, and the Bund, the largest and most effective Jewish labor union of the Diaspora, disappeared.

The Bund was a central component of a cultural movement and social formation that was central to Jewish life not only in Eastern Europe but also in New York City and a few other urban centers in the United States and Canada from the 1880s to the early 1920s. It takes its name from its slogan of Yiddishkeit (Jewishness), the programmatic advocacy of a distinctive Yiddish-speaking linguistic and minority culture with its own literature, entertainment, schools, and press, and beyond that a permanently developing secular, national way of life in the Jewish Diaspora.

Yiddishkeit had approximately the same historical trajectory as its strong Bundist component. It reached its peak in the early years of the twentieth century and was in sharp decline and disintegration by the 1920s, manipulated and largely suppressed by the Soviet authorities, rejected by the Hebrew-speaking community in Palestine, and undermined by the rapid assimilation of American and Canadian Jews to English-speaking culture. Yiddishkeit's last vestiges were extinguished in the Nazi death camps.

Yiddishkeit exists now only in museum nostalgia and artificial academy memory. Yet it was a vibrant language bloc, cultural movement, and social force among millions of Jews in Eastern Europe and America for almost half a century, and it is still passionately remembered by old pensioners in Tel Aviv and Miami.

In 1910 Yiddishkeit was a vibrant and seemingly highly durable culture. In Odessa, Vilnius, Kiev, Warsaw, and New York, its institutional base was strong, through schools, newspapers, book publishers, theaters, adult education groups, and speakers' tours. It was confidently creating a distinctive literature of poetry, novels, short stories, and dramatic and historical writing. It was effectively absorbing vanguard ideas from philosophy and the behavioral sciences, and transmitting them in popularized form to millions of Yiddish-reading Jews in Eastern Europe and the United States and Canada.

It was transforming the Yiddish language itself from a marginal patois of the streets, heretofore given literary form mainly in religious handbooks for women, into a vibrant, expressive, supple literary language capable of communicating on any subject. As it became more literary, Yiddish in its grammatical structure tended to become more like modern German, but in the hands of its masters it was a special, distinctive cultural instrument, with its own peculiar voice ringing of the ghetto streets and hermeneutic minds liberated from rabbinical yeshivas to accommodate modernity.

Yiddishkeit of 1880 to 1920 was mostly secular in orientation but with a sentimental nationalist attachment to the Jewish past, especially ancient patriarchs, prophets, and heroes. It had a soft spot for zaddikim as long as they had no power and were waning as leaders in Jewish society. It loved the Diaspora's physical environment—icy Russian and Canadian winters; greening Polish springs; hazy autumns in Kentucky and Tennessee, as well as the colorful clotted pushcart streets of Manhattan's Lower East Side and Brooklyn.

Yiddishkeit was thoroughly leftist but not communist. It was humanitarian, liberal, and democratic, often naively so. It imagined that it could in the eastern Pale or New York ghetto create an autonomous world of Yiddish culture, uniting the best of modernity and modernism with a Jewish heritage from which stern Halakah had been mostly filtered out, leaving a sentimental and idealistic substratum.

Yiddishkeit's main information highway was the daily newspaper and the literary weekly and monthly. It was very much driven by the techniques of popular journalism, seconded by domestic theater, vaudeville, and, in its closing years, film. Its spirit endures in the artfully contrived nostalgic evocations of Isaac Bashevis Singer. But an equally quick and perhaps more authentic recall of this vanished culture can be gained simply by watching the Molly Picon films from the 1930s made in Poland.

Yiddishkeit was extremely prolific in literary production of all kinds—poetry, drama, fiction, and history. But its greatest poet, Haim Nachman Bialik, chose, as a Zionist, to write almost entirely in Hebrew after his early work in Yiddish, and his mature masterpieces are in Hebrew.

The large volume of Yiddish drama is marked by sentimentality and overplotting to satisfy a commercial audience. The one play generated by Yiddishkeit that is still performed, S. Ansky's *The Dybbuk*, portrays the superstition and demonology of the premodern, Hasidic world. The dramatists of Yiddishkeit, while consciously imitative of Henrik Ibsen's realism, failed to produce a play that dealt persuasively with their own society.

Five important writers of fiction were products of Yiddishkeit. But Abraham Cahan, the editor of the then immensely popular newspaper *The Jewish Daily Forward* in New York, wrote *The Rise of David Levinsky* (1917), a clinical account of social mobility in immigrant New York society, in English. And the greatest of all writers who came out of the world of Yiddishkeit, Isaac Babel, wrote in the 1920s in Russian. His *Red Calvary*, about the strange encounter between Cossacks and Jews during the Russian Civil War around 1920, derived from his own experiences, is the finest piece of fiction writing to come out of Eastern European Jewish culture.

The three major fiction writers generated by the culture of Yiddishkeit who wrote in *mama lushen* (the "mother tongue" of Yiddish) were Isaac Leib Peretz; Mendele Mocher Sforim, "Mendele the Bookseller" (Sholem Abramovich); and the still famous Sholem Aleichem (Sholem Rabinowitz).

Peretz, who was very influential as an ideological advocate of Yiddish language, schooling, and autonomous Diaspora culture, was an effective if somewhat sentimental teller of Hasidic tales.

Mendele makes for hard reading today. His elaborately plotted novels tell of life in the shtetl villages and small towns of the 1870s and 1880s, on the eve of modernity. They contain graphic, trenchant descriptions of the consequences of ignorance, poverty, and superstition in the decaying Hasidic and rabbinical world. Mendele in these passages showed he had the ability to be the Yiddish Zola, but his need to tell a romantic story and gain readers mitigated his social criticism.

At least half of Sholem Aleichem's prolific output was an exercise in contrived nostalgia—he wrote for the Jewish newspapers in New York humorous accounts, laced with sympathy and pathos, of life in the old country while he was living in the Bronx. Sholem Aleichem's sentimental stories about the village poor, the life and times of Tevye the milkman, were further sentimentalized when the stories were turned into the musical comedy *Fiddler on the Roof* in the 1960s.

Much more subtle is Aleichem's volume of stories about Motel-Payse, the cantor's son—his growing up in a small town, his personal agonies, his social escapades. There is psychological insight as well as nostalgic humor here—a Yiddish Booth Tarkington.

None of these three eminences of Yiddish fiction are anywhere near the level of Isaac Babel:

> In the Red Cavalry stories, Cossack vitality is opposed to Jewish other worldliness, intellectuality, and weakness: the fullness of life is associated with Cossacks, the whiff of death with Jews.

When Cossacks are hurt, they wreak vengeance; when Jews are hurt, they have only words . . . The Hasidic world . . . is dying . . . One of the greatest prose writers of twentieth-century Russia, Babel was also the most Jewish. [Alice Stone Nakhimovsky]

Babel was eliminated by Stalin in 1939. Both a product of Yiddish-keit and a writer who clearly surpassed it, he is the endpoint of the world of Yiddishkeit. Yet while Sholem Aleichem is a familiar name today among middle-class American Jews, Babel is almost unknown to the Jewish public.

The voluminous historical writing of Simon Subnow, Yiddish-keit's prominent historian, exhibits defects similar to those of the leading fiction writers in the Yiddish language. Dubnow was by pro-fession a journalist, who worked in Odessa and Warsaw and finally in Riga, Latvia, where he died at an advanced age at the hands of the Nazis in 1941. Dubnow's important historical work was done in the first quarter of the century. He had no professional training as a his-torian, and regrettably this shows in his work, which is deficient in research and critical rigor. But he wrote the first history of the Jews in Poland and got the story more or less right. Later he embarked on an ambitious multivolume *World History of the Jewish People*, which was popular and was eventually translated from Yiddish into English.

Dubnow is always reasonably well-informed, but never deeply engaged in the historical material. He lacks sociological insight. He is a confirmed Diaspora-type nationalist, who never gives an inch to the Christians. He writes an even, smooth, if unexciting prose.

His greatest contribution to Jewish historiography was not his voluminous narratives, educational as they were for the Yiddish readers of his day, but his disclosure of the richness of Jewish archival material in Eastern Europe, going back to sixteenth-century Poland. This stimulated the founding of the Jewish Scientific Institute (YIVO) to collect and preserve this material. Vast amounts of docu-mentation were lost at the hands of the Nazis and much is still held hostage by Russian agencies, but a splendid YIVO archive in New York is Dubnow's monument. From its rich collection will eventually be written the history of Yiddishkeit.

The Jews in Poland had been speaking a Yiddish patois since they came from Germany in the sixteenth century. But Yiddishkeit was something well beyond this basic language usage. It not only modified Yiddish into a more literary language but sought to employ it as the base for a distinctive, permanent Diaspora culture responsive to modernity.

Yiddishkeit had only a couple of generations to show its intellectual and artistic possibilities before it went into rapid contraction in the 1920s under the combined blows of Soviet hostility, Zionist Hebraism, and American Jewry's rapid changeover to an English base in a highly assimilated culture. Babel's marvelous fiction gives us an indication of the intellectual and philosophical heights that Yiddishkeit might have reached in another two or three generations of expansion and maturation, instead of contraction and decline due to irresistible external forces.

Another indication of Yiddishkeit's high potential lay in the Jewish art theaters on New York City's lower Second Avenue in the first third of this century under the leadership of great directors Jacob Ben-Ami, Maurice Schwartz, and Jacob Adler. By the 1930s, as audiences dwindled, a younger generation of Yiddish actors such as Paul Muni, John Garfield, and Edward G. Robinson made brilliant careers in the Hollywood studios run by an older and less-educated generation of Jewish film producers. In the 1980s the venerable Stella Adler, who had a short Hollywood career, was still training NYU theater students in the dramaturgy of the Lower East Side that her father, among others, had represented in the waning glorious moments of Jewish art theater in the 1930s.

In 1920 there were two prolific Yiddish poets of extraordinary quality writing in New York City, Mani Leib and Moshe Leib Halpern. By 1950 they were almost unknown; there was hardly left a Yiddish-reading audience for their work, which would have placed them in the elite group of twentieth-century Americn poets had they written in English. An intriguing book by Ruth Wisse, published in 1988, has resurrected their lives and art, but it had to be more a work of literary archaeology than literary criticism.

Columbia and Harvard and a few other universities today offer instruction in Yiddish but for American Jews below the age of sixty it has become an esoteric foreign language, to be mastered only with much exertion. Literary Yiddish is more difficult for Anglophones to learn than the German language from which it is principally derived because of the large number of colloquial phrases and loose grammatical constructions that the Yiddish novelists and poets employed.

To all but a few Yiddish scholars like Professor Wisse, Mani Leib and Moshe Leib Halpern, whose poetry was very familiar to millions of New York Jews when Woodrow Wilson was in the White House, are now as remote as Solomon Ibn Gabirol. Rarely in the history of the world literature have prominent and popular writers so rapidly disappeared from common view.

As I was growing up in Winnipeg, Canada, in the 1940s, an outpost of by then archaic Yiddishkeit, it was peculiar and pathetic to encounter traveling envoys of Yiddish language and literature appearing like lost souls to expound on the beauty and suppleness of the language, giving readings from Peretz to small but enthusiastic audiences. Yiddishkeit was already in 1945 Canada a pathetic time warp revelatory of a vanished world whose last vestiges had disappeared in the Holocaust.

In 1988, while I was teaching at Tel Aviv University, I used to go to Dizengoff Square in the middle of Tel Aviv on a warm Saturday evening and address in Yiddish anyone who looked over the age of sixty. Often I got a delighted response. We sat on the plastic benches, ate bad Israeli ice cream, and talked at length of the old country and the way it was.

Yiddishkeit, backed up by the Bund, aimed to create a permanent national home and distinctive culture for the Jews in the Diaspora. In the 1880s, especially in the heartland of Yiddishkeit, a small minority of intellectuals and activists were questioning the desirability and feasibility of remaining in the Galuth (Diaspora) and began to direct their attention toward a return to their ancestral homeland in Palestine.

All the forces that constituted Jewish responses to modernity contributed to the emergence of modern Zionism in the late nineteenth century. Yiddishkeit heightened national consciousness and the desire for a cultural renaissance. The Haskalah inaugurated the revival of Hebrew as a living language, and this Hebraist literary trend sharpened thinking toward a cultural center in Palestine. Market capitalism generated the billionaire patriarchs, fiscally patrician patrons who were willing to support new agricultural settlements in the old homeland. Socialism and labor movements stirred up visions of a new Jew, casting off the bourgeois character of Jewish employment and life in the Diaspora and returning to work in the Holy Land as a therapy to upgrade Jewish behavior and mentality close to the soil.

Along with these forces contributing to the emergence of Zionism were the beginnings of doubt that modernity would work out for
the Jews. Could they really be assimilated and absorbed into
postmedieval industrial society? Or would vestigial resistance from
Christian anti-Semitism, compounded by the social tension and class
conflict that went along with modernity, as well as a rising tide of
ideological racism in the late nineteenth century, stop or even
reverse the process of Jewish emancipation and assault the Jews with
a wave of deprivation and persecution?

Was European culture systemically enlightened now, or was it
going to turn ugly and chauvinist and restart marginalization and
oppression of the Jews?

These questions began to be asked as early as the 1860s by
Moses Hess, a socialist colleague of Marx. Karl Marx was sure the
Jewish problem was an effect of bourgeois society. With its replacement by the classless society of the future, anti-Semitism and
pogroms would disappear, he claimed. Moses Hess questioned this
and presented a view of cultural despair—that is, anti-Semitic
Catholicism and racism operating on a separate track from the economic one, an essentially non-Marxist argument.

The Zionist tempo picked up after pogroms in Odessa and other
places in southern Russia in the early 1880s. Then a Jewish physician, Leon Pinsker, published *Auto-Emancipation*, in which he contended that Jewish emancipation in Europe was illusory. Western civilization was drenched in Judeo-phobia, and it had started to act up
again. There was only one way to Jewish security, a return to freedom—Zion.

Palestine in the 1880s was a sleepy malaria-ridden backwater of
the decaying Ottoman empire. A few thousand Jews lived in Palestine, nearly all there for religious reasons and existing on handouts
from back home. The sultan in Istanbul was not a bit eager to see
significant Jewish immigration to Palestine and certainly not an influx
of troublemaking younger people. He had no sympathy with a vision
of Palestine as a Jewish homeland. The Arab population in Palestine
was content to work its vineyards, orchards, and sheep-runs. It tolerated a small group of old praying Jews. It wanted no young people's
immigration to threaten their hold on land and water resources.
Zionism faced profound obstacles.

Nevertheless small groups calling themselves Lovers of Zion
began to proliferate in Russia in the 1880s. They saw themselves as

mainly study groups, principally for history and Hebrew language, but occasionally a handful of members would uproot their families and head for the Holy Land, where they were not likely to find employment and also would have to live off charity from the West.

The luminary among the Lovers of Zion emerged in the 1890s in Odessa, the sparkling port town the Jews loved, despite occasional pogroms there by Ukrainians. He was Asher Ginsberg, known by his pen name of Ahad Ha'Am ("One of the People"). He and his wife were both products of old prominent and affluent Hasidic families, and Ahad Ha'Am was more or less observant. In his Yiddish and Hebrew writings, in which he demonstrated high literary skills, he envisioned the Lovers of Zion groups coalescing in an effort to make substantial agricultural settlements in Palestine, to serve as a foundation in the Holy Land for a Hebrew-speaking cultural center for world Jewry.

Politics was not important, in Ahad Ha'Am's view. It did not matter who ruled Palestine, or what the format of the agricultural settlements would be—they could be oriented to either market capitalism or socialism. What mattered was helping young people to go there and establish a Hebrew-speaking base for later immigration, and in the meantime serving as moral arbiters for world Jewry. Support from billionaire patriarchs would help to start this immigration and to fund the support agencies the Zionist immigrants would need.

The billionaire patriarchs, like the Rothschild family, the French Baron Maurice de Hirsch, and the American Loeb and Schiff families, were starting to subsidize Jewish operations in Palestine.

At that point everything changed in Zionism with the sudden emergence of a messianic-type although thoroughly secular leader, Theodor Herzl, the Paris correspondent of a prominent Jewish-owned Viennese newspaper. Herzl's background was thoroughly middle class. Although he obtained a law degree, he soon abandoned practice. Because he had married into a wealthy family, he could afford to take off time from his journalistic work for purposes of Zionist agitating. In the early 1890s he was probably already suffering from the fatal consequence of venereal disease that brought about his death in 1904 at the age of forty-four.

Herzl was a handsome, tall, elegantly bearded, immaculately well-dressed figure, bound to impress the Jewish masses by his appearance. He had only a rudimentary Jewish education and was amazingly ignorant of Jewish history, which he later learned on the job.

He was a new kind of Jewish leader, thoroughly assimilated and without traditional background.

Herzl had made a marginal reputation as the writer of frothy comedies for the Viennese stage and of a highly personal style of journalism that today we would call tabloid. For his newspaper he reported on the sensational trial in Paris of Captain Alfred Dreyfus, a Jewish officer from a prominent Alsatian family, who was convicted of selling military secrets to the Germans and sentenced to life imprisonment in the dreaded French penal colony of Devil's Island off the coast of Latin America.

All the intellectual elite and much of the general population of Paris lined up either for or against Dreyfus, and this split between the liberal left and the Catholic right endured until 1945. The prominent radical journalist and novelist Émile Zola, the liberal politician Georges Clemenceau (later prime minister), and the Jewish novelist Marcel Proust, among many others, worked to overturn Dreyfus's conviction on perjured testimony. After a new trial, he was pardoned, and one of his chief accusers among the army officers committed suicide and another fled the country.

Herzl was deeply moved by the public controversy surrounding Dreyfus. He took note of the resurgence of the anti-Semitic French Catholic right, given additional voice through racist theories borrowed from the then fashionable Social Darwinism, a pseudo-sociology that posited a hierarchy of races, with the Jews assigned to a low rung. The Dreyfus case made many Jews who were well-accommodated to modernity and saw themselves as fully assimilated citizens feel uncomfortable. Herzl reacted to this bourgeois Jewish discomfort. He was keenly aware of the rise of anti-Semitism in Vienna, where the mayor had been elected on an anti-Jewish platform.

Yet as described by his best biographer, Ernst Pawel, Herzl's sudden conversion to Zionism was not merely a reaction to the Dreyfus case and his sense of rising anti-Semitism. If the Dreyfus case revealed Jewish isolation, it could also be construed to indicate just the opposite—the number of distinguished French Gentiles like Zola and Clemenceau who had come to Dreyfus's support and secured the reversal of his conviction was also significant. The Dreyfus case showed that the French system of justice ultimately worked in the case of a Jew subjected to a conspiracy, and that the Jews had plenty of support in liberal Gentile society.

It was not so much that Herzl was convinced by the Dreyfus

case that the Jews were doomed if they stayed in Christian Europe and that they had to seek refuge in their own homeland. It was that Herzl, by whatever psychological process, now saw himself as a kind of Moses destined to lead the Jews back to their ancestral land.

Herzl's plays are full of sentimental junctures and reversals of fortune, and he refashioned his life along romantic lines. His parents had always indulged him, and his family now allowed him to become a full-fledged Zionist agitator, not only making speeches to Jewish groups all over Europe but seeking audiences with the German emperor and the Turkish sultan to abet the gaining of Palestine as the Jewish homeland. His audiences with exalted political figures resulted in nothing tangible but impressed the Jewish masses. His reputation in the Jewish world of Eastern as well as Western Europe rose like a rocket, and he was emboldened to call the first world Zionist congress to meet in Basel, Switzerland, in 1896.

In the hitherto placid little world of Zionism, Herzl's initiatives were not universally welcome. Ahad Ha'Am, the leading Zionist thinker in Eastern Europe, deeply resented Herzl's intrusions and essentially disagreed with his political program, for Ahad Ha'Am saw Palestine not as the goal of mass migration but as an elite cultural center for world Jewry.

Nevertheless, it was impossible to refuse Herzl's call to the first Zionist congress, where the official language for debate was German. An executive committee for the world Zionist organization, headed by Herzl, was selected, and funding was secured from the usual philanthropists. In less than a decade this Viennese fantasist accomplished more for Zionism than anyone in the previous fifteen hundred years.

Shortly before his premature death, Herzl came close to splitting the Zionist movement by expressing sympathy for a British offer to resettle Jews in Uganda in Africa (actually a country much more suitable to successful agriculture than the desiccated Palestine of the time). With his lack of Jewish background, Herzl could not at first perceive the unique meaning of Palestine in Jewish consciousness. But ever the astute politician, he came around, and political Zionism proceeded on its course after his death.

By 1910 a new charismatic figure had appeared on the Zionist scene, this time in Palestine itself. This was the young David Ben-Gurion, who had been among the leaders of the second aliyah (migration) of committed young socialist Zionists to Palestine. They aimed to establish agricultural collectives and not only redeem the country for the Jewish people but transform the allegedly overbourgeoisified Jewish temperament as well. Under the influence of the Russian Jewish philosopher A. D. Gordon, a disciple of Leo Tolstoy, the socialist Zionists believed that working the land with one's own hands in collective settlements would create a "New Jew" completely divested of centuries of ghetto angularity.

Working the land with one's own hands in a collective farming environment was guaranteed, argued A. D. Gordon, to replace Shylock with a bronzed Jewish man or woman of the greatest moral purity. This belief in the positive impact of youthful direct action was a popular one in Europe of the time. It led directly to the Hitler Youth movement as well as to Ben-Gurion's brand of socialist Zionism.

The destiny of the several agricultural collectives that were then founded, in which using hired Arab labor was forbidden and middle-class soft-handed young people tried to be progressive, tough farmers under very difficult circumstances, was inevitably a mixed one. In a sense, all that the founding of these collectives accomplished was an increase in demand for support from patient and generous Jewish philanthropy, which was now asked to subsidize young socialists as well as aged Hasids in the Holy Land. One of the collectives established in the second aliyah—Degania, on the shores of the Sea of Galilee—flourished and is still a showplace for tourists to visit. Gordon's pathetic little collection of Palestinian flora and fauna is lovingly preserved there. It looks like a bad high school science lab.

Ben-Gurion was the son of a middle-class Polish family, who entered into the Zionist movement in his adolescence and never knew or wanted any other life. With very little formal education, he was a voracious reader and an autodidact. Despite his reputation as a hero of the kibbutz (agricultural collective), he actually stayed in one for only a short interval. By 1914 he had decided to become a lawyer—which accorded with his political ambitions—and applied for entry to law school in Istanbul. When the Turkish authorities insisted that he produce a Polish high school diploma, he brazenly forged one and was admitted.

From the start of his career, Ben-Gurion's main interest was political, the securing of supreme power for himself in the *yishuv* (Jewish community) in Palestine. He was certainly a doctrinaire socialist who

thought the kibbutz would be by far the best foundation for an ultimate Jewish state in Palestine. Through his leadership in the Histadrut, the national labor union, he came by the 1920s to control
much of the direction of the *yishuv*'s economy.

Yet Ben-Gurion, while fully capable of three-hour ideological
speeches to kibbutz or Histadrut workers, was essentially a pragmatist, willing to do just about anything to gain and hold personal
power. He was not above petty corruption, the personal misuse of
public funds. Despite his socialist ideology, he had no qualms about
making deals with market capitalists and no compunction about
accepting aid from the Jewish billionaire patriarchs. He was fortunate
in having as a colleague Beryl Katznelson, an astute and careful
hands-on manager of the Histadrut and socialist enterprises, giving
Ben-Gurion freedom to pursue his political career, travel frequently
to Europe and America, and make deals.

In 1915 Ben-Gurion was still a Turkophile, seeking to be on
the good side of the ruling government in Palestine. When Turkey
entered the World War on Germany's side, Ben-Gurion proposed
organizing a Jewish military brigade to fight on the Turkish side.

The proposal did not set well with another Polish Jew who was
rapidly emerging as the leader of Zionism in Britain, Chaim Weizmann. His middle-class Polish family had sent him to get an education in Germany, and after he obtained a Ph.D. in chemistry, Weizmann secured a teaching post at the then thriving University of
Manchester in Britain.

The Manchester location was fortunate for Weizmann, since the
city's substantial Jewish population was led by a group of wealthy
businessmen who were sympathetic to Zionism and who made
important connections for Weizmann with prominent politicians and
government officials.

Weizmann himself turned out to be extremely resourceful. He
spoke English flawlessly and dressed carefully, and he and his
sophisticated wife were very social people who soon moved in
exalted circles. Weizmann was a vehement Anglophile and correctly
foresaw that the war would give the British government the opportunity to dismember the fading Turkish empire and, among other
moves, seize Palestine for its own imperial control.

By 1916 this likelihood was also clear to Ben-Gurion. He ceased
his efforts to organize a Jewish brigade for the Turkish army, for

which the sultan had evinced no enthusiasm, and instead left for America to raise funds and volunteers for a brigade to fight on the British side. With characteristic insouciance, Ben-Gurion learned English from a book on the boat from Alexandria to New York. Not surprisingly, he did not learn it very well, and his lecture tour of American cities, even when he spoke in Yiddish, was not well-received. The head of the Zionist organization in Milwaukee, Goldie Myerson (many years later, under the name of Golda Meir, to be his close political colleague and ultimate successor as Israeli prime minister), refused to let him speak in her city.

From these modest beginnings, given a big boost when, as Weizmann and later Ben-Gurion had expected, the British took Palestine from the Turks in 1917, the Zionist movement developed. After the messianic comet of Herzl had passed across the Jewish horizon, it was left to these three Eastern European Jews—Ahad Ha'Am, Ben-Gurion, and Weizmann—to shape the future of Zionism. Each had a distinctive vision of Zion's future. Ahad Ha'Am wanted a relatively small and select Jewish population as the base for establishing a cultural center in Palestine for world Jewry. Ben-Gurion wanted mass immigration and the creation of a socialist state, based on agricultural collectives and a powerful national labor union.

Weizmann was the least ideologically directed of the three. He liked the idea of Zion as a cultural center but thought of it as a place for scientific research as well as traditional or humanistic learning. He could tolerate socialism but was himself a political moderate who saw the benefits of the heavy application of market capitalism in Palestine. Weizmann concentrated on the immediate future, the need to get British government support for the principle of a Jewish homeland in the old Holy Land.

Ben-Gurion was the only one of the three who thought for a while about the Arab problem, but seeing no immediate solution, he put it aside.

Of the three giants of Zionism, Weizmann most resembled Herzl, and was in effect his successor. Strong similarities existed between them. Both enjoyed moving in the highest circles of society; they not only tolerated but admired imperial power; they were at ease with market capitalism; they were sophisticated, upscale Europeans.

Ben-Gurion was more of a political infighter, a leader of the masses. He was ill-prepared to negotiate with the rich and the powerful. This limitation was balanced by his extraordinary courage and perseverance. Ahad Ha'Am was a secular zaddik, alone with his learned and subtle thoughts, forever polishing his elegant Hebrew essays. Because he died in Palestine in 1927, Ahad Ha'Am's stature as a Zionist giant is below Weizmann's and Ben-Gurion's. But he had great influence in his day.

Weizmann was a world statesman, Ben-Gurion the popular leader and socialist organizer, Ahad Ha'Am the guru. They were a formidable trio, and even though there was little personal friendship and occasional acrimony among them, they were successful in laying the foundations for the triumph of Zionism and the emergence of a Jewish state.

Their great flaw was they had no empathy for the Palestinian Arabs, or any taste or understanding for Islamic culture, or even much concern for the million Jews still living in Arab countries outside Palestine. The Zionist achievement as of 1914 was a modest one and could have been as easily reversed as built upon. Only two hundred thousand Jews lived in Palestine in 1914, and five times that number of Arabs. The political problem of Turkish rule hostile to major Jewish settlement remained, and even if it was probable by then that the sultan would lose Palestine to Britain's Near Eastern imperial ambitions, there was the immense problem of establishing a viable modern economy to support major immigration in this impoverished, desiccated land.

Despite able and determined leadership provided by Ben-Gurion and Weizmann, the prospects for a national Jewish home and a modern state and society in their difficult environment were remote. The possibility of a world Jewish cultural center in the ancient Holy Land, as imagined by Ahad Ha'Am, was greater, but even this required substantial resources and the moving of eminent scholars from Europe and America to Palestine, and these were major obstacles.

In the following four decades, Zion's future as a Jewish state and society would greatly improve because of British imperialism, friendly for a time, and because the deteriorating situation for European Jews in the 1930s and 1940s would drive successive waves of immigrants to seek refuge in Palestine.

But a third factor conducive to the later triumph of Zionism was already in place in 1914, and in the long run this factor was as important as the other two in providing the foundations for realization of Zionist aims. This condition was the support that Jewish Palestine received from the late nineteenth century onward from the new organizations of world Jewry headed by the billionaire patriarchs.

Since the eleventh century, indeed since Talmudic times, Jews had enjoyed strong local communal organizations, sometimes bound together in regional associations, headed by rabbis and the commercial and banking capitalists with whom rabbinical families were often tied by marriage. The historian of the premodern Jewish community, Salo W. Baron, following his early training in the German legalistic school of institutional history, was probably too much of a formalist in his historical interpretation. Baron perhaps exaggerated at times the functional powers of leadership and social control exercised by the community organizations and their rabbinical-capitalist executives because formal documents stipulated this authority, and checking these legal claims against operational situations is hard to do. But on the whole this was the situation actually in play in the Jewish communities, from eleventh-century Muslim Spain to eighteenth-century Catholic Poland.

A major consequence of the deconstructive impact of modernity on nineteenth-century Jewry was an alteration in the structure and personnel of communal organization and leadership. With Jewish emancipation, social mobility, and assimilation and secularism, the rabbinate in the late nineteenth century lost their accustomed authority, and except in isolated Hasidic communities built charismaticaly around a zaddik, the rabbis descended to the level of religious hirelings. They were now synagogue placeholders hired and fired by the affluent elders of the synagogue. There was always here or there an occasional rabbi who by the strength of his personality and learning earned a strong leadership role. But by and large the rabbinate lost its authoritative power in Jewish society in the late nineteenth century.

On the other side, the power in the community of the capitalists grew all the more. Enormously wealthy investment bankers—Rothschild and Warburg in Europe; Kuhn, Loeb, and Schiff in the United States—joined with other highly visible corporate capitalists like Maurice de Hirsch to assume a dominant position in Jewish communal organizations everywhere. This was partly because of their political and social connections and general visibility and also because of their charitable giving and patronage of the arts and letters.

Alongside these billionaire patriarchs emerged a new ruling group by the early twentieth century in the Jewish communities, for the most part displacing the now status-reduced rabbinate. There were prominent members of the learned professions, usually lawyers and physicians, and Jews who had been successful in politics or held high positions in government.

What was also conducive to this change of direction in Jewish communal leadership was that modernity's shrinking of space and time, through new technology in communication and transportation, made much more possible than before the forming of national or international committees to supervise crucial aspects of Jewish life. The Israelite Alliance in France, the American Jewish Committee (mostly German Jewish), and the American Jewish Congress (a wider membership open to Eastern European immigrants) were examples of such committees. Similar organizations came into existence in every country with a significant Jewish population by the 1920s. The World Jewish Congress served as an umbrella organization for national Jewish organizations in particular countries.

Partly because of the time and leisure needed for travel to meetings, and partly by the impress of their wealth and power-driven names, the billionaire patriarchs loomed large in these regional and international Jewish organization. They were used to hiring managers for their corporations, and hence a new type came to prominence in these Jewish organizations—the professional fund-raisers and managers. The managers seemed to have a high degree of autonomy but their decision making was always in fulfillment of the policies of the billionaire patriarchs who dominated the boards of these organizations. A particularly effective international Jewish organization, well-run by professionals, was the Joint Distribution Committee to provide emergency aid to Jews in war zones and refugee camps.

The major reason that Zionism survived its struggling early period before 1917 was that it received the endorsement and patronage of many billionaire patriarchs and their charitable organizations right from the start of modern Zionist ventures in the 1880s. A Jewish Palestine was a good investment for these astute corporate leaders because it was an underdeveloped land controlled by a feeble Muslim sultanate and occupied by poor Arab peasants and a small handful of malleable landlords and merchants.

A few million dollars of investment between 1880 and 1917 used for land purchase got the Jews a significant toehold in this underdeveloped country, enough to provide a start if later opportunities presented themselves. The land was usually purchased from Arab absentee landlords.

For all of Ben-Gurion's socialist theorizing, Zionism and modern Israel were a result of a shrewd business decision by a group of billionaire patriarchs staking out a position in the Near Eastern political and economic market. This is what made the long-run difference, not Odessa and Warsaw intellectual products pathetically pushing plows and milking cows and growing oranges they weren't sure what to do with.

Was Zionism a negative or positive response to Jewish emancipation and immersion (full immersion west of Poland and partial immersion even in Eastern Europe) in modernity? It was both. Zionism was attuned to an early warning system that, despite the prosperity of modernity, this great historical experiment was flawed and might not work out. Society and culture reshaped by modernity, and momentarily giving Jews full access to it, was beginning to turn around—so said the warning light emitting from the Russian pogroms of the 1880s and again in 1903 from the Dreyfus case in France, and similar such outrageous incidents elsewhere—and could ferociously reject the Jews on aggravated grounds of anti-Semitism.

So the Zionists contended, claiming the only solution was to prepare a homeland in the ancestral Holy Land. If anti-Semitism rose within the technology and mentality of modernity, why its hateful ferocity and new world-spanning technology would leave the Jews alone in Palestine was not addressed by the Zionists.

The Zionists postulated a world in which an abused minority had withdrawal rights from international society. They could retire from the game to their own enclave and would be left alone. Zionists still talk like that while demonstrating full well by Israeli behavior that isolation is impossible and that Jewish survival in the Holy Land depends on American policy and international economic and political activity. But in Herzl's time it looked simpler, or perhaps Herzl the magician pretended it was simpler.

While Zionism was in one sense a negative response to modernity, in another sense it was a highly positive response because it drew upon the other positive responses to modernity—the Haskalah;

market capitalism; socialism; Yiddishkeit's romantic nationalism and cultural solidarity—to develop its appeal and its character. Therefore Zionism can be viewed less as a response to early warning that modernity would betray the Jews than as a conviction that modernity had so transformed Jewish history that the age-old yearning about ineffable return could at last be realized.

For a number of Jewish scientists, philosophers, and writers, however, the baseline of modernity represented something more critical than the responses we have examined. These were the Jewish leaders of the modernist cultural revolution who were not content with modernity's alteration of well-being, behavior, and ambience. They sought to push on from there to a new view of nature and humanity.

The names of the Jewish modernists stand in the front rank of almost every intellectual and artistic field with the possible exception of the visual arts, but even there the names of painters Chaim Soutine in Paris and Marc Chagall first in Russia and later in Paris, and the Italian sculptor and painter Amedeo Modigliani, can be placed at least in the second rank of creativity.

In other cultural and intellectual areas in which the modernist revolution between 1900 and 1930 proceeded, Jews assumed leadership roles of the most seminal and critical importance. In the modernist novel, there are no more important names than Paris's Marcel Proust (his father was a non-Jew, but his mother was a Weil, one of the eminent French Jewish families) and Prague's Franz Kafka. In historiography, London's Lewis B. Namier and Paris's Marc Bloch achieved comparable distinction. In symphonic music stood the towering figures of Vienna's Gustav Mahler and Arnold Schoenberg. In jazz-derived popular music New York's George Gershwin excelled.

The Frankfurt School of "critical theory," (neo-Marxist sociology) organized by Max Horkheimer in the late 1920s, produced two of the most influential cultural theorists of this century—Walter Benjamin (a close friend of Gershom Scholem) and Theodor Adorno (his father was Jewish—he took this Italian Catholic mother's surname in a vain effort to avoid Nazi oppression). The two main themes in the writing of the Frankfurt School closely reflect their authors' Jewish backgrounds. First, while the cultural superstructure is held to be determined by the material base in its formation, eventually literature, music, and the arts obtain a high degree of autonomy from the material context. This privileging of intellect continues Jewish mainstream elitist thinking going back to the rabbinical world.

Second, while committed to the socialist left, Benjamin especially showed a fear of the implication of the rise of mass culture in "the age of mechanical reproduction." The Jewish rabbis' fear of the ignorance and vulgarity exhibited by the common man is paradoxically imitated in the writings of these leftist cultural theorists. Benjamin and Adorno became intellectual gods for the New Left of the 1960s and later. The Jewish New Left academics repeated the Frankfurt school's ambiguous attitude to mass society.

There is a parallel between the Frankfurt School's concern with the mass mind and the prime theme in the novels of two other Central European Jews, Franz Kafka and Aaron Appelfeld—the inundation of a refined liberal culture by barbarism and terror. In retrospect Benjamin and Adorno seem to be typical Central European Jewish intellectuals of the second quarter of this century. Ambivalence and ambiguity are present at the center of their theory. Literature and the arts are regarded as products of a material and social base; yet they have a high degree of structural autonomy. The masses are ideologically admired yet also feared. This ambivalence and ambiguity in the thought of Benjamin and Adorno reflects the complex position of Jews in Central Europe and the anxiety about the Jewish future after the shattering of the German and Austrian empires in which the Jews had prospered.

The Frankfurt School's cultural theory bridged Marxism with the newer thinking in the modernist movement. That made the Frankfurt School politically radical but only moderately innovative in the context of the modernist movement, which at its core aimed at a more decisive departure from the nineteenth-century frame of mind. Again, it was Jewish thinkers who led the way to this high modernism in the natural and human sciences between 1910 and 1935.

Five Jews almost single-handedly transformed key academic disciplines, with profound implications for Western thought in general. They were Zurich's and Berlin's Albert Einstein in physics; Vienna's Sigmund Freud in psychiatry; Paris's Émile Durkheim in sociology; New York's Franz Boas in anthropology; and Vienna's and Cambridge University's Ludwig Wittgenstein in philosophy.

Even more than a half-century later, in the last decade of the twentieth century, the main assumptions and purposes of each of these disciplines is still following the direction set down by these Jewish thinkers between 1900 and 1935. Take away the structural impact of their theories, and the whole academic world as we know it would implode.

Maimonides showed the way for Thomas Aquinas and Christian scholasticism; Spinoza anticipated the rationalism of the eighteenth-century Enlightenment. But only once before had ideas propounded by a group of Jews had such a massive impact on general culture, and that was the era of postexilic Judaism and Pauline Christianity and Qumran and Philonic Judaism, from 300 B.C. to A.D. 100.

Historians of twentieth-century thought may note in passing the biographical fact that these seminal thinkers were all Jews, but they have not pondered its significance beyond possibly remarking that this was the first emancipated Jewish generation to have full access to academia, and this resulted in the start-up burst that occurs when a hitherto largely excluded minority group is fully integrated into the dominant academic culture.

Something more profound and structural was involved in the Jewish role in the modernist revolution than this sociological phenomenon of the supersession of marginality. There was an ideological drive at work. Modernism was a wide-ranging cultural revolution that rejected exhausted Victorianism and stipulated the opposite in just about every field of science and the arts.

Modernism advocated and valued the small, the fragmented, and the particular against the big, the complete, and the general; self-referentiality (the thing refers to itself, the picture is understood within its frame, the text within the words of the text) against extended referentiality (the thing can only be understood in reference to something else); the difficult and academically elite against the simple, popular, and vulgar; in general, the microcosmic plane against the macrocosmic plane that Victorianism reflected in the age of imperialism, industrial expansion, and patriarchy when it found truth in the broadest, most universal, and temporally most extended way any problem in any field could be perceived.

Modernism sought the truth by concentrating on the smallest possible unit that could be defined and controlled for purpose of examination: the atom, the particle of energy, the sentence, the text, the actual materials in painting, the chromatic scales in music, the particular moment in history, the dream or the traumatic experience in psychology, quantifiable data in sociology, kinship and gift-giving in anthropology.

Victorianism liked to build on the heritage of the past. Modernism, assuming this heritage, wanted to put it aside and concentrate on what could be discovered anew in the laboratory, in the research library, in the psychiatric patient's free association and sexual memory, in the application of color to canvas, in words and sentences, in quantifiable social trends, in the anthropological fieldwork experience.

The Victorians said: Carry along the past and extend it into the present and the future. The modernists said: Start all over again, go back to the most basic unit, rethink everything, starting with the smallest observable unit. Modernism was zero-base thinking, a restarting of cultural formulation.

The problems with modernist thinking are as obvious as the grand impact of its accomplishments in every field. Whether zero-base thinking is really possible, whether you can start all over again without replication of some assumptions from the past, whether you can do research without an initial hypothesis to control and shape the data, and whether you can understand where these assumptions come from—this is the intellectual challenge of the modernist program.

There is also a moral challenge in starting over, received values are put aside and an extreme relativism or moral agnosticism operates that leads to no accepted sanctions against violence and terrorism. Modernism, so hyperrationalistic in its style, brings on the nightmare of irrationality, a world that has been unhinged from the institutional controls and conditioning values built up over time. If modernism generated the greatest expansion ever in the natural and behavioral sciences, and an efflorescence in the arts almost unprecedented in its richness, so the argument goes, it also set the context for terror and genocide unprecedented in human history.

Not surprisingly, the years from 1935 to 1960 evidenced a retreat to Victorianism: to historicizing, moralizing, and generalizing modes of thought. Then the postmodern intellectual movement in which three Jews—Claude Lévi-Strauss, Jacques Derrida, and Harold Bloom—have played leadership roles restarted the modernist revolution, but with the effort to safeguard against its corrosiveness and angularity and moral agnosticism.

Early twentieth-century modernism was a Jewish response to emancipation and to Jewish immersion in modernity, just as were the Haskalah and Reform Judaism, market capitalism, socialism, Yiddishkeit, and Zionism. It was the response of a generation of Jews who came to maturity in the closing years of the nineteenth century and who were the first generation of Jews with full access to European academia and the arts, the first thoroughly emancipated generation of Jews in a cultural and intellectual sense.

Their response was a fundamental reexamination of the postulates of European thought as it had existed in the nineteenth century. As new men, as recent outsiders, they had no personal stake or family participation in Victorianism or professional responsibility to it. They were not restrained by prior commitments from undertaking the zero-base reconsideration of physics, psychology, sociology, philosophy, anthropology, and the arts.

Judaism as well as Victorianism was their target. In every field their theories damaged Judaism as much as they did Victorian culture. This is partly because the Jews in responding positively to Victorianism had imbibed the ingredients of Victorian culture—its liberalism, its market theory, its socialist doctrines, its cultural and political nationalism—and incorporated them into the center of the mentality of the emancipated middle-class Jews.

But modernism went beyond attacking this Victorian shape and surface of Jewish thought. It also took aim at the structure of historical Judaism itself.

Einstein's physics, by revealing the identity and interchangeability of matter and energy, took away the Jewish idea of a transcendent spiritual God imposing His power on the world of matter, thus providing scientific support for Spinoza's advocacy of immanence against Jewish transcendence.

By revealing the power in the subconscious and the role in human behavior of the repressed libido, Freud introduced into ethical consideration a whole new dimension that made Jewish ethics one-sided and obsolete—the superego but without the id, and therefore a vulnerable and inadequate foundation for moral theory. He also perceived in Jewish devotion to patriarchy unresolved Oedipal feelings and incomplete personal development.

Durkheim reduced religion to a set of social functions among others, desacring its claim to uniqueness, making it purely instrumental and without authority outside its social usefulness.

Boas elaborated a cultural pluralism that removed the claim for the superiority of one culture over another; if this protected the Jews from Christian and anti-Semitic claims that Judaism was an inferior religion, it also made Judaism and traditional Jewish culture lacking in priority over any other religion and culture and made of the concept of chosenness and its attendant forms and institutions just one more set of anthropological practices devoid of social authority.

Wittgenstein, by limiting philosophical inquiry to analysis of simple speech and excluding metaphysical concepts and even ethical propositions from philosophical discourse, left every major idea in the Bible a rhetorical assertion without philosophical or logical support.

This modernist onslaught motivated two young and brilliant Berlin academic Jews in the early 1920s to find solace in mysticism. Martin Buber drew from Hasidism the idea that we establish our individual authenticity, we gain consciousness of our moral being in dialogue—interaction, love, communal activity—on "the narrow ridge" between I and Thou, and out of this existential dialogue we can also in time find a relationship with God. Hasidim dancing in a circle carrying the Torah scroll, holding each other's hands and thereby finding security and happiness, and, if they dance together long enough, experiencing God: This is Buber's message. Join hands and the life force will be with you.

Buber's mystical philosophy is similar to the idea of *élan vital* propounded in Paris in the early 1920s by another Jew, Henri Bergson, who also tried to evade the techno-chilling consequences of modern science. Buber's authenticating Hasidic-like dialogue is paralleled in Bergson by "the creation of the self by the self."

Similar attitudes prevail today in the evangelical Christianity of the American South and the New Age West Coast theosophies. These are all efforts to avoid the bleak implications and difficult academic-level thinking central to modernism. Babba, Bubba, Buber—it comes to about the same thing.

Gershom Scholem left Germany early to help found the Hebrew University and, against modernism, he spent a lifetime researching and expounding the history of Jewish Gnosticism, Cabala, and messianism. Buber offers the experience of personal dialogue, Scholem the experience of history against modernism's hyperrationalistic elimination of the intellectual foundations of Judaism.

In the terror, chaos, and catastrophe that began to descend on the Jews in the 1930s, Buber's existential neo-Hasidic mysticism and Scholem's recovery and application of the wellspring of Jewish Gnosticism and messianism offered some hope and comfort.

With the marginal exception of Mordecai Kaplan's inconsequential Reconstructionist Judaism of the 1940s, there was never a serious effort to reconsider the foundations of Judaism in the light of Einstein, Freud, Durkheim, Boas, and Wittgenstein, the greatest Jewish minds of the early twentieth century. All was swept away in the European destruction, and when the survivors staggered bleeding among the ruins, the only way of life, and only way of thinking that appealed was Zionism and socialism, and market capitalism. The modernist response to modernity was never applied to Judaism even though the intellectual leaders of modernism were mostly Jews of the generation of 1900.

This fact, along with the Holocaust and the rise of Israel, is the most astonishing aspect of twentieth-century Jewish history. It has been ignored by Jewish historians, or consciously refused admittance to historical discourse, because to confront it would have revolutionary implications for the future of the Jews.

CHAPTER TEN

The Wall of Hatred

Chaim Nachman Bialik, a Russian Jew who died in Palestine in 1937, was the greatest Hebrew poet since Solomon ibn-Gabirol in the twelfth century. A close associate of Ahad Ha'Am, he was a product of the renaissance of Hebrew letters in Odessa around 1900. Bialik's decision to write his mature poetry in Hebrew rather than in Yiddish, in which he was also splendid writer, was a severe blow to Yiddishkeit and an important sign that in the new Zion, Hebrew, not Yiddish, would be the national language. Deeply learned in Jewish traditions, but fully cognizant of contemporary cross-European cultural developments, Bialik stands in the front rank among Jewish writers of the twentieth century.

Bialik was deeply moved by the pogroms at Kishinev in Bessarabia (Russian-controlled Romania) in 1903, whose consequences Jewish officials sent him to observe. He was further depressed by Herzl's death in 1904. Out of this dark context came his poem of wrath and doom, "Davar"(the Word), which prophesied that the new century would be not a time of emancipation and progress for Jews as the nineteenth century had been, but a time of terrible trouble and devastating isolation:

Look, how the night envelops us, we are crushed
By darkness, we grope like the blind;
Something has gone wrong, no one knows what.
No one sees, no one tells,
If the sun has risen for us or set—
Or set forever.
And chaos is all around, all around terrible chaos
and no escape.

[transl. David Aberbach]

No biblical prophets ever came closer to forecasting the coming terror and catastrophe of the Jews.

The First World War of 1914–18 was fought on the Eastern Front precisely in the old Pale of Settlement, producing vast destruction of Jewish settlements and costing hundreds of thousands of Jewish casualties. By this time the tide of an intense anti-Semitism was on the rise and gained momentum in the malaise that followed World War I. The expanding and prosperous Jewish communities in the United States and Canada suffered a severe check in the 1920s and 1930s from anti-Semitic discrimination and the closing of opportunity, particularly with regard to open access to the learned professions. The Jews in Stalinist Russia bore the brunt of the Great Purge of the 1930s. The *yishuv* in Palestine experienced the outbreak of successive waves of Arab violence and then the loss of support from British imperial power.

All this misery led up to the Holocaust, the Shoah, the greatest catastrophe in two thousand years of Diaspora history. The Jewish world population, which had been eleven million in 1914 and had risen to seventeen million in 1939, was reduced again to eleven million in 1945. The old Polish and German Jewish communities were wiped out, and severe losses were experienced by the Jewish populations of Russia, France, Greece, Italy, Holland, Austria, Czechoslovakia, and Hungary. In the late 1940s and 1950s, the centuries-old Jewish communities in Arab lands were driven out and most of these Oriental Jews resettled, but in circumstances of poverty and miserable disorder, in Israel.

"Something has gone wrong, no one knows what," lamented Bialik in 1905. In retrospect, we can empirically designate certain things that went wrong that not only caused the deaths of millions of Jews and the dispersal, persecution, and deprivation of millions more, but threatened the very survival of the Jews.

But empirical explanations, no matter how cleverly couched in the language of historiography and sociology, can never fully explain what happened between 1914 and 1950. We are left with the dark Cabalistic vision that God withdrew His Shekinah, His shadow from the world, allowing the momentary victory of Satan, the time of *tzimtzum,* the breaking of the vessels, the disturbance of the universe.

The onslaught against the Jews, the jeopardy to their sheer physical survival, as well as the deprivation and misery loosed on them between the early years of the twentieth century and its midpoint, was so vast and universal a phenomenon as to defy rational analysis and to beg for mystical and theological explanations. Yet in the past three decades an enormous amount of excellent research and writing has been done on twentieth-century anti-Semitism and the Holocaust, and certain patterns and general causes are readily highlighted from this historical inquiry.

The overall causes for Jewish suffering and catastrophe in the first half of the twentieth century fall into two groups—the social and the ideological. One might also speak of these two kinds of causes for the misery and destruction of the Jews as the impersonal and the willful. The first group or kind of causation—the social, the impersonal—speaks to structural changes of a broad and systemic nature in Western and world society and economy, a change in environment and context that, although not clearly recognized as such at the time by Jewish leaders and their Gentile sympathizers, was bound to make things more difficult, and possibly disastrous for the Jews.

The second group or kind of causation responsible for Jewish troubles—the ideological, the willful—involved conscious hatred for the Jews among certain populations and a fervent determination to do the Jews harm, justifying this Judeo-phobia as morally dictated and rationally or scientifically compelling.

In dealing with the ultimate social, impersonal causes of the tidal wave of anti-Semitism, deprivation, discrimination, violence, and finally genocide against the Jews, it must be stressed again that the emancipation of the Jews in the nineteenth century in Western Europe and the Americas stemmed not only from liberal doctrines but also from the needs of the state. Jewish emancipation and advancement was due in part to liberal ideas of civil rights and political equality, but it was also and mainly the consequence of the need of the nineteenth-century state to maximize the human resources at its disposal, and this implied favorable and equitable treatment for the Jewish minority because of the contributions in commerce, industry, and learning that Jewish citizens could offer to the state.

A positive attitude toward Jews, flecked even with philo-Semitic sentiments, and freedom of the Jews to gain upward social mobility reached its peak in the 1870s, precisely after twenty-five years of European peace, prosperity, improvement of educational opportunities, and expansion of the middle class had generated a relaxed and progressive attitude in Western culture and society. Even in czarist Russia, the 1860s and 1870s were marked by significant liberalization, economic progress, and dissemination of bourgeois learning, bringing Russia to the edge of modernity.

By the 1880s a reversal of fortune in world society was under way, slowly building up social tensions, combative business pressures, feelings of anger and despair among large numbers in the population everywhere, to be followed in the 1890s by an international arms race and imperial rivalries among the great powers that threatened in periodic crises to end the long peace and finally did so in August 1914.

The first and perhaps most basic social problem was that cycle of the massive capitalist expansion that began in the early nineteenth century and most visibly in the late 1840s came to an end. The market economy entered into a new and much more difficult period. In this era of matured capitalism, the steady market expansion that had begun with the Industrial Revolution around 1790 and then had been given a new boost by a middle-class consumer expansion between 1848 and the early 1870s was exhausted. World capitalism was choking for lack of access to new markets, and aside from controversial and expensive opening up of new markets by imperial military forces in Africa and East Asia, they were hard to find.

Consequently there was a debilitating and disappointing long depression in Western Europe and the United States from 1873 to 1896. After 1910 there was again business stagnation. Employers tried to pass along the adverse consequences of market stagnation to their workers through cuts in salaries and layoffs, precipitating from 1910 to the outbreak of World War I militant and extensive strikes and a general atmosphere of intense labor conflict.

In this acrid and volatile ambience, compounded further in Russia by the ill-advised tactics of a neoreactionary and inept regime, the Jews were bound, in every country, and at all levels of society, to find themselves living and working no longer in a liberal, progressive, and generally benign or even welcoming atmosphere, but just the opposite. The descent of the world economy into the Great Depression in the decade after 1929 stimulated a savage and almost universal outburst of anti-Semitism.

In the difficult world of the late nineteenth and early twentieth centuries, of mature and at times crisis-ridden capitalism, when the human resources the Jews could provide to the state were no longer at such a high premium as earlier, resentment against and hatred for the Jews was bound to increase, and governments, sensitive to economic concerns and imperialist and international pressures and conflicts, were not anywhere near as protective and helpful toward their Jewish minorities as they had been.

Instead the temptation was to divert attention from a government's ineptitude in combating depression and unemployment by venting hatred and anxiety upon the Jews.

There is a sad parallel between the fate of the Jews in the twentieth century and their circumstances in Ashkenaz in the twelfth and thirteenth centuries. No longer seen as the dispenser of extraordinary talents and resources in society, they were exposed by the Gentile ruling class in both eras to the passions and animosities stirred up by economic and political change.

Increasingly between 1880 and 1914 and again with almost unprecedented fury in the 1920s and 1930s, the Jews were vilified as corrupt, devious, and antisocial schemers in the higher levels of finance, commerce, and industry. In the 1930s the Jews were condemned for fraud, fiscal manipulation, and social parasitism whatever the nature of the national regime—whether liberal capitalist in Britain, France, and the United States; or fascist in Germany; or communist in Soviet Russia. Wealthy Jews were condemned not only for financial scandals such as tricky stock offerings but also for disproportionate domination of the expanding and socially ever more important information industry—newspapers and book publishing houses, and later film companies and radio networks.

Vestigial centuries-old anti-Semitism, having been deflated and somewhat marginalized but not effaced from culture, religion, and society in the previous happy and liberal era, now came back as a raging fire directed against elite businessmen and financiers as well as the Jewish middle and working class. The figure of Shylock was reinflated and sent to harrow even the billionaire patriarchs among the Jews, who previously had lived in a rarefied atmosphere of gentility and refinement. This discomfort made them more cautious in combating the anti-Semitic inferno than they would have been had it impacted only on Jews of more modest circumstances.

The Jewish middle class also aroused widespread resentment, all the way from Moscow to Budapest and London to New York and beyond, as greedy bourgeois intruders who had gained shocking and ever-escalating overrepresentation in admission to colleges, universities, and professional schools, and in the learned professions of law, medicine, and academia.

Working-class resentment and hostility against the Jews was stirred by the great westward wave of Jewish immigrants from Eastern Europe, the five million who settled in and sought employment in the United States, Canada, Western Europe, and Latin America. These lower-class, initially Yiddish-speaking, and frequently still devout Jews were seen not only as culturally and religiously alien, politically radical, and civilly dangerous, but as immediate threats to the job security, opportunity, and well-being of the Gentile working class and petty bourgeoisie.

It must be recognized, as it rarely is in histories of the Jews, that these expressed resentments and indictments against the Jews were not entirely fictitious libels or maliciously revived and activated stereotypes simply disseminated by paranoid hate merchants from the grab bag of the bad anti-Semitic premodern past. There was just enough empirical truth in these negative, overblown, and overgeneralized images to give them persuasive force.

The complaints against Jewish behavior at various social levels must always be perceived contextually within a period of mature capitalism, static opportunity levels, and repeated depressions and fiscal crises in the period from 1875 into the 1930s. Gentile businessmen, would-be professionals, and industrial workers, running up against closed employment doors, narrow privileging of university education and entry to the learned professions, economic inelasticity, and other frustrations and anxieties, looked around and blamed not the system under which or the era in which they lived, or their own lack of responsive resourcefulness, but the Jews.

There was a high degree of personal blaming of Jews for impersonal social conditions that severely affected individuals and families. These social forces were hard to define and well-nigh impossible consciously to moderate, at least before 1945. So it may be argued that the Jews were convenient scapegoats for these systemic ills. That is true, but it is also true that the Jews were not entirely blameless victims, and the complaints against them were not totally without foundation.

Jewish financiers were involved in a series of nasty scandals in France in the 1880s and again in the 1920s, and also in England in the first decade of the twentieth century. Jewish entrepreneurs did loom large in the information industries: in newspapers and book publishing in Berlin and Vienna and in the publishing world and radio networks in New York in the 1930s. The heads of the Hollywood film studios that developed in the three decades after 1910 were almost entirely Jews, mostly from immigrant families. Their view of the world—although it tended to be conservative, patriotic, conventionally moralistic, and family oriented—was communicated to billions of people worldwide in their films.

Of course, the response to these alleged indices of the nefarious activities of Jewish big businessmen is that a great many Gentiles as well as a handful of Jews were involved in financial scandals, and that Jews moved into the publishing and entertainment industries because these were accessible undercapitalized fields in which ingenuity and hard work could generate rapid success. That does not hinder the convenient use of such Jewish business activities to focus complaints about the Jews doing dirty work in finance and gaining dominant positions in dissemination of information.

Jews in the early decades of the century, especially in Western and Central Europe, were significantly overrepresented, relative to their share of the population, among college and university students and in the learned professions of law, medicine, and by 1930 academia, especially in the natural and behavioral sciences. This was despite ever-escalating use of quotas designed to restrict Jewish access to higher education and the professions.

Again it could be argued that as intelligent and highly literate people, Jews were prone to seek university education and pursue careers in the professions and that their record as students and performance in the professions were superior and constituted a positive contribution to society. Plenty of liberal Gentiles agreed with this view. But again in a time of static or contracting economy, when colleges and universities and the professions could not accommodate many eager to be there, Jewish success in this area inevitably inspired middle-class resentment.

Again the Shylock image was used; Jews had intelligence but they lacked "character," it was claimed, the moral stability that learning and professional practice required. Jews would learn anything, say anything to get ahead.

Whatever the pros and cons of this argument (which was still going on fiercely in the United States and Canada in the 1950s), two things are factually evident: First, quotas were imposed to limit Jewish access to higher education and to the professions. Second, despite this, Jewish overrepresentation was remarkable. Twenty percent of the students at Harvard in 1910, until a smaller quota was enforced, were Jewish. More than half the students in 1930 at the City College of New York, which had no quotas or tuition fees, were Jewish. Half the lawyers in Budapest and the psychiatrists in Vienna in 1930 were Jewish. At the University of Berlin in that year half the junior nontenured faculty was Jewish, but less than ten percent of the senior tenured faculty, because of a strict quota. Jewish overrepresentation in higher education and the professions aroused ideological derision among socialist Zionists as well as resentment among middle-class Gentiles in Western and Central Europe, the United States, and Canada.

Whatever the tensions and complaints generated by Jewish business practices or their roles in universities and the professions, the consequences would have been marginal if a great fear had not been produced in the West by the five million immigrants from Poland, Russia, and the Ukraine between 1880 and 1920. There was concern that these immigrants, prepared to work in insalubrious conditions (sweatshops) for low pay and no benefits would take away jobs from Gentile workers at a time of periodic layoffs and employment contractions. There was also an intense dislike of the appearance and behavior patterns of the newly immigrated Eastern European Jews among middle-class and affluent Gentiles who, at least in the short run, were not competing with them for jobs.

There was revulsion against their Yiddish tongue, their lack of cleanliness, their propensity to petty crime, and generally their alien appearance among old established Jewish families as well as Gentiles. These old Jewish elites, Sephardi and German Jews holding their noses at the new arrivals, were keenly aware of the bad reputations and fearful resentments that the Eastern European Jews stirred up, whether in Berlin, London, Paris, or New York.

The billionaire patriarchs—the Rothschilds, the Schiffs—and other wealthy Jews hastened to counteract hostilities to the Yids from Poland by every means at their disposal—by establishing antidefamation leagues and undertaking counterpropaganda against the slandering of the Jews; by funding settlement houses (pioneering social work agencies), health clinics, trade schools, family counseling clinics, and in New York even privately financed investigations into Jewish criminal gangs.

Whether even greater and more expensive efforts by the old Jewish elites would have stilled the sentiments and fears produced by the Eastern European immigrants is debatable. They made great efforts but at a level well below their maximal funding capability. No billionaire patriarch or even ordinary wealthy Jew impoverished himself or his family by founding settlement houses and health clinics for the new immigrants.

The problem was that the tide of immigration was so rapid, vast, and chaotic, and the leadership provided in Eastern Europe by rabbis, fading there already, was so poorly transferred to immigrant Jewish society in Western Europe and the Americas, that meliorative efforts of the old elite were bound to have only a palliative and marginal effect in counteracting the hostility that the immigration stimulated.

The passing of the younger generation of immigrant Jews through state-supported schools and their immersion in a secular national culture in their new countries, as well as the general impact of modernity, was effective in a generation or two in mitigating some of this hostility. Yet complaints continued. Now the trouble with Jews was not that they looked and behaved like aliens but that they were too acculturated, were slyly and cynically cloning the manners and dress of the Gentiles. As long as the market economy was static, contracting, or racked by crisis, and employment and professional opportunities were constricted, the transfer of this large Jewish labor force from East to West, irrespective of its rapid acculturation, was bound to breed furious anti-Semitism.

Again the argument can be made that, whatever problems an activity engaged in by groups of Jews entailed for Gentiles—cheating in financial deals, dominating the information and entertainment industries, cutting a wide swath through universities and the professions, working cheaply in sweatshops—Jews should be considered as individuals and bear no collective responsibility, blame, or even group consideration for these developments that provide a social context for the perilous rise of Judeo-phobia in the first half of the twentieth century.

Some Jewish liberals and civil libertarians and antidefamation officials repudiate any discussion of these as factors fueling anti-Semitism. They were merely actions of individuals, they say. This nominalism can reach the point that Jewish history becomes a history of rabbis, and books like that are around.

My response is first that this individualism is only an American attitude, grounded in the Constitution of 1787, the Bill of Rights of 1791, and the Fourteenth Amendment of 1868 and its application to the states and all citizens by Supreme Court decisions.

Europe, even England with a common-law tradition that has been heavily drawn on by American constitutionalism, retained a firm dedication to groupthink, sensitivity to collective social action, and identification of Jews as a distinct minority even if they had been emancipated to receive individually civil and political rights. Some English Gentiles were anti-Semitic, but even those who were not were highly conscious of Jews as a distinct group with identifiable behavioral characteristics. English Jews themselves are therefore a clannish in-group with strong collective feelings, comprising an identifiable minority within British society and culture. Canadian Gentiles place individual Jews in collective categories, and Canadian Jews, while not as strongly clannish as British Jews, have a very strong sense of groupthink.

The first and most important social, impersonal cause of the deterioration of the Jewish position in the first half of the twentieth century, irrespective of the defensive efforts of Jewish communal organizations and antidefamation agencies, was the economic stagnation of mature capitalism, which lessened the advantage to the state of Jewish entrepreneurial intelligence and rationality from what it had been earlier in the nineteenth century, because inadequate opportunity existed to turn such superior human resources to national benefit.

Jewish enterprise, ambition, and innovation aroused the resentment and fueled the hatred of every Gentile social group because the Jews represented tough competition within the zero-sum game, the stagnating structure of mature capitalism. This was the fundamental Jewish difficulty and most important ignition of anti-Semitism of the first half of the twentieth century and was only alleviated by the post–World War II economic boom, revived economic expansion, and renewed call for and appreciation of the talent and energy that the Jews could then offer to society.

That the Soviet Union was less generous to Jews in the second half of the twentieth century than capitalist countries is due to the much smaller expansion of the Russian economy at that time, so that jealousy of the Jews and the wish to restrain their exercise of talents endured in the Soviet Union, while in Western countries, Jews again found a hospitable ambience from the late 1940s to the mid-1980s.

Two other general social or impersonal factors had unfortunate consequences for the Jews in the first half of the twentieth century. One was the unprecedented magnitude of the loss of life in the First World War. There were ten million deaths, including one million among civilians, including thousands of Jews living in the eastern Pale, the site of titanic battles between German and Russian armies.

This mortality deteriorated the value of human life, inured the public to atrocity stories, and foregrounded the use of violence in social life in a manner that was unthinkable in the peaceful Europe of 1875.

This meant that if the Jews were to be subject to persecution, such oppression could very well take the form of lethal violence set in a Europe where such genocidal conduct was not immediately subject to condemnation. World War I debased the moral currency and inured Europeans to the intrinsic horror of the collective taking of human life. World War II debased the value of human life almost to point zero, but the great reversal downward, so menacing for a vulnerable and hated minority like the Jews, was the period 1914–18.

The other important social, impersonal change that negatively affected the position of the Jews was the great expansion of the mass media—cheap mass-circulation newspapers, film, and radio. Even though Jews themselves played important roles in this communication revolution, the result was disadvantageous for them as a group. Coupled with universal state-induced literacy, the advent of the mass media at an unprecedented level and through new technical channels in the earlier twentieth century greatly facilitated the dissemination of state propaganda. It also enhanced the capacity of militant groups within the state to broadcast anti-Semitic ideas to literate mass consumers and convince them of the truth of hostile allegations against the Jews.

Whatever the skill of Jewish counterpropaganda, it was difficult and expensive from then on to impede anti-Jewish hate campaigns through the vehicle of the mass media. Obscure paranoid Jew-baiters could rise quickly from the gutter and address millions through the mass press and the new radio. The voice of anti-Semitism was given personal and more forceful expression through radio broadcasts. The demagogue's impress on the mass mind was very difficult for Jewish antidefamation agencies to countervail.

Alongside the operation of these three social forces—the deterioration of market capitalism and the resultant intense competitive pressures; the debasement of the value of life; and the enhanced power of the mass media disseminating a hate campaign against Jews—ideological causes for Jewish suffering existed in the first half of the twentieth century. We call these willful factors, because they involved a conscious wish on someone's or some group's part to vilify and damage the Jews. Historians usually give priority to these ideological, willful causes of the rise of twentieth-century anti-Semitism, but the ideologies would not have had great impact and such terrible consequence without the broader context of social, impersonal causes.

The Jews incurred the hatred of the two largest religious congregations in the world, Roman Catholicism and Islam. In retrospect this fact of ideological opposition to the Jews appears to have overwhelming and terrible importance. But at the time this dual opposition to the Jews from Roman Catholicism and Islam, highly visible by the end of the 1920s if not earlier, was not clearly perceived by Jewish leaders and opinion-makers. Its significance is still outside the sharp focus of Jewish thought. Jewish history books do not tell their readers this devastating generalization: In the early twentieth century the Jews succeeded in incurring the implacable hatred of the two world religions, with a combined membership approaching two billion people.

In this circumstance, could the Jews have lived out the twentieth century without a lethal catastrophe? The catastrophe did indeed occur in Europe in the 1940s and another one threatened in the Zionist homeland between 1948 and 1973.

The Roman Catholic ideological opposition to the Jews for the most part terminated in 1965 when the Second Vatican Council, pursuing the liberalization of the Church, removed the taint of deicide from the Jews living in the Diaspora and subsequent to the generation of Jesus Christ. They were no longer to be held collectively responsible for the death of Jesus, although the Vatican Council did not clearly negate the New Testament Gospels' ascription of guilt to the Jerusalem Jews of Jesus' time. This change in Catholic ideology, the most important in Jewish-Christian relations since the first century A.D., was followed in 1994 by the Vatican's full recognition of the state of Israel and the exchange of ambassadors between Rome and Tel Aviv.

In 1994 Islam's opposition to the state of Israel and Muslim religious leaders' implacable hatred of the Jews still continued, although there was hope for moderation if a political settlement between Israelis and Palestinians could be worked out.

Roman Catholic opposition to the Jews in the early twentieth century was a carryover of nearly two millennia of rancorous hostility, but it was exacerbated after 1900 by conflict that arose from modern political and cultural situations. In addition to the perpetuation in Church teaching and among the Church hierarchy of traditional Catholic Judeo-phobia, three new sources of conflict emerged between Catholics and Jews.

The first was Jewish adherence in Western European states to governmental efforts to divest the Church of its traditional control over the education of Catholic citizens and its right to enjoy a state-funded educational operation. This issue flared up in the late nineteenth century in both Germany and France. Committed to a nondenominational civil society under the aegis of secular liberalism, Jews vehemently supported political efforts to divest the Church of its old dominance in education and its privilege of state support for its schools.

In France, where the great majority of the population was nominally Catholic, and where there existed in the late nineteenth century a particularly militant group of clergy and Catholic intellectuals, the Catholic educational issue became a particularly volatile, protracted, and bitter one. Jews were vehement supporters of the French liberal left politicians who wanted to secularize completely the state-supported French school system, and this move to secularization of French education was on the whole victorious. The militant neomedieval group among the French clergy, with the important addition of laymen who were journalists and writers of polemical literature, remained intransigent in their opposition to this triumph of secular liberalism in France, and singled out the Jews as their most committed enemy.

At the time of the Dreyfus affair in the 1890s a particularly virulent kind of Judeo-phobia had emerged among French Catholics, in which all Jews were identified as anti-Catholic whatever their personal involvement in the dispute over education. This was an updated version of the medieval Catholic view of Jews as being the other in society, the enemies of the faith, the harbingers of wrong ideas and moral failings. Jews in the Catholic view were the enemies of Christian culture, the violators of historical tradition, the perverters of truth, the adherents of a religious group that not only had rejected Christ but now sought aggressively to divest the Church of its traditional and rightful place in French civilization.

From the point of view of these militant Catholics, and they included many of the most active clergy and prime intellectuals, the Jews had declared war on the Church, had hurt the Church, and must be punished by minimally being divested of their political and cultural leadership and driven from the powerful place they had come to assume in French public life.

A paramilitary organization called the Action Française was only the most noisy of several Catholic groups engaged in anti-Semitic furor. This right wing of French Catholicism issued a steady stream of ideological polemic against the Jews that profoundly influenced French political leadership under the German occupation during 1940–44 and the Vichy puppet regime, and led directly to the deaths of thousands of Jews resident in France and the misery of many more.

Since the Catholic Church in the French-speaking Canadian province of Quebec was heavily under the influence of the militant wing of the Catholic Church in France, the intensified hostility to Jews that emerged from the Parisian situation was transmitted to Montreal and inflamed Judeo-phobia there in the 1920s and 1930s. Because a substantial quota of posts in the Canadian federal government were reserved for Quebec Catholics (who comprised forty percent of the country's thin population), the intense anti-Semitism that prevailed in Canadian governmental circles in the 1930s and 1940s must be seen as being at least in part inspired by the backwash of the ideological attack on Jews that flowed out of Catholic France to Montreal.

There was an adverse practical consequence of this French Catholic influence upon the Quebeçois who held high posts in the Canadian government. Although Canada was underpopulated and in search of immigrants, and although it had welcomed Eastern European Jews to Canada before World War I, it refused to admit any Jewish refugees from Hitlerism to Canada in the 1930s and early 1940s. "None is too many," remarked a high-placed Canadian immigration official about the Jewish immigration quota to Canada.

Thus hundreds of thousands of European Jews who could have been saved by admission to Canada were refused. They were victims of the ideological onslaught on the Jews by French militant Catholicism seeping into Quebec and from there into the Canadian government. Jewish support for the liberal left secularists in France produced problems in Canada.

The centuries-old hatred for Jews that characterized Catholicism in Central Europe, leading to Polish and Croatian collaboration with the Germans in the killing of millions of Jews during World War II, was also reinforced by the ideological militancy coming out of angry and intellectual French Catholicism.

Polish culture since the early nineteenth century had been strongly under Parisian influence. French was the second language of Polish Catholic intellectuals. Renewed hostility to Jews in the more militant and intellectual wing of the French Church in the 1920s and 1930s had an impact in Warsaw and Krakow. The Croatian Catholic elite looked for guidance to both Poland and France. Again Jewish support for the French liberal left secular politicians in their victory over the Catholic clergy at the turn of the century had devastating consequences in terms of Jewish mortality four decades later.

The second exacerbation of Catholic ideological opposition to the Jews occurred in the United States. There Jewish organizational leadership, particularly the American Jewish Congress, took the side of secularist civil libertarians who insisted that the First Amendment to the American Constitution should be interpreted to build an absolute high wall between church and state.

The First Amendment of 1791 had prohibited the federal government from creating "an establishment of religion." The moderate interpretation before the 1920s was that the restriction referred to the establishment of a state church as existed in England. However, the civil libertarians, supported by the American Jewish Congress and the majority of Jewish communal leadership, argued for a much more radical interpretation. They contended that the First Amendment prohibited any kind of state funding of the operations of religious groups, such as parochial schools. They claimed that it even prohibited prayer in public schools.

Furthermore, in view of the judicial trend toward using the Fourteenth Amendment of 1868 to mean that all first ten amendments applied to state as well as federal governments, the governments of states with a large Catholic population, such as Maryland, New York, and Louisiana, would fall under this absolute high wall separation of church and state.

This radically secular new view of the First Amendment was distressing to both the hierarchy and the laity of the American Catholic Church from the 1930s onward. The Church had a large and expensive parochial school system for which it sought state subsidy. Catholic taxpayers supported public schools while sending their children to parochial schools and believed that some of their tax money should flow back to Catholic schools. Now this was being disputed by civil libertarians supported by the American Jewish Congress and other majoritarian Jewish organizations. The AJC's skillful legal staff was in the forefront of the expensive litigation on this matter. Jewish money was being used to seek a Supreme Court decision directly contrary to the interests of millions of American Catholics.

It was also contrary to Jewish interests in a way. If state support could go to Catholic parochial education, it also could be directed toward support of Jewish synagogue schools and adult education. A major reason that the children and grandchildren of Eastern European immigrants were slipping into assimilation into American secular culture and then removing themselves from Jewish communal life, and then through acculturation and intermarriage with Gentiles abandoning their self-identification as Jews, was the poor quality of Jewish childhood and adult education. The synagogues lacked the resources to create a first-rate system of parochial schools, and did little in the way of adult education. Orthodox Jews were most sensitive to this problem as they were most eager to send their children to

Jewish parochial schools. In their stand on the First Amendment, the American Jewish Congress and the majoritarian Jewish organizations were undermining the interests of the Orthodox minority as well as that of the Roman Catholics.

The Supreme Court ultimately decided, between 1960 and 1985, in favor of the high wall between church and state, thereby endorsing the arguments that high-powered lawyers from the American Jewish Congress had been making since the late 1930s.

The role of the Jewish majority in advocating this decision adverse to American Catholic interests (and those of the Jewish Orthodox minority) was bitterly resented by the Catholic clergy and laity, and embittered Jewish-Catholic relations for a long time. Ironically in the 1990s the religious groups still assiduously trying to breach the high wall of segregation between church and state and find ways to get state support for their schools were ultra-Orthodox and Hasidic communities in New York City and its suburbs. The Catholics by then had given up the battle, but at the cost of having to cut back severely on their parochial school system.

The important U.S. Supreme Court decisions establishing an absolute wall between church and state in the face of bitter and voluble Roman Catholic expressions came between 1960 and the early 1980s. But the struggle had begun in the 1930s. It was then that the Jewish communal leaders began to indicate their break with American Catholicism by joining up with the most vociferous anti-Catholic Protestant groups.

It certainly did not have to go this way. An alternative scenario would have been Jewish alliance with Catholics in favor of state support for parochial schools. The Catholics in the Eastern United States contained many working-class and lower-middle-class Irish and Italian immigrant groups. There was common ground for a Jewish-Catholic alliance in the 1930s and 1940s against the Protestant ascendancy: Sociologically, a large segment of the Catholic population resembled the New York Jewish population. A prominent plank in a Jewish-Catholic alliance would have been state support for parochial schools, Jewish as well as Catholic. As a matter of fact, Jews joined with the majority of Catholics in support of the Democratic party under Franklin D. Roosevelt in the 1930s and 1940s. But the Jewish leaders threw in their lot with the Anglo-Protestants against the Catholics on the church-state schools issue, a tremendously important one for

Catholics with their vast, underfunded parochial system, which only state fiscal support could have made viable in the long run.

Why did the American Jewish Congress and other Jewish community organizations take this radical line? There were three factors at work. One was an ideological commitment to the liberal-left view of the American Constitution in which absolute separation of church and state was a prime ingredient. Jewish lawyers who were graduates of Ivy League law schools imbibed there this innovative interpretation of the First Amendment.

Another factor at work was the burden of memory. If one thing was known in the 1930s and 1940s about the history of the Jewish Diaspora it was that Catholics had persecuted Jews. The notorious Spanish Inquisition and the expulsion from Spain in 1492, seen through a scrim that made these historical incidents even more dark and painful than they really were—this burden of history inhibited American Jewish leadership from trying to foment an alliance with the Catholics and instead pushed them into the arms of the most intransigent anti-Catholic Protestants.

A third factor was that in the 1930s and 1940s Anglo-Protestants seemed unimpeachably the power center now and forever in American society. Jewish leaders felt good about currying favor with the Protestant overlords. The Catholics had numbers and strong voices, but the numbers were based on the urban underclass and at least one of these voices—the radio priest Father Charles Coughlin in Boston—was a vociferous anti-Semite.

The schools issue gained increasing involvement by Jewish leadership until, by 1950, most of the cost of litigation in the federal court was being borne by Jewish sources and the point man for the anti-Catholic side was Leo Pfeffer, a prominent Jewish civil rights lawyer. (Paradoxically, Pfeffer was an observant Orthodox Jew; he served his coreligionists poorly by getting the courts virtually to eliminate state support for parochial schools.)

By the early 1940s, burning resentment against the Jews had surfaced in American Catholic academic and intellectual circles. In 1960 this hostility was finally publicized in the Jesuit journal *America*. The results, as Naomi W. Cohen has stressed, were of very mixed value for American Jews. The other road not traveled, a Jewish-Catholic alliance, might very well have been tactically more advantageous for the Jews. At least it would have mitigated the vehement hostility to

Jews evident among American Catholics in the 1930s and 1940s. Never has a policy so easily defended as righteous been so productive of tragic consequences. The Jews desperately needed Catholic support in the early 1940s to pressure the federal government to save the Jewish remnant in Nazi-occupied Europe. They got no Catholic support. A Jewish-Catholic alliance against the Protestant ascendancy on the schools' issue and church-state matters might very well have saved millions of Jews. Jewish national leadership in America from the 1930s to the 1980s thereby demonstrated a self-righteous, shortsighted, dogmatically ideological attitude that was highly problematic and at bottom ill-advised.

The third exacerbation of Catholic ideological hostility to Jews arose from the complex and subtle debates about modernism.

The writings of Jewish leaders of modernism in the behavioral sciences, particularly Sigmund Freud in Vienna and Émile Durkheim in Paris, evidenced not only an intense moral relativism but also a specific vein of hostility to traditional Catholic doctrine. While in general Catholic intellectuals were opposed to the modernist movement, a stream of Catholic modernism exhibited a bitter hostility toward Jews, believing that Jews had led modernism astray and turned it into anti-Christian secularism and relativism.

This was the view of T. S. Eliot, the American expatriate to London, who became a celebrated English poet, dramatist, and critic, and the intellectual leader of literary modernism in the English-speaking world.

Eliot was not a Roman Catholic but an Anglo-Catholic, a High Anglican in full agreement with the postulates of Catholic literary culture. A scion of a prominent St. Louis, Missouri, family, the holder of a Ph.D. in philosophy from Harvard University, and a powerful editor in the London publishing world, T. S. Eliot was in his younger days a vehement and outspoken anti-Semite. This is apparent in some of his early poetry and is explicit in a public lecture he gave at the University of Virginia in 1931. Eliot agreed with the theme in militant French Catholicism that the Jews were the betrayers and corrupters of a Western civilization founded on Christianity and the Latin classics. While Eliot for professional reasons was careful what he said about Jews in his later writings, his widow has never opened his private papers to biographers because they are replete with anti-Semitic utterances.

Eliot's two chief associates in the important and influential English movement of literary modernism did not mitigate their anti-Semitic expressions. One was Ezra Pound, another American expatriate, now regarded as perhaps the greatest English poet of the twentieth century. He made anti-Semitic broadcasts from Fascist Rome during World War II and ended up in permanent incarceration in a mental hospital in Washington, D.C. Another was the experimental novelist and critic Wyndham Lewis. He was such a committed Jew-hater that he published a pamphlet praising Hitler, which made him unpopular in Britain and forced him to take refuge for several years in a Catholic college in Canada.

With respect to the complex relationship between modernism and anti-Semitism, the Jews were in a double bind. First, they played a significant and visible role in modernism. They occupied, albeit not exclusively, a vanguard position in it. In response, traditionalists, who felt that radical, secular modernism was undermining—destructuring, as it were—traditional culture and Christianity, that its internationalist bent and moral relativism were threatening national cultures and traditions, attributed the ill they perceived to Jews and felt that Jews were serving Western culture poorly, and that they were effecting this through the vehicle of modernism.*

Jews had launched an assault, according to this view, on traditional, Christian, historical, and national cultures, and modernism, its secular internationalism, was their weapon. The traditionalists—especially Catholics—displaced their antimodernism into a fanatical hatred of Jews. Fervent nationalists often viewed Jewish intellectuals as cynical cosmopolites who were using modernist ideas to delegitimize patriotism.

Why should there be an anti-Semitic strain in modernism such as in the Eliot-Pound-Wyndham Lewis circle? The question is difficult but answerable. The Jews were seen as the archrepresentatives of the nineteenth-century culture against which modernism was rebelling, and were regarded as historically and religiously minded. Particularly so were the Jewish immigrants from Eastern Europe, who had been coming to Western Europe in larger numbers since

---

*This and the next three paragraphs are adapted from Norman F. Cantor, *Twentieth-Century Culture* (New York: Peter Lang Publishing, 1988), pp. 128–29, by permission of the publisher.

1900. The Jew, mostly Polish, who then came into the West were traditionalist in their religious practices, and were expected to stay that way.

The Jews were indeed a historical people. Their sense of identity was corporate and was expressed through historical consciousness—tendencies against which modernism rebelled. Also, the Jews were the visible beneficiaries of nineteenth-century liberalism. Nineteenth-century liberal historicism and secular universalism had advocated the emancipation of the Jews, had protected them, had given them civil rights, and had argued for their right to participate fully in European society.

Therefore, the Jews were hit with a double bind. They were regarded as the archfiends of modernism, who were eroding traditional European Christian and national culture, and, at the same time, they were perceived as the archbeneficiaries of everything that represented, to the radical modernist mind, superseded nineteenth-century culture. The way in which modernism developed contributed significantly to the rise of anti-Semitism between 1900 and 1940, and the exceptional strength of anti-Semitism in academic literature departments between 1920 and 1950.

Eliot-Pound literary modernism became extremely fashionable at leading American universities in the late 1920s, 1930s, and 1940s, and with it came strong reinforcement of the anti-Semitic conviction that Jews should be refused appointment to humanities departments because they lacked sensitivity to the high Christian traditions central to Western civilization.

No Jews were teaching in the distinguished English departments at Harvard and Yale in the 1920s, 1930s, and early 1940s. Lionel Trilling, not only a Jew but one who was in his younger days active in Jewish intellectual circles, obtained tenure in the Columbia English department only at the direct intervention of the university president, Nicholas Murray Butler. The chairman of the English department told another young Jewish literary critic, Clifton Fadiman, who applied for a teaching position at Columbia that the Jewish quota, which was one, had been filled, and Fadiman had to satisfy himself with a career as an editor for book clubs and a panelist on quiz shows.

Even in the early 1950s the Princeton English department, another bastion of the T. S. Eliot tradition of literary modernism, tried to avoid having even Jewish graduate students; when one with an Anglicized name slipped in, he was urged to leave.

Did the ideological war between the Jews and the Catholics in France, the United States, and England play a part in Pope Pius XII's refusal to condemn explicitly the Nazi policy toward the Jews and the resulting Holocaust during World War II? In his expression of regret about war and violence, Pius XII never brought himself to utter the word "Jew."

Since the Vatican has never opened its archives on Pius XII's record during the war to researchers, how big a role the Catholic-Jewish conflict in France, the United States, and England played in shaping his reticence is uncertain. His apologists never cease to point out that the pope offered refuge in the Vatican to some Jews resident in Rome in the early 1940s, though they usually neglect to add that these privileged refugees were subjected to efforts to convert them, and at least three distinguished ones, the grand rabbi of Rome himself and two German Jewish medievalists (who later had celebrated careers in American Catholic universities) went over to the Church.

The standard explanation for Pius XII's reticence on the Holocaust is that he feared that a public confrontation with the Nazis would result in harm to German and Italian Catholics. This makes him appear as a wily diplomat but scarcely a committed witness to the Christian truth. Another explanation for his behavior is that as papal legate to Germany between the wars he became a firm Germanophile and therefore tended to the view (also temporarily popular with many English conservatives) that the good instincts of the German people would prevail in time and moderate the policy of the Berlin government.

Whatever the other influences on Pius XII in the context of widespread anti-Jewish attitudes prevailing in Catholic culture at the time, all the way from militant Parisian clergy to angry American bishops to disdainful English literary modernists, it is understandable how the pope could have given saving the Jews such low priority in Vatican policy. This context does not excuse him, but it helps to explain him.

In retrospect, it is amazing how little weight Jewish leadership in the interwar years seemed to give to implications of the deep tensions existing between Catholicism and the Jewish world. Jewish leaders seem to have convinced themselves that the importance of a still conservative Church in Western society had been suppressed by a new era of liberal secularism. This optimistic view was proved fatally wrong.

It was not enough in the 1920s and 1930s for Jews to contend with Catholicism. They also aroused the ire of the other world religion, Islam, because of Zionist activism and the increasing Jewish settlements in Palestine.

For almost half a millennium Jews—about a million of them in 1920—had lived quietly in Mediterranean and Near Eastern countries under the rule of the government of the Ottoman Turks in Istanbul, after it was taken from the Byzantine Greeks in 1453. The Turkish sultan had augmented the Jewish population of his vast domains by welcoming Sephardi Jews from Spain after 1492. In the sixteenth and seventeenth centuries the Jews prospered in commerce in the Turkish empire and held some lower-echelon governmental posts as well.

Beginning in the eighteenth century the fortunes of the "Oriental" Jews, as they were called in Israel when they were forced to migrate there around 1950, slowly declined. They became much poorer. This was partly because the economy of the Arabic world in which they lived deteriorated and partly because the Turkish government came to prefer Armenian and Coptic Christians as middle-class merchants and administrative officials. By the early twentieth century, with occasional exceptions, especially in Iran and Syria, the Jews in the Turkish empire were humble artisans and small tradesman eking out a pauperized but on the whole physically secure existence. In the late nineteenth century they began to receive aid from the charitable billionaire patriarchs in Western Europe.

Unfortunately for the Oriental Jews, as well as for the *yishuv*, the Zionist community in Palestine, the Zionist venture into Palestine was contemporary with the spiritual rebirth of Islam, the upsurge of nationalism in Arabic-speaking countries, and the general revitalization of this long dormant Arabic world.

The Palestinian situation undoubtedly inflamed Arabic feelings and Islamic perceptions, but other factors were at work in the eastern Mediterranean—the early twentieth-century modernizing political revolution in Turkey, the breakup of the Turkish empire, and the emergence of newly independent Arabic states in the 1920s under British and French imperial guidance

Culture was as important as politics in the Arab revival. Pan-Arab nationalist ideology was fostered, often by Lebanese or Palestinian Christians—such as the historian Philip Hitti, a native of Beirut, and later the literary critic Edward Said, who came from East Jerusalem. It is significant that Arab Christians played a prominent role in the rise of Arab nationalism and hostility to Jews. They imported into the Islamic culture traditional Christian anti-Semitism and gave it a new facade.

Another source of Muslim revival was the influence of English Arabists who had developed a love for the Arabic language and culture and a respect for the Muslim religion, and tried to communicate these attitudes to a wide public through journalism and books. Some of these Arabists were political activists like T. E. Lawrence, a British official who lived for a while in Saudi Arabia and worked to stimulate Arab nationalism. Some were academic scholars, like Hamilton Gibb, who taught for several decades at Oxford and Harvard. They were motivated by a selective carryover of the more benign Victorian imperial ideals as well as by their devotion to Arabic and Muslim lifestyles.

These Arabists drew upon Christian traditions of anti-Semitism and militant imperialism to condemn Zionists and Jews in general in favor of Arabs, whom they viewed as pure, idealistic, and uncorrupted in contrast to the effete and corrupt Jews. The voice of the English Arabists can be heard in the then phenomenally popular philosophy of history propounded by University of London professor Arnold Toynbee in the 1930s and 1940s in which Judaism is dismissed as "a fossilized religion."

By the 1940s English Arabism had spread across the Atlantic to affect high-level officials in the American departments of State and Defense. They defended their anti-Zionist policy recommendations on strategic grounds, but their communications also reflected the influence of English Arabism reinforced by Christian anti-Semitism.

The leaders of the *yishuv* in Palestine and Zionist leaders abroad realized the importance of the Muslim and Arab revivals belatedly. Nor did they for a long time perceive that the more successful Zionism became, the more intransigently ideological the Palestinians and many other Arabs were likely to be in opposition. Ironically, the English Arabists owed a great debt to German and Viennese Jewish scholars at the turn of the century who had opened up the scientific study of Islamic history and Arabic language. Not until the 1950s did the Israeli universities found their own departments for the study of the Arabic and the Islamic world, which belatedly led the Israelis to a much better understanding of the Arabic mind and Islamic culture.

After ignoring the Arab opposition for more than two decades, the Zionists were convinced of the seriousness of the Arab problem by outbreaks of Arab terrorism in 1920 and 1929, by an organized, wide-ranging rebellion in 1936, and by the slow reactions of the British power in Palestine to counter these threats. The Zionists reacted by agreeing to a partition of Palestine proposed by the British government in 1937 and to another partition proposed by an international U.S.-backed commission in 1947. The Arabs refused both compromises, and the future of Palestine was left to be determined by war.

It is always hard to engage in retrospective contrafactual speculation, but it is reasonable to guess that much of the Arab and Muslim ideological hatred for Zionism and for the Jews in general could have been mitigated, if perhaps not entirely prevented, if in the first thirty-five years of the century the Zionists had adopted a more generous, sympathetic, and cooperative attitude toward the Palestinians and the Arab and Muslim world in general. Since Jews were living peacefully if not prosperously in Arab lands in 1900, there was nothing fundamentally conducive to conflict between Arabs and Jews except the Zionist issue. Even a more adulatory rhetoric on the part of the *yishuv* in addressing the Arabs, an old culture and a proud people, would have helped.

Instead the Jewish attitude was heavily conditioned by nineteenth-century imperialist chauvinism and white racism. The Jews were to learn dearly how conscious of their glorious past and insistent on their own rights the Arabs and Muslims could become, and that these apparently backward people could learn to fight European-style.

The Arab nationalists, Muslim militants, and English Arabists in the first half of the twentieth century created a hateful ideological image of the Jews just as the Catholic militants did. Jews were heartless secularists, destroyers of ancient Near Eastern societies, imperialists, and white chauvinists. Catholic and Arabic images overlapped and hardened into an atmosphere of venomous hatred in the world against the Jews.

In addition to Catholic and Arabic-Muslim hatred of the Jews in the 1930s, a double strand of hatred emerged from the Soviet Union, the Bolshevik Russian state, in whose establishment communist Jews had played such an important part. This Soviet source was bifocal. It stemmed both from the Ukraine, with its pogromist traditions; and from the Moscow Kremlin itself, from Joseph Stalin, even though the Ukrainian peasants and the Stalinist government were implacable enemies. Anti-Semitism was the only thing on which they could agree.

Thus in Eastern Europe a front of hatred against the Jews developed that had several constituents: militant Catholicism influencing Poles and Croatians, updated Ukrainian pogromism, and anti-Semitism from the center of the Soviet regime itself. Even if these groups could not agree on anything else, they could agree on hating and killing Jews. Here was a disaster waiting to happen.

With the heritage of Greek Orthodox Christianity and of the ferocious resentment built up in the sixteenth and seventeenth centuries against the Jewish agents of the Polish landlords who exploited and oppressed them, the Ukrainians could draw on a deep well of Judeophobia. Even when in the twentieth century substantial numbers of Ukrainians immigrated to Manitoba in Canada, they carried Jew hatred with them, resulting in Ukrainian gangs beating up Jewish schoolchildren on the streets of Winnipeg in the early 1940s.

Back home in the rich agricultural basin of the Ukraine, nationalist leaders repudiated the Bolshevik regime and tried to establish an independent republic, leading to intensive civil war between 1918 and 1921 until the Red Army finally prevailed. It was a source of additional anguish to the Ukrainian nationalists that the czarist generals they followed were beaten by the Red Army directed by the Jewish communist Leon Trotsky.

Out of this violent climate emerged the *Protocols of the Elders of Zion*, which purported to be an account of the leaders of world Jewry, plotting their economic and political takeover of all societies.

This was the time, just before and after World War I, when Jewish international welfare organizations such as the Joint Distribution Committee, funded by billionaire patriarchs and professionally staffed mainly with American experts, were sending aid to the starving Jews in Kiev and other Ukrainian and Polish centers. The authors of the *Protocol* forgery—possibly the czarist secret police early in the century—were obviously impressed by the Jewish money they saw in action and the Jewish skill in managing welfare operations. This insight, plus old hatred for Jews in the Greek Orthodox tradition, plus the large number of Jewish Bolsheviks—first in the revolutionary movement and later in high positions in Moscow—inspired the readers of the *Protocol* after the October Revolution to envisage a perfidious Jewish attempt to take over the world.

The *Protocol* pamphlet in the 1920s became a worldwide bestseller. Henry Ford, the anti-Semitic American automobile magnate, paid for its distribution in the United States. It still can be found at every newspaper kiosk in the Arab world.

While the Ukraine was under counterrevolutionary control, the White Army carried out fierce pogroms against Jews. This was to be expected. What was unexpected and hotly debated in Jewish leftist circles in the 1930s was the Stalinist attack on two prominent Russian Jewish groups. The first victims were the so-called Old Bolsheviks, mainly Jewish colleagues of Lenin who had held high positions in the government, and their associates, often also Jews. The second group consisted of prominent Jewish writers and theatrical producers, the cohort of literary intellectuals like Isaac Babel who in 1917 had thrown in their lot with the Bolsheviks.

These two groups were physically eliminated and members of their families also shot or sent to slave labor camps in Siberia. The best of the Jewish political and literary elite of the Soviet Union and their families and friends were suddenly removed from the Russian scene where they had loomed large since the Russian Revolution.

Stalin, an ethnic Asiatic from Russian Georgia, gained control over the Communist party and the Soviet government in the late 1920s after his political struggle with Trotsky. To Jews in the highest reaches of the communist regime, the defeat and exile of Trotsky might have represented a warning to them also, but they treated the struggle between the two Bolshevik titans as an ideological and political one, not an ethnic one, and they supported Stalin. As master of the Soviet state and its huge secret police apparatus, Stalin first crushed the dissident Ukrainians by artificially creating a famine in what was the richest agricultural area in Europe, and allowed two million Ukrainian peasants to starve to death.

Then Stalin turned against the Jews between 1936 and 1939. First the Old Bolsheviks were tried for treason in fraudulent show trials—conspiring with the exiled Trotsky was a favorite accusation—and shot. Their families were either shot or consigned to Siberian slave labor camps. Jews right through the whole Soviet civil service were purged. Perhaps two hundred thousand Jews were shot or sent to die in the frozen prison camps.

Finally in 1938–39 Stalin turned against the Jews prominent in literature and theater and purged them as well. In the cases of some leading writers like Isaac Babel they weren't even given a fraudulent trial; they simply disappeared. The last vestiges of the dream of Yiddishkeit, which a handful of Jewish writers and Communist party officials had tried to perpetuate under Soviet auspices, were eliminated with them. These pathetic communist adherents of Yiddishkeit had gotten Soviet permission to create a Jewish autonomous republic in the wasteland of Birobidzhan in Asia, and communist propaganda in the West talked up this impoverished settlement as a glorious Soviet alternative to imperialist Zionism. Now the Birobidzhan pretense was abandoned.

Stalin also moved against leading Jewish communists in other countries. His trick was to invite them to conferences in Moscow, or for sabbatical leave in a Russian propaganda institute, and then, when they turned up in Moscow, to have them accused of being capitalist-imperialist-Trotskyite traitors, put on trial, and shot, or simply rubbed out in the dead of night by the Soviet secret police.

Some historians believe that this maniacal Stalinist purge of communist Jews had a rationale behind it. As early as 1936, they say, Stalin was planning his accommodation with Hitler that resulted in the Hitler-Stalin pact of 1939 and the ensuing partition of Poland between Germany and the Soviet Union. To prepare for this ideological and diplomatic reversal, Stalin wanted to remove Jews from power and influence in Russia and as much as possible from communist circles in other countries as well, because he feared that the Jewish communists would never go along with his plan for the infamous demarche.

If this foresight, along with his native Judeo-phobia and paranoia, motivated his onslaught against the Jews, Stalin probably underestimated the capacity of Jewish communists to modify their fantasies in accordance with the change of party line from Moscow. Despite the plentitude of circumstantial evidence that Stalin in the late 1930s was undertaking a Jewish purge, which resumed again after the war, most Jewish communists in Paris or New York still refused to believe this was happening and clung to their Stalinist faith. What disturbed them most was not the purge of the Jewish Old Bolsheviks but the disappearance of some great Jewish writers like Isaac Babel. But they still kept the faith.

Whenever the Jewish Stalinist loyalists in the United States or Canada got restless, Stalin would send out some second-rate Jewish journalist from Moscow, who had been fearfully preserved for just such an occasion, to address Jewish leftists in Yiddish or bad English, and tell them that things were still wonderful for Jews in the Soviet Union.

The prominence of Jews in Soviet Russian political and cultural circles before Stalin mostly eliminated them, and the highly visible role of Jewish communists in the Western world, from Berlin to New York, in the interwar period, certainly contributed to the solidification of the wall of popular hatred against Jews.

The Harvard historian of Bolshevism, Richard Pipes, has stressed that the exportation of revolution from Moscow had the effect of strengthening the hand of "national extremists who exploited the population's xenophobia by stressing the role of foreigners, especially Jews, in inciting civil unrest." Unfortunately, there were circumstantial and anecdotal, even some statistical, verifications for the popular anti-Semitic double-faced image of the Jews around 1930 as both slippery entrepreneurs and conspiratorial communists. Nowadays of course it has become politically incorrect in the controlling American Jewish precincts to verify the existence of this provocative polarity in the interwar era.

The wall of activated hate that enveloped the Jews in the 1920s and early 1930s, from Paris to New York to London, to Beirut to Rome to Moscow, generated a sharp and lethal anti-Semitic intellectual thrust in the form of a variant of race theory.

Histories of the Holocaust normally begin their account of the background to the catastrophe of the early 1940s by pointing to late nineteenth-century racism. This is not entirely wrong, but it gives a false impression of the intellectual origins of the Nazi-directed Holocaust. It was not that racism created the virulent anti-Semitism that led to the Holocaust. It was rather that the various ideological hatreds of the Jews we have delineated—from Catholicism, from Islam, from Stalinism—shaped and employed the legacy of the nineteenth-century race theory in a way that became lethal for the Jews.

Since 1945 and more intensively since the 1960s all forms of racialist thinking are excluded from rational and enlightened discourse, especially in the United States, where the liberal civil libertarians have made racial doctrine intrinsically wrong, evil, and undiscussable. Modern anthropology, as defined by the German Jewish expatriate Franz Boas, for three decades head of the anthropology department at Columbia University, declared nineteenth-century race theory without scientific foundation.

But this behavioral egalitarianism and universality was itself an ideology. Whether mankind can be divided into biologically designated racial groups had been neither proven nor disproven, merely excluded from civil discourse as a result of what the Nazis and other such hate-mongering groups did with it.

Furthermore, racism is itself a central doctrine in traditional Judaism and Jewish cultural history. The Hebrew Bible is blatantly racist, with all the talk about the seed of Abraham, the chosen people, and Israel as the light to the other nations. Orthodox Jews in their morning prayers still thank God daily that he did not make Jews "like the other peoples of the earth." If this isn't racism, what is? That highly regarded medieval book, Judah Halevi's *Kuzari*, is blatantly racist. Halevi will not even allow that a convert to Judaism is the equal of a natural-born Jew.

Martin Buber, the much-praised theologian and mystic, was still talking in the early 1920s about the distinctiveness of Jewish "blood." Early Zionism was greatly affected by a positive view of racism. Herzl was inclined that way, and his close associate Max Nordau, for two decades a prominent Zionist leader in Europe, was the author of a classic of racist theory, *Degeneration*.

From about 1830 to 1900 Jews in Western Europe, especially in Britain, benefited rather than suffered from racist attitudes. Jews of Sephardi origin, if they were affluent, were regarded in aristocratic circles as esoteric creatures possessing superior bloodlines, and intermarriage with a converted Jew was entirely permissible in the best social and political circles. The behavior of the British prime minister Benjamin Disraeli is an example of this attitude. Far from trying to play down his Jewish ethnicity, Disraeli, the shrewdest of politicians, emphasized it by turning up in Parliament in a hairdo and clothes that fit the racial stereotype of a Mediterranean Jew.

Racist theory only became unpopular among Jews as a polemical variant of racism aimed at them slowly developed in the first two decades of the twentieth century and was used by anti-Semites who wanted to do great harm to Jews.

It was not racism per se that hurt the Jews but one particular form of it that the Nazis picked up and used to articulate and justify their Jew hatred. Militant Catholicism pretty well came to the same bottom line of advocating the exclusion of the Jews from Western civilization, but the Nazis did not want to draw on any prevailing religion, although they often played ball politically with the Church and its weak and compliant pope.

The form of racism that became a deadly curse for the Jews was a subset of hierarchic Social Darwinism, which had wide acceptance as a legitimate sociology between 1880 and 1920. Darwin's population biology was regarded in the late nineteenth century as scientifically verifiable (although some still dispute this today).

Darwin's model of a struggle for existence among animal species in nature (he got the idea from Ricardo's vision of market economy) so that some positively evolve while others, less adaptable to their environments, are conditioned by this "natural selection" to extinction, was applied by the Social Darwinists to human races. Some races are more "fit" than others, stronger physically and mentally, and these superior beings naturally dominate in mankind. Others, less fit because they are "primitive" or "degenerate," are slated for subjugation by the superior races.

Social Darwinism was sometimes used to sustain a progressive point of view, but normally it served as an intellectual instrument of the right, particularly white imperialist forces. It was popular in Britain as sustaining the myth of the white man's burdensome privilege of ruling over the colored races.

In the 1890s Social Darwinists, including some in universities, began to turn out hierarchic tables in which Jews were placed near the bottom of the list of races, just above blacks. If universalist multiculturalist equality rather than Social Darwinism had been fashionable, this particular pseudo-scientific polemic against the Jews would not have been possible, of course. Still, it was not Social Darwinism per se that was so devastating for the Jews. It was the wall of hatred collapsing on them from all quarters, which used Social Darwinism as an ideological vehicle against the Jews.

It is again the fashion of historical accounts of the background to the Holocaust to say that the fascist movements and governments that emerged in the 1920s and 1930s embraced this polemically anti-Semitic variant of hierarchic Social Darwinism just when it came under attack by academic social science, led by Franz Boas at Columbia University. This conventional identification of fascism with anti-Semitic racism, however, is not borne out by empirical data.

"Fascism" is a term invented by Benito Mussolini (a former socialist editor) for his rightist Italian movement of the early 1920s. It gets its name from Mussolini's adoption of the fasces, the ancient Roman ceremonial ax, as the symbol of his movement. Some historians dislike using the term "fascism" to apply to rightist groups other than Mussolini's. But if fascism has generic meaning, it refers to military dictatorships hostile to democratic liberalism and fanatically opposed to communism and Marxism.

There were four such fascist operations between 1920 and 1945: Mussolini's in Italy; Hitlerian Nazism (Hitler did not call himself a fascist); militant Catholic movements such as the Action Française in France that fed into the collaborationist Vichy government during the German occupation, 1940–44; and the General Franco party and government in Spain that overthrew the republican government in the Spanish Civil War of 1936–39.

The most insightful study of the sociology of fascism is by the German right-wing historian Ernst Nolte. In his view, what Italian, French, and German fascism have in common (he excludes Spain) is a counterrevolution against modernity's abstract liberalism and atomizing destruction of middle-class family and communal bonds. Fascism seeks to recover bourgeois community while still using the technology that modernity provided. (In Nolte's sociological language, the fascist revolt against modernity and liberal democracy therefore represents "anti-transcendence").

Whatever the validity of a common sociological pattern in movements and governments conventionally termed "fascist," only two of these—the German and French—were in fact anti-Semitic.

Mussolini was not personally anti-Semitic. The fascist movement that took over the government in the early 1920s had considerable support from affluent Jews, and Jews served in Mussolini's government. The advent of fascism made little difference to the old Jewish communities of Italy. Only in 1938, when he made the ill-fated Pact of Steel with Hitler, did Mussolini come under pressure to apply the

Nazi anti-Semitic laws in Italy. Even then he characteristically daw-
dled to the extent that in 1940 some French Jews fled from the militant Catholic and collaborationist Vichy government over the Italian
border to find easier circumstances. Only when Mussolini became
completely dependent on Hitler and the German army in 1941 did
he begin to treat the Jews closer to the German manner, but two-
thirds of Italian Jews did survive the war.

Franco's conservative Catholic regime had no record of anti-
Semitism. True, virtually no Jews lived in Spain when he took power.
Nor did Franco, unlike his liberal successors in the late 1970s, offer
an apology for 1492. Yet he allowed thousands of Jews fleeing over
the Pyrenees to enter Spain. Some carried visas to other countries
and were only in transit, but some were allowed to stay in Spain.

Whether Hitler and the Nazis had a coherent doctrine and were
far-right anti-Semitic ideologues, or were just a gang of criminals
who would advocate anything, including Jew hatred, that gained
them power, is a matter of some dispute among historians. Nothing
in Nazi doctrine, however, is more consistent than Judeo-phobia.
Even Nazi hatred of the Soviet Union was interrupted by the Hitler-
Stalin pact of September 1939, which remained in force until Hitler's
invasion of Russia in June 1941.

Efforts to account for Hitler's continued and genocidal hatred of
the Jews point—aside from political advantage—to a social and psychological explanation. The social explanation refers to his growing
up in Vienna at the turn of the century in a city virulent with anti-
Semitism, a city where the mayor in the early twentieth century was
elected on an anti-Semitic platform. (It is characteristic of Austrian
temperament that when a state museum held a historical exhibition
in 1985 on the career of that mayor, they neglected to mention his
anti-Semitism.) The psychological explanation is that Hitler believed
that his beloved mother had suffered from the bungled treatment of
a Jewish doctor.

With respect to the Jews, Hitler said as early as 1922: "The anni-
hilation of the Jews will be my first and foremost task." He kept his
word.

Essentially, the Nazi view of the Jews was a racist version of the
more cultural one espoused by militant French Catholics: The Jews
were a foreign bacillus that had to be removed from European civilization. The Nazis were, however, more outspoken in promising to

use violence to achieve this end and more thorough in implementing physical extermination. Of course, they also had more opportunity than the French Catholics.

Although theoretically Nazism and Catholicism were enemies, it is significant that the initial strength of Nazism lay in the Catholic south. Munich and Innsbruck in the Catholic south of Germany were fervent centers of Hitlerian belief by 1932, while Protestant Berlin had to be forced into the Nazi fold after the Nazis took power in the early 1930s.

German Catholicism in the 1920s was neither as activist nor as flagrantly anti-Semitic as French Catholicism. But the German Catholics had also been bruised by the "cultural struggle" over education in the late nineteenth century and there was among the hierarchy and professors in the German Catholic world a deep legacy of hostility to the Jews as liberal secularists and supporters of Bismarck and the Protestants in this cultural conflict.

There was also a deeper ingredient of hostility to Jews in German Catholicism. It had strong roots in the Catholic Counter-Reformation of the seventeenth century and beyond that, in a primordial love of the Catholic Middle Ages. German Catholicism was steeped in old learning and liturgy and there was in south Germany and its Catholic-dominated universities a tradition of devotion and scholarship that can be traced back to the Dominican friars of the late Middle Ages, the ancient and inveterate enemies of the Jews. When the Nazis exulted in the beer halls and paraded in the streets of southern Germany in the 1920s and early 1930s, they could draw upon this complex Catholic legacy of regarding Jews as enemies of Christian civilization. That the Nazis were visibly and more immediately a threat to Christian civilization did not prevent them from finding widespread support in German Catholic society. The hesitancy of the Catholic bishops in denouncing Hitler, and the silence in Rome, allowed for Catholic support to play a significant role in the rise of the Nazi hordes to power. Of course, this is not talked about nowadays.

By 1930 the appeal of the skillful demagogue Hitler and his National Socialist party to the German voter made the Nazis one of Germany's three leading parties. Germany had endured twelve years of military defeat, fiscal chaos, political instability, cultural upheaval, and, with the onset of the worldwide Great Depression, economic crisis once again. In the context of this desperate situation, the Nazis obtained the loyalty of millions of resentful petty bourgeoisie and skilled workers. The military and some big-time industrialists did not refrain from hedging their bets by also supporting Hitler.

Yet if the liberal Social Democrats and the Communist party had joined hands, they could easily have gained a majority in the German parliament and kept Hitler out of power. But the Communists received orders from Moscow not to align with the Social Democrats, a standard Stalinist policy toward the liberal socialists.

In 1932 the Nazis won a plurality in the German parliament and the aged German president, a World War I general, offered Hitler the position of chancellor and the opportunity to form a government. As soon as the Nazis took over the government, they used their control of the police to eliminate political opponents and labor unions and to begin to move against the Jews.

Both in Germany and abroad in 1933 there was a widespread feeling that an irreparable disaster had not occurred. Observers refused to recognize that a gang of criminals and anti-Semitic fanatics had taken over the most technologically advanced country in Europe. Rather they said that lethal anti-Semitism was just a propaganda facade used by Hitler to gain power and would not mean much in practice; the gaining of power would make Hitler more responsible and more moderate; and Hitler was just a transitory figure, and the German military and industrialists would soon replace him with a more conventional conservative leader.

None of these hopes was realized. The Nazi government proceeded to strip the Jews of their citizenship, their property, their freedom, and their lives. The Nuremberg Laws of 1935 divested the Jews of their German citizenship and expelled them from civil service positions. This actually turned out to be fortunate for many Jewish professors and scientists. Thrown out of their jobs, they departed to other countries, especially the United States and Britain, with their families, and thereby were saved from the lethal terror that followed.

During *Kristallnacht* in 1938, Nazi gangs in uniform, ostensibly in revenge for the assassination of a minor German diplomat by a Jew in Paris, roamed the streets of German cities smashing windows, looting Jewish property, and burning down synagogues. This terror removed the last hope that the Nazi war against the Jews could be averted. By 1938 one hundred thousand of the four hundred fifty thousand Jews in Germany had departed to Palestine or the United States. The rest were trapped, and only twenty thousand German Jews survived the war.

Anyone with one Jewish grandparent was designated a Jew. Conversion to Christianity or distinguished military service in World War I made no difference. It was strictly a racial matter.

What had begun in Germany was repeated in every other country that the Germans conquered and ruled between 1938 and 1945. Although billions of dollars of Jewish property was expropriated, the attack on the Jews was actually disadvantageous to the Nazi war machine. German, Danish, Hungarian, and Italian physicists who were Jewish or whose spouses were Jewish congregated in the United States and built the atom bomb that Hitler's scientists had tried and failed to make. Jewish slave labor in concentration camps was highly skilled, and by 1942 critically needed in Germany's munition plants. Yet the Nazis killed off this valuable labor supply and clogged the railroads by transporting millions of Jews to death camps.

No one knows for sure how many Jews died in the Nazi Shoah, the Holocaust. The most commonly agreed upon figure is 5.8 million. It was not less than five million; it could have been seven million. The variation is due to the Soviet Union never having released information on how many of its Jewish civilians died under Nazi rule between the time Hitler invaded Russia in June 1941 and his armies were driven out in late 1944.

In 1939 there were three hundred thousand Jews in France; a third were killed by the Nazis, most but not all immigrants and refugees who lacked French citizenship. Of three hundred fifty thousand Jews in Czechoslovakia, only twenty-five thousand survived the war. Of one hundred ninety thousand Austrian Jews, only fifteen thousand survived. In 1939 there were one hundred forty thousand Jews in Holland, many of them in families that had been there since the seventeenth century; seventy-five percent died at the hands of Nazis or Fascists. Of seventy-five thousand Jews in Greece, many there since the sixteenth century, only ten thousand survived the war. Among Jews in Russia and Lithuania and the other Baltic states who were under Russian rule in 1941, it is a safe guess that at least 1.5 million perished at the hands of the Germans and their collaborators.

Of the 3.3 million Jews in Poland in 1939, only two hundred thousand survived the war; most of these survivors departed in the 1950s to escape renewed anti-Semitism under communist aegis.

Of the close to six million Jews who died in the Holocaust, their murder was effected in these ways: about 1.5 million killed by shootings, especially in 1939–41; a like amount from starvation or being worked to death as slave labor; and the balance, about three million, from systematic extinction by gassing in death camps like Auschwitz Birkenau in Poland between 1942 and early 1945.

There is nothing like the magnitude of this genocide in world history. The Germans were the most advanced people technologically in Europe and showed their skill at systematic technology in the way they killed Jews. At least twenty-five percent of German adult males were directly involved in killing or severely abusing Jews in one way or another. At least eighty percent of the German people knew what was going on. Not more than two hundred Germans are known to have publicly protested. Most of them were shot by the Gestapo.

This record of mortality does not of course complete the record of Jewish misery at Nazi hands. Before Jews were killed, they were herded into ghettos, starved, and deprived of the last shred of human dignity. Babies and the aged, children and adults, women and men—it made no difference. The Jews shot by special rifle brigades in the first two years of the war were forced to dig their own mass graves before being gunned down. Jewish town councils were recruited to assist in establishing priorities for the dispatching of people in cattle cars to the death camps. In the camps, Jews were selected to assist in organizing lethal routines and burning the bodies.

There was little Jewish resistance. The Jews were unarmed, they had no military leadership, and they felt totally isolated from the rest of humanity. The Orthodox rabbis and zaddikim preached fatalistic compliance. How could there be resistance under such circumstances? The one major act of rebellion came in the Warsaw Ghetto in April 1943, where the Jews with very little in the way of weapons fought a pitched battle against German tanks and cannons for several weeks before the ghetto was burned to the ground along with nearly all of the several thousand resisters, mostly young Zionists. Miraculously, a few of the Warsaw resisters survived and turned up in Israel after the war.

Some Jews joined partisan bands, especially in Russian territory, or formed their own partisan groups in the forests. The history of these partisans is poorly documented; again, the Soviets have released very little information. There is some evidence that Jews were not welcome in Russia partisan bands and that Jewish partisan groups received little or no support from the Russian military.

The literature on the Holocaust is substantial. There are three major historical works—by the Americans Raoul Hilberg (the pioneering scholar in the field) and Lucy Dawidowicz, and by the Israeli Leni Yahil—and innumerable memoirs and novels. Three films about the Holocaust are worth seeing: *Shoah*; *Europa, Europa*; and *Schindler's List*.

Two museums are devoted to the Holocaust, one in Jerusalem and the other in Washington, D.C. Both are heavily visited.

There is no lack of information or insight about the Holocaust. Yet several questions continue to be disputed: First, how early did the Germans plan the systematic extinction of the Jews as distinct from indiscriminate and ad hoc slaughter? Second, how much involved in the genocide were other peoples in Europe besides the Germans, and who were the worst offenders? And third, and most disputed and painful to discuss, why were the Jews left to die at Nazi hands with very little specific effort to save them—how do we account for the abandonment of the Jews and the negligible efforts made by Jewish communities in the free world as well as by the Allied governments to stop or mitigate the Holocaust? The last question involves the Jews themselves in the countries blessed by not coming under Nazi rule, and is still a highly uncomfortable issue in Jewish circles, whether in Tel Aviv, New York, London, or Toronto.

In regard to the first question, the German historian Ernst Nolte generated a controversy, principally in his own country, by arguing in the mid-1980s that Hitler and the Nazi government initially had no plans for systematic murder of the Jews. This program developed, he argued, only late in 1942 after the Germans began to sustain important losses from Soviet counterattack and the German conquest of Russia became doubtful. (The Princeton historian Arno Mayer propounded a similar thesis.) Detractors claimed that Nolte was developing a German apology for the Holocaust: The Germans did all of Europe a favor by attacking Soviet Russia, and when they began to sustain heavy losses, they lost their moral bearings and took out their bitterness on the Jews.

Nolte's argument is important from a Jewish perspective because if the systematic elimination of the Jews was not yet set in the first half of 1942, it is all the more likely that a deal could have been worked out by the Allies or Jewish representatives with the Nazis to buy the release of millions of Jews—provided there was somewhere to send them.

The main argument against Nolte is the surviving records of the Wannsee Conference, a meeting of second-level German officials in January 1942 in a garden suburb of Berlin to begin talking about the systematic elimination of the Jews ("the final solution"). The problem with the Wannsee Conference as a sign of early German systematic planning to eliminate the Jews is that the officials were not top-level and the discussion they held was on a rather generalized level.

No document exists that shows Hitler personally ordering the startup of the Holocaust. But top people in government or big corporations who are ordering underlings to do something nasty normally do not put it in writing, the counterargument goes. Hitler had declared in the most explicit terms since he first appeared on the political scene in 1922 that he intended to annihilate the Jews, and he confirmed this many times in his speeches before and during the war. Why do we need to find his signature on a specific administrative document, ordering planning for the Holocaust?

The second question is the extent of complicity of groups other than Germans in the management and implementation of the Holocaust. The answer to this question is fully clear although still uncomfortable in certain quarters: The complicity of the French, Austrians, Poles, Ukrainians, Croatians, and Bosnians was very great, and indisputable. Without their help the Germans would logistically not have been able to annihilate as many as six million Jews—perhaps not more than half that number.

The role of the Vichy government, the rightist collaborationist administration in France under the Nazi occupation, and of the French and administrative and police officials generally, was to provide important assistance to the Nazi rulers by identifying and rounding up Jews to be shipped eastward to their deaths. The French officials acted on their own initiative and collected for shipment several hundred children even though the German officials had not asked for them.

The service of the Austrians, Poles, Ukrainians, and Croatians was not only surveillance and collection of Jews but participation in the killing fields and the death camps by the hundreds. Without such close participation, the Germans would not have been able to meet the high targets they developed for genocide of the Jews.

The militant French Catholic Church and the old anti-Semitic Ukrainian Greek Church must bear a heavy share of responsibility for the hateful attitude toward the Jews that in many eyes legitimized killing them. In Croatia a nationalist military clique was eager to terminate its inclusion in Yugoslavia and looked upon massacring Jews as a way of demonstrating solidarity with the German conquerors who could grant them their wish; as in Poland, militant Catholicism was also a factor.

Militant Catholic hatefulness that had emerged earlier in the century against the Jews inspired Austrian and Polish participation in genocide. The Vichy government also sought to humiliate and segregate Jews by every means possible, because Catholic ideology denied Jews the right to live in Christian society.

The superficial character of the nineteenth-century liberal sentiment in society was demonstrated by the way in which militant Catholicism and old-line Greek Orthodox hostility surged to the surface under the German occupation, swept away the constraints of constitutionalism and law, and impelled many thousands of French, Austrians, Poles, Ukrainians, and Croatians to participate eagerly in the Holocaust.

The Jews had miscalculated that liberalism and modernity had moved European civilization into a new, irreversible era of humanity in which pogromism and ghettoization were superseded. This was very bad judgment.

Militant French Catholics bore such animosity to the Jews that their active participation in the lethal Vichy roundup and dispatching of Jews to the death camps naturally followed. In defense of the Catholics, the Jews by their alliance with the aggressive secular liberal left in France brought down on themselves the renewed hatred of the Church's leadership and intellectuals. But that does not excuse the French Church for what happened. No political or cultural divide between Catholics and Jews can be cited to defend the dreadful record of the French Church against the Jews in the Second World War.

Nor is the record of celebrated French intellectuals pardonable. The French novelist Céline spent the war in Paris spewing anti-

Semitic diatribes in support of Hitler. When Paris was liberated, Céline fled for a while to Denmark and then returned peacefully to Paris. His novels with their anti-Semitic vitriol are still much prized in French literature courses in American colleges. In French-speaking Belgium, a young literary critic, Paul de Man, wrote anti-Semitic articles for a French-language collaborationist newspaper. After the war he moved to the United States and ended up as the star of Yale University's humanities faculty. Simone de Beauvoir, the feminist philosopher, spent the war comfortably working for the collaborationist, anti-Semitic Paris radio. Such stories of cultural eminences in the French world and their inglorious record during the war can be greatly multiplied. French culture, so heavily derived from Catholicism, remains intensely anti-Semitic at its core.

The same indictment pertains to the Catholic Church in Poland, which was thoroughly inhibited by its centuries-long hostility to the Jews from doing anything significant to oppose the Nazi death camps.

Polish Catholics worked in the concentration camps and for the death squads by the thousands. The Church hierarchy never advised them not to accept such employment. Poland was turned into the most savage killing field in modern history while the Church hierarchy looked on quietly.

The Poles now make the defense that Poland was under heavy, brutal German occupation. This in no way excuses millions of Poles from extensive collaboration with the Germans in turning Jews over to the death squads. It does not excuse the indispensable employment of hundreds of Poles in the death camps.

As a measure of Polish attitude toward the Jews, the Polish government in exile in safe London did not, until the war was close to ending, cease spewing anti-Semitic propaganda in direct continuation of the hatred uttered by Polish Catholic politicians and government officials in the 1920s and 1930s. The Polish government in London discouraged the Polish resistance at home, well-armed by the Allies, from offering significant help to Jewish resistance fighters.

Nothing can remotely excuse the role of Polish Catholics in the Holocaust. They stand condemned along with the Germans, Austrians, Vichy Catholics, and Ukrainian Greek Orthodox death squads.

The Catholic Croatians who beat up on the Jews were joined by their neighbors, the Bosnian Muslims. The grand mufti of Jerusalem, who had led the Arab rebellion in Palestine until the British colonial power decided he was a menace and he fled to Berlin for protection, made speeches against the Jews on German shortwave broadcasts. The Bosnian Muslims responded actively to his demands to eliminate the Jews and support Hitler. After the war the British did not think it prudent to prosecute the grand mufti, of the eminent Jerusalem Husseini family, for treason. He died peacefully just as a young Austrian Catholic, Kurt Waldheim, who, as an officer in the German army, participated personally in the roundup of Greek Jews for the death camps, became foreign minister of his country and then secretary general for the UN.

In only one European country under German occupation did the native government and the people organize to save Jews. That was in Denmark where the greater part of the small Jewish population was ferried to safety across the sea to neutral Sweden. Otherwise there are only individual instances of "righteous Gentiles" who risked their own safety to harbor and help Jews.

In an effort to make it appear that the Jews were not alone, in recent years the Holocaust museum in Jerusalem had made a big fuss about these righteous Gentiles. How many were there? Ten thousand in all of Europe seems a reasonable estimate. Their courage and humanity ought to be recognized, but statistically they were insignificant. Jews themselves now seem reluctant to admit how totally the wall of European hatred collapsed on them in the early 1940s, how alone they really were. The implications remain highly disturbing.

The third question arising from the Holocaust is the most troubling in its moral implications. It is also the most difficult to answer, and the response is most likely to generate controversy, especially in world Jewish society itself. Why were the Jews abandoned by the Allied governments, and why were the Jews in the free world communities so ineffective in helping the Jews under Nazi death threat? Why didn't at least one national community of Jews intervene or even make a highly visible effort to intervene to stop the Holocaust?

The general answer to this question is that the Jewish societies who could have helped the Eastern European Jews and mitigated the Holocaust, primarily American Jewry and the *yishuv* in Palestine, were so embedded in the concerns and attitudes that arose from their immediate environment and so impeded by their countries' political and cultural structures that they could not find ways to break out of these national limitations and act effectively to avert or at least mitigate the catastrophe in Eastern Europe.

Another way of saying much the same thing is that the Jewish national communities in the free world that could conceivably have intervened to help Eastern European Jewry were inhibited and distracted by the wall of hate in their own ambience. American Jews were hypersensitive to intense anti-Semitism in the United States, and the *yishuv* in Palestine was at loggerheads with both the Arabs and the British imperial government.

Yet the ultimate judgment of history must be that despite these real and heavy obstacles, strenuous and perhaps hazardous efforts made in the United States and Palestine, and perhaps also in Canada and Britain by the Jewish societies there could have saved millions of Holocaust victims, perhaps as many as a third of the approximately six million who died at the hands of the Germans and their collaborators in the worst genocide of all time.

CHAPTER ELEVEN

The National Societies

"The law of the country is the law," said the Talmudic rabbis. The Talmudic lesson was that Jews living in the Diaspora in exile from Jerusalem had to accommodate themselves to the prescripts of kings and governors. The Jews were told that they had no choice. This policy ordained a certain passivity, an acceptance of the lot the goyim and their power centers had given to Jews within the particular political and social framework of various countries.

The Talmudic policy of enjoining obedience to the law of the kingdom in which Jews lived sometimes had the downside effect of dissuading Jews from taking preventive evasive action against tyrannical rulers and walls of hatred. It is partly responsible for the Holocaust of the 1940s, narcotizing the Jews of Poland to stay put when their leaders should have been taking the most affirmative action possible in the early 1930s, if not earlier, to organize mass emigration.

Talmudic obedient passivity toward the state in which the Jews lived could thus contribute to disaster. But it also had the positive effect, in more normal times, of conditioning Jews to settle down and to habilitate themselves as best they could within the social, political, and cultural structure where they were domiciled.

It was a Halakic program for adaptation and accommodation. It presupposed a certain minimum of humanity on the part of the rulers and an ultimate limit to abusive and discriminatory treatment in hope for a better day. The fanciful story of the Jews in Persia (completely without historical foundation) told each year at Purim in the depths of harsh late winter dramatizes what the Talmudic rabbis taught. Just as the evil Haman is about to rain vast harm on the Jews, he is removed by Jewish Queen Esther's intercession with her Gentile husband, and it is Haman who suffers, not the now celebrating Jews.

This romantic reversal of fortune remained the perpetual Jewish hope. It did not happen in Eastern Europe in the early 1940s as it did not happen in 1648 or 1492 or 1096 or 312, previous days of dire defeat and lethal persecution. But what happened in Eastern Europe under the Nazis was unprecedented, beyond human reason and imagination, something that no policy could anticipate.

The son of a French rabbi, the founder of sociology as a science, Emile Durkheim (d. 1917) provided a theory of social action and group behavior to supplement and deepen rabbinical enjoining that for the Jews the law of the country was the rule. Durkheim proposed the theory of functionalism. Any given society is a closed box whose sides are functions of one another. They interact with one another to form a stable culture. Particularly in the twentieth century, with ample precedents in medieval Sepharad and pre-Hitler Germany, the Jews everywhere were absorbed into this functional operation of society. They were acted upon by the dominant culture and social behavioral patterns. As a result, the Jews in various countries in the twentieth century were powerfully affected by the nexus of ideas, lifestyles, and attitudes prevailing where they lived.

The power of modernity, backed up by demands of the state upon the Jews, and implemented further by interaction with their non-Jewish neighbors, eroded the Jews' capacity or will to remain as distinct minorities, significantly separated from the societies around them. As the twentieth century wore on, the Jews in each country took on the special qualities of the national cultures in which they were physically and temperamentally embedded. A certain distinctive Jewishness remained in substratum, although steadily weakening after 1950, but world Jewry by the last decade of the twentieth century had divided along the lines of national societies, their differences in identity becoming as remarkable as their Jewish commonality.

Along with vestiges of religion, the state of Israel and devotion to it worldwide became the uniting bond among world Jewry. By 1970 it was the civil religion of Zionism, as much as or more than the old faith, that kept Jews together wherever they lived. Zionism counteracted the powerful pull of the Gentile cultures and behavioral patterns of the societies in which Jews lived, molding them into discernible national societies held together by the fragile threads of old religion and new pride in and devotion to the state of Israel, which came into being in 1948 and emerged triumphant in 1967.

Highly active and successful—within limited scope—Jewish organizations operated internationally. The World Jewish Congress, the World Zionist Organization, the Joint Distribution Committee, the Jewish Agency for Israel, and the Friends of the Hebrew University stand out in this regard. They had professional management and were highly skilled in fund-raising. But they involved only a thin elite of billionaire patriarchs, professional managers, and political activists. Outside Israel and other areas where distribution of charity was immediately important, these international Jewish organizations affected very little the consciousness and behavior of the mass of Jewish populations in particular countries, even the better-educated and more affluent groups.

In their daily lives, in expectations for their families, in their cultural involvements, the Jews were primarily shaped in their attitudes and behaviors by the institutions, public discourses, lifestyles, and media centers of the particular countries in which they lived. Orthodox Jews in the Diaspora were most frequently exceptions to this general pattern, but not as much as often claimed, and in any case the Orthodox never amounted to more than fifteen percent of Jewish populations in the Diaspora (or even in Israel, for that matter).

It is wrong to extrapolate from turnouts for an Israeli bond dinner or from lists of contributors to the Hebrew or Tel Aviv universities the actual composition of the cultural shape, the personal commitments, the immediate obligations and involvements of Jews within their Diaspora-located national societies. While Zionism became a kind of civic religion that bound Jews together, it only affected a marginal segment of Jewish consciousness in the Diaspora.

This is readily shown by the simple fact that among the three million Jews who "made aliyah" (immigrated) to Israel from its founding in 1948 to the present day, not more than five percent came for truly voluntary or autonomous reasons. All the others were driven toward Israel by immediate or prospective deterioration of their political and economic environment in their birthplaces in the Galuth. Israel was a land of landed refugees, not immigrant zealots, despite all the efforts of Zionist publicity to disguise this fundamental fact.

There are two models or paradigms for viewing Jewish history between 1940 and the end of the twentieth century. One is simple and flattering to the Jews. It was used, for instance, by Paul Johnson (a British Catholic, sometimes leftist journalist, presently neoconservative historian) in the last chapter of his best-selling history of the Jews; the chapter is called "Zion." It is a model enunciated a hundred times a month from pulpits and lecterns, especially in North America and Israel, and it goes like this.

Two monumental events in the twentieth century challenged the attention and sympathy of anyone anywhere who had a degree of Jewish identity. One was the catastrophe of the Holocaust. The other was the exhilarating opportunities involved in the creation of a Jewish state in Israel.

Jewish national societies failed to respond effectively to the Holocaust; they did respond appropriately to the emergence of Israel. This is an important reason that the Jews of Eastern Europe were annihilated, while Israel against great odds survived and became a flawed but dynamic and powerful state.

The medieval motif that the Messiah would come at the point of greatest darkness and prevalence of evil was in a way borne out. And the ancient pattern of catastrophe followed by redemption was repeated.

Then it was destruction of Jerusalem and the dispersion of the people of Judea followed by the consolidation of traditional Judaism in the Talmud and the entrenchment of rabbinical leadership. In the twentieth century the historical pattern was the Holocaust followed by the triumph of the Zionist state and the raising of the blue and white flag of an independent state of Israel over Jerusalem.

From failure to triumph, from catastrophe to redemption, from the centrifugal impotence of the Jewish national societies to save the Eastern European Jews from the Nazis to the crystallization of a new Jewish worldwide identity in commitment to Zionism and the state of Israel—this is the overriding theme in the development of the Jewish communities in the twentieth century, it is assumed in this model of recent Jewish history.

Without denying a certain short-term and rough validity to this triumphalist Holocaust-to-Israel modality, alternatively there is a more complex, unfinished, and problematic model of contemporary Jewish history.

The Jews in each major country of their domicile were being functionally pulled into the culture and behavioral patterns of the environment in which they lived. While not entirely forgetting their traditional religious heritage and while maintaining a visceral loyalty to Israel, the Jews in each national society were working out distinctive patterns of thought and action that were likely to intensify as time went on and drive them slowly and perhaps irretrievably apart. This process also refers to Israel itself as it becomes the focal point of economic development and Jewish-Arab cultural synthesis in a peaceful and more market-oriented Near East.

The national society paradigm of latter-day Jewish history is useful to understanding the past as well as the present and the future. The embedding of the Jews within powerful ambient cultures was sufficiently operational in the 1930s and 1940s to explain the universal impotence and regrettably evident lassitude of Jews within their national societies in the face of the Nazi threat and the developing Holocaust.

Four Jewish national societies are most important in the later twentieth century and therefore worth focusing on historically: Canada, Britain, Israel, and the United States.

In 1940 Canada had two hundred thousand Jews in a population of eighteen million. Today it has three hundred thousand in a population almost twice as large. The Jewish physical presence in Canada has thus sharply declined while its social and cultural impact has significantly increased because of a great advance in the wealth of Canadian Jews and their status in the learned professions and in higher education.

In 1940 Montreal had the largest Jewish population in Canada, around seventy-five thousand. The other main population centers of Canadian Jewry were Toronto and Winnipeg. There were still in those days many Jewish storekeepers spread out in the small towns across the vast, frozen country. The Jews were nearly all from Eastern Europe. Perhaps half had been brought in by the railroads in the late nineteenth and early twentieth centuries to boost the meager population and stimulate commerce that the railroads could carry.

The Jews were nearly all a petty bourgeois lot, living in distinct—

almost ghettoized—areas of cities. Until the emergence of a new Canadian-born generation in the 1940s they were usually fluent in Yiddish as well as English. The colleges and universities did not welcome them, although they were beginning to penetrate these institutions as students, but not as faculty. The legal and medical professions tried hard to keep the Jews out by quotas on admission to professional schools and other discriminatory practices. The press was not generous to them, following the lead of Catholic, Anglican, and sometimes Protestant churches in venting religious hatred upon them.

The Jews worked hard as storekeepers, tailors, and cattle dealers, and in similar marginal occupations. Their communal leadership was feeble, their rabbis thoroughly undistinguished, their charitable institutions underfunded and ineffective in combating the pain of massive unemployment during the Great Depression of the 1930s, which hit Canada very hard.

Graphic accounts of this defenseless, courageous, economically marginal Canadian Jewish existence in the 1940s have been written by Mordecai Richler (in Montreal, with plenty of acid humor) and Adele Weisman (in Winnipeg, thoroughly gloomy).

Among Canadian Jews there was in 1940 only one wealthy family—the Bronfmans, centered first in Winnipeg and then in Montreal. They made their money as liquor suppliers to Al Capone and other American bootleggers over the border, skirting the law before the repeal of Prohibition in 1933. In 1940 the Bronfmans were still hard at work building their liquor empire and had not yet emerged, as they would in the 1960s, as philanthropists and community leaders.

The two cultures that shared rule in Canada were French Catholicism in Quebec, violently anti-Semitic and reinforced in this attitude by France; and English provincial Anglicanism and Protestantism of the world of Liverpool, Birmingham, and Glasgow, which had dispatched millions of proletarian immigrants to Canada over the decades. Although they were not as ideological as the French Catholic variety of anti-Semite, these British Canadians had inherited the mother country's provincial hostility to the Jews as close competitors for goods, jobs, and services. A visceral hostility and contempt for Jews was central to Anglophone Canadian culture in the 1930s and 1940s.

In this bitter context it is no surprise that Jewish immigration to Canada was cut off in the 1930s (given additional justification by the need to save jobs for the native Canadians in the midst of the Depression), and that the Canadian government during the war, liberal as it was in many ways, adamantly refused to admit any Jewish refugees into Canada from Europe. Jewish community spokesmen were too self-conscious and deferential to undertake a significant public protest.

As an additional complication, English Canada had military conscription, while French Canada did not until 1942, and this was not effective in Quebec, whose natives refused to serve. In the midst of this acrimony there was a widespread feeling among the masses that Canadian boys were dying overseas to help the Jews—it was a Jew's war. The government, already faced with turmoil over conscription, did not want to give plausibility to this popular belief by admitting Jewish refugees.

Canadian Jews at home (their military service record was undistinguished) had a good war, and some new fortunes were made, especially in the needle trades and in wholesaling (black marketing mostly). In the 1950s and 1960s there was vibrant upward social mobility among Canadian Jews. They moved out of their near-ghettos into better parts of town. When the Quebecois became visibly more chauvinist and militant, there was a massive Jewish migration from Montreal to Toronto, which in its educational institutions, its professional ranks, its artistic activities, and its business activities took on a discernible Jewish presence.

The Liberal Prime minister in the 1960s, Pierre Trudeau, a Quebec Catholic but a secular progressive, for the first time opened the Canadian civil service to Jews in significant numers. In a country with a top-heavy welfare state and a huge, well-paid bureaucracy, this was a major turning point for Canadian Jews. Trudeau's liberal left philo-Semitism powerfully contributed to the vilification to which he was subjected by the Canadian press, which was dominated by WASP and French Catholic old-line anti-Semites.

Jews all over the country poured into the medical, legal, and accounting professions. Jews for the first time by 1970 were hired in university faculties. Jews sat on the Canadian Supreme Court and were visible as commentators and producers on radio and television. Canada's most important diplomatic post, that of ambassador to Washington, was held for more than a decade by a Jewish Rhodes scholar and former Oxford don.

Along with the now billionaire patriarch Bronfmans, a new family rose to great presence internationally from their base in Toronto real estate and the construction industry—the Reichmans, Orthodox Jewish immigrants of Balkan origin, who came to booming postwar Canada with considerable capital earned in Africa and invested it wisely (until reversals in the 1980s). The number of postwar Jewish immigrants remained modest, however. In the east, German and Italian immigrants greatly outnumbered the Jewish ones; in Winnipeg, the Jews took second place now to their old enemies the Ukrainians.

By 1990 Canadian Jews were prosperous and comfortable and socially accepted. They formed a rapidly aging population as younger people migrated to Los Angeles and other American cities in large numbers.

Canadian Jews were fervent Zionists. Devotion to Israel, rather than flaccid synagogue activity, was their identifying religion. They produced few actual immigrants to Israel, while lavish in their charity to Zion. Indeed, per capita, Canadian Jews have probably been Israeli benefactors to a greater degree than American Jews.

A fervent intellectuality with a Yiddish base that had characterized Canadian Jews in the early 1940s disappeared entirely. They were thoroughly adapted to modernizing suburban middle-class culture. They had no journals and no forums of their own. But they relished the opportunities of the country clubs, the season tickets to hockey and football games, and—in the east and the far west—the ski resorts. In the whole country they had only one rabbi of some international reputation as a thinker and scholar—Emil Fackenheim in Toronto, in the Buber intellectual mold.

It looked in the 1930s and 1940s that Jews were coming to play a significant role in Canadian political life—on the leftist side. The inherited socialism from Eastern Europe in those decades impelled Jewish activists to take a prominent role in the formation of a socialist party, then called the CCF and now the Social Democratic party. It is hardly an exaggeration to say that this party's founders were either Methodists or Jews.

The Social Democrats, while they occasionally had important successes at the provincial level, have always remained a weak third party in federal politics. Partly for this reason Jews slowly gave up on socialist politics, and as the decades pass, Jewish participation in socialist activism has declined to a very low level.

The other reason for Jewish withdrawal from socialist political activism was ideological. The post-Yiddish generation coming along after 1960 wanted to participate in the structural heights of Canadian capitalism, not combat it in company with trade union leaders and radical clergymen, among whom residual provincial British anti-Semitism endures to the present day.

Meanwhile, efforts of Jewish lawyers principally to get into the upper reaches of the Liberal and Conservative parties had little success over time. The Jews weren't needed there, and both old-line parties assiduously had to court Quebec if they hoped to win a federal election. The Francophone Catholics had no taste for Jewish party leadership.

Anglophone Canadians were generally a quiet, cautious, soft-spoken lot, deep into their families and their business and professional interests, lacking in enthusiasm of any kind (except for sports), whether intellectual or political. It was English provincial culture gone prosperous and effete but not more intellectual. The Jews were thoroughly assimilated into this culture; they made no waves and were personally content.

The Jewish intermarriage rate with Gentiles in Canada was about half of the fifty percent rate that existed in the United States by 1990, although it was slowly increasing. This means that the Canadian Jews are likely to continue to be an identifiable ethnic group for the indefinite future. But with a steady or declining population in total while the general population is slowly increasing, the Jewish group presence in Canada is eroding.

There was a Jewish flavor to cultural life in Montreal and Winnipeg in 1940 that is now absent. Only in Toronto, with its one hundred twenty-five thousand Jews in a population of three million, is there something of a Jewish presence. But it is as individuals rising to prominence in big business, academia, the learned professions, and the arts that this impact is exhibited.

In the 1980s Canadian Jews acted as a group only to combat German and Slavic Holocaust deniers and to try to get them evicted (in Alberta) from teaching posts in public schools. Otherwise, as a group Canadian Jews—except for passionate defense of Israel, whatever its policies—had no common agenda. Canadian Jews in the 1990s had become an exotic breed, distinguished by their individual accomplishments, thoroughly satisfied with their country, and fully acculturated to upper middle-class suburban lifestyles, an immense departure in every respect from the situation in 1940.

As with almost every other facet of culture and society in

English-speaking Canada, Canadian Jews were profoundly influenced by what was happening in the United States. In some respects, Canadian Jews were the most Americanized of Canadian ethnic groups. The primary sign of affluence for a Canadian Jew was three months each winter in California, Florida, or Arizona. Canadian Jewish doctors and academics felt a strong pull southward.

British Jewry was more insular than the Canadian Jewry, more inclined to work out a distinctive destiny and lifestyle. Almost any book that deals critically with the history of British Jewry since 1930 seems to cause acrimonious conflict among prominent British Jews and their newspapers. There are two reasons for this. First, British Jewry is badly fractionalized along several lines: an extremely wealthy and politically influential narrow elite in British Jewry's main centers in London and Manchester on the one side, and the mass of British Jews who have modest middle-class and petty bourgeois status; the rigidly Orthodox versus the somewhat more liberal Jews in religious matters; the old Sephardic oligarchy versus the Eastern and Central European immigrants and their scions. Second, there is a miasma of bad conscience about the object failure of British Jewry to do anything effective or even publicly symbolic to get the wartime Churchill government to try to impede the Holocaust.

In 1939 there were three hundred thousand Jews in Britain (and about the same number today) in a population of forty-six million. Demographically their presence was marginal, but since more than two-thirds lived in London and the suburbs of Manchester, they had some visibility. It is instructive that when a Jew appeared in a British movie in the 1930s or early 1940s he invariably was a somewhat seedy tailor or pawnbroker.

The halcyon days were far gone when British Jews were thought of as exotic Mediterranean or other upscale types hobnobbing with royalty and intermarrying with the nobility. Aside from the Rothschilds and other old private banking families and a few families who had made millions in textile manufacture or the retail trades, the Jews in Britain were in 1939 a plebeian lot. The thick anti-Semitism of the time, spreading slowly upward from the Gentile lower classes, who competed with immigrant Jews, to the ruling classes, was pervasive and bitter. There were severe limitations on the entry of Jews to the better private schools, to Oxford and Cambridge colleges, and to the learned professions. The Jews were made to feel alien and unwanted.

For a time in the mid-1930s fascist gangs marched through Jew-ish-populated North London, picking fights. As late as the early 1950s a gang of students at Oxford would break into the room of a Jewish student resident in college and seek to beat him up. Under these cir-cumstances, British Jews were prone to keep their heads down and their mouths shut. Appointment of a Jewish professor who was a British citizen in any university was rare and almost unheard of at Oxbridge. Paradoxically, British universities were generous in wel-coming Jewish refugee professors, especially in the sciences, from Central Europe—they realized how much those professors could contribute academically.

As in Canada, the government was deeply concerned that Chris-tian young men conscripted to fight in the war were not perceived as being sacrificed for the Jews. In addition to this general caution, high officials in the foreign and defense ministries were personally and openly anti-Semitic.

Under these circumstances it was unlikely that the British wartime government, beyond issuing warnings that justice would be meted out to war criminals after the ultimate British victory, would do anything tangible to slow down the Holocaust. The key was Prime Minister Winston Churchill himself, a brilliant, charismatic, and immensely complicated man. He alone could have taken action on behalf of the doomed continental Jews. But he did nothing for them. Churchill himself, as a scion of the old high aristocracy, was not heir to an anti-Semitic culture. He was personally sympathetic to Zionism, although in his exalted romantic mind Zionism became a means to bolster the British empire in the Near East. At a bad point in Churchill's fortunes in the early 1930s, he had been saved from hav-ing to sell his beloved country house by a wealthy Jew who, unso-licited, had bailed him out. He did not forget this favor.

But Churchill refused to do anything special for the Jews under German occupation. He would not send British planes to bomb the railway tracks to the death camps, although British pilots were sent off on all sorts of risky missions. He would not make secret deals with Nazi agents in Lisbon, Zurich, or other neutral cities, although after the winter of 1942, when it was evident the Germans could not win the war, such dealing was possible.

Churchill was a highly intelligent man and something of a per-sonal philo-Semite. But he did not raise a finger for the Holocaust-threatened Jews. Like his great friend and ally President Franklin

Roosevelt of the United States, he was hypersensitive to the depth of anti-Semitism in his society and haunted by fear that special efforts to save the Jews would raise cries of "it is a Jew's war" and "British Christian boys are dying to save the rotten Jews." He backed off completely.

Later Churchill justified his inaction on the grounds that everything had to be focused on the military task at hand. The sooner the war ended, the more Jews would be saved, he claimed. Churchill may have sincerely believed this, or persuaded himself that he did.

The British Jewish community and its quiescent, timid leaders did nothing publicly to pressure the government, although political agitation in the streets of London during the war for one cause or another was surprisingly prevalent. But there were no street marches for the doomed Jews; no rabbi chained himself to the railing of Parliament or threw himself on the doorstep of the prime minister's residence at 10 Downing Street. A few civilized private conferences with prominent officials, a few restrained letters to the *London Times.* That was all.

In retrospect, thinking about it makes one sick. No wonder the Anglo-Jewish elite is hypersensitive to historical accounts of the 1940s.

The greatest disappointment is Chaim Weizmann, who was in London for most of the war. He did nothing significant to save the Jews of Europe. He was invisible on the public scene—nothing like his activism during the First World War. The fact of the matter is that Weizmann was burned out and in a state of deep depression. In the late 1930s the machinations of his archrival for leadership in the Zionist world, David Ben-Gurion, had pushed him out of the leadership of the World Zionist Organization. In effect he was in retirement, to be summoned by Ben-Gurion in 1948 to become the first president of Israel, a strictly figurehead position. Weizmann's decline in the late 1930s was very bad luck for the European Jews. He might have been able to do something.

Only in the late 1960s, during the great (and short-lived) British economic boom, did the social and fiscal position of British Jewry appreciably improve. For the first time, led by Isaiah Berlin and Max Beloff, Jews became prominent in academia. They significantly improved their role in the legal profession. In addition to banking, textile manufacture, and retailing, they occupied leading positions in publishing (George Weidenfeld) and journalism, and eventually in politics for the first time since the age of Disraeli.

In 1945 the chairman of the British Labor party, which defeated Churchill's Conservatives and took power to introduce the welfare state, was Harold Laski, a University of London professor who was the scion of a wealthy Manchester family. He was constantly subject to a barrage of anti-Semitic libels and was given no position in the Socialist government.

After 1979 when Margaret Thatcher's Conservatives came to power, Jews were prominent in the Thatcher wing of the Conservative party, committed to waking Britain from its economic somnolence by dismantling parts of the welfare state and liberating the market economy. The very middle-class Mrs. Thatcher liked smart and rich Jews, and at one point she had three Jews in her cabinet, including the number two cabinet officer, Nigel Lawson, the chancellor of the exchequer. He had a falling out with the Iron Lady but was brought back by her successor, John Major.

Jews remain in Britain a small, marginal, quiescent, and not thoroughly popular group, but their situation has significantly improved since 1945.

Because of bitterness at alleged ingratitude of the Zionists and anger at the way the Israelis drove the British out of Palestine after the war—and residual philo-Arabism—the British upper classes are overwhelmingly anti-Israel and pro-PLO. But this has not translated into anti-Semitism. It still hangs like a miasma in British culture but is less threatening to individual Jews than it was in the 1930s and 1940s.

Frederic Raphael, a London Jewish writer of social-oriented fiction, has since the early 1960s chronicled the fate of the successive younger Jewish generations in Britain in a long series of novels and plays. Over time, Raphael's North London Jews have become less beholden to or concerned with their families and have become much bolder in pursuing ambitious careers. By the 1980s they see themselves much more as individuals than a comparable group in the 1960s, more confident that their talents will be rewarded and much less concerned that being Jewish will hold them back. Traditional Judaism rarely plays any role in their lives and consciousness, and this Jewish elite appears to be on the road to full assimilation and intermarriage that their cohorts in North America have already taken, should the anti-Semitic ambience in Britain further attenuate.

As personal opportunities for English Jews improve, Jewish identity in Britain declines. A leading Anglo-Jewish historian, Bernard Wasserstein, remarked in 1994 that "Anglo-Jewry slowly, but with seeming inevitability, slides toward assimilation and dissolution."

Britain is one country where the rabbinate remains a powerful force in community life, but since the rabbis are forever hair-splitting about points of the Halakah, their potential to take activist roles is thereby diminished. Prominent Jewish academics along with a group of billionaire businessmen dominated the Jewish horizon in Britain.

For all the marginality of British Jewry, it is remarkable that the British learned most of their philosophy since 1930 from one Jew, Ludwig Wittgenstein (Bertrand Russell's chosen successor in the chair of philosophy at Cambridge), and much of their history from two other Jews, Sir Lewis Bernstein Namier and Sir Geoffrey Elton. Not accidentally, all three were emigrants from Central Europe. Jews from the continent could do what native-born British Jews were not allowed to do—show the British how to think philosophically and historically.

Namier was the dominant historian in Britain in the 1940s and 1950s. Yet he never was given a chair at Oxbridge (even though he was educated as an undergraduate at Oxford and spent all his life after adolescence in Britain), such was the anti-Semitic hatred toward him. That he was a fervent Zionist and active collaborator with Chaim Weizmann hurt him severely. He taught at Manchester and London.

Namier was the historian of the eighteenth-century English government. He had a romantic attachment to the freewheeling corrupt old aristocrats who manipulated elections and controlled Parliament in the eighteenth century. He hated ideology, both liberal and fascist.

Sir Geoffrey Elton was the son of Victor Ehrenberg, the distinguished refugee classicist from Prague. Ten years old when he came to London, where his father became a professor, he grew up in the British army during the war and spoke afterward with a slight trace of working-class cockney and had a passion for British beer. Elton held the senior chair of history at Cambridge University.

He was the historian of the sixteenth-century English government. Like Namier—although less romantically—he too was a conservative and an admirer of the old landed society and its institutions, which he regarded as a beautiful and incomparable blend of freedom and authority. Elton was one of the few British academics to support Margaret Thatcher.

Not only were Namier and Elton great researchers, vigorous writers, and skillful academic politicians; they were also both products of rabbinical patrician lineage. Namier was a direct descendant of the Vilna Gaon, the learned opponent of the early Hasidim. Elton on his mother's side was descended from a prominent early seventeenth-century Prague rabbi, also a great Halakic scholar, who in a famous legend created a golem (android).

Since the implication of Wittgenstein's philosophy was also anti-ideological and conservative, the three great British Jewish humanists of the twentieth century all came down heavily on the side of conservative patriotism and accommodation within the rigid British class structure. It was a social and political system in which Jews had done tolerably well. On the other political side was the pathetic figure of socialist Harold Laski, treated roughly in his own day and now forgotten.

Wittgenstein, Namier, Elton, and Laski all had one thing in common: They were great teachers and gathered around themselves circles of brilliant young disciples, many from overseas, who went on to illustrious academic careers. They were rabbinical figures within British academia.

Since British academics in the 1940s and 1950s cast a long shadow over American and Canadian universities, their influence in Anglophone North America was almost as important as in Britain itself. By the 1980s no Jewish academic in Britain had anywhere near the stature of Wittgenstein, Namier, Elton, and Laski, and as a result, many of the British Jewish academics immigrated to the United States to find more attractive careers there.

In 1940 the Jewish population of British-ruled Palestine had barely reached six hundred thousand (within an Arab population of 1.5 million), only twice the size of the Jewish population of Canada or Britain. This is one fact that teaches caution about the traditional triumphalist and teleological histories of Israel and its Palestine predecessor. The second is that the Jewish population, split about evenly in 1940 between rural and urban areas, struggled hard to make a living. Most Jews in the *yishuv* (the Palestine community) lived in modest circumstances. Poverty was endemic, despite generous charity by overseas billionaire patriarchs. Unemployment was a severe problem.

Contrary to Zionist mythology, portraying the heroic handsome kibbutz (collective farm) and moshav (cooperative farm) workers and their happy bronzed children, the Zionist experiment after a half-century was not much of a success.

To appease the angry and well-organized Arabs, the British government in 1939 in its infamous White Paper cut off nearly all future Jewish immigration to Palestine. But the fact is that the economic situation of the *yishuv* was so marginal that without massive amounts of foreign aid, not available in the closing years of the Great Depression, Zionist Palestine could not have absorbed a major influx of refugees from Nazi Europe. It had a hard time taking care of its existing population.

This is one of the two main reasons that David Ben-Gurion and his socialist colleagues in the Palestinian Jewish leadership were relatively quiet during the first four years of the war and undertook no strenuous efforts to save the Holocaust victims. The other reason for their passivity was ideological. Socialist Zion had been predicated on the creation of a New Jew, while prospective Eastern European refugees were normally the products of the old petty bourgeois and decaying religious culture that in socialist Zionist eyes fomented bad behavior.

A romantic glow covers historical accounts of Zionist Palestine. The British and the Arabs are assigned the bad-guy roles, and the Jews are regarded as heroes and saints. The actual history is more complex and sadder.

In 1917, as the British army took Palestine from the Turks, the government in London issued the famous Balfour Declaration, named after the foreign minister who drafted it, A. J. Balfour, a Conservative intellectual who was personally a philo-Semite, as was to a lesser extent the Liberal prime minister in the coalition wartime government, the idiosyncratic Welshman David Lloyd George.

It is a myth of Jewish history comparable to the story of Moses and the Exodus that the Balfour Declaration, guaranteeing Jews "a national home" in Palestine, vaguely saving Arab rights, was issued as a personal favor to Chaim Weizmann for his successful work on the chemistry of British explosives. Weizmann did such work, for which he gained patents after the war that made him affluent to the extent that from 1924 until he became president of Israel in 1948 he did not draw a salary from his Zionist affiliations but lived off his patents.

Weizmann's successful research indeed solidified his good relations with the leading government officials and allowed him to lobby them personally on behalf of the Zionist program when the British army marched into Jerusalem.

But two other factors were also at work in the making of the Balfour Declaration. First, it came at a time when Britain and France were hard-pressed in the war against Germany, and the British hoped that endorsing Zionism would increase support for Britain in the United States. (The influence of Jews on the American government was overestimated.) Secondly, and more important, the British would come out of the war as the dominant Near Eastern power, and the Zionist enclave in Palestine was at first seen as a boost to strengthening British imperial presence in the eastern Mediterranean.

Weizmann, speaking for the Zionists, confirmed the expectation that a Jewish enclave in the Near East would serve as a British imperial base. If Balfour and Lloyd George had interviewed the rising politician in the *yishuv*, David Ben-Gurion, they would have realized that this was an overoptimistic assumption.

By 1922 the British had become increasingly committed to building their imperial structure in the Near East through collaboration with and control of various Arab princes. These potentates were still somewhat ambivalent about a Jewish Palestine, but the British knew by 1922 that they had made a naive overcommitment in 1917. Yet they set about, as honorable gentlemen, at least to go through the motions of fulfilling their obligation to the Jews.

The British governor in Palestine for most of the 1920s was the London Jewish lawyer and politician Herbert Samuel. He was not a fervent Zionist but was sympathetic to development of the *yishuv* while he tried to be evenhanded in his treatment of the increasingly rebellious and hostile Palestinian Arabs. He was a good administrator, and no subsequent British governor of Palestine did as good a job—or got on as well with the socialist leadership of the *yishuv*.

Arab hostility flared into violence in 1920 and 1929, and the more the Jewish population slowly increased, and the more land the Jewish National Fund, a charitable but aggressive development corporation, bought from lackadaisical or absentee Arab landlords, the more intransigent became the opposition of the Palestinians to the fulfillment of the Balfour Declaration. Between 1936 and 1938 this opposition flamed into a well-organized rebellion, put down by the British with difficulty.

But Jewish Palestine had other problems besides Arab opposition and British inconstancy. They arose from the socialist leadership of the *yishuv,* its ideological commitments, and its highly centralized Jewish economy. Put simply, they arose from the mind-set and behavior of Ben-Gurion. He was at the same time the leader of a federation of socialist parties, eventually called Poale Zion, Labor Zionist; the controller of Histadrut, a Soviet-style combination of national cooperative, labor union, and corporate business; and the head of the Jewish Agency, which the British recognized as the semiofficial spokesman for the *yishuv.*

Ben-Gurion was also a prolific writer in the Hebrew press and had slowly become a powerful if verbose orator. He was not a good administrator and in fact was a bit of a crook—he dipped into Histadrut funds for his own personal use, including trysts with his mistress in sundry European spas. But he had a loyal and capable colleague, Beryl Katznelson, to do the day-to-day administrative work while Ben-Gurion pursued policy, politics, and ideological pronouncements. His petty corruptions set the pattern for later Israeli officials.

The Labor Zionists created a welfare state that controlled the greater part of the economy as well. In the 1930s it still saw the future in the agricultural collectives and cooperatives. But this was a risky economic policy because turning Palestine's sandy and rocky soil into productive agriculture, while possible, was a high-cost venture for which faltering agricultural sales abroad, during a time of worldwide farming surplus and prolonged depression, could not pay. Focusing on the kibbutzim also left the urban workers underemployed or at best poorly paid.

The socialist economy that Ben-Gurion and Katznelson created also spawned a top-heavy and slow-moving bureaucracy that plagues Israel to the present day. The squelching of the market by socialist controls and regulation discouraged capital investment from abroad. Charitable funds flowed in, but little in the way of investment to develop the economy.

The Ben-Gurion economic plan for the *yishuv* was unsuccessful.

It created a few showpiece kibbutzim but it also stymied economic development and fostered Soviet-style poverty and damaged a very fragile ecology. For example, in the 1950s the Hula swamps, a large wetland in the north of the country, were drained at great expense and with much celebration, but much of the drained land turned out to be unsuitable for intensive agriculture, and meanwhile wildlife was endangered.

In 1940 the *yishuv* under Ben-Gurion's leadership had failed to meet its basic goals. The Arabs were rebellious and intransigent, the British were disenchanted and weary, and the Jewish economy was a mess. This is not the way standard Zionist histories portray the development of the *yishuv*, although Shabtai Teveth, Ben-Gurion's authorized biographer, is almost as frank about the failures of his policy as he is about the defects in the great man's character.

The fact is that the Jewish economy in Israel from the first decade of the century to today has never been a viable one. The Jews in Zion have never been able to support themselves. The balance sheet has always been negative.

They have survived only by covering their deficits with foreign aid—Jewish charity lavishly allotted from abroad and, since around 1970, extensive American government aid.

A brilliant right-wing Zionist leader in the 1930s, a native of Poland, clearly saw these social problems and prescribed radical solutions. He was Ze'ev Jabotinsky, a charismatic orator and a keen admirer of European fascism. Jabotinsky's followers, a noisy but small minority of the Palestinian Jewish voters, were then called Revisionists (today Likud). For the economy Jabotinsky advocated dismantling the bureaucratic socialist framework and freeing up the market to attract investment. He has been proved right about that. His other remedy, still rejected by the overwhelming majority of Israelis, was to use military force to expel the Arabs from the country.

In addition, Jabotinsky advocated the forming of an armed Jewish underground not only to resist the Arabs but also to take violent action against the British if they did not fulfill their commitment to Zionism and reopen Jewish immigration. This was at first rejected by Ben-Gurion and the socialist majority. But by 1943 as word of the Holocaust spread and the British still would not open Palestine to the refugees from Nazism, Ben-Gurion essentially came around to Jabotinsky's position.

The kibbutz-based Haganah, established as a Jewish defense force (with British help) during the Arab rebellion of the late 1930s, began to transform itself into a liberation army. By 1945 the only difference between the Haganah and its Palmach (attack corps) and the Revisionists' main military organization, the Irgun Zvi Leumi, was that the latter condoned terrorism against the British, including assassination of British officials and killing of hostages.

In the past three decades, the record of the *yishuv* in countervailing the Holocaust has been the subject of dispute. Could more have been done by Ben-Gurion, the Jewish Agency, and the socialist Zionist leadership in saving a larger remnant of Eastern European Jews? The answer is probably yes.

In the mid-1930s the Zionist leadership made a short-lived but momentarily effective deal with the Nazi government by which, in exchange for the *yishuv* breaching the worldwide Jewish boycott against trade in German goods, a group of German Jews was allowed to immigrate to Palestine and received some compensation from the German government for Nazi seizure of their property. More of such complex backstairs deals might have been possible, but none was ever attempted again.

A close study of Zionist diplomacy in the late 1930s by the Israeli historian S. B. Beit Zvi concludes that Zionist efforts to get countries to take in Eastern European refugees fell short of what could have been done. The fact is that the *yishuv*'s Labor Zionist leadership was not very interested in Jews gaining refuge in countries other than Palestine.

In 1944 the *yishuv* leadership received an offer from Nazi officials in Hungary to exchange the lives of Hungarian Jews, who were undergoing the process of shipment to the death camps in return for military trucks and other such non-lethal materiel. The *yishuv* leadership checked with Allied representatives in the Near East, who characteristically opposed the opening of negotiations. The *yishuv* leadership meekly and needlessly acquiesced and failed to follow up on the possibility of dealing with the Nazi authorities in Hungary. Hundreds of thousands of lives might have been saved.

Instead of dealing with the Nazis, Ben-Gurion and the *yishuv* leadership focused on getting the British to allow Jewish refugees from the developing Holocaust into Palestine, leading to bitter confrontation with the British in the last two years of the war. Ben-

Gurion's long-term policy, and within this policy the relatively low priority he gave to saving Jews under Nazi rule, was indicated by the results of the Biltmore Conference (so-called because it was held at the Biltmore Hotel in New York City) in 1942. The participants were Ben-Gurion and the *yishuv* leadership and a wide representation of American Jewry, mostly leaders of Zionist organizations. The resolutions of the Biltmore Conference gave priority to forging ahead toward the creation of an independent Jewish state in Israel.

Ben-Gurion and his colleagues knew that this constituted a challenge to the British government. It was not the most likely way to win over British and world opinion to giving urgent attention to the saving of the Jews from Nazi Holocaust. By the time of the Biltmore Conference, Ben-Gurion was ready to write off the European Jews. He also realized that his assertion of the winning of Jewish independence in an autonomous state was likely to generate conflict with the British government and its army in Palestine.

A man of infinite courage and bold determination, Ben-Gurion was prepared to pursue this radical policy. Weizmann would have preferred to concentrate for the present on saving the remnant under Nazi rule. He would have favored long and patient negotiation with the British. He would certainly not at this time have proclaimed the earliest possible gaining of independence as the goal of Zionist policy. But Weizmann had been shunted to the side in world Zionist circles, and Ben-Gurion, by force of his charismatic personality, got his way.

By 1943 an occasional leaky ship laden with refugees would turn up at the port of Haifa, to be turned away by the British authorities—in one instance to sink off Constantinople with five hundred people aboard. The last vestiges of the *yishuv's* confidence in British humanity then evaporated. The outlook of the Labor Zionists and the Revisionists grew closer, although they never created a united resistance front. Independence, the birth of a free Israel, seemed the only solution.

Already in 1937 the Zionists had reluctantly accepted a British proposal for the partition of Palestine between Arabs and Jews that would have given them a small country of their own. The arrogant and intransigent Arabs rejected the proposal. In 1947 a United Nations Commission offered another partition, this one allotting slightly more territory to the Jews. Ben-Gurion was willing to accept it. This proposal was also rejected by the Palestinians, who had become more ambitious and optimistic about their political future as they counted on support from the surrounding Arab governments, whose strategic locations and oil resources appeared to make them much stronger in the postwar world than ever before.

In 1947 the British, impoverished by the war and frustrated by the deadlock between Arabs and Jews, and feeling the effect of the terrorist attacks launched by the Irgun and an even more extreme Revisionist group, Lehi (the Stern Gang), suddenly announced their intention to withdraw from Palestine, just at about the same time as the British government gave up its rule in India. The British decision to abandon Palestine was made by the foreign secretary in the postwar Labor government in London, Ernest Bevin, a prominent labor union leader. He has entered into Zionist memory as an anti-Semite. Bevin certainly was pro-Arab and cool to Zionist ambitions. He gave priority in British policy to winning the cold war against the Soviet Union. For Bevin, this necessitated appeasing the Arabs.

The process of British withdrawal was such that it threatened to turn over most of Palestine to the Arabs. Ben-Gurion saw an opportunity that might never come again. He declared the existence of the state of Israel and prepared for the inevitable fight to the death against the Palestinians and their supporters among the neighboring Arab countries. His action was one of exceptional courage, and the cost was severe. Six thousand Jews fell in the Israeli War of Independence, 1947–48, a tremendous toll for such a small population.

Initially the Israelis were poorly armed, inadequately trained, and disorganized, but the officers of their liberation army, drawn almost entirely from the kibbutzim, in the end prevailed. Their strategy was often unwise, but they fought with desperate ferocity. Militarily they carved out a much larger state than the UN partition plan had allotted them, although they could gain only the western half of Jerusalem. The rest of the Holy City, along with much of the West Bank of the Jordan River, fell to the British-trained and British-armed Jordanese army.

At one point in 1948 not only were the Israelis facing Palestinian armed bands, but five Arab armies were marching on Israel, although only the Jordanese army was militarily effective. No moment in Jewish history stretching back to the time of King David was marked by such personal heroism as distinguished the behavior of both Jewish military and civilians in the War of Independence, the first Arab-Israeli war. The story has been well told by Dan Kurzman.

In addition to their personal courage and self-sacrifice, the Israelis prevailed becaused of a number of factors. First, they had received a modicum of military training from a philo-Semitic, Bible-thumping British general, Orde Windgate. Secondly, their declaration of independence was immediately recognized by both the Soviet Union and the United States. The Stalinist Soviets (who were soon to turn viciously anti-Israel and pro-Arab) recognized Israel to make trouble for the British empire, which was collapsing in any case.

The American story is complex. The secretaries of the American departments of State and Defense urged American President Harry S. Truman not to antagonize the Arabs by recognizing Israel, but Truman overruled them. A variety of motives have been attributed to Truman: He wanted to strengthen the support of Jews for the Democratic party; or he was a philo-Semite, having once had a generous Jewish partner in a failed haberdashery store in depression Kansas City. Maybe he just thought it was the right thing to do.

Truman compromised with his dissenting cabinet by imposing an American embargo on the shipment of arms to Palestine, a stricture that fell mostly on the Jews. The Zionists, however, had plenty of money from emergency fund-raising in the United States and Canada, and arms were smuggled out through the Brooklyn docks to Israel. In postwar Europe plenty of arms caches could be purchased by Zionist agents.

The big problem was finding airplanes, and here the third factor accounting for Jewish victory in the War of Independence was at work the support of the Czech Communist government, of whom the head, Rudolf Slansky, and most of the top officials were Jewish. They were short-lived carryovers from the 1920s when Jews were the core of communist leadership in Central Europe. In the latter stages of the war, the Germans had made most of their planes in Prague, which was hard to reach by Allied bombers, and, ironically, these surplus German planes formed the core of the first Israeli air force, usually flown by pilots who were alumni of the American, British, and Canadian air forces. Slansky and his Jewish colleagues were forthwith purged by Stalin's representatives. He has not received appropriate recognition in Zionist memory.

In the uneasy truce that was worked out in 1948 bringing the first Arab-Israeli war to an end (Egypt made a peace treaty with Israel in 1980; Jordan, in 1994) the new state of Israel faced enormous problems of absorbing not only close to a million refugees from Europe, survivors of the Holocaust, but in the first four years of its existence, another million "Oriental" or Sephardic Jews who were driven out of Arab countries where in many instances they had lived peacefully for a millennium or more.

Middle-class Oriental Jews, expelled and divested of their property, often suffered severe status declension in their forced immigration to Israel. Shunted off to bleak "development towns" away from the major population centers, they faced a difficult employment situation and turned into a deprived proletariat, a condition that is still only partly mitigated. Although nearly equal in numbers to Ashkenazic Jews, the Orientals comprise only twenty percent of the students in Israeli universities. Politically, the Orientals have also remained relatively weak.

During the height of immigration in 1949–50 the treatment of the Orientals by the Israeli government was not generous; a brilliant book by Tom Segev shows how much the attitude of the Ben-Gurion government was infected with Western racism.

While absorbing the Jewish refugees from Arab lands, the Israelis were seizing the property of several hundred thousands of Arabs who had departed from their Palestinian homes during the War of Independence. In recent years there has been much controversy over whether the Palestinians left voluntarily, on recommendation of their leaders with the rash promise of returning soon with victorious Arab armies, or whether they were expelled by the Israelis through terror and physical force. A careful study by the Israeli historian Benny Morris has concluded that both causes were at work.

The Israeli government in the 1950s faced huge domestic problems of resettling, housing, and employing two million people, as well as defending its frontiers from Arab incursions. It came through these crises reasonably well. Ben-Gurion as prime minister demonstrated charismatic leadership, and his senior officials in the Labor Zionist government, mostly products of the kibbutzim, demonstrated extraordinary energy and resourcefulness.

Of course the government could not have operated fiscally without vast amounts of Jewish overseas aid. It was also helped greatly by the beginning of German reparations, which was opposed bitterly by Menachem Begin, Jabotinsky's heir as leader of the rightist opposition, but readily accepted by Ben-Gurion. The dealing with the Germans he should have tried in the 1930s and 1940s he was now eager to effect. Of course, it was a different German government with which he was now involved.

Israeli frontiers were protected against periodic Arab incursions by the well-developed Israel Defense Forces, armed at first principally by France, whose government was at the time pro-Israeli in compensation for the dismal French record on the treatment of Jews during the war. It also helped that the largest French aircraft manufacturer was a Jew.

The Israeli foreign intelligence service, the Mossad, and the domestic intelligence service, Shin Beit, also gained a reputation for prodigious capacity to ferret out secrets from the Arab government and even from Soviet sources. Profound knowledge of all aspects of European politics and society that came readily to Jews from their historical experience was now compounded by close study of Arab language, culture, and politics in Israeli universities.

The Israelis became so skilled in intelligence work that the American Central Intelligence Agency, not staffed by philo-Semites by any means, came to rely on the Israelis for important information. It was the Israelis in 1956 who obtained the complete text of Nikita Khrushchev's famous secret speech in Moscow denouncing Stalin, after the CIA had failed to obtain it. How the Israelis obtained it was typical of many of their intelligence coups. A Polish Jew with access to high levels in the Communist Warsaw government, who was given a confidential copy of the document, simply flew to Israel with it and handed it over to Israeli intelligence.

Egypt in the mid-1950s had emerged as the greatest threat to Israel, and in 1956 in the Suez War, the Israelis joined with the British and French to punish the Egyptians. American intervention forced the Israelis to withdraw from their gains in the Sinai peninsula, but they had discovered that they could beat the Russian-armed Egyptians, and this gave IDF renewed confidence and set the stage for the triumphs of the Six-Day War in 1967.

Domestically what distinguished Israel in the late 1950s and 1960s was a process of modernization centering on the development of an excellent educational system. The public school system under the Labor government was lavishly supported and on the whole kept free of sectarian interference. The hitherto impoverished Hebrew University in Jerusalem, founded in 1924, and the new Tel Aviv University were richly supported both from government funds and from fund-raising in the United States and other countries, and emerged as strong institutions. The Weizmann Institute of Science, in Rehovot near Tel Aviv, which Weizmann had founded in 1937 because he was dissatisfied with the progress of the Hebrew University (which he also helped to found), became a world-class center of scientific research.

The economic development of Israel, held back by almost Soviet-style regulation and central planning of industry and the megaton Histadrut labor union and exorbitant taxation, did not match the military and educational success of the new state. For the moment, the implications of this economic failure were covered up by the inflow of aid from abroad, the burgeoning tourist industry, and immensely skillful government propaganda.

But underneath all the commotion and surface success, Israeli society was settling into a sharp three-class division that intensified in the following decades. On top was about five percent of the population consisting of high government officials, the bureaucratic bigwigs of banks and state corporations, and business entrepreneurs. They lived well, spent much time abroad, and were part of the international bourgeoisie. They built villas in the more salubrious parts of Jerusalem and along the coast stretching from the northern suburbs of Tel Aviv forty miles through Herzlia to Caesarea, the favorite residence also of the Roman rulers of Palestine.

Another twenty percent of the population were professionals—physicians, lawyers, professors and teachers, second-echelon bureaucrats, and successful owners of small enterprises such as retail shops and restaurants, along with the upper ranks of the army officers. They endured on modest salaries but lived in comfortable Western-style apartments and gave their children good educations at home and abroad. They had no capital but carried themselves with dignity and were crucial in stabilizing the new country.

The balance of the population—three-quarters of them—were poor, struggling from week to week on small salaries or welfare checks, crushed by taxation, living in substandard housing, existing mostly on a diet of fortunately abundant supplies of vegetables and fruit.

The agricultural dreams of the socialist Zionist founders vanished. The population was now mainly urban. The kibbutz population by 1970 was insignificant in numbers—three percent of the people and declining. Yet the kibbutzim continued to produce a large proportion of the army officers and high government officials. Facing difficulty selling their agricultural produce abroad, many kibbutzim turned to manufacturing and the tourist trade to make ends meet, with mixed results. By 1980 most farming collectives and cooperatives were carrying heavy debts to the banks.

The army was the great leveler and common educator of Israel. Everyone except the ultra-Orthodox, including women, had to put in two years of military training, and afterward men had to serve one month a year of reserve duty until they reached age fifty-five. This was a very heavy tax on the country's energy and intelligence, but it did have the educational impact of helping to foment a common citizenship out of a variety of immigrant cultures. It probably also, along with the grim economic circumstances for most people and the constant threat of Arab incursion and terrorism, conditioned a tough, materialistic, and almost cynical national temperament. The Israelis emerged by the 1970s as an eminently capable and shrewd but not very idealistic or generous people.

They had come a long way not only from the Hasidic ghettos but from the chivalrous idealism of Herzl, Weizmann, and Ahad Ha'Am. The Israelis liked to boast that their native-born were sabras, cactuses tough on the outside but sweet and soft inside. Over time, the toughness increased and the soft interior shrank.

This was understandable. They lived in a state of siege, forever threatened by incursions, terrorism, and outright war. From the end of the War of Independence in 1948 until 1993, eighteen thousand Israelis died at Arab hands. Not only were Arab terrorist incursions into Israel on all fronts frequent, but even Jewish athletes at the Munich Olympic games in 1972 were cut down by the Arab militants.

After military training, Israelis were urged to keep their guns and carry them on their persons. It is a tribute to their innate decency that the violent crime rate among Israeli Jews is negligible.

The Israelis were deeply bothered by the extremely effective propaganda launched against them abroad by the Palestine Liberation Organization and its spokesmen, not only its nominal head Yasser Arafat, but suave scholars like Edward Said. The United

Nations in 1975 condemned Zionism as a form of racism, a libel that was not rescinded until 1991.

The press in Britain, Canada, France, and frequently also the United States railed against Israel as an imperialist and racist power, and the American TV networks learned that projecting images of Israeli soldiers attacking Arabs, even if motivated by self-defense, made for attractive and dramatic viewing. There were no more persistent critics of Israel than American leftist journalists, many of them Jews. They held Israel to a much higher ethical standard than they imposed on the Arabs.

By the mid-1960s the Israelis felt that they were being treated unfairly in the forum of world opinion as well as threatened physically by Arab armies and terrorist organizations. When in June 1967 the Egyptians closed the Gulf of Aqaba to Israeli shipping, a technical act of war, and the Egyptian blowhard President Nasser thundered bellicose threats, the Israelis had had enough. Their highly skilled air force made a preemptive strike on Egyptian airfields and destroyed Nasser's Russian-supplied air force in a couple of hours. Israeli tank columns raced across the Sinai peninsula and turned the Egyptian tanks into scrap metal. East Jerusalem was taken from Jordan and the reunited City of David proclaimed as the capital of Israel.

Throughout the world, in Soviet countries as well as in the Western world, Jews gathered in front of TV sets and watched the graphic pictures of the Israeli triumph. It sent a thrill up and down the spines of these people, so beaten upon, so insulted and demeaned for close to two millennia. It was the greatest Jewish victory since David slew Goliath. The Jews had struck back at last.

From millions of heads, through millions of minds, went the strains of the Israeli national anthem "Hatikva"—hope. "Wherever there beats a Jewish heart . . ." begins this stirring anthem. The Israelis had characteristically lifted the melody from a symphonic poem by the Czech Gentile composer Bedřich Smetana.

The smashing of Egypt and Jordan in the Six-Day War of 1967 seemed at the time one of the best things that ever happened in Jewish history. But in retrospect it appears as the beginning of great troubles for Israel. Not only was East Jerusalem taken, but the West Bank of the Jordan and Gaza as well. Israel became an imperial occupying power ruling millions of discontented Arabs in the "territories" as well as the twenty percent of the Israeli citizenship who were Arabs.

Sinai was given back to Egypt at the end of the 1970s, but Israel remained in control of the territories and experienced all the agonies of an occupying power. As a result, the image of Israel abroad, no doubt affected by visceral anti-Semitism, changed from that of a land of heroic, democratic people to that of an imperial state exploiting less fortunate neighbors. Not Switzerland but Sparta or Prussia or even Nazi Germany was held up as the Israeli model.

And there was just enough plausibility in these damaging allegations to make them stick, especially among people who did not like Jews anyway. Israeli agriculture (other than the kibbutzim) and construction industries exploited cheap Arab labor. Although the Israelis greatly improved health facilities and transportation infrastructure in the territories, the populations there lived in bad housing and unsanitary conditions, and their educational institutions were much inferior to Israel's.

Whether the Israelis could have negotiated a general peace with their Arab neighbors and the Palestine leadership in the PLO immediately after the Six-Day War is debatable. The government headed by Golda Meir and Moshe Dayan didn't try very hard. They had won a great victory. They were not prone to sweeping concessions. A triumphalist tone entered into the Israeli government.

The military and intelligence services relaxed and were ill-prepared for the Yom Kippur War of 1973 launched by Egypt and Syria. The armies of these countries were now well-trained and armed by the Russians, and the first week of the war was a near disaster for the Israelis on both fronts. What was most threatening was the loss of a large part of their supply of tanks on the Syrian front. A supply bailout by the American government saved Israel from a military disaster. The American arms airlift advocated by American Secretary of State Henry Kissinger, a Jew, allowed General Ariel Sharon's risky but successful tank crossing of the Suez Canal and surrounding of the Egyptian army that led to UN intervention to end the war.

The Israelis barely managed to push back the Syrians on the Golan Heights. On the northern front they learned that they had found an enemy who was their equal. The image of the Arabs as soft and incompetent vanished in 1973.

Overcome by its triumphalist vapors, the Labor government had done little for the Orientals in the late 1960s and 1970s, and in the election of 1977 the Orientals supported the rightist opposition in the form of the Likud party led by Jabotinsky's disciples, Menachem Begin and Itzhak Shamir, which replaced the Labor government. The Likud party remained in power for nearly all of the next fifteen years. While Begin withdrew from the Sinai at American urging, his stance militarily was an aggressive one, resulting in the Lebanese invasion of 1982.

The Lebanese War of 1982, featuring an Israeli advance on Beirut, represented the radical effort of General Sharon, then defense minister, with the acquiescence Prime Minister Menachem Begin, to solve the Palestinian problem by military means.

The Reagan administration in the United States, particularly its idiosyncratic Secretary of State Alexander Haig, was pro-Israeli to a greater extent than any previous American administration. The Israelis were heavily armed by the Americans, and Sharon determined to use this military strength to force the PLO from Lebanon, from which they had been launching cross-border incursions into northern Israel. Amid the various factions struggling for power in bleeding Lebanon, Sharon also intended to set up a Christian group as the dominant force in the country. The PLO was forced to retreat from Lebanon and set up headquarters in Tunis. That did not greatly reduce the effectiveness of their operations. Sharon's efforts to set up a Christian government in Beirut allied to Israel came to nothing when the Christian leader was assassinated and the Syrians intervened to restore the strength of Muslim factions.

American and European TV pictures of Beirut under Israeli bombardment hurt Israel's image. Even worse was the massacre of a Muslim refugee encampment by Lebanese Christian soldiers allied to the Israelis. An Israeli court of inquiry found that Sharon was reckless in not taking precautions against such a possibility.

Begin was so devastated by the Lebanese War, in which the IDF took its greatest casualties since 1948, that he withdrew abruptly from public life, leaving the government in the hands of Shamir, a taciturn former intelligence official and Stern Gang terrorist against the British before independence.

Clearly the Israelis had gone too far in the direction of militarism, which was becoming an unbearable burden on the population.

Domestically the Likud government was more sympathetic than Labor to a market economy, but it only marginally made the structural changes needed to attract heavy investment from abroad.

To please the ultra-Orthodox and retain their political support, lavish government aid was given to their sectarian educational institutions at the expense of the public schools, which deteriorated. Government support of the universities, whose faculties were overwhelmingly opposed to the Likud, was sharply cut, and Israeli higher education and scientific research went into steep decline just at the point when they were turning into world-class institutions.

Corruption of a serious nature spread through the upper stratum of Israeli society and politics. The heads of all major banks in the 1980s were convicted of stock market manipulation. Government aid was secretly lavished on favored individuals and groups, particularly ultra-Orthodox sects whose votes were needed by Likud. Industrialists and retired generals became covertly active in the world arms trade, with government consent. The Iran side of the Reaganite Iran-Contra scheme was largely hatched in Tel Aviv.

Israelis had always been proud of their socialized medical system operated by a Histadrut subsidiary. By the late 1980s it was bogged down in a bureaucratic morass and running huge deficits.

Lavish subsidies and cheap housing were offered to any Jew who moved to the conquered territories, and as a result more than one hundred thousand Jews came to live in heavily defended pockets of the West Bank. Perhaps a quarter of them were Orthodox religious idealists determined to recover "Judea and Samaria"—or the "land of Abraham"—for the Jewish people. The majority were simply looking for bargain housing within commuting distance of Jerusalem and Tel Aviv. While the Israeli road system was generally substandard and the railroads were much as the British had left them, an elaborate road system began to be built to connect the West Bank "settlers" to the rest of Israel and make all the more difficult the prospect of an Israeli withdrawal.

An intransigent Arab response was only a matter of time. The unemployed and poorly educated young Arabs on the West Bank and in Gaza were an ideal recruiting ground for popular insurrection, and the *intifada* began toward the end of 1987. The Israeli occupation army—mostly reservists unenthusiastic about the difficult assignment of restoring peace in the territories—never developed a consistent policy about how to deal with children throwing stones and burning tires.

The majority of a new generation of Israelis were sick of all this, sick of the greater Israel that included the territories, sick of triumphalism and militarism. They wanted to trade conquered land for peace, to give up the repellent Gaza and most of the West Bank. A new Labor government coming to power in 1992 under Itzhak Rabin, one of the last of the generation of kibbutz and moshav military heroes of the late 1940s and 1950s, determined to carry out peace negotiations.

The Zionists abroad, especially in the United States, were not enthusiastic about Rabin's peace initiatives. They had steadfastly supported Begin and Shamir in their aggressive policies. The militant Likudnik General Sharon was a favorite speaker in New York synagogues. Diaspora Jews had come to identify Israel with militancy and triumphalism and to think of Arabs as a race of cowardly terrorists. *Commentary,* the most influential American Jewish magazine, under Norman Podhoretz's skillful and aggressive editorship, had strongly supported the militant policy of the Likud government. It was hostile to the Israeli groups that had sought accommodation with the Arabs and was highly critical of Rabin's peace efforts.

The signaling of a possible new day when Rabin shook hands with Arafat in the White House Rose Garden in September 1993, and serious peace talks with the PLO commenced, sent a shock wave through Diaspora Jewry. They would have to start thinking differently about Israel, the Near East, and even their own identity if the peace negotiations were successful and the Israelis withdrew from the territories—and possibly even gave up most of the Golan Heights, gained and held with so much Jewish blood, to the fierce, inscrutable Syrians.

If peace was achieved with the Palestinians and Syrians, American Jews would have to think of Israel differently, as a smaller, peaceful, normal country, not the Lion of Judah.

The American Jews, along with many of the Israelis, had incorporated heroism into their culture. That it was vicarious, surrogate heroism—the Israelis fought and died, the Americans supported them fiscally and morally and basked in the Israeli military image—made it even more attractive than being on the ground and hazardously participating personally in the Israel Defense Forces. Now all this might evaporate. The suburban Jewish American's reflected image of himself as a fighter was put at risk.

The three hundred thousand Russian immigrants who poured into Israel in the 1980s and early 1990s felt otherwise. They keenly welcomed the peace offensive. They had no interest in the territories, no desire to cultivate a military tradition. They were unaffected by biblical references; very few of them had ever read the Bible before they came to Israel and learned Hebrew. They wanted jobs and security for themselves and their families.

While Stalin had obliterated Jewish religion, Jewish memory, and even the Yiddish language, and purged Jewish political and intellectual elites, he had allowed a younger generation of Russian Jews (despite the usual discriminatory quotas) to obtain good educations and professional training. Russian Jews left for Israel because the Soviet Union, as it disintegrated in the late 1980s, was allowing traditional anti-Semitism to seep up through the cracks and because they simply wanted better jobs and more affluent lifestyles. Most of the Russian immigrants really wanted to go to the United States, but the Likud government convinced Washington to cut off Soviet Jewish immigration, to force the Moscow emigrants to turn toward Jerusalem, an astonishingly cynical act.

Perhaps a quarter of the Russian immigrants were not ethnically Jews at all. The rabbis protested, but they were shunted aside. (The rabbis also complained that the black Ethiopian Jews, airlifted en masse to Jerusalem, were not ethnic Jews, but here also they were ignored.)

The Russians represented a new sizable bloc among the four million Israeli voters. They would have to be listened to. Their occupational ambitions could only be satisfied if Israel developed a wealthier high-tech economy, and this required a massive capital investment, which in turn presupposed a Near Eastern peace. By bringing in the Russians, the Likud undermined their own militant policy.

Israel in the early 1990s is a country rife with paradoxes and anomalies. It is a country that stops dead for the Sabbath from noon on Friday until sundown on Saturday, but less than twenty percent of its Jewish population attends Sabbath religious services. It is a country where every inch of its ancient soil is revered and where archaeological discoveries are greeted with national celebration, but which treats its fragile ecology with a recklessness that astounds an American or a Canadian. It has no pollution controls on its automobile emissions and spews raw sewage into the Mediterranean, fouling its own beaches.

Israel is forever digging (bootlessly) for oil but doing little to forestall an imminent shortage of water. It worries about attracting and settling immigrants but not about bringing back home three hundred thousand Israeli emigrants, many highly educated and skilled, living in the United States.

It is a boisterous democracy but seemingly incapable of legislating constitutional freedom of speech. It talks about the world unity of the Jewish people but refuses to recognize marriages performed in Israel by Reform rabbis and still in many ways accords its women inferior status to men. The Talmudic law that only a husband can inaugurate a divorce action still prevails in Israel. In any government office, the top official is nearly always a male, whose work is mainly done by a woman "assistant."

Israel establishes museums to depict Jewish history but actually does little or nothing to cultivate the glorious Yiddish past of Ashkenazic culture. It has more automobiles per road mile than any country in the world but no automobile industry; all its cars are imported. It spends millions on its tourist industry but only a few minutes a day on the state TV and radio are broadcast in English, while Jordanese TV and radio have many hours of English-language broadcast.

The Israelis point with justifiable pride to their fine universities but allow their most distinguished professors to hold chairs jointly abroad and absent themselves from their Israeli students for half a year or longer.

One could go on and on relating the paradoxes and ambivalence of the Israelis, of which they do not like to be reminded. When a visiting Fulbright professor tried to point them out, in a confidential document in response to a questionnaire from the Israeli Fulbright Commission, the commission shamelessly induced the U.S. cultural attaché in Tel Aviv to censure him.

The context in which these Israeli problems should be seen is not the Zionist mythology that all would be perfect in Israel if only the Arabs would somehow disappear, but the realization that this is a very young country, not yet fifty years old as an independent state, and composed of people brought from disparate ends of the earth and blended together out of highly diverse cultures.

If there was ever a country characterized by diversity and multi-culturalism—and that condition exists even without considering the Muslim and Christian minorities—it is Israel.

The greatest Israeli novelist, S. Y. Agnon, who won the Nobel Prize for literature, put it well in *A Guest for the Night* (1939). He portrays an unfinished country, with many problems, many issues yet to be resolved. This is still true. The character of Israel is still in its early phase of formation. Agnon, however, also shows a people of great courage and dignity, trying to work out their problems.

The worst thing about Israel in the 1980s and early 1990s was that it had allowed itself to become thoroughly dependent on American government aid for both military and civilian purposes—at least five billion dollars a year. When it is factored in that Jewish charitable sources abroad provide annually a similar sum, Israel has to be recognized as a severely debtor nation, a colonial country, unable to provide for itself, greedily and recklessly used to living off other peoples' money.

This is a mighty obstacle to facing its own problems, to healing its fragile economy, to building up its own export industries, to making effective use of its tremendous reservoir of educated and skilled manpower.

Since the Rabin-Arafat agreement of September 1993, Israel has made significant progress in developing peace with the Palestinians and in the long run with its Arab neighbors. There is a long way to go, but a real start has been made. It is on the economic side that Israel must make a similar dramatic breakthrough by dismantling its Soviet-style command economy. The following sobering item appeared in the *Jerusalem Post* international edition of April 23, 1994:

> Recently published research sponsored by Canada's Fraser Institute and the U.S.-based Liberty Fund show that in a survey of hundreds of economics professors around the world, Israel ranked nearly last in degree of economic freedom, ahead only of several former Communist countries and India.

Israeli reliance on American aid, its status as a debtor and mendicant nation produces a complex variety of ill effects. Within Israel, a disproportionate share of American aid goes to support the elite five percent of the population in the higher ranks of the civil service, the state corporations, the army, and the learned professions, therefore augmenting the strains of class polarization in Israel, making it resemble in this regard a Third World country.

The vast funds gained annually from private sources among American Jewry means deprivation of urgent communal needs in the United States, of which education is the most obvious sufferer. In a sense, the Israeli elite, is devouring its own seed-corn—taking short-term advantage at the price of long-term penalties. The more American Jewish aid goes to Israel, the more the sad inadequacy of Jewish educational institutions at all levels in the United States is unrepaired. This means the younger generation of American Jews, lacking a Jewish consciousness because of the sorry state of Jewish education, is less likely than that of their parents to perpetuate the Zionist ethos that first gripped American Jews in the 1940s; as a result, Israel will become more isolated in time. The Israeli elite, made sleek and comfortable on American aid, is living on borrowed time. Significantly, eighty percent of American Jews have never visited Israel, and the proportion who will visit seems likely to decline rather than increase as the aging American Jewish population experiences high mortality among its senior citizens, whose vehement Zionist commitments will erode among the rising generation.

Israel then is a country of co-dependents, living off the foreign dole, obsessing with fiscal substance abuse, reluctant to take the strong measures necessary to create a First World market economy and compete on the world economic stage. The Israelis have become intoxicated, not like many of their distressed forefathers with mystical religion, but with military glamour and triumphalist images, a dangerous and self-destructive mind-set in the sober, competitive world at the end of the twentieth century.

The hope for Israel is that if peace with the Arabs is consummated at last, the Israelis will look at themselves in the mirror, see themselves realistically for what they are, both good and bad, and resolve to terminate their long weekend of militarism and economic dependency, and become the great nation they are fully capable of becoming.

From around 1960 the Israelis have asserted a voice as leader of world Jewry, and Diaspora Jews who were conscious of their Jewishness have focused much attention on them. For such a small, still relatively poor country, with such a modest total population size, it is amazing how much attention has been given to the Israelis. The space in the *New York Times* accorded to Canada in a given year can be measured in inches. In the case of Israel it would be measured in feet. If anything, Israel has been overexposed in the world's press, encouraging grandstanding by Israeli politicians rather than attention to hard business.

There are good grounds for thinking of Israel as one of the two leading national societies of Jews in the world, and by the early 1990s their numbers were only a million below the United States' five million Jews. Yet the history and destiny of American Jewry is also crucial for the shaping of twentieth-century Jewish history. Today's Russia, the Ukraine, and Belarus combined probably have among them another three million ethnic Jews, but the great majority of them have little self-identification as Jews as a result of the heavy hand of Stalinist cultural obliteration.

Given Israel's Arab and economic problems and the effacement of Jewish identity in the Soviet Union, the destiny of the Jews from 1920 onward has been heavily conditioned by the American situation.

If pressure were to have been brought on the Allied governments during World War II to help the Jews, the four million Jews then in the United States, by virtue of their numbers and their economic and political circumstances would have had to have taken the major role, possibly along with the *yishuv* in Palestine, in this initiative. Yet they failed to act effectively, and this impotence remains a stain on the conscience of American Jews and a controversial issue.

Down into the 1920s the promise offered by the poem on the Statue of Liberty, written by an American Jewish woman, Emma Lazarus, about offering hope and solace to the poor, wretched, huddled masses of Eastern Europe, appeared to be in course of fulfillment. Never in the long history of American immigrant groups had one adjusted better, become more rapidly assimilated to the prevailing culture, and shown more decisive social mobility. The rapid success of the Jews stood in contrast with the slower acculturation and economic success of Irish and Italian groups.

One reason for this was the innate intelligence and rationality of the Ashkenazic Jews, the high degree of their literate intelligence given the opportunity to ally itself with business, higher education, and the learned professions.

In 1900 the Jews appeared to have migrated from the squalor, poverty, filth, and criminality of the Eastern European Pale to much the same crowded circumstances in the tenement and pushcart world of the Lower East Side of New York City. Millions lived in extremely crowded and insalubrious conditions and struggled as petty tradesmen or were ground down in sweatshops of the needle trade.

The memorial to this initial era of misery and exploitation (1890–1920) is a building just east of Washington Square in lower Manhattan, then a factory building, now a classroom building for New York University. There in 1903 occurred the infamous Triangle Shirtwaist Company fire, when three hundred young Jewish women, caught in a fire in the sweatshop where they worked, found the fire exit locked by the bosses to cut down on pilferage and were overcome.

But in the next twenty years, significant improvement in immigrant Jewish life occurred. Subways, schools, unions, and physical dispersion to the outlying boroughs of New York City were the key factors. The International Ladies Garment Workers Union and other unions improved salaries and working conditions. The boom that marked World War I increased demand for Jewish labor and greatly reduced the inflow of cheap labor. The exclusion of Jews by the immigration act of 1924, preceded by diminution of intake since 1917, was bad for Jews still caught in Eastern Europe but fortunate for those already in the country as the labor pool stabilized.

The building of subways to Brooklyn and the Bronx in the first decade of the century allowed Jews of modest income to escape from the tenement hellholes of the Lower East Side and find cheap housing in fresh air in the outlying suburbs.

The New York public school system did more than anything to provide for assimilation and social mobility of the younger generation. The WASP and Irish teachers in these schools did not fail the Jews. They did their job well, insensitive as most of them were to Jewish diversity. City College provided free college education for those who could meet its high entrance standards.

For those who could not, and whose families could scrape up the modest tuition, there was close by to the Lower East Side the Washington Square campus of New York University. The university trustees built a splendid new campus for men on University Heights in the Bronx, where the Jewish quota was a rigid fifteen percent, and were preparing to close down the old Washington Square campus, which consisted of four ramshackle buildings, when the Jewish immigrants poured in and the WASP trustees realized they had a tuition goldmine. By 1920 more than half of its students were Jews, women as well as men, and the talk in Manhattan was of "NYJew."

The New York billionaire patriarchs—"Our Crowd"—from German Jewish families funded some basic social services when the early waves of immigrants arrived in the late nineteenth century. By 1900 they could see that these unwashed masses from the shtetlach were doing well on their own and reduced their commitments. But they kept a close eye on the burgeoning of Jewish organized crime. Secretly the uptown families cooperated with the police to hire private investigators to infiltrate the Jewish gangs.

It was the Jews, by and large, not the Italians, who created what later was called the Mafia. In the 1920s the Italians began to replace the Jews in the New York organized crime industry, but as late as 1940 if you wanted a spectacular hit you were looking for a representative of the Lepke Buchalter Gang, also known as Murder Inc. Jews also were also prominent in the gambling trade and developed Las Vegas in the 1940s. It was a Jewish gambler who fixed the 1919 baseball World Series—what became known as the Black Sox scandal.

Why did Jews as an immigrant group do better than the Irish or the Italians? Perhaps it was innately superior genes, better selective breeding. Certainly it was due to the failure of the rabbis and zaddikim to transfer their control and conservative leadership across the Atlantic, while the heavy hand of the Catholic Church lay upon daily life in the Irish and Italian communities almost as much in early twentieth century America as in Europe.

Jewish communal life was shattered and family life modified to give freedom to the younger generation to live their own lives and pursue their own trades, educations, and careers.

Yiddish was abandoned with astonishing rapidity. *The Jewish Daily Forward* and three other daily Jewish newspapers in New York in 1914 had a combined circulation of a million copies. By 1930 these papers were struggling to stay in business. The Eastern European Jewish tradition of pursuing the learned professions and the more upscale colleges was visibly under way by 1920. And the Jews spread out from New York City to create substantial populations in Chicago, Philadelphia, Baltimore, Minneapolis, Cleveland, Detroit, and Los Angeles.

In Hollywood, a new industry developed, the making and distributing of films, almost completely dominated in the first fifty years of its existence by immigrant Jews and still dominated at its top level by Jews.

The Hollywood film reached its zenith as an art form in the first decade of sound motion pictures in the 1930s. The ethos it projected was that of the earnest, patriotic, immigrant Jews who headed the movie studios. Hard work, honesty, idealism, and loyalty to family and country were the values that the Hollywood films inculcated. An activated ethical context is ever present in the Hollywood movies, whether dramas or comedies, even in the Fred Astaire/Ginger Rogers musicals. Do the right thing and be rewarded: That is the immigrant's hope and expectation in his new country.

Since the United States was still generally a nation of immigrants, the Hollywood ethos interacted well with the value system of its working-class and petty bourgeois audience. It was easily compatible with Calvinist Protestant traditions. It also make the bold entrepreneurs who founded the great Hollywood studios very rich.

Jewish leadership affected radio (and then TV) the way it shaped the Hollywood film. Parallel to Louis B. Mayer, Jack Warner, and David Selznick in Hollywood were William Paley and David Sarnoff in radio. They were the founders, respectively, of the CBS and NBC networks. And they inculcated the same ethos in their programming—patriotic, family-oriented, puritanical, vaguely liberal, fully compatible with the Protestant culture of the interwar era.

If the trend line of Jewish advancement as it existed in the early 1920s had continued, the immense wealth and power enjoyed by the American Jews around 1970 would already have been theirs by the 1940, and they would likely have exercised their wealth and power to save millions of the Jews in Eastern Europe, who in many instances were their own relatives. But two adverse developments in the 1920s and 1930s blocked further Jewish melioration and empowerment—surging anti-Semitism and the Great Depression.

The immigration act of 1924 was principally directed against Eastern European Jews, to cut off the flow of immigration of poor Jews from the shtetlach, and it was fiercely enforced and almost one hundred percent effective. It was not in fact significantly breached until Senator Edward Kennedy's immigration act of 1965. In the short run, the quota wall against the Jews heretofore passing through the immigration station on New York's Ellis Island actually helped the

New York immigrants by freezing the labor pool and making their services more valuable. In the long run, it was a major contribution to the Holocaust, for it excluded entry of Jews from Hitler's Europe.

In the late 1930s and early 1940s time and time again international meetings were held on the refugee—that is, mainly the Jewish—question. No one ever determined whether the Nazis would release their imprisoned Jews—for a steep consideration, of course—because there was nowhere for them to go. The United States would not take them, and that was the obvious place, and if the United States would not modify its exclusionary immigration laws, neither would anyone else. Therefore, next to the murderous intentions of Germans, Poles, and Ukrainians, what did most to kill the Jews was their immigration exclusion from the United States that began in practice in 1917 and was confirmed in 1924.

This closing of Jewish immigration, leaving Ellis Island a ghost town symbolizing a vanished era, was first of all a consequence of the great wave of anti-Semitism that arose in the United States in the early years of the century and reached its peak in the 1930s. Anti-Semitic fervor spilled through all classes and groups in Gentile society and ran like a fever through major American institutions.

The elite eastern private colleges in the 1920s imposed strict quotas on the admission of Jewish students, from Princeton's three percent to Harvard's fifteen percent to Columbia's twenty-five percent. Jewish applicants to medical schools—despite the building of major hospitals by Jewish philanthropists in several cities, so that Mount Sinai and Beth Israel became common names in American health care—also found it difficult to gain admission. Jewish students did better on admission to elite law schools, but then found that the major corporate law firms would not hire them and the elite Jewish law firms were too few to accommodate the flood of prospective brilliant Jewish attorneys flowing out of law schools in the 1920s and 1930s.

The banking and insurance and public utilities industries excluded Jews from executive positions, as did the automobile and oil and gas companies. Anti-Semitism was conducive to segregated housing. There were suburban and beach communities where Jews could not buy or rent houses, but the college admission and employment situation hit hardest because it impeded the social mobility of Jews coming out of immigrant communities.

Jews in the 1930s were proscribed from teaching jobs in the

humanities departments of major universities. Some Jews were admitted to graduate programs in these places, but when a Jew came to apply for a college teaching job, his dissertation supervisor warned prospective employers that the applicant who had Anglicized his name was in fact Jewish. Under these circumstances it is not surprising that places like City College or Brooklyn College, where Jews were hired, had better faculty than Princeton or Amherst.

In the 1930s anti-Semitism was an accepted ingredient in American public discourse at all levels. The English poet and critic T. S. Eliot was applauded on elite campuses when he disparaged Jews during his lecture tours. At Princeton, Jews were excluded from the more fashionable student dining clubs. Hate merchants spewed anti-Semitic diatribes not only in books and pamphlets but in the new medium of the radio. A Catholic priest, Charles Coughlin, drew millions of listeners with his anti-Semitic Sunday sermons. Several years went by before the Church hierarchy silenced him.

The Great Depression was the other development that hit American Jews hard and drained their self-confidence and capacity for collective action. Limited in access to the professions and excluded from executive positions in most industrial corporations, Jews were heavily concentrated in the 1930s in the retail and service industries and manufacturing markets, such as clothes and textiles, that sold directly to a shrinking consumers' market. The billionaire patriarchs were frightened and quieted by the stock market crash and less inclined to public interventions.

In these adverse circumstances, the Jewish response was a political one. They became fanatical and well-nigh universal supporters of Franklin D. Roosevelt's New Deal and his Democratic party. FDR would end the Depression, they expected, and that would make a big difference to the economically vulnerable Jewish middle class.

Just as important, with the help of Felix Frankfurter, the disciple of Louis Brandeis and a leading professor at Harvard Law School (and later appointed by FDR to the U.S. Supreme Court), Jewish graduates from Harvard and other elite law schools were funneled to Washington to work at relatively high positions in the newly created or greatly expanded New Deal regulatory agencies.

Roosevelt had a liberal left agenda of building a regulatory and to some degree a welfare state. The young Jewish lawyers were ideal personnel for this task. They personally worshipped FDR. They warmed to his moderately left, Keynesian ideas, which often confirmed inherited Jewish family socialist leanings. They were brilliant, incessantly hardworking public servants. They had no commitment to the old free-market economy.

In New Deal Washington there was a strange replay of the centuries-old tradition of the court Jews, as Benjamin Ginsberg has noted. Although a patrician, FDR was devoid of the anti-Semitism characteristic of his class. He was on friendly terms with the Jewish financier Bernard Baruch. He appointed Frankfurter to the Supreme Court, and Henry Morgenthau, the scion of a billionaire Jewish family, was a member of his cabinet as the secretary of the Treasury. Brilliant young Jews felt a deep personal loyalty toward Roosevelt.

Some of the responsibilities thrust upon the young Jewish lawyers in New Deal Washington took them far from their background. Abe Fortas, a Tennessee Jew who graduated from Harvard Law School, was responsible for writing major laws on the environment and agricultural support mechanisms, which took him far from his middle-class Jewish background. Some of the federal agricultural laws drafted by Fortas in the 1930s are still on the books.

Working in a New Deal agency proved to be the avenue for breaking the anti-Jewish barrier in major Gentile law firms in New York and Washington. The New Deal Jewish lawyers with their expertise in the new regulatory state were useful to old-line law firms serving corporate interests, and in the early 1940s those firms began to hire Jews for the first time.

The failure of American Jews to respond courageously and effectively to the torment of Eastern European Jews in the early 1940s has to be understood in the context of their difficult situation in the 1930s. They faced a wall of anti-Semitism that extended into the State Department and the immigration service. Their economic and professional prospects were still questionable, making for caution and disinclination to public confrontations.

They were overcommitted and extremely grateful to FDR and incapable of mounting a public challenge to him when he refused to take any action that could have saved large numbers of Jews from the Holocaust—either by pushing to change the exclusionary immigration laws or undertaking the military and diplomatic measures during the war that Churchill also refused to undertake. FDR won four elections, but to do this he had put together a large and unwieldy coalition of disparate groups, among most of which Jews were held in suspicion and low esteem. Roosevelt did not wish to risk his political hold on the country by special efforts to save the Eastern European Jews.

FDR's political consultations in 1944 with the Jewish labor union leader Sidney Hillman brought a derisive cry from the President's Republican opponents. Their taunting chant of "clear it with Sidney" was code for "FDR consults with leftist Jews." In this context it would have taken a willingness to risk his political career for FDR to have tried to save the European Jews. He was an idealist and a courageous man, but he had no inclination to risk political martyrdom.

Finally in 1944 Henry Morgenthau made a belated personal appeal to Roosevelt and forthrightly criticized the anti-Jewish attitudes of the State Department and the consular hierarchy. By then it was too late to do much, and it is questionable whether Morgenthau ever got more than sentiment out of FDR, who was a charismatic leader, in some ways a visionary, but a shrewd patrician politician above all.

Even when a few thousand Jews caught up in the Hitlerian nightmare qualified for visas, the WASP anti-Semites in the State Department's consular service conspired to keep them out. In 1940 Breckinridge Long, the assistant secretary of State for consular matters (i.e., the person in charge of giving out visas abroad) urged American consuls simply to stall when a rare qualified Jewish applicant appeared, "to put every obstacle in the way, which would postpone and postpone the granting of the visas." There is a special place in hell for the likes of WASP bluebloods like Breckinridge Long, who made a very bad situation for the Jews even worse.

The ultimate reason, beyond these contextual political ones, that the American Jews failed to mitigate the Holocaust was their own weak leadership. The leading public spokesmen on the Holocaust threat were two Reform rabbis, Stephen Wise of New York and Abba Hillel Silver of Cleveland. They gave sermons, they wrote letters to Washington, and they talked in private with the President. They held one large public meeting in Madison Square Garden that got some but not great attention in the press. Otherwise they did nothing.

They did not lead a march on Washington; they did not chain themselves to the fence around the White House. They were too civilized, too fearful, too co-opted by FDR and the liberal wing of the

Democratic party. Indeed they acted like court Jews who disdained above all to upset the king and instead waited patiently for a better day. It was a time-honored policy of Jewish leadership, now exercised with incredibly lethal consequence.

If Wise and Silver had made a huge public fuss, the anti-Semites would have had plenty to feed on, but they might have saved a couple of million Jewish lives.

The loudest noise on behalf of the Eastern European Jews came from two relatively obscure figures, disciples of Jabotinsky and his rightist Revisionists. One was Hillel Cook, the nephew of Palestine's most revered rabbi. He showed that incessant public campaigning on the Jewish issue could get public attention and raise the consciousness of American Jews. He did what Wise and Silver, from the pulpits of their elegant synagogues, failed to do.

Even more remarkably, Ben Hecht, a veteran popular dramatist and film writer, wrote and produced a Broadway play that severely criticized the British for exclusion of Jewish refugees from Palestine. American intellectuals and the social elite found the play vulgar and propagandist. Indeed it was, but it also played to packed audiences, not all Jews. The play was produced in 1944—too late to have a practical outcome. Hecht demonstrated what the organized Jewish leadership should have done. They should have undertaken a public campaign of high visibility, fostering guilt among the Gentiles and pressing Roosevelt for action. Their hearts weren't in it.

Two things can be said on behalf of Wise and Silver and the old-line billionaire Our Crowd patriarchs who also failed to act to save the Jews from the Holocaust. First, it was two decades before the African-American civil rights movement led by Martin Luther King. Except for Communist agitation in the 1930s, or that of the Klu Klux Klan in the South, neither a fortunate model, a contemporary American ambience of political agitation and civil disobedience was lacking, and civil disobedience in wartime raised special problems.

The Depression also cast a heavy pall over Jewish life in America and eroded a sense of community. This malaise is illustrated in the finest novel about Jewish American life in the immigrant era, Henry Roth's *Call It Sleep* (1934). A boy who grows up in the New York of that time feels completely isolated, even from his family, which is headed by an abusive father. There is no structural safety net, nothing he can latch on to outside his personal experience—no institutional nexus or communal cover to protect or mentor the boy.

The long chain of Jewish heritage and its attendant institutions have vanished in the fiery crucible of American materialist and consumer society.

This nihilistic ambience was no context for the anxious and risky summoning of Jewish collectivity to demand action by the President against the Holocaust. All had been swept away, the slate of Jewish history wiped clean. Martin Luther King could draw upon the Southern black churches as a base. Wise and Silver, what did they have? The Reform synagogues with their flowers and organ music and Protestant-sounding sermons? There was no passion there, no depth of feeling, no wellsprings of commitment either religious or social to summon up at the crucial moment and save the Jews from the burning ground.

The failure of American Jewry to take action against the Holocaust, their inability to engage in highly visible public protest and to bring pressure on the Roosevelt administration, represents the nadir of the leadership role the rabbinate had for two millennia exercised in Jewish life.

Reform Judaism, to which Wise and Silver adhered, in general had responded slowly and feebly to the tide of Eastern European immigration. In the 1930s it appealed mainly to non-Eastern immigrant Jews, and among the immigrant families only to the affluent and well-educated.

Reform Judaism was weakened internally by a bitter dispute over whether to endorse Zionism, a dispute eventually settled in the late 1940s in Zionism's favor but at the cost of further distracting the liberal denomination from the crisis in Europe.

Reform Judaism had lost the intellectual vitality that characterized it in the Kantian nineteenth century. It was now conformist, superficial, a new kind of formalism to set as an alternative to the fustian formalism of the orthodoxy of the time.

Orthodoxy retained the loyalty of only ten percent of the American Jewish population. It seemed bewildered by the strenuous challenge of a secular and consumerist culture. Even its efforts to build a major university committed to Halakic tradition, Yeshiva University, were largely a failure. Yeshiva was underfunded and lacking in distinguished faculty and had very little impact on the American scene.

By the 1930s the larger Jewish religious denomination was Conservative Judaism. The term was used only in the United States and Canada, but this approach was already prominent in Britain by the start of the twentieth century. A rabbi who taught at Cambridge University, Solomon Schechter, the discoverer of the genizah archives, was brought over to head the Conservative Judaism's training institute for rabbis, the Jewish Theological Seminary, on Morningside Heights in New York, alongside Columbia University.

JTS produced an enormous number of ordained rabbis to take the pulpits of the ever expanding list of Conservative synagogues, and it was a very respectful center of Jewish learning. But Conservative Judaism was an awkward compromise that signified the lassitude and indecision affecting Jewish religion in America. What Conservative Judaism offered, however, was what many rapidly assimilating immigrants and, even more, their children and grandchildren, wanted. It was consumer-driven.

The immigrant population shied away from the abbreviated and Anglicized liturgy that Reform Judaism offered. They felt it was too uncomfortably Gentile, too much "temple" and not enough "synagogue." Conservative Judaism allowed them to retain essentially the Orthodox service, slightly pruned of its more prolix and obscure qualities and with a modicum of important prayers translated into English. But Conservative Judaism had no firm stand on anything else. Some Conservative Jews were observant, most were not. It was a spiritual buffet. Buy your ticket and take your choice.

Conservative rabbis did not prohibit their members from driving their cars to synagogues on the Sabbath, a big stumbling block for Orthodox congregations. Therefore Conservative communities could develop in the suburbs where most Jews lived, beyond walking distance to a synagogue. Many Conservative Jews kept kashruth at home but ate in nonkosher restaurants—pork in Chinese restaurants was somehow deemed especially acceptable.

While offering reasonable compromises on all sides, Conservative Judaism lacked a spiritual core. Two professors at the Jewish Theological Seminary in the 1940s and 1950s, Mordecai Kaplan and Abraham Joseph Heschel, were keenly aware of these problems and from very different standpoints tried to give Conservative Judaism a positive focus.

Kaplan founded what he called Reconstruction, but he continued to belong to the Conservative rabbinical association and to teach at the Jewish Theological Seminary. Twice Hebrew Union College in New York, the eastern training institute for Reform Judaism, offered him a professorship and twice he almost took it, only to back out at the last minute. His impact there would have been much greater; he really belonged, if anywhere, in the Reform camp. For instance, he published in 1941 a new prayer book that was even more radical in its excisions than the standard Reform one. He wanted to remove Kol Nidre, the Yom Kippur prayer, because some people thought it gave plausibility to anti-Semitic claims of Jewish duplicity—by asking God to cancel contractual oaths (the explanation being that the oaths arose out of the individual Jew's relationship to God, not contracts with other people).

The trustees of the Jewish Theological Seminary would have been glad to see Kaplan leave and pressed the head of the seminary, the Talmudic scholar Louis Ginsberg, to fire him. Ginsberg, who had been Kaplan's student, refused. Why did Kaplan not switch to the more appropriate forum of Hebrew Union College? Timidity and inertia, it would seem, but someone so passive could not inspire the religious revolution in American Jewish life he seemed at times to want to lead.

Kaplan had some very good reforming ideas. He stressed that the synagogue had to be a popular community center involved in child-hood and adult education, and he personally exercised a strong influence in that direction. But he was essentially a sociologist, not a theologian. He was a follower of the American pragmatist philosopher John Dewey (as were many New York Jewish intellectuals of his generation). He focused on the synagogue's role in society but had little to say about the religious message the synagogue should enunciate. Indeed, he suggested that an atheist could be welcomed as a synagogue member.

To carry out a religious reformation, you not only have to believe that your spiritual vision is the right one, but that what you propose in the way of a religious community is much better than prevailing choices. Kaplan failed by a wide margin to fulfill these requirements for a new Jewish reformation and hence his Recon-structionist movement, which momentarily looked promising in the 1940s, had a very modest impact. It was absurd, and doomed his movement to failure, that he remained a professor at the Jewish Theological Seminary, the center of Conservative Judaism, while advocating the radical Reconstructionist program. Kaplan was a conflicted and timid man, and his failure had severe negative consequences for American Judaism.

Abraham Heschel, the most widely revered American Jewish rabbi of his generation, had much indeed to say about religion. But it is hard to find anything original in his writings. They follow directly in the Hasidic tradition, somewhat toned down for the American environment. He was a saintly man, and perhaps it was his personality that won him such admiration. The explanation for his popularity cannot be found in his writings.

Neither Heschel nor Kaplan was willing to face the critical intellectual issue that Conservative and Reform Judaism both encounter: In light of the modernist intellectual revolution, how should Jewish theology be revamped to bring it into the twentieth century? Never mind John Dewey or the Ba'al Shem-Tov: What is the significance of Freud, Einstein, Durkheim, Boas, and Wittgenstein—the Jewish big five of modernism—for modern-day Judaism? That was the issue.

No rabbinical thinker wanted to face it then, and none wants to face it even today. In light of this situation Reform and Conservative Judaism, whatever their successes as consumer satisfiers or community organizers, are cultural failures. That was true in 1945. It is still true five decades later.

The failure of Conservative—and Reform—Judaism to develop an innovative and intellectually compelling departure in Jewish thought became all the more important during the era of unprecedented and upward social mobility and prosperity for American Jews in the three decades after the war.

By the early 1960s the anti-Semitic miasma of the 1930s and 1940s was fast dissipating. Jews were moving in unprecedented numbers into Ivy League colleges, the faculties of the major universities, and positions in Gentile old-line law firms. In the 1960s two Jews received appointments to the U.S. Supreme Court. Some further anecdotal examples of Jewish upward mobility can be instanced. The first half-Jew (aside from Salo Baron, on an endowed professorship of Jewish history) to teach in the Columbia history department, Richard Hofstadter, was appointed in 1945. The first full-blooded Jew, the son of a Brooklyn rabbi, Richard B. Morris, was appointed in 1948. By 1960 Morris was the chairman of the department and a third of the department was Jewish.

In the 1930s and early 1940s the predominantly Jewish component of the "New York Intellectuals," a group of critics and fiction
writers who transformed the Trotskyite monthly *Partisan Review* into
a highly influential organ at the vanguard of literary and art criticism,
had to make their careers outside of academia, for the most part in
journalism. By the late 1950s the same kind of Jewish intellectual and
writer was finding a secure place on the campus. Indeed some of the
original *Partisan Review* crowd were habilitated on university faculties. Philip Rahv, the most effective editor of the *Partisan Review,*
ended up on the Brandeis University campus. Irving Howe now
taught at his alma mater, City College in New York. Along with a
long string of conventional socialist tracts, Howe wrote *The World of
Our Fathers* (1976), a sentimental but insightful recreation of shtetl
and Lower East Side culture that became a bestseller. Jewish intellectuals continued to produce innovative literary and art criticism from
such hitherto exalted WASP ramparts as Harvard, Yale, and Cornell.

By the mid-1970s about a third of the faculty in the humanities
and social science departments of the top twenty-five universities
were Jewish. Forty percent of the entering class at Yale Law School
in 1974 was Jewish. A quarter of the undergraduate body of Harvard
College by 1970 was Jewish, and forty percent at Columbia College.

The Jewish advance continued for the next two decades on all
fronts. The head of the Du Pont Corporation in the 1970s, the president of Princeton in the 1980s, and the president of Yale in the 1990s
all were Jewish. By the early 1990s Jews were also taking a front line
in federal politics. In the Congress elected in 1992 Jews were represented in both houses in a proportion five times greater than their
proportion in the population. Both senators from California were
Jewish women. President Bill Clinton's White House had by far the
largest number of Jews as officials in the history of the American
presidency.

In the course of a little more than a year (1993–94) President
Clinton appointed two Jews to the U.S. Supreme Court, Ruth Bader
Ginsberg and Steven Breyer. This was the first time in a quarter century that any Jew had sat on the Supreme Court, although they were
well represented on the other federal courts. Both Ginsberg and
Breyer already had distinguished records as federal judges. Both
were also privately millionaires.

That two of the nine Supreme Court judges are Jews (which has happened twice before in the twentieth century) is appropriate recognition of the major role Jews have played in the legal profession as a whole. In the great corporate law firms in New York, Washington, Chicago, and Los Angeles, Jews are widely represented, far beyond the traditionally Jewish-dominated firms.

It was now very hard to recollect the intense anti-Semitism that prevailed in the American Bar Association in the first four decades of this century. While in the 1940s and 1950s medicine had seemed to be the profession most attractive and rewarding to Jews, and in the 1960s and 1970s it was academia that seemed exceptionally hospitable to brilliant and highly productive Jews, in the 1980s, as both the medical and academic professions suffered novel problems, it was the law that seemed to be attracting more of the best minds of the younger Jewish generation than any other learned profession.

At least the legal profession at its highest corporate level is now deemed equivalent to medicine, which is bothered by structural and political problems, and preferable to depression-ridden academia as a life career for the best and brightest of the post–college age Jewish generation, for women as well as men. Whether this shift is good for the country is a moot matter.

The last Gentile bastion in Hollywood, the Disney studio, came under Jewish executive leadership in the early 1990s. One TV network was already headed by a Jew (Laurence Tisch at CBS), and Jews are prominent executives and producers at the other two major networks as well.

The content of Hollywood film and network TV under Jewish aegis in the 1980s differed significantly from the programmatic texture of the movies and radio networks that the Jewish film and broadcasting magnates of the previous generation had disseminated. There was now virtual abandonment of the puritanical structures derived from mainline Protestant culture. Now there was almost unlimited concession to market demands and common depiction of violence and sex in films and on television. The Jewish entertainment entrepreneurs were now usually much better educated than their predecessors but the products they offered were frequently more vulgar in content, presented, however, with the greatest technical skill imaginable. Traditional Jewish morality, similar to American Calvinism in its puritanical parameters, seemed to have no restraining effect on the Jewish entertainment magnates' programmatic decisions. Yet at the same time the sentimental liberalism of the Holly-wood film of the 1930s and 1940s was perpetuated into film content and TV programming of the 1980s and 1990s. Political liberalism was now given sharper focus with emphasis on multiculturalism and eth-nic diversity, environmentalism, and feminism.

Through the mid-1970s and most of the 1980s New York City had its first full-blooded Jewish mayors, Abe Beame and Edward Koch, respectively (Fiorello La Guardia, mayor in the 1930s, was reputedly half-Jewish). Even the leading Near Eastern experts in the State Department in the late 1980s were mostly Jewish, despite the remark of Secretary of State James Baker: "Fuck the Jews. They don't vote for us."

Baker was right in pointing to the small minority of Jewish voters for his Republican party. In the Reagan years there was a significant shift of Jewish support to the Republicans, but after Reagan the tradi-tional Jewish overcommitment to the Democrats reasserted itself. In the presidential election of 1992, close to half of the funds for Demo-cratic candidate Bill Clinton came from Jewish sources.

Jewish academics and other intellectuals played the dominant role in the fashioning of the New Left culture of the 1960s and 1970s. Sometimes, as in the influential writings of the historical sociologist Immanuel Wallerstein, this New Left theory was only a modestly updated version of mainline Marxist-Leninism. More often it was a blend of the imaginative cultural Marxism of Benjamin, Adorno, and the Frankfurt School of the 1930s with the more radical side of the Freudian tradition. The leader in this direction was Herbert Marcuse, a product of the Frankfurt School and the highly visible guru of the Jewish-sponsored Brandeis University in the 1950s and 1960s.

The highly successful American feminist movement of the 1970s and 1980s involved Jewish leadership as well. Jewish women had played no role in the first American feminist movement in the first three decades of the twentieth century. It was different this time around. Perhaps the two most prominent personalities in the women's movement, Gloria Steinem and Betty Freidan, were Jewish. A third leading feminist theorist, Elizabeth Fox-Genovese, was half-Jewish. The author of the all-time bestselling novel, translated into twenty-seven languages, celebrating feminine sexuality was an upper-middle-class, New York Jewish woman, Erica Jong.

The age of Jewish ease and self-satisfaction had dawned. By the

1980s Jewish billionaires had achieved a level of dominating comfort that was unprecedented for them in American history. When the Tisch family had a wedding, they took over the Metropolitan Museum of Art for that convivial purpose. This set tongues to wag at their ostentation, but it bothered them not. Jews played a major role in the Wall Street expansion of the 1980s, including insider trading. Ivan Boesky, one of the two billionaire Jewish Wall Street felons, was a prominent benefactor of the Jewish Theological Seminary.

Jewish investment bankers played a major, perhaps predominant role in the frenetic Wall Street speculative ventures of the 1980s. In "the Predator's Ball" of the 1980s, as a best-selling journalistic account of these fiscal ventures termed it, the Jewish dance card was full, although when a Gentile novelist, Michael Thomas, made the Jewish presence in Wall Street speculative ventures a prominent theme in a novel, he was denounced in the *New York Times Book Review* for anti-Semitism.

Various techniques and instruments were used in the Wall Street boom of the 1980s. But the most consequential—and lucrative—was the floating of "junk" (low grade) bonds to provide capital for involuntary takeover of one company by another. The economic and social implications of the junk bond instrument remain in dispute. Some well-informed fiscal experts see it as a very positive contribution to the development of American business, allowing aggressive and innovative financiers and executives to take over old, routinized, and underperforming companies or to bring together in one umbrella organization several companies who could now function in synergistic and productive cooperation.

Other writers, including the veteran fiscal critic Benjamin Stein, see the junk bond device as a huge fraudulent Ponzi scheme generating temporary money pools that could be looted by ruthless investment bankers and corporate executives and their overcompensated lawyers. It has been pointed out that the combined companies funded out of junk bonds are often so badly in debt that immediately they have to sell off valuable components of the corporation to generate quick cash, making a mockery of the fine talk about synergistic opportunities. It has also been pointed out that the billionaire owners of these bloated enterprises founded on junk bonds often try to save costs through devastating layoffs of workers who have given decades of sincere and competent service to the company now taken over. *Other People's Money,* a popular play of the mid-1980s about the takeover of a small New England company by a Wall Street sharpie leaves no doubt about the latter's Jewish ethnicity.

The prime inventor of the business takeover scheme through the floating of junk bonds was a Californian financier, Michael Milken, who was associated with a leading Wall Street investment firm. Hailed in some quarters as a financial genius and despised in others as a cynical predator, Milken eventually ran afoul of committing technical violations of the Wall Street criminal code. He was sentenced to ten years imprisonment by a Gentile woman judge who was married to a prominent Jewish journalist. Eventually, she found grounds for sharply reducing Milken's sentence.

When Michael Milken came out of prison he offered his services as lecturer on high finance to the University of Southern California. Even more amazing than Milken's chutzpah was his ability to persuade the university to accept his brazen offer. He then proceeded to tape and market his lectures.

In addition to Milken and Boesky, the two prominent Jewish Wall Street felons, other Jewish billionaires or their companies were involved in dubious practices. Steve Ross, who became head of the largest media combine, Time-Warner, was in his early years besmirched by a scandal involving illegal management practices at a dinner theater he owned in Westchester County. In the end, a close associate and personal friend took the rap for Ross.

Another high-profile Jewish billionaire imitated Steve Ross in emerging unscathed from a matter of business criminality. One of the vice presidents of his company pleaded guilty, and the federal prosecutor generously accepted the Jewish billionaire's claim that he didn't know what was going on in the higher reaches of his own company. The crime in this instance was extortion—using prostitutes to entrap business competitors.

The skill of some Jewish billionaires in skirting the limits of the law but somehow emerging unscathed, with the aid of high-priced New York Jewish attorneys and a compliant press, was remarkable.

Another prominent behavior pattern of high-profile Jewish billionaires in recent years has frequently been jettisoning the usually Jewish first wife in favor of a trophy Gentile second wife.

In 1993, the two most highly paid corporate executives in the United States were Jewish. One was the head of a Hollywood studio, the other a Wall Street investment banker.

Jewish billionaires in the 1990s demonstrated that they had arrived at the pinnacle of social prowess and cultural importance by buying professional sports teams, hitherto the proud preserve of WASP and Irish magnates. By 1993 the New York football Giants, the most honored name in professional sports, two other National Football League teams, and two of the major league baseball franchises were in Jewish hands. One of these Jewish owners carried so much weight with the other owners that he engineered the firing of the baseball commissioner and took over as acting commissioner, representing the owners before a congressional committee. In the 1930s American Jews had thought they were doing well when they produced a couple of boxing champions. The Jews did not have to show their sweaty bodies anymore; they owned the teams.

As in Berlin and Vienna before Hitler, the Jewish role in publishing was an important one. By 1950 Jewish families owned two of the three most influential newspapers in the United States, the *New York Times* and the *Washington Post*. Furthermore, both families were directly involved in the daily operation of the papers and in setting their editorial policies.

The *New York Times* assumed the role of speaking for the Eastern establishment; its politics were that of the centrist liberals working in tandem with the more progressive conservatives. America's rise to power in the two decades after World War II was based on this centrism and a broad humanitarian political consensus, which fully accorded with the outlook of the Ochs-Sulzberger family, which owned the *Times* and closely supervised its operation. The *Washington Post*, in the hands of the Meyer-Graham family, became the voice of the liberal left Democrats. It achieved new celebrity when it confronted and powerfully contributed to bringing down the Republican Richard Nixon administration.

The behavior and mind-set of the Ochs-Sulzberger and Meyer-Graham families was austerely aristocratic and paternalistic. They were court Jews within a boisterous democratic republic and greatly helped to give stability and reforming thrust to the inherently polarized and conflicted American political system. Without their persistent if not uncritical support of Isreal, the survival of the beleaguered Jewish state would have been unlikely.

In the 1930s and 1940s, smart, courageous New York Jews had started up book publishing companies that became Alfred A. Knopf; Random House (Bennett Cerf); Simon and Schuster; and Farrar,

Straus, and Giroux. Now these publishing houses, built on the courage and good taste of their founders, are usually part of vast media empires. But Jews are still prominent as editors—Michael Korda at Simon and Schuster, Jason Epstein at Knopf, Roger Straus still running the show in his own company.

Two Jews, Robert Silver and Barbara Epstein, had started the *New York Review of Books* in the 1960s. Thirty years later, although it is owned now by a Southern WASP, this highly influential weekly has the same editors and still reflects the tastes and assumptions of the New York Jewish liberal left academic crowd.

All over the country by the 1980s Jewish names proudly adorned not only hospital buildings—that practice had begun in the 1950s—but buildings and institutes on distinguished university campuses. Billionaire Jews became as important in the funding of American higher education as they had already been in the provision of its medical facilities.

Larry Tisch was the leader in this new trend. At New York University by the end of the 1980s his name adorned not only the university hospital but also its school of the performing arts, perhaps the best in the country, and the building that housed its undergraduate school of business. These designations were richly deserved not only because of the Tisch's personal benefactions but also because of his close management of New York University. As chairman of the board of trustees from 1977 onward, Tisch was the effective head of New York University. He controlled its development as closely and as skillfully as he managed the CBS TV network. Tisch set a new style of hands-on management of a major university by the chairman of the board of trustees, theretofore regarded as a mostly honorific position. And he did an excellent job, firmly guiding NYU to much improved status within American academia.

Jews in the four decades after 1950 came home in American society to suburban comfort, to penetration of academia and the privileged bastions of the learned professions, to corporate business, to politics and government and controlling levels of the media. Jews were overrepresented in the learned professions by a factor of five or six. In 1994 Jews were only three percent of the American population but their impact was equivalent to an ethnic group comprising twenty percent of the population.

Nothing in Jewish history equaled this degree of Jewish accession to power, wealth, and prominence. Not in Muslim Spain, not in early twentieth-century Germany, not in Israel itself, because there were no comparable levels of wealth and power on a world-class scale in that small country to attain.

Why did this happen? After the miseries of the 1930s and early 1940s, why did Jews experience so much success and upward social mobility in the decades after the war? No sociological study of this phenomenon has yet appeared, but it is a safe assessment that four causes were at work.

First, from a year or two after World War II until the oil crisis of 1973, there was a steady expansion of the American economy, and this expansion resumed for a time in the Reagan era of the 1980s. The Jews since 1850 had always done well in a period of fiscal and business growth. Their exceptional talents were admired and their central participation as managers, investors, and professionals was eagerly recruited during the upward phase of the long business cycle.

Second, the Jews had proved themselves valuable and reliable in serving the American power and moneyed elite on the latter's own terms, from inside the establishment. By the third postimmigrant generation they were not only thoroughly assimilated in their lifestyles to WASP ways but apparently fully committed to continuance of the elite's substance and style of domination.

Fears in the 1940s that the Jews might be politically unreliable, that they might be sympathetic to communism, died with alleged atom spies Julius and Ethel Rosenberg in 1953. They were prosecuted by a Jewish prosecutor, condemned to death (in Ethel's case at least, unjustifiably, the definitive study by Ronald Radosh reveals) in an extravagant show of overcompensated loyalty by a Jewish judge. The Rosenbergs' bodies were offered up to the Gentiles as the Jews' expiation for their leftist inclinations in the 1920s and 1930s. A physicist in Britain convicted at the same time as the Rosenbergs of the same crime got a sentence of twelve years and served five years in jail.

After the Rosenbergs, there was no problem about Jewish loyalty. Two of the assistants to red-hunter Senator Joseph McCarthy in the early 1950s were Jewish boys, Cohn and Schine (the third assistant was Robert Kennedy). The Jewish heads of Hollywood studios pushed to find ex-communists in the film industry they could showcase as blacklisted.

In the 1960s there was again a momentary flicker of doubt about

Jewish political reliability. A disturbingly large number of leaders of the campus New Left were Jewish. Some were "red diaper babies," children of the 1930s Communists. But most came from the new suburban Jewish middle class of the 1950s and early 1960s and reflected their parents' weariness with the desolate boredom and fiscal stress of suburban living.

The New Left reached its zenith in May 1968 and was dead as a political movement by the fall of 1971. Once the Jewish radicals saw the blacks taking over, they went back to graduate school and law school, and the radical movement dissipated.

By the Reagan-Bush years, Jews who had been Trotskyites and Democratic Socialists in the 1940s were now stalwart neoconservatives, expounding the glories of the English liberal-conservative traditions and the American market economy.

Two highly visible publishing and speaking couples, Norman Podhoretz and Midge Decter, and Irving Kristol and Gertrude Himmelfarb, in fact turned neoconservatism into a traditional mishpachah (family) enterprise, gobbling up not only editorships and institutes and faculty chairs for themselves but good jobs in the Reagan-Bush administration for son or son-in-law. It was a wonderful example of the Jewish outerborough style of the 1930s turned into careers of rightist loyalty to Anglo-conservatism—from New York City's corner delicatessen to Washington patronage and columns in the *Wall Street Journal* and national speaking tours courtesy of the National Endowment for the Humanities.

By 1993 Rabbi Michael Lerner, a noisy New Left leader on the West Coast in the late 1960s, had emerged as Hillary Rodham Clinton's private counselor in "the politics of meaning." Jewish communism was as remote as Karaism. The Jews' political reliability was thoroughly proven.

The third reason for the decline in anti-Semitism in the United States in the quarter of a century after 1960 and the concomitant rise of Jewish leadership and privilege in every important aspect of social and economic life was the effective work of the Anti-Defamation League. Founded as an agency of the innocuous Jewish national fraternal organization B'nai B'rith, learning the arts of public debate from the civil rights movement of the 1960s and taking advantage of the spirit of egalitarianism and political correctness that followed in the wake of the civil rights movement, the ADL became remarkably effective in combating prejudicial remarks and hurtful actions against Jews. No other ethnic group in American society by 1975 could come close to matching the way in which the ADL protected Jewish reputations and negotiated for Jewish access to place and power. Even the ADL's somewhat bold policy in the 1980s of identifying anti-Zionism or even severe criticism of Israel with anti-Semitism gained a large degree of public acceptance.

The fourth reason for Jewish advancement was the Holocaust itself. *Cui bono?* asks the moral philosopher. Who benefits from an act? The Jews of America greatly benefited from the Holocaust. Hitlerism thoroughly discredited anti-Semitism in white upper middle-class circles. Anti-Semitism was no longer seen as a country club sport or a legitimate venting of primordial feelings, but a torch brought into social relations that could burn the house down. Anti-Semitism was no longer socially acceptable in white affluent and power circles in the Northeast and on the West Coast. Even the Southern bigots learned to watch what they said.

It is no accident that Steven Spielberg chose to film *Schindler's List,* based on a book published in 1986, in 1993. As soon as anti-Semitism began to reemerge as part of legitimate social discourse, on campuses and in the press, propounded by Black Muslims, Spielberg saw that the rest of the country needed a graphic reminder, a booster shot, of what the Holocaust was really like to quench the incipient Judeo-phobe fire.

Behind these four specific reasons for the rise of the Jews in the United States in the thirty-five years after 1950, there was a general sociological condition at work. This was the era of the spreading out of urban populations into the suburbs and the rise of a distributed society ten to forty miles beyond the metropolitan centers, along with shopping-mall culture. The Jews early on fit in with this suburban development. It was a Jewish builder, William Levitt, who demonstrated on Long Island immediately after the war that suburban housing could be built for people of modest as well as affluent means.

Although as late as 1960 there were restrictions on Jewish penetration of some old WASP suburban enclaves, they too slowly gave way to Jewish access, which particularly flourished in upscale communities like Great Neck, Long Island; Scarsdale in Westchester County, New York; Shaker Heights, Ohio; a long strip of towns along the north shore of Lake Michigan beyond Chicago; the San Fernando Valley north of Los Angeles; and Palo Alto and Marin County located, respectively, south and north of San Francisco.

Jewish professionals and affluent businesspeople were ideal members of these upscale suburban communities because they were well-educated, ambitious, resourceful, and conscientious taxpayers and citizens. They subscribed to the model of good suburban families set by WASP tradition: They tolerated high taxes for good schools; they participated in volunteer work; and they were extremely attentive to the upkeep of their hard-won property. Aside from putting up a synagogue that usually resembled a concert hall and was discreetly tucked away behind thick vegetation, they made no intrusions upon the derivative Protestant culture of the affluent suburbs. When the rare colony of ultra-Orthodox and Hasidic Jews moved in, as happened in Rockland County, New York, there was plenty of local tension. But this was an unusual situation. Almost universally, the Jewish suburbanites gratefully accepted the mores, style, and social attitudes of Protestant suburbia and were scrupulous supporters of the inherited power structure and Ivy League mentality that graced the affluent suburbs.

This had the effect, over a decade or two, of showing the WASP elite that the Jews of the new generation, well-educated and affluent, fit in harmoniously with the dominant culture. Suburban integration of Jews and Gentiles greatly helped to make Jews acceptable in law firms, the staffs of renowned hsoptials, and corporate boardrooms. These fashionable suburban addresses also helped Jewish adolescents to get admitted to highly selective colleges in the 1960s and afterward. Thereby suburbia, especially in its more affluent and exclusive manifestation, contributed significantly to Jewish advancement in the thirty-five years after 1950 as much as it also pushed the Jews who lived in these gilded enclaves deeper into a filtered, homogenous, dominant WASP culture.

In spite of this suburban acculturation, and upward and social mobility, the Jewish upper-middle-class never forgot the experience of the 1930s and the memory of FDR. They remained heavily committed to the liberal wing of the Democratic party and to liberal progressive causes.

Jews had played a key role in the civil rights movement, in African-American liberation. They provided much of the funding in the early decades, sacrificed a couple of their children, and offered much professional help. Jews had made the National Association for the Advancement of Colored People possible, and one of the two NAACP lawyers who won the *Brown* v. *Board of Education* case, which struck down the legality of segregation in 1954, was a Jew, Jack Greenberg, now a professor at Columbia University Law School. (A docudrama in 1994 on PBS TV about *Brown* completely ignored the NAACP's Jewish lawyer, a sign of the times).

Black leaders by the 1980s did not want to be reminded how much they had depended on Jewish help for many decades. This is understandable. Israelis never mention how much their country's existence owed to British imperialism. The African Americans wanted to assert their autonomy, their own identity. No harm in that.

There was an old well-spring of anti-Semitism among Harlem blacks in particular going back to the 1920s. This is not surprising because the Jewish storekeeper, landlord, and schoolteacher were in the front line of authority that affected the daily lives of African Americans. Hardly any blacks ever had a personal encounter with a WASP billionaire. But middle class Jewish businessmen and civil servants they ran up against daily. Even when, as was often the case, the Jew was generous, the black could not help but feel the sting of submission.

Therefore time and time again, from the 1920s on, militant leaders of black America, especially in Harlem, used the Jews as a foil to represent "the man," the figure of authority and oppression. In 1969 this ethos exploded into a struggle between black militants and the Jewish-dominated New York City schoolteacher's union, a conflict that left deep scars and contributed to Jewish defection from the teaching profession, which had been highly regarded among New York Jews in the 1930s and 1940s.

Around 1990 began a new wave of black anti-Semitism. The Jew was held responsible for every bad thing that had ever happened to African Americans, even slave-trading and slavery! Intellectual leaders of black America such as Harvard's Henry L. Gates and Princeton's Cornel West, however, strongly counseled against this facile anti-Semitism.

Gates remarked that "Black anti-Semitism hurts blacks, first and foremost, in part because it compromises the moral credibility of our struggle against racism, but equally as important, because it leads us into the politics of distraction and distortion. Getting the source of our problems wrong is an obstacle to setting them right."

The black philosopher Cornel West characteristically took the high moral ground:

> The present impasse in black-Jewish relations will be overcome when self-critical exchanges take place within and across the black and Jewish communities not simply about their own group interest but also, and more importantly, about what being black or Jewish means in *ethical terms*.

Although vigorously condemned by the Anti-Defamation League and denounced from scores of rabbinical pulpits and by *Commentary* magazine, no friend of the blacks in the first place, the expressions of black anti-Semitism in reality did not represent any threat to American Jews.

What was actually harmful to Jews, at least to Jewish males of the younger generation, was the affirmative action quotas ("targets") that African Americans—but also many Jewish feminists—demanded in higher education and for entry to the professions. Although prominent Jews did not want to talk about it (their own sons were protected), middle-class Jews by the early 1990s were dismayed to find that it was getting harder for their sons to get appointments in academia or entry into the elite law schools than it had been two decades before. Jewish males were at the bottom of the affirmative action preferences list after the minorities and women were taken care of.

All white males were now disadvantaged, but somehow Jewish males were at the bottom of the preference list. And strange tricks were played even with regard to minority designation to push the Jews down the preference list. Thus Hispanics were in the top rung for affirmative action, but Jews of Latin American provenance with Hispanic names, even though their families might have lived in Argentina or Chile for generations before coming to the United States, were not given Hispanic preference. Law school admissions officers had to scrutinize applications with deconstructive care to filter out a Latin American Hispanic named Jew, but by 1990 they were doing just that. The Nazis who weeded out Jewish applicants to German universities in the early

1930s would have applauded this Jew-filtering zeal of the elite law school admissions officers.

On a straightline projection, given current hiring practices, the percentage of Jews on the faculties of the major universities, which has been steadily declining since the mid-1980s, will continue to decline. By 2010 Jews will comprise less than fifteen percent of faculties, far below the thirty-five percent peak of the late 1970s.

This is something that American Jews now ensconced in the power elite do not want to talk about because it would call into question the affirmative action programs that they themselves endorse and apply within their institutions. The younger Jewish males are in status declension, but do not talk about it. The older generation will probably be gone to affluent and honored retirement before it becomes a public issue. As for now, the families of wealthy and powerful Jews do not feel the impact of the new discrimination; there is always a route open for their scions. Just pick up the phone. It is only the middle-class Jews who get those slim, cold rejection letters from the elite colleges and law schools and become Ph.D. cab drivers, and who cares about them? Who ever cared?

Brandeis University had been founded in a suburb of Boston in 1948, mainly with the support of Jewish philanthropists in New York City, precisely to countervail the discrimination against the entry of Jews into elite colleges and professional schools that had prevailed in the 1930s. In the 1950s under a dynamic president, the historian Abraham L. Sachar, Brandeis flourished and became one of the best liveral arts colleges in the country. But as the barriers against Jews eroded in the 1960s, Brandeis's original purpose became unnecessary. It never developed the law and medical schools that had been the original goal of its founders. New York Jewish philantropists turned their attention elsewhere—not only to Israel but to Columbia and New York universities, which now welcomed Jews onto their boards of trustees. Under weak presidential leadership in the 1970s and 1980s following Abe Sachar's retirement, Brandeis suffered severe fiscal problems. Therefore in the 1990s, when Jewish males were again threatened under the banner of afirmative action with discrimination by elite colleges and professional achools, Brandeis University could do little to help them.

Jewish women by the early 1990s were doing very well, thank you. Social acceptance of the egalitarian demands of the women's movement were beneficial to them because of their intelligence and access to elite education. They did not have to get fat and brassy sitting around in their designer living rooms anymore, propping up their husbands and organizing Hadassah tours of Israel.

They could dress for success, go to law school and business school, and cut a swath through law firms and corporate executive offices and throw their weight around as cosseted vice presidents of the more upscale publishing houses and magazines. Or they could dress down and frumpy, in Maoist baggies or pseudo–Left Bank dark dresses and serve as chairmen of departments at NYU or Hunter, doing their jobs with exceptional competence.

The vicissitudes in the world of middle-class work are the real problems that American Jews face in 1994, not a handful of enraged Black Muslims spewing venom on the campus and on street corners, unsettling as it is to hear echos of the old wall-of-hatred rhetoric cranking up again.

The diminution in the fortunes of middle-class Jewish males is a hot issue for the Jewish establishment to handle because there is no commonality of interest. Rich men's sons are immune; Jewish women are actually benefiting from the new affirmative action quota system. It is the middle-class Jewish male who is being diminished and emasculated—again.

Once again Jewish fortunes are driven by the business cycle. The problems now slowly licking at the feet of the American Jewish male have come after the running out of the postwar economic expansion during the past two decades. There is a shortage of jobs and a surplus of qualified personnel in academia and the learned professions generally.

The boom days appear to be over. American capitalism has entered a mature, postexpansion phase. As always, Jewish social mobility is immediately threatened when the downturn begins. In a competitive world, some people have to be put at the back of the line of educational privilege and professional employment. Affirmative action profiles tell the male Jews to get to the back of the line.

For the moment the Jewish wheel of fortune has just begun to turn down, and only yet a few notches. Visibly the Jews are still riding high in terms of wealth and power.

In these recent decades of American Jewish expansion the failure of Reform and Conservative Judaism to challenge modernist culture and redefine Jewish theology has been keenly felt. This deficiency is projected into the writings of the best Jewish writers of the postwar era, the novelists Philip Roth and Saul Bellow and the filmmaker Woody Allen. Although they express it in different ways, all three writers expound the same theme.

Jewish males of educated sensibility, high talent, and inexhaustible energy can find no outlet for their capacities, no satisfying other with whom to integrate. Their deep feelings and brilliant insights are left dangling in the air. There is a lack of consummation or fit application of their socially valuable skills and their intrinsic good intentions.

Therefore the American Jewish male, as seen by Roth, Bellow, and Allen, becomes a misfit; an evader; a wimp; a noodnik; a fool; a madman; a pathetic failed searcher for dignity; fulfillment, normality, power. Neither systematic masturbation, nor fleeing to exotic climes, nor copulating with the nearest available shiksa helps him much, but these are the unsatisfying, inconclusive, and ridiculous solutions he tries. The novel or film is excruciatingly funny, wildly absorbing, but on reflection devastating in its indictment.

American Jewish culture, say its best writers and filmmakers, involves a fatal bifurcation of personality, an unfulfillment of ambition, an inapplicability of reason and intelligence, a turning one's back upon a burning-out individual. Jewish feminists are just beginning to feel this condition as well. How far can things go with Hildegard of Bingen or Mary Wollstonecraft?

Rabbinic Judaism still provides its age-old, time-tested solutions—the fulfillment of mitzvoth, the study of Torah and Talmud, the mythologizing of history, the cultivation of Jewish home and family. Rabbi Irving Greenberg and Blu Greenberg have made as strong a case as can be made for the Orthodox, Halakic way in the American setting. But when orthodoxy would not give up its compulsive rigidities, the immobile Sabbath, the arbitrary dietary schemes, the jejune liturgy, it missed its great opportunity to satisfy more than fifteen percent of American Jewry.

The majority may envy a little the Halakic minority in having found peace and a firm context for behavior and feeling. But there is no chance that they will go that way. Are they going to give up driving out to the Hamptons on Friday nights? Are they going to give up dining in three-star restaurants? Are they going to endure regularly four-hour repetitions of flinty medieval prayers in impenetrable off-key Hebrew or flat English? No.

The Israelis, eighty-five percent of whom have similar impatience with orthodoxy even in its most up-to-date face (not go to the beach on the Sabbath?) have had a kind of solution: service to the army and the state, the neo-Spartan, new-Prussian modality of behavior and sensibility. A prime reason for the irrational popularity of Zionism among American Jews since 1948, especially when associated with periodic battlefield victories, is the Americans' vicarious projection onto the Israeli Prussian means of integration of self and other, a surrogate union of the dialectic of history and the majesty of pseudo-imperial power.

This was never more than a palliative, however, not much more real than masturbating, running off to exotic places, or making out with the closest shiksa, although more dignified and to be blessed from the lazy rabbinical pulpits.

If only a political crusade could be launched again, like the New Deal or the civil rights movement, some great cause to consume Jewish passions and use up excess intelligence and energy. Bill and Hillary . . . another disappointment, like ridiculous Ronnie from Hollywood and his crackpot market capitalism of the L.A. freeways.

A self without an object, a mind that cannot use up its brain cells, unexpended energy, the American Jewish malady. If peace comes in the Near East, even the cheap Israeli narcotic will be taken away.

All societies have their totems, the heroic images that represent the societies' yearnings for perfection and highest expectation of themselves. The totem of Israeli society was Moshe Dayan, who fought courageously in the War of Independence, who became identified with Israel's military triumph in the Six-Day War. Lean, handsome, with a romantic black patch over the eye he lost in the War of Independence, celebrated if controversial amateur archaeologist, womanizer, brilliant speaker, shrewd politician, he represented what the Israelis wanted to think of themselves and what they wanted the world to think of them.

The portrait of her father presented by his daughter, Yael Dayan, a feminist journalist and politician, in her memoir *My Father, His Daughter*, perhaps the most insightful book ever written about Israel, does not detract much from the romantic image of Moshe Dayan, but it communicates also the distance, the coldness, the selfishness, the remoteness, perhaps the hollowness of this brave man, and these are perhaps also qualities many sensitive Israelis see in themselves. There is a coldness, a mystery, a distance from humanity about them that anyone from another country who lives and works in Israel for half a year will be impressed by.

If Moshe Dayan is the totem of Israeli society, the symbol of recent and contemporary American Jewish society is Laurence A. Tisch. On a stocky body is a large, round, bald head with piercing bright eyes forever seeking out vulnerability in the person he is addressing, forever looking for an opening, an advantage. The body clothed in a fifteen-hundred-dollar designer suit, just emerged from his limousine, the voice loud and clear, the words always well-articulated, a half-smile frequently opening his lips to reveal the large white teeth, Tisch is what the American Jewish moneyed and professional elite—the opinion-makers who alone count in American Jewish national society, the rabbis having been turned into hesitant, marginal hirelings, the academics being soft people auto-erotically shirking from power—admire as the dynamic embodiment of business acumen and social domination.

In the eyes of the American Jewish elite, these are the only games, besides travel and decorating houses, worth playing, and in recent years Larry Tisch has been regarded by them as the most valuable player in the Jewish league.

Like his network of friends, colleagues, and admirers, Tisch is extremely well-informed while being self-consciously anti-intellectual. They all hold the opaque humanities professors and the leftist-bearing social scientists in contempt, regarding them as equivalent to low-level clerks in their business or professional establishments.

They are the kinds of people who judge the quality of a book, which they do not read, although they may buy it, by the review it gets in the *New York Times Book Review*, and it is not really worth thinking about until it appears halfway up the *Times* best-seller list. They know that nearly all professors can be readily bought and that nearly all writers are for hire cheap, so why focus on what they write about?

In five generations of development Ashkenazic Jews have come from revering the word to revering the thing, and Larry Tisch is the Ba'al Shem-Tov of the American Jewish opinion-maker, their shaman.

Here is the great leader that four generations of American Jewish history have created, a person of genuine insight and good information, insatiable in his yearning to dominate and to demonstrate his capacity to manage, control, develop, innovate in the hotel and real estate business where he started, but even more in the intangible, kinetic fields that America had made so much its special fields of cultural acumen and world communication—entertainment and higher education.

The Morgans, the Rockefellers, the Harrimans, the Roosevelts, the Kennedys, the titans of bygone eras, they have been superseded by the Jew as flawless achiever, Larry Tisch. This is the American totem, as Moshe Dayan is the Israeli one. "Blessed be God who has preserved us unto this day."

CHAPTER TWELVE

The Future of the Jews

In the later 1990s, the reshaping of the parameters of Western thought by Jews that began in 1900 will continue to occur. The Jewish role in modernism is paralleled by a prominent Jewish role in postmodernist thought. One aspect of the future of the Jews at the beginning of the twenty-first century that can be asserted with confidence is the continuing major impact of individual Jewish thinkers in shaping the direction and manufacturing the texture of Western thought. The postmodernist consciousness as the end of the twentieth century approaches is a mind-set that Jewish thinkers have left their indelible stamp upon, just as the modernist intellectual upheaval at the beginning of this century was at its very center profoundly affected by Jewish thinkers.

These historical facts may be as profoundly disturbing to many Jews as to a multitude of Gentiles. First, the Jewish middle-class populace is uneasy that the radical structuring of Western thought in the modernist movement and then further significant restructuring in postmodernism should carry such a heavy Jewish association. This realization, it is felt, somehow exposes the Jews as a whole and makes them vulnerable to criticism. Second, if to the great breakthroughs of the Jewish modernists earlier in the century is now added the vistas of Jewish postmodernists, the task of reconciling the sacred chain of traditional Judaism with the innovative ideas of great Jewish thinkers of this century makes an already overwhelming burden all the more difficult and formidable.

These concerns are not to be taken lightly. They are reasonable. But such bourgeois Jewish feelings do not alter the facts of history, stretching into the near future.

The transformation of Western thought inaugurated by five Jews—the physicist Albert Einstein, the psychologist Sigmund Freud, the sociologist Emile Durkheim, the anthropologist Franz Boas, and the philosopher Ludwig Wittgenstein—during the age of high modernism in the first four decades of the twentieth century was perpetuated in the postmodernist era in the four decades after 1955 by four Jewish thinkers of a younger generation. Two of these—Noam Chomsky and Harold Bloom—were Americans; two—Claude Lévi-Strauss and Jacques Derrida—were French. Whatever the implications of these historical facts, they must be encountered, not suppressed.

Chomsky was a professor of linguistics at M.I.T. who revolutionized and in fact created anew the field of linguistics. Although Chomsky was a vehement critic of Israel (as well as a prime leader of opposition of the 1960s to the Vietnam War), his theory of language development in individual minds was entirely in line with Hasidic and Cabalistic traditions and certainly compatible with the Torah and the Talmud. We learn language, said Chomsky, because we have an innate language capacity, especially active in the ages between three and fourteen. This is an idealistic, Platonic view of linguistic development in which mental capacity is previous to the specific language. Chomsky's view, disseminated by the missionary effects of his many students and disciples, came to dominate the discipline of linguistics by 1970. It is interesting that the leading American theorist in the field of linguistics in the 1930s, Edward Sapir of Yale University, was also Jewish. Linguistics is a science resembling the language-focused texture of the Talmudic, Cabalistic, and Hasidic frame of mind. Chomsky's oracular style of behavior and his penchant for uttering opinions on any social problem made him a secular rabbi.

Harold Bloom, who taught at Yale, where he held a senior chair in literature, and at New York University, exhibited a similar rabbinical style. He sat in his seminars, his pale fleshy zaddiklike face uttering definitive judgments to his adoring students and others who traveled many miles just to hear the truth from his lips, expounding dramatically innovative literary criticism. Essentially Bloom had two ideas. One was that the history of literature comprises the influence of one writer and one text upon another and misunderstanding or misinterpretation from one text or writer to another was a key factor. Assuredly this doctrine of intertexuality was exemplified as much by the history of rabbinical thought as by the development of English poetry. Bloom's other idea was the continuing centrality of Gnostic dualism in Christian as well as Jewish thought, right into the American evangelical tradition. Bloom consciously proclaimed himself Gershom Scholem's disciple and he played an important role in the 1960s and 1970s in making Scholem's immensely important work better known in America.

Claude Lévi-Strauss came from a Belgian rabbinical family and studied anthropology at Paris in the 1930s with Michel Mauss, the nephew and intellectual heir of another rabbinical scion, Emile Durkheim. From insights gained in the 1930s while doing fieldwork among Amazon peoples, and influenced as well by the school of gestalt psychology that flourished at the New School for Social Research in New York where he taught during the War after he fled from the Nazi occupation of Paris, Lévi-Strauss developed the social theory which he eloquently expounded in 1956 in *Tristes Tropiques,* one of the three most innovative books of the twentieth century. (The other two are Freud's *The Interpretation of Dreams* by another Jew, Freud, and James Joyce's novel *Ulysses,* which is at least ostensibly about a day in the life of an early twentieth-century Dublin Jew).

Lévi-Strauss also had two main ideas. One was the doctrine of the social other—the universal split between the hegemonic, imperialist, mechanistic, environment-devastating, and tradition-breaking political and industrial West, and the rest of mankind. This is the cardinal doctrine of all leftist-leaning thought since 1960. Lévi-Strauss's companion idea was that of a universal binary code that comprises the structure of all societies and all thought. Bitterly resisted by the empirical Anglo-American school of anthropology founded by Franz Boas, Lévi-Strauss's structural anthropology has come not only to gain wide acceptance in social science but also to shape literary and art criticism. The advance of computer science with its binary mathematical code had given additional credence to Lévi-Strauss's universal structuralism that he began to expound in the 1950s.

Boas and Lévi-Strauss fought against racism but from different ends of the theoretical spectrum. Boas insisted that no ethnic group or culture is superior to another because empirically no category of comparative judgment can be established. Every people must be evaluated within its own context and within its own forms of social action. Lévi-Strauss believed that no social or ethnic group can be viewed as superior to another because the same structural code runs universally through mind and society everywhere. He even claimed that the "savage mind" and the mind of the academic scientist are functioning structurally in much the same way. Boas's and Lévi-Strauss's theories came to the same conclusion—no racial hierarchy, no privilege—but by different routes.

In the late 1950s the Jewish population of France rose rapidly from three hundred thousand to half a million, and the character of this population was also altered by the addition to the static, highly assimilated, old Jewish population in France of Sephardic families fleeing from Arab victory in the Algerian War. As French citizens, the majority of Algerian Jews chose to relocate in France, the others migrating to Israel. Most of the Algerian Jews remained poor and undereducated but from a middle-class Algerian family came the extremely influential philosopher and literary critic Jacques Derrida. He taught droves of eager graduate students at Paris and also was an important presence in at least three American universities.

Essentially Derrida's theory of deconstruction is Freudianism applied to literary culture. Beneath the surface textual expression and explicit meaning, there is another, contradictory level of meaning, and yet further levels of different meanings. Thus control of the literary text is taken away from the author whose "death" is proclaimed and the text given autonomous freedom to deconstruct itself. A vigorous and prolific writer and a powerful platform lecturer, Derrida has come to have an enormous influence in the English-speaking as well as Francophone world and his theory of deconstruction has influenced novels and poetry, film, architecture, and painting.

The Jewish background to Derrida's philosophy is evident. Essentially he is propounding a hermeneutic theory of the text that is fully within the Talmudic, Cabalistic, and Hasidic traditions. As an Algerian Jew, Derrida was the scion of a mistreated and underprivileged minority and therefore likely to take a radical and oppositional attitude toward canonical literary culture.

The impact of the doctrines of Chomsky, Bloom, Lévi-Strauss, and Derrida will reverberate into the next century.

The Jews are a superior people intellectually and as long as Jewish genes exist, the extraordinary impact Jews have had in twentieth century thought will continue indefinitely. The heyday of the Jewish male scholar and scientist may indeed be over as the political makeup of the academic world restricts male Jewish entry through prejudicial affirmative action screening and promotion processes. In the foreseeable future Jewish academics will not in such great numbers enjoy the privilege of status and reward that they occupied from 1960 to 1985. But the situation is not likely to be as bad as they heyday of anti-Semitism on the campus from 1920 to 1945. And even when the Jews suffered severe discrimination and outright deprivation within academia, in the bad old days, they still found a way to make their impact felt. "Jews have to be better than anyone else," my mentor in the Princeton History Department used to tell me in the early 1950s, and they were. The Jews were among the very best scholars and scientists and in spite of the miasma of anti-Semitism, they still entered the academic arena, albeit in small numbers compared to the glory days of the 1960s and 1970s, and made their very special contribution of transformative initiatives in Western thought.

Whatever happens to the Jews in the twenty-first century, short of another ghetto or shoah, their intellectual impact will continue. Chomsky, Bloom, Lévi-Strauss, and Derrida, the second wave, succeeded the five intellectuals titans of modernism, and the postmodernists will be succeeded by another generation of ethnically Jewish important intellectuals in the early decades of the twenty-first century.

The four Jewish leaders of postmodernist thought expounded doctrines that could be perceived as more compatible with and less confrontational against the sacred chain of the Jewish Talmudic, Cabalistic, and Hasidic tradition than the modernist wave of 1900–1940. A possibility of healing, of reunification of traditional Jewish thought with later twentieth-century theory was offered by salient ingredients in the writings of Chomsky, Bloom, Lévi-Strauss, and Derrida.

That did not mean, however, that the rabbinate and quasi-canonical Jewish journals such as *Commentary,* funded by the establishmentarian American Jewish Committee, rushed to celebrate and embrace Chomsky, Bloom, Lévi-Strauss and Derrida and emphasize the prospect of integration of their ideas with the older Jewish intellectual tradition. There was something about each of the four Jewish postmodernists that made them ill-regarded in dominant Jewish circles. Chomsky was a vehement critic of Israel and was pro-Arab. Bloom argued that the narrative thrust of the Pentateuch comprised a novel written by a princess of the Davidian line in the first millennium B.C., thereby reducing the Pentateuch to fictional characters and peeling away the historicity of the Bible. Lévi-Strauss propounded the politically radical doctrine of the social other which was used polemically by Edward Said and other haters of Israel and besides espoused a universalist structuralism that made upper-middle-class Jews in the United States and Canada feel uncomfortably submerged in an egalitarian continuity. Derrida was too much a Freudian, too inclined to call into question traditional textual meanings and thereby threatened not only traditional readings of the Bible but the bromides offered in rabbinical sermons and the pieties of American Jewish community leaders.

The possibility of at least partial rapprochement between the Jewish intellectual vanguard and the ideas of the postmodernists after the radical rapture fomented by the Jewish modernists of the earlier generation has not been therefore significantly developed. Simple ignorance of what Chomsky, Bloom, Lévi-Strauss, and Derrida have said and practical restorative implications of their theories have played a big part in this inertia. Jewish rabbinical seminaries are much less intellectually alive and au courant these days than Christian, particularly Catholic ones. Jewish Studies programs are committed to cultivating the past rather than reshaping the future, as their cautious, conservative, wealthy benefactors would heartily prefer. It required infinitely more intellectual prowess and moral courage than Jewish communal leadership possessed, to have fashioned a new Judaism out of the radical doctrines of the five great modernists of the early twentieth century. It would not be such a reach to reconstitute Judaism through the doctrines of the postmodernists. But little along these lines has been attempted.

If we come to assess the future of the Jews from today's vantage, we must first say that there is a lassitude, a torpor, in current thought about Judaism that produces a weak base for meeting the critical collective challenges that press upon the Jewish world today.

The genetic intellectual superiority of the Jews will be extended and as long as its carriers are individually free and privileged to pursue their interests in science, philosophy, literature, and the arts, highly advantageous consequences for humanity will follow.

But Jewish identity, the collective existence of the Jewish people, this from present vantage is threatened in the near future.

Recorded and scientifically sustainable Jewish history extends from the time of King David around 1000 B.C. to the time of Itzhak Rabin's second premiership of Israel and his efforts to negotiate peace with the Arabs in 1993 and 1994. Three millennia of continuous history. Perhaps only the Chinese have a comparable historical duration of richly textured development.

That Jewish history has endured so long does not mean that inevitably it will continue the way it has been. It is hazardous for a historian to predict the future. Events not now foreseen may change things appreciably, such as in this instance a powerful religious revival in which the sacred chain of biblical and postbiblical Judaism will encounter and embrace, rather than shrink from, modernist and postmodernist culture, and an intellectual and emotional rebirth will occur.

But in 1994 there is no sign that this is likely to happen, and saving an unforeseen reversal of current trends, it appears from present perspective that the history of the Jews as we have known it and them is probably approaching the end.

A remnant of Jews committed to traditional Judaism—about fifteen percent of the Jewish populations of Israel and the United States—will remain fifty or a hundred years from now. But as for the rest, their Jewish identity will have become submerged in the powerful ambient culture—that of American suburban middle-class materialism in America and a newly vibrant Near Eastern Arab culture in the case of Israel.

If the majority of ethnic Jews still maintain their conscious identities as Jews in these circumstances, it will be a Jewish identity much modified and attenuated by interaction with the powerful interactive surrounding cultures.

We must not think that it is either history's mandate or God's will that the Jews should continue to exist as an identifiable and distinctive group in any way near even their current modest numbers. Great Jewish communities have disappeared before, and they were the most intellectual and creative ones of the post–second exilic era. The progressive Alexandrian community declined into relative insignificance between A.D. 100 and 400. The great community of Iberia disappeared between 1350 and 1550, partly because of forced conversion and exile, but partly and probably more because of a massive departure of Jews into the magnetic Christian culture of the Iberian peninsula.

While in the end it was the Nazis who were mostly responsible for the extinction of the phenomenally creative German Jewish community as it was in 1900, the fact is that with an intermarriage rate of fifty percent and a conversion rate almost as high, without Hitler German Jewry would have almost disappeared as a separate group by the end of the twentieth century, although half a million individuals (the number of Jews in Germany in 1933) would have saved their lives and continued their vibrant contributions to German culture and science.

"Demography is destiny," said the eminent British historian Geoffrey Barraclough in the 1960s, and in the case of the Jews the population trends signal the approaching end of Jewish history as we have known it. Fifty years from now there will be about the same number of Orthodox Jews in America—not more than fifteen percent of the current five million—as there are today. There is no way their Halakic behavior can appeal beyond a population level that this difficult lifestyle appeals to today.

As for the other eighty-five percent of the Jews in America, they are on a one-way ticket to disappearance as an ethnic solidarity. The message of the 1990 U.S. census is dire, so much so that the rabbinate is reluctant to discuss its significance publicly.

Fifty-two percent of Jewish marriages in 1990 were intermarriage with Gentiles, and since at best only one in three spouses convert to Judaism and less than one in three children of these mixed marriages are raised as Jews, the extrapolation is the steady disappearance of American Jewry over the next century or so. What would have happened in Germany by the year 2000 without Hitlerian intervention is now happening in America.

A sociologist at the Jewish Theological Seminary, Jack Wertheimer, in 1993 pointed to a symbolic fact of great importance. So many of the members of their congregations are couples with a converted spouse that rabbis, other than the Orthodox, can no longer warn in their sermons against intermarriage with Gentiles—it would insult a large minority of their congregations. The point of no return for Jewish group survival has been reached.

Additional pieces of data are relevant and signatory. First, perusal of the *New York Times* Sunday marriage page reveals that out of two dozen or so marriages normally listed there, at least four are intermarriages between Jews and Gentiles—almost as often a Jewish woman taking a Gentile spouse as a Jewish man doing that, contrary to the intermarriage pattern of twenty years ago. Beyond the raw statistics is the important social fact that these are the American elite, the suburban bluebloods, the rising professionals.

The Jews—as they were in mid-nineteenth-century England—are no longer a despised minority to the WASP elite but the opposite. They are an exotic breed who make good spouses and enrich the Episcopalian and Protestant bloodlines. A new intermarried elite is being created as in fifteenth-century Spain and early twentieth-century Germany.

Another social fact is that even including the Orthodox with their relatively large families, the Jewish production of children in America falls below the replacement ratio of the 2.3 children per family needed to sustain the current population level. While thousands of Jews annually depart from the Jewish community by failing to practice Judaism and exhibit no Jewish identity, those who remain fail to procreate to sustain even a stable population—at a time when, due to immigration, legal and illegal, the general American population is burgeoning, especially among Hispanics, Asiatics, and African Americans.

By 1990 the traditional Jewish family structure that was the mainstay of synagogue centrality in Jewish life had all but collapsed. Only fourteen percent of American Jewish households now contain the conventional, heterosexual married parents with children. Even in these households the deterioration of the American middle-class family's income through a working father, as well as the professional ambitions of well-educated Jewish women, has driven Jewish mothers to seek employment outside the home to sustain basic needs or pursue upward mobility, imbalancing traditional parental roles in the Jewish family.

The huge number of single-parent Jewish families and unmarried couples and gay couples constituted a social revolution that made obsolete and irrelevant the teachings of conventional Judaism that assumed the traditional married-parents-with-children household. Rabbis were bewildered how to relate the collapse of Jewish family life to the moral heritage of Judaism that had presupposed a standard family structure.

Even if Jews did not commit racial suicide by intermarriage, their numbers in American society would slowly and steadily deteriorate to insignificance over the next two centuries. But intermarriage and abandonment of Jewish identity and failure to raise children of mixed marriage as Jews will greatly accelerate the process of group extinction—except for the three-quarters of a million Orthodox who will persist as walking museums of the long-ago Ashkenazic past.

Again, if there was a religious revival, and if the infrastructure of Jewish childhood and adult education was not sacrificed at the altar of overachieving Zionist fund-raising for Israel, this process could be halted and reversed, but in 1994 such prospects are remote.

The religious and cultural revival of American Jews could not be led by the current complement of rabbis of whatever persuasion.

Particularly within Reform and Conservative denominations, the quality of recruited personnel for the rabbinate in the past two decades has been mediocre among the male candidates. Women rabbis are of better quality, but they are still too few and too little accepted to be able to provide moral and intellectual leadership.

A visible number of women rabbis today exist only among Reform congregations, but even in their liberal context they are very rarely other than assistants to a male rabbi. Innovative rabbis are in any case not tolerated by the domineering and obtuse synagogue boards that hire and retain them. Alternatively, the religious and cultural revival of American Judaism cannot be undertaken by Jewish academics. They are not interested, are not knowledgeable in Judaism, and rarely possess the charismatic qualities that leadership demands.

If some younger Jews feel the need for a revival, they have no one to lead them. They form synagogue havurot groups, New Age spiritual societies, but these will have no long-range impact without powerful leadership that intrinsically cannot come from the present weak rabbinate and could not come from anywhere else. A tradition of lay religious leadership does not exist in Judaism as it does in some Christian groups, such as Methodism.

Therefore the current alarmingly adverse social indicators show that the imminent erosion and breakup of the American Jewish community will continue to pursue their ravaging way unchecked.

There are also problems with the future of Israeli Jews. What lay beneath the Rabin peace negotiations with the Arabs is essentially Israeli yearning for economic normality. The Israeli economy has never been viable, never been self-sustaining. Now ten percent of the population is unemployed, including many thousands of highly educated recent Russian immigrants who will not stand for this adverse situation. The only hope is development of Israel as a high-tech economy, as the Near Eastern Singapore or South Korea.

Yasser Arafat, the head of the PLO, in 1993 had on his hands the blood of thousands of Israelis killed by Arab fire in the past quarter-century. Yet there was no one else with whom to negotiate. The Rabin government first tried to negotiate peace directly with leaders of the West Bank Arab community. This went nowhere because they were forever looking over their shoulders at Arafat, afraid to make a peace that the PLO would repudiate. There was no one else to negotiate with except Arafat, and the time was running out for such negotiations because the militant Muslim fundamentalists, Hamas (whom the Israelis had formerly encouraged as a counterweight to the PLO), were gaining support in the occupied territories.

While Arafat continued to make provocative speeches proclaiming that a capital for the Palestinian state in Jerusalem was still his goal, thereby riling many Israelis who broadly accepted peace negotiations with the Arabs as inevitable, the Arafat problem for the Rabin government in the short run was not that the PLO leader would be too stong and intransigent but that he would be too weak and ineffective as an administrator of the territories. Arafat had to put in place fiscal and control systems that would satisfy the World Bank, the U.S. government, and other donors of promised aid. He had to deal with immensely difficult problems in the fields of health, education, and industrial production. Whether Arafat had sufficient administrative skills to deal with these issues was moot. He was, therefore, possibly a transitional figure. Meanwhile, the Rabin government had to depend on him.

Rabin's problem was almost as great on the Israeli Jewish as on the Palestinian side. His government in 1994 retained a majority in the Israeli parliament only with votes from Arab representatives. The mood of the Israeli public swung significantly from day to day. The Likud looked forward to regaining power in the election of 1996. But it seemed unlikely that the peace process could be reversed. Among other reasons, the American government, which sustained Israel's military capacity, would not allow such a reversal.

The Rabin government did not seek American Zionist advice before beginning negotiations with the PLO. Rabin regarded the American Jews as having no rights in determining the future of Israel, only obligations to provide fiscal and political support.

The Labor government could point to a long tradition of wanting to make peace that had been interrupted, they argued, by nearly two decades of Likud intransigence. Rabin and his foreign minister, Shimon Peres, were putting Israel back on track after the Likud years. Perhaps the American Jews had forgotten that and had become accustomed to an image of a militant greater Israel, but that image was an aberration from the best Zionist traditions, they argued.

As long ago as 1948 Chaim Weizmann had offered Israeli economic and technological cooperation to the king of Jordan and had been refused, just as peace feelers later put out—halfheartedly some would claim—by Ben-Gurion and Golda Meir had led nowhere.

In any case it was the dawn of a new era in 1993. The time had come for the Israelis to recognize reality and get out of ruling most or all of the territories as quickly as they could. They would have to risk the possible problems of later political development of the territories under Palestinian control.

There was the additional risk that the wall of hatred against the Jews in the Muslim world was so high and pervasive that any peace arrangement would come undone in the context of the Jew-hating ingredient in world Muslim culture. Israel was discouraged that Muslim countries from Jordan to Malaysia were banning the showing of the Holocaust film *Schlindler's List,* because it was considered too favorable to the Jews and too hostile to the Germans. The Israeli government hoped for and expected a slow modification of Muslim attitudes, believing that the governing and business elite in Muslim countries, seeing the advantages of peace with Israel and cooperation with Israelis in economic development, would have the courage and skill to mitigate the fanaticism of the Muslim masses that the PLO had done so much to instigate in previous decades.

In the 1930s and 1940s the first president of the Hebrew University, Judah Magnes, a Reform rabbi from Cincinnati, had brought down upon himself much Zionist abuse because of his insistence that the only solution to the Palestine problem was a binational Jewish-Arab state in Israel. Although no one seems to have noticed, the plan agreed to by Rabin and Arafat in 1993 was not far from this Magnes solution.

There would now be two political entities—Israel and Palestine, the latter developing out of the autonomous territories of the West Bank and Gaza—each with its own executives and legislatures. But it is politically naive to give so much importance to these formal political structures. The two states would have to engage in very close cooperation on economic matters, water supplies, technological developments, ecology, and police, and in the modern world these areas of governmental activity are fully as important as the traditional structures of executives and legislatures.

Another derivation from the Rabin-Arafat negotiations seems to have been overlooked—what would happen now to the Arabs with Israeli residence and citizenship, who comprised twenty percent of Israel's population, and whose birthrate was much higher than the Jewish average in Israel? Their position in 1993 was that of African-Americans in the American South in the early 1960s. They formally had political and civil rights but were still second-class citizens. They were meagerly represented in the Israeli learned professions. They comprised less than five percent of the student body of Israeli universities, and in only one institution—Haifa University, located next to the largest enclave of Israeli Arabs in the Galilee—were they a visible campus presence, with seven percent of the student body. Furthermore, no concessions were made to them—they had to learn Hebrew to attend Israeli universities, much superior to the Arab West Bank colleges at the best of times, and the latter postsecondary institution had been greatly disrupted in the *intifada*.

Over time, and it could be a short time, as the Palestinian autonomous entities in the West Bank and Gaza turn into a Palestinian state, would the Israeli Arabs be content to be separate from the Palestinian political nation, and if they were, would they continue to tolerate their second-class status in Israel? Not much thought appears to have been given to these critical prospects, which soon could be pressing and difficult issues, raising the kinds of problems that have dissolved Yugoslavia and Czechoslovakia and ravaged Northern Ireland.

The bacillus of nationalism, once inserted into a body politic, readily becomes highly volatile. The Zionists of all people should

know that. All attention in 1994 was given to West Bank Jewish settlers who opposed the peace agreement, but in the long run the
problem of the Israeli Arabs and their self-identity could be a much
more difficult one, threatening the stability of Israel.

The Israeli government and popular majority were betting that
economics and technology would prevail over politics and culture—
modernity would mitigate Arab nationalism and militarism.

Peace will bring American and European investment, the Israeli
government expects. The Israeli economy will be transformed to a
high-technology one and be a focal point for a Near Eastern common market. If the French and Germans could join together in a
European Economic Community after centuries of fratricidal conflict,
so can the Jews and Arabs, who a millennium ago shared easily the
great commerce of the Mediterranean and beyond in the Goitein-
genizah world.

So it can be again. In 1993 three hundred business people and
civil servants in Amman, Jordan, were hard at work learning Hebrew
in anticipation of the Near Eastern common market. King Hussein of
Jordan looked upon peace with Israel as merely the first step toward
an economic union with the Jewish state. A look at the map shows
that the cheapest way to ship Mercedes cars from Germany to
Kuwait is not through the obsolete and expensive Suez Canal but
through the port of Haifa and then by road ferry south through the
desert (some road improvement will be needed, but that is cheap
and easy).

The Arabs, facing their own severe fiscal strictures and vast
unemployment, need this Judeo-Arab economic pact and common
market as much as the Israelis. Somehow the Jewish extremists will
be bought off and the Arab ones repressed. A new generation of
young Arabs will be students, not stone throwers and street rioters.

Fifty years from now, in a immensely thriving Near Eastern economy, perhaps it will be as hard to remember what caused the Arab-
Jewish conflicts as it is to explain the Roman-Jewish wars.

If economics and technology repress political memory and
dampen religious fervor, there could still be a momentous challenge
facing the Israelis a few decades into the future. The superstructure
of culture follows the structured economic base. Currently, synagogue attendance per capita in Israel is actually no greater than in
America. The proportion of Orthodox Israelis is no more than in the
United States. Even on Yom Kippur, Israeli beaches are crowded

with materialist sun worshippers. In the exploding economy of the early twenty-first-century Near East, there is an imminent possibility that the four million Israelis will be absorbed by the revived ancient and vibrant culture of the Arab world and sucked into its lifestyle and behavior pattern, as happened to the much more observant Jews of medieval Muslim Spain.

The romanticization of Iberian Jewish history as the golden age of the Diaspora has covered up a reality that is highly relevant to the new cultural age which the Israelis will be entering after peace with the Arabs. Attention should be paid to the fact that the great Jewish writers of Muslim Iberia wrote their most important works in Arabic, that Sephardim dressed like Arabs, that their lifestyle and sexual behavior became similar to that of their Arab neighbors. So it very well could be again.

The Israelis will provide economic, technological, and educational leadership in the newly pacified and modernized Near East. But allow a couple of decades to pass, and a new Israeli generation time to emerge, and the impress upon Israel of Arabic language and behavior is liable to be profound.

It will not be easy for Israelis to resist the vibrations emanating from the ambience of a hundred million Arabs. After a time they will probably not want to resist. They will see themselves not as intransigent Westerners, as a last outpost of Victorian imperialism, the ultimate heirs of the French crusaders who slaughtered Jews and fought Arabs, but as the finest product of a developing highbred, syncretic Near Eastern culture in the twenty-first century.

If intermarriage between Jews and Christians in America is the norm, why not intermarriage between Jews and Muslims in the Near East? That prospect may seem impossible to most Israelis today, at least among the older generation, but the Israelis have always been blind to the powerful impact of anthropological functions. By the second half of the twenty-first century intermarriage is sure to follow between Jews and Arabs. Those who work together play together; those who play together copulate. It is the law of nature.

The cultural and ethnic blending of Jews and Arabs will mitigate the tensions between Israelis and Palestinians. A new Judeo-Arab Near Eastern elite will emerge in the next century.

One can bewail the strong indications that the sacred chain is running through its last links, and Jewish history as we have known it is approaching its end. But look at it in the context of divinity. The

Jews have fulfilled their role in history. They have been a light to the world. They gave the world monotheism and puritanical ethics, and spawned the two world religions, Christianity and Islam. They gave the Western world its scheme of genesis, destiny, and eschatology. They provided a permanent heritage of the prophetic preaching of social justice.

And in the twentieth century the Jews gave the Western world a group of thinkers who created the modernist and postmodernist culture in the sciences, the behavioral disciplines, and the arts as we experience them.

The Jews served their own purpose, and God's purpose, and mankind's purpose. Pragmatically, they are no longer very much needed as a distinct race. The Jewish heritage would endure if the Jews disappeared as a major group in the world in the twenty-first century.

Whether the Jews came as shepherds out of Mesopotamia as the Bible says; whether they were originally sectarian or social activists among the Canaanites who turned into an exclusive endogamous group; or whether they were beings who came by spaceship from some distant planet, for three thousand years this special people lived and propagated and imparted their unique ideas to mankind.

The Jews suffered incomparable miseries because they were witnesses to the truth that God is transcendent and purely spiritual and can be conditioned by no magical instruments.

The Jews achieved incomparable glories, especially of an intellectual kind, but—given the chance in ancient times and recently in the state of Israel—also of the heroic, military kind. Now the Jews' innate superior qualities will be perpetuated by intermarriage through the bloodlines of millions of people and diffused through American, Arab, and other societies. Their intermarriage with scions of the WASP elite in the United States will generate a new American patrician class, part-Jewish, as occurred in Iberia in the sixteenth century among families partly descended from Jewish converts.

But distinctive Jewish identity is running out, as the largest, most affluent, and vibrant Jewish community in the United States is demographically disappearing not only through assimilation, the pathological breakdown of family life, and failure to reproduce at the replacement level, but through the racial suicide of a runaway rate of intermarriage.

A similar melding of Jews and Arabs in the Near East will take time, but it is likely to happen if an effective peace between Israelis and Palestinians can be implemented.

The two Jewish national societies on which the future of the Jews depends, those of Israel and the United States, by 1994 face problems so critical and complex as not be resolvable unless charismatic and enlightened leadership in these communities is willing to speak truth to the Jews and encounter these issues head on. Even then, solutions are not readily conceivable.

The Jews of America face not only the steady erosion of Jewish identification through assimilation and intermarriage, but also the peculiar situation that while middle-age Jews enjoy unprecedented power and affluence, younger postadolescent Jewish males are being excluded from equal access to the learned professions, and with that from the continued accessibility of Jews to the high social status enjoyed by the older generation. A quiet process of reversion back to the discriminatory quotas of the 1930s and 1940s is under way in the guise of diversity and multiculturalism. Postadolescent Jewish females are for the moment enjoying the benefit of affirmative action and do not experience a commonality of interests with the status-declining younger Jewish males.

While these critical issues occasionally surface in discussions in *Commentary* and other Jewish media, there is no sign that any sharp focus upon them leading to meliorative action is coming from the lackadaisical and timid rabbinate or any other prospective leadership source.

In 1994 the Jews of Israel, perhaps belatedly by about two decades, are embarked on a concerted peace campaign that could provide the context for desperately needed economic and technological growth. They are aware that one hundred thousand Jews on the West Bank, of whom a quarter are intransigent religious idealists— and among these, devout Americans stand out—present a problem that has to be dealt with to achieve the ends of the peace process.

But no one in Israel appears to be giving thought to two more difficult implications of the gaining of a general peace—first, in the short run, the prospect of activated nationalism on the part of one million Israeli Arabs, their discontent with their second-class citizenship in Israel, and the likelihood that they would want to join with a Palestinian state that is in the offing; and second, in the long run, social consequences of the Near Eastern common market that the Israelis want to bring about rapidly, which would contribute to the loss of cultural and ethnic distinctiveness of Jews that is already proceeding with furious pace in America.

In this context, perhaps the Lubavitcher Hasidim in Brooklyn, urgently awaiting the Messiah's imminent appearance, were on the right track. In the current circumstances, nothing short of the appearance of the Messiah—or a comparable upheaval—can save Jewish group identity over the next fifty years.

In order to reverse the current strong trend to radical shrinking and early dissolution of the American Jewish community, save for an esoteric remnant, the following would have to be done starting immediately:

All of the funds annually shipped to Israel from Jewish sources in the United States and Canada would have to be invested in Jewish primary, secondary, and post-secondary education at home. This would involve, among other things, massive subsidizing of Jewish parochial schools, residential Jewish high schools, Hebrew-speaking summer camps, and adult education institutes; and the rescue of Yeshiva and Brandeis universities from their current penury and the founding of at least three more Jewish colleges to be located respectively in the Midwest, the South, and California.

Jewish scholars would have to reinterpret Judaism in light of modernist and postmodernist thought. Since almost no rabbi currently has the intellectual and learned capacity to do this, a panel of Jewish professors in the leading universities, the best minds among ethnic Jews, would have to be called upon for this task. They would be given an absolute time limit of three years to produce a new Jewish theology that accords with natural science, social and behavioral sciences, and humanistic thought of the end of the twentieth century.

A new Jewish liturgy would have to be devised, jettisoning eighty percent of the current boring medieval-derived synagogue liturgy and making use of the music, literature, and art of the current age. An elite group of Jewish composers, poets, novelists, and theater, film, and TV people would do this work and the synagogue councils would have to promise beforehand that they will implement their new liturgy which should be completed on an absolute deadline of two years. Furthermore, this liturgy will be revised every five years. It will be prescribed to the liturgical craftsmen that no Jewish synagogue service will last more than ninety minutes, with another thirty minutes allowed for sermons. Henceforth at least half of the sermons in Jewish synagogues within a calendar year must be delivered by lay people drawn from academia, the other learned professions, government service, and the media. One quarter at least of all sermons in a given year should be given by women and one quarter by people less than fifty years of age.

A subsidized national Jewish-focused weekly newsmagazine on the model of *Time* and *Newsweek* will be created and distributed free to schools, synagogues, and universities, and to anyone who requests a subscription.

Any Jewish college student who graduates magna or summa cum laude from the two hundred best colleges in the country and who wishes to study to be a rabbi or cantor or teacher in a Jewish school will receive a four year, $20,000 a year fellowship plus free tuition.

All rabbis must have at least an M.A. degree within seven years of beginning their pulpit and a doctorate within fourteen years. A fund to provide sabbatical leaves for rabbis to pursue advanced study will be established.

These provisions, if instituted, would probably save the Jewish people as a collective entity. So will the coming of the Messiah. The latter is a more likely prospect to be attempted than the former.

The Jewish people as a whole, as an ethnic entity, is threatened with erosion and communal extinction. What the Holocaust began physically will in the twenty-first century be accomplished culturally.

The Jews are going home now into the mist of history, into the remembrance of times long past, to rest with their God. *Am Yisroel Chai!* The Nation of Israel Lives! was the age-old cry. No longer.

Now this cry falls frozen on the advancing horizons of the coming new millennium.

Good Reading
on Jewish History

As the vigorous outpouring of publication on Jewish history continues, the bibliographical needs of the general reader and college student are best served by an annotated guide that constitutes a selected library of books that are both authoritative in their learning and accessible to the educated lay reader and preferably are a pleasure to read.

This is the purpose of the following Select Bibliography. It will be noted that the majority of these books have been published since 1980 and these are therefore still likely available through booksellers or by phoning the customer service department of the publishers. All of these titles can be found in a good university or first-rate college library.

I. The Ancient World: The Second Millennium B.C. to A.D. 600

Allegro, John M. *The Chosen People*. Garden City, N.Y.: Doubleday, 1972.

A Manchester scholar's very controversial and idiosyncratic but persistently interesting account of ancient Jewish religion which it is here claimed originated mostly in Iraq and was also marked by an underground variety involving psychedelic drugs. The latter claim, not popular in Jewish circles, was also espoused by Columbia University's Morton Smith toward the end of his career.

Alter, Robert, and Frank Kermode. *The Literary Guide to the Bible*. Cambridge, Mass.: Harvard University Press, 1987.

Critical essays on the books of the Hebrew Bible by leading scholars and general essays on the literary character of biblical literature comprise most of this volume. Uneven but intriguing.

Barnavi, Eli, ed. *A Historical Atlas of the Jewish People*. New York: Knopf, 1992.

The first part of this Israeli project is very helpful in sorting out the complexities of ancient Jewish history. The maps are superb and the archaeological illustrations well chosen.

Bickerman, Elias J. *From Ezra to the Last of the Maccabees: Foundations of Postbiblical Judaism*. New York: Schocken, 1962.

The Columbia University authority on Judaism in the Hellenistic era summarizes his many studies on this important subject.

Bloom, Harold, and David Rosenberg. *The Book of J*. New York: Vintage, 1990.

The renowned Yale critic highlights a novel embedded in the Torah, written by a woman of the royal court, a suggestion already made by R.E. Friedman. The new translation by Rosenberg will make you stop and think. This is the first translation of part of the Pentateuch that actually reads differently than the King James Version. This book was a bestseller in the United States.

Cohen, Shaye J. D. *From the Maccabees to the Mishna*. Philadelphia: Westminster, 1987.

By the head of the Judaic Studies Program at Brown University, formerly at the Jewish Theological Seminary, this work of deep learning and clear insight is also well written, guiding the reader through half a millennium of crucial religious development. An enduring, classic work.

Eilberg-Schwartz, Howard. *The Savage in Judaism*. Bloomington, Ind.: Indiana University Press, 1990.

A controversial but important and up-to-date anthropological reading of parts of the Bible that leaves the reader wanting more of such.

Fox, Robin Lane. *The Unauthorized Version, Truth and Fiction in the Bible*. New York: Viking, 1991.

This book by an Oxford don covers much the same ground and says much the same things about the Hebrew Bible as the earlier book by

Richard Friedman, but in a more personal, crankily British way, with a discussion of the New Testament—also significantly a Jewish product—added on.

Frederikson, Paula. *From Jesus to Christ*. New Haven, Conn.: Yale University Press, 1988.

The Jewish origins of Christianity, brilliantly explicated by a Boston University professor who is herself a convert from Christianity to Orthodox Judaism.

Friedman, Richard Elliott. *Who Wrote the Bible?* New York: Summit, 1987.

If you are going to read one book about the Hebrew Bible, this classic by a University of California professor is the one. It marvelously sums up the results of more than a century of scholarship in a succinct, clear, and thoroughly convincing manner.

Goodenough, Erwin R. *Jewish Symbols in the Graeco-Roman Period*. Abr. ed. Princeton, N.J.: Princeton University Press, 1988.

A representative selection from the great Yale scholar's seminal analysis of Hellenistic Jewish culture.

Hadas-Lebel, Mireille. *Flavius Josephus: Eyewitness to Rome's First-Century Conquest of Judea*. New York: Macmillan, 1989.

A highly readable and authoritative account of the great war of A.D. 66–70 through the life and perception of someone who was there. The author teaches in a French University.

Küng, Hans. *Judaism: Between Yesterday and Tomorrow*. New York: Crossroads, 1992.

A great man has written a very important book. Father Küng, a German theologian, is the world's leading liberal Roman Catholic thinker. The first part of this book summarizes biblical religion and history as well as anyone has ever done. The rest of the book reflects on the implications of ancient Judaism for later eras and today.

Neusner, Jacob. *The Bavli: An Introduction*. Atlanta: Scholars, 1992.

Formerly at Brown University, now the holder of a research chair at South Florida University, the prolific Neusner has devoted much of his long and distinguished career to explicating the Talmud. Here is a convenient summary of his views, clearly stated. An indispensable guide to the Talmud.

✓ Otzen, Benedict. *Judaism in Antiquity*. Sheffield: JSOT Press, 1990.

Among the legion of books by Protestant scholars surveying ancient Jewish history, this one by a Danish historian is probably the briefest, the most readable, and most persuasive.

Sarna, Nahum. *Exploring Exodus, the Heritage of Biblical Israel*. New York: Schocken, 1986.
———. *Songs of the Heart: An Introduction to the Book of Psalms*. New York: Schocken, 1993.

A Brandeis professor and prominent Conservative rabbi gives his learned and heartfelt readings of the Bible. Too pious for my taste but admirable of their kind.

✓ Segal, Alan F. *Rebecca's Children: Judaism and Christianity in the Roman World*. Cambridge, Mass: Harvard University Press, 1986.

The common origins of rabbinical Judaism and early Christianity; a clear-headed, sympathetic account by a Columbia professor.

Shanks, Hershel, ed. *Understanding the Dead Sea Scrolls: A Reader from the Biblical Archaeology Review*. New York: Vintage, 1993.

Dispassionate and insightful essays, the best introduction to this muddled subject.

Smith, Morton. *Palestinian Parties and Politics that Shaped the Old Testament*. 2d ed. London: SCM, 1987.

Bickerman's Columbia colleague and disciple straightens out the Pharisees and the Saduccees. A readable analysis of a very difficult subject.

✓ Steinsaltz, Adin. *The Essential Talmud*. New York: Bantam, 1976.

The great Israeli rabbinical scholar delivers what he promises. Dry, but succinct and readable.

✓ Zeitlin, Irving M. *Ancient Judaism: Biblical Criticism From Max Weber to the Present*. New York: Polity, 1984.

A Toronto sociologist's updated and expanded version of Max Weber's classic sociological study of the same main title. Immensely valuable synthesis of seven decades of scholarship.

II. Medieval and Early Modern Times: 600 to 1800

Ashtor, Eliyahu. *The Jews of Moslem Spain*. 3 vols. Philadelphia: Jewish Publication Society, 1979.

An Israeli historian's bold and near-successful effort to communicate very deep research in a literary form that is immediately accessible to the general reader.

Baer, Yitzhak F. *Galut*. Lanham, Md.: University Press of America, 1988 (1947).

The prominent historian of Jews in Christian Iberia ruminates on the course of Diaspora history. Fiercely Zionist, intellectually challenging.

Baron, Salo W. *A Social and Religious History of the Jews*. 2d ed. Vol. 8, *Philosophy and Science*. Philadelphia: Jewish Publication Society, 1971 (1958).

The most readable of Baron's many volumes, this discussion of medieval Jewish philosophy and science is marked not only by immense learning but also by subtle insight into a very complex subject.

Biale, David. *Eros and the Jews: From Biblical Israel to Contemporary America*. New York: Basic Books, 1992.

Jewish sexuality through the ages. Lots of laughs, some insights.

Dubnov, Simon M. *A History of the Jews in Russia and Poland From the Earliest Times*. New York: KTAV, 1975 (1920).

In many ways obsolete but still very much worth reading. The classic work of Yiddish historiography.

Faur, José. *In the Shadow of History: Jews and Conversos at the Dawn of Modernity*. Albany, N.Y.: State University of New York Press, 1992.

Overlapping somewhat with the first volume of Y. Yovel's work, this is an illuminating account of intellectual Marranos in the transition from Judaism to Christianity.

Gerber, Jane S. *The Jews of Spain*. New York: Free Press, 1992.

A convenient and readable overview, somewhat romanticized.

Goitein, Solomon D. *A Mediterranean Society*. 6 vols. Berkeley: University of California Press, 1967–1993.

Two thousand pages of deep immersion in the social and economic life of the Jewish merchant class in the Arabic Mediterranean world from 950 to 1250. A world of its own. The prose is readable enough but the very loosely structured work requires infinite patience and leisure to read through. The result is worth it—like reading all of Proust, another product of the Jewish mannerist imagination. Volumes III and V are probably the most accessible to the general reader. Volume VI is a cumulative index.

✓   ——. *Jews and Arabs: Their Contacts Through the Ages.* 3d ed. New York: Schocken Books, 1974.

Until someone produces a volume of carefully edited selections from Goitein's *A Mediterranean Society,* this short, thoughtful, and highly personal survey will provide easy access to the master's many decades of research and reflection on medieval Arabic Jewish culture and society. Goitein knows the Arabs as well as he knows the Jews.

Green, Arthur. *Tormented Master: A Life of Rabbi Nahman of Bratislav.* Tuscaloosa, Ala.: University of Alabama Press, 1979.

A careful biography of an early prominent Hasidic zaddik, Nahman of Bratislav, this work provides many insights into East European Jewish life around 1800.

Heer, Friedrich. *God's First Love: Christians and Jews Over Two Thousand Years.* New York: Weybright and Talley, 1970.

Heer was a prominent Viennese liberal Catholic intellectual historian. This book is probably the best of many accounts of Christian anti-Semitism down to 1900.

Idel, Moshe. *Kabbalah: New Perspectives.* New Haven, Conn.: Yale University Press, 1988.

A Hebrew University professor's followup and modification of Gershom Scholem's pioneering work.

Israel, Jonathan I. *European Jewry in the Ages of Mercantilism.* 2d ed. New York: Oxford University Press, 1989.

The Jewish role in early modern capitalism, by a University of London professor. Somewhat dry and hyper-academic but worth careful study for its highly illuminating account of Jewish economic and social roles. A seminal work.

Kadourie, Elie ed. *Spain and the Jews. The Sephardi Experience 1492 and After.* New York: Thames and Hudson, 1992.

An extremely valuable collection of important essays by leading scholars. The papers by Henry Kamen and Haim Beinart are especially significant.

Katz, Jacob. *Tradition and Crisis: Jewish Society at the End of the Middle Ages.* New York: Free Press, 1961.

A summary of a lifetime of research and reflection by the Hebrew University historical sociologist. Especially valuable for the discussion of communal and family structure.

Lewis, Bernard. *The Jews of Islam*. Princeton, N.J.: Princeton University Press, 1984.

Covering much the same ground as Goitein's *Jews and Arabs,* this book presents a very (perhaps too) succinct summary of Lewis's authoritative perceptions on Jewish-Muslim relations through the long centuries.

Maccoby, Hyam. *Judaism on Trial: Jewish-Christian Disputations in the Middle Ages*. Rutherford, N.J.: Farleigh Dickinson University Press, 1982.

Absorbing if somewhat idiosyncratic narratives with an excellent translation of Nachmanides's account of his disputation.

Mahler, Raphael. *A History of Modern Jewry*. New York: Schocken Books, 1971.

The title of this lengthy and authoritative study of the social foundations of Hasidism and its early phase should be "the origins and significance of Hasidism." A monumental and readable piece of high scholarship by the veteran YIVO scholar.

Scholem, Gershom. *Kabbalah*. New York: Dorset, 1987 (1974).

A highly readable summing up of Scholem's life-long research on medieval Jewish mysticism and its legacy.

—————. *Sabbatai Sevi: The Mystical Messiah*. Princeton, N.J.: Princeton University Press, 1973.

The single most impressive work of humanistic scholarship ever written on post Biblical Jewish history. A masterpiece that deals with not only messianism but also mysticism and the intellectual background to Hasidism.

Sharot, Stephen. *Messianism, Mysticism, and Magic. A Sociological Analysis of Jewish Religion*. Chapel Hill, N.C.: University of North Carolina, 1982.

An Israeli sociologist gives a succinct and subtle appraisal of the social and cultural meaning of Jewish mystical and messianic movements from the sixteenth century to the present. A classic work and a delight to read.

Sirat, Colette. *A History of Jewish Philosophy in the Middle Ages*. New York: Cambridge University Press, 1990 (1985).

Somewhat difficult and technical, this survey by a Parisian scholar is immensely useful for its biographical information, pithy summaries of theories, and extensive quotes from medieval writings.

Stillman, Norman A. *The Jews of Arab Lands*. Philadelphia: Jewish Publication Society, 1979.

The American scholar Stillman, Goitein's student, provides a wonderful anthology of contemporary writings, brilliantly translated, with helpful introductions for the period down to 1800. A classic.

Stow, Kenneth. *Alienated Minority: The Jews of Medieval Latin Europe.* Cambridge, Mass.: Harvard University Press, 1992.

An authoritative narrative of the decline and fall of Ashkenaz.

Yerushalmi, Yosef H. *From Spanish Court to Italian Ghetto: Isaac Cardoso.* Seattle: University of Washington Press, 1981.

The Sephardic Diaspora in charming biographical form.

Yovel, Yirmiyahu. *Spinoza and Other Heretics.* 2 vols. Princeton, N.J.: Princeton University Press, 1989.

Nothing less than an intellectual history of Western Sephardi society from 1500 into the eighteenth century by a Jerusalem professor. Bold, idiosyncratic, original; a seminal work.

III. The Modern and Contemporary Era: 1800 to 1994

Aberbach, David. *Bialik.* New York: Grove, 1988.

Not the definitive study of the poet and sage that needs to be written, but an interim essay that is well-informed and insightful.

Alcalay, Ammiel. *After Jews and Arabs: Remaking Levantine Culture.* Minneapolis: University of Minnesota Press, 1993.

Original and suggestive essays on aspects of Israeli culture in an unusual Middle Eastern context.

Alderman, Geoffrey. *Modern British Jewry.* New York: Oxford University Press, 1992.

A London University professor caused a commotion in the placid world of British Jewry with this hard-hitting but thoroughly well-grounded and convincing book. A model of what the history of a national Jewish society ought to be.

Beit Zvi, S. B. *Post-Ugandan Zionism on Trial: A Study of the Factors that Caused the Mistakes Made by the Zionist Movement during the Holocaust.* 2 vols. Tel Aviv: Beit Zvi, 1991.

The author's discussion of the subject as announced in the subtitle is relentlessly persuasive. He couldn't find a publisher who dared to bring out the book, and no wonder. Compelling reading.

Beller, Steven. *Vienna and the Jews 1867–1938: A Cultural History*. New York: Cambridge University Press, 1989.

The world of Freud, Schoenberg, and Wittgenstein, artfully analyzed.

Burt, Robert A. *Two Jewish Justices: Outcasts in the Promised Land*. Berkeley: University of California Press, 1988.

A succinct and thoughtful discussion of Brandeis and Frankfurter and their relationship, by a Yale law professor.

Chamish, Barry. *The Fall of Israel*. London: Canongate, 1992.

A detailed account of gross corruption in Israeli government and big business in the 1980s. Much of this information got into Israeli newspapers, but here it is in one book by an outraged Canadian living in Israel.

Chernow, Ron. *The Warburgs*. New York: Random House, 1993.

The billionaire patriarchs at work and play, prolix but valuable because of the author's access to the family's private papers, and easy reading.

Dayan, Yael. *My Father, His Daughter*. New York: Farrar, Straus, 1985.

A biographical portrait of the Israeli hero and statesman Moshe Dayan written by his daughter, a feminist journalist and politician. A work of deep insight.

Englander, David, ed. *The Jewish Enigma: An Enduring People*. New York: Braziller, 1992.

An up-to-date and insightful collection of overviews by a group of English and American scholars.

Feingold, Henry L., ed. *The Jewish People In America*. 5 vols. Baltimore: Johns Hopkins University Press.

An ambitious effort at a comprehensive narrative sponsored by the American Jewish Historical Society and addressed to the lay reader. Inevitably uneven, but volume 3 on the period 1880–1920 by Gerald Sorin and volume 4 on the period 1920–45 by Feingold, are very much worth reading.

Friedman, Maurice. *Encounter on the Narrow Ridge: A Life of Martin Buber*. New York: Paragon, 1991.

Not only an authoritative biography of the sage, but an intellectual history of early twentieth century German Jewry.

Gilman, Sander. *The Jews's Body*. New York: Routledge, 1991.

A prominent Cornell professor's psychiatric ruminations on anti-Semitism and the Jewish question in modern culture.

Ginsberg, Benjamin. *The Fatal Embrace: Jews and the State.* Chicago: University of Chicago Press, 1993.

An original and provocative essay by a Johns Hopkins political scientist about modern Jews, political power, and anti-Semitism.

Greenberg, Louis. *The Jews in Russia: The Struggle For Emancipation.* New Haven, Conn.: Yale University Press, 1965 (1949–51).

Partisan and somewhat obsolete but still not superseded. Highly readable.

Harshav, Benjamin. *The Meaning of Yiddish.* Berkeley: University of California Press, 1990.

A comprehensive and inspiring history of Yiddish language and the culture it expressed, by an Israeli scholar. A classic.

Hilberg, Raul. *Perpetrators, Victims, Bystanders: The Jewish Catastrophe 1933-1945.* New York: HarperCollins, 1992.

The pioneering American historian of the Holocaust gives his explicit conclusions after thirty years of research and reflection. Persuasive and important.

Howe, Irving. *The World of Our Fathers: The Journey of East European Jews to America and the Life They Found and Made.* New York: Schocken Books, 1989 (1976).

A brilliantly written combination of insight and sentiment. A runaway bestseller.

Kalmar, Ivan. *The Trotskys, Freuds, and Woody Allens: Portrait of a Culture.* New York: Viking, 1993.

A Toronto anthropologist's reflections on the folkways of the tribe. Many smiles, plenty of insight.

Kolsky, Thomas A. *Jews Against Zionism: The American Council for Judaism 1942–1948.* Philadelphia: Temple University Press, 1990.

A lively account of the losers—Reform rabbis who opposed Zionism. A vanished but interesting sub-culture.

Kurzman, Dan. *Genesis 1948: The First Arab-Israeli War.* New York: Da Capo, 1992 (1970).

The War of Independence graphically narrated by an American writer. Partisan but frank in revealing Israeli failures as well as triumphs.

Levin, Nora. *The Jews in the Soviet Union Since 1917: Paradox of Survival*. 2 vols. New York: New York University Press, 1988.

An absorbing and well-informed narrative history in the grand manner. A formidable achievement.

Linderman, Albert S. *The Jews Accused: Three Anti-Semitic Affairs: Dreyfus, Beilis, Frank 1894–1915*. New York: Cambridge University Press, 1991.

Reflective and probing examination of key aspects of the Wall of Hatred.

Mendes-Flohr, Paul. *Divided Passions: Jewish Intellectuals and the Experience of Modernity*. Detroit: Wayne, 1991.

Not comprehensive, but offering important studies of key aspects of this immensely complex and important subject by a Hebrew University professor.

Meyer, Michael A. *Response to Modernity: History of the Reform Movement in Judaism*. New York: Oxford University Press, 1988.

A somewhat dry and academic account, with an institutional focus, but well-researched and valuable. The author teaches at Hebrew Union College in New York.

Mosse, Werner E. *Jews in the German Economy, The German-Jewish Elite 1820–1936*. New York: Oxford University Press, 1987.

Rising above a vast fog of polemics and apologetics, this is an authoritative summation of the facts, worthy of close consideration.

Nakhimovsky, Alice Stone. *Russian-Jewish Literature and Identity*. Baltimore: Johns Hopkins University Press, 1992.

First-rate literary criticism, beautifully written.

Oz, Amos. *Israeli Literature: A Case of Reality Reflecting Fiction*, Colorado Springs: Colorado College, 1985.

Cultural insights by Israel's best known commentator. Essentially the voice of the Israeli liberal establishment. How the *New Yorker* wants to see Israeli culture.

Pawel, Ernst. *The Labyrinth of Exile: A Life of Theodor Herzl*. New York: Farrar, Straus, 1988.

An extremely insightful biography, placing Herzl in his cultural ambience and portraying Herzl's weaknesses as well as his greatness.

✓ Raviv, Dan, and Yosef Melman. *Every Spy a Prince: The Complete History of Israel's Intelligence Community*. Boston: Houghton Mifflin, 1990.

This bestseller by two Israeli journalists is concrete and circumstantial, telling of the intelligence confusions and failures as well as the celebrated successes. Sometimes you wonder how the Arabs could have lost.

Reinharz, Jehudah. *Chaim Weizmann*. 2 vols. New York: Oxford University Press, 1985, 1993.

Rose, Norman. *Chaim Weizmann*. New York: Viking, 1986.

Rose's biography is much the more readable of the two and communicates Weizmann's humanity and grandeur. A first-rate memorial to a very great man, whatever your feelings about Zionism. Reinharz provides more information but is hard going and lacks focus. All things considered, Rose's is the better work.

Sachar, Howard M. *A History of the Jews in America*. New York: Knopf, 1992.

Lengthy and comprehensive, somewhat dull but highly informative, especially on communal organizations.

———. *A History of Israel*. New York: Knopf, 1993.

Triumphalist and partisan, but a convenient narrative.

Schult, Mel. *Judaism Faces the Twentieth Century: A Biography of Moedecai Kaplan*. Detroit: Wayne, 1993.

This long-awaited biography of Kaplan could be better written but it is intrinsically fascinating. Kaplan's failure to foment a religious rebirth seems to be due at least partly to defects in personality.

Segev, Tom. *The First Israelis, 1949*. New York: Free Press, 1986.

———. *The Seventh Million: The Israelis and the Holocaust*. New York: Hill and Wang, 1993.

Israel's top investigative journalist pulls no punches in describing the way it really was. Not what you are going to hear at an Israeli Bond dinner or from your local synagogue pulpit.

Stillman, Norman A. *The Jews in Arab Lands in Modern Times*. Philadelphia: Jewish Publication Society, 1991.

The fate of the "Oriental" Jews since 1800 portrayed in contemporary documents with extremely valuable editorial introductions.

Teveth, Shabtai. *Ben-Gurion: The Burning Ground 1886-1948*. Boston: Houghton Mifflin, 1987.

The first volume of the authorized biography that is remarkably frank about Ben-Gurion's personal and policy failures, yet communicates his courage, dynamism, and vision. Not well written but still fascinating. Teveth is an Israeli journalist.

Weintraub, Stanley. *Disraeli*. New York: Dutton, 1993.

Disraeli as a Jew. Detailed and delightful.

Wertheimer, Jack. *A People Divided: Judaism in Contemporary America*. New York: Basic Books, 1993.

A prophet crying in the wilderness. Wertheimer is a historical sociologist teaching at the font of Conservative Judaism, the Jewish Theological Seminary. Wertheimer sees the future of the Jewish community and faith in the American setting to be in grave peril. When he published a summary of this book in *Commentary*, he was publicly censured by the head of the Conservative national rabbinical organization. So much for self-criticism and free speech in the American Jewish community. Wertheimer took this censure calmly.

Wistrich, Robert S. *Between Redemption and Perdition: Anti-Semitism and Jewish Identity*. Boston: Routledge, 1990.

A Jerusalem professor's sensitive probing of the relationship between anti-Semitism and anti-Zionism. This book aroused fierce criticism in Britain where in academic and media circles it is fashionable to maintain that it is possible to make a sharp distinction between anti-Semitism and anti-Zionism, a position also held in some American leftist precincts, such as the *Village Voice*.

Wyman, David B. *The Abandonment of the Jews: America and the Holocaust, 1941–1945*. New York: Pantheon, 1984.

The pioneering work on this highly controversial subject was Arthur Morse, *While Six Million Died* (1964). Wyman's book is based on extensive additional archival research and is authoritative. What annoyed Arthur Schlesinger, Jr. and other liberal Democrats is that FDR himself comes through badly, not just a handful of anti-Semitic WASPS in the State Department. Unsuccessful efforts were made in 1994 to dissuade PBS from running a documentary film based on Wyman's excellent book. Read it and weep.

Yahl, Leni. *The Holocaust: The Fate of European Jewry*. New York: Oxford University Press, 1990.

A comprehensive and definitive narrative history by an Israeli scholar.

Zipperstein, Steven J. *The Jews of Odessa: A Cultural History, 1794–1881.* Stanford, Calif.: Stanford University Press, 1991.

A very important study of the emergence of the leading intellectual center of Russian Jewry.

———. *Elusive Prophet: Ahad Ha'Am and the Origins of Zionism.* Berkeley: University of California Press, 1993.

A superb account of Ahad Ha'Am in his time and place, giving full explanation of his importance in Zionist history, by a Stanford scholar.

Zuccotti, Susan. *The Holocaust, the French and the Jews.* New York: Basic Books, 1993.

A devastating and incontestable indictment. You will never eat in a French restaurant again. Zuccotti is a student of Columbia's Robert Paxton, who did the pioneering work on this subject twenty years ago.

A Mini-List

You only have time to read a half dozen books on Jewish history? Or you want a handy list of highly discussable, relatively short books for your synagogue or adult education group? I would choose the following. (Full bibliographical information is given above.)

Cohen, Shaye J. D. *From the Maccabees to the Mishna*
Friedman, Richard Elliot. *Who Wrote the Bible?*
Hilberg, Raul. *Perpetrators, Victims, Bystanders: The Jewish Catastrophe 1933–1945*
Lewis, Bernard. *The Jews of Islam*
Rose, Norman. *Chaim Weizmann*
Sharot, Stephen. *Messianism, Mysticism, and Magic*

INDEX